Russian Style

I0883423

Russian Style

Performing Gender, Power, and Putinism

Julie A. Cassiday

THE UNIVERSITY OF WISCONSIN PRESS

The University of Wisconsin Press
728 State Street, Suite 443
Madison, Wisconsin 53706
uwpress.wisc.edu

Copyright © 2023
The Board of Regents of the University of Wisconsin System
All rights reserved. Except in the case of brief quotations embedded in critical articles and reviews, no part of this publication may be reproduced, stored in a retrieval system, transmitted in any format or by any means—digital, electronic, mechanical, photocopying, recording, or otherwise—or conveyed via the Internet or a website without written permission of the University of Wisconsin Press. Rights inquiries should be directed to rights@uwpress.wisc.edu.

Printed in the United States of America
This book may be available in a digital edition.

Library of Congress Cataloging-in-Publication Data

Names: Cassiday, Julie A., author.
Title: Russian style : performing gender, power, and Putinism / Julie A. Cassiday.
Description: Madison, Wisconsin : The University of Wisconsin Press, 2023. | Includes bibliographical references and index.
Identifiers: LCCN 2023014986 | ISBN 9780299346706 (hardcover)
Subjects: LCSH: Sex role—Russia (Federation) | Gender expression—Russia (Federation) | Popular culture—Russia (Federation) | Drag performance—Russia (Federation) | Russia (Federation)—Social conditions—21st century.
Classification: LCC HQ1075.5.R9 C377 2023 | DDC 305.30947086—dc23/eng/20230811
LC record available at https://lccn.loc.gov/2023014986

ISBN 9780299346744 (pbk.)

For Emily, without whom none of this would have happened.

Contents

List of Illustrations ix

Preface xi

Introduction 3

1 A Genealogy of Post-Soviet Pop Performativity 27

2 The Soviet Legacy of Traumatized Bodies 59

3 *Travesti* and the Post-Soviet Drag Queen 78

4 Queer Performativity in Putin's Russia 103

5 Post-Soviet Postfeminism 129

Conclusion 163

Notes 179

Bibliography 217

Index 245

Illustrations

1 An Ulianovsk cadet twerks as he sweeps in the "Satisfaction" video from January 2018 4

2 The meme of Putin as a gay clown banned as extremist material in 2017 39

3 The meme of Putin draped in an oversized condom on a poster during the 2011–2012 protests 43

4 Zaza Napoli posing in her full feminine glamour 54

5 Olia Poliakova emerging from a barrel of caviar for the 2012 video "Russian Style" 55

6 Fierce wearing "the medals of a nonexistent power [that] would go out of style" in the final scene of Fedor Bondarchuk's *9th Company* (2005) 66

7 Vladislav Mamyshev-Monro, photograph of actress Liubov' Orlova in her casket from the series "Happy Love (Liubov' Orlova)" (2000) 84

8 Verka Serduchka performing "Dancing Lasha Tumbai" on behalf of Ukraine at the 2007 Eurovision Song Contest 88

9 Anatolii Evdokimov *en travesti* as Eve, reenacting the creation of the world (2012) 94

10 Dima Bilan performing "Believe" with composer Edvin Marton and Olympic figure skater Evgenii Pliushchenko on behalf of Russia during the 2008 Eurovision finals 111

11 Sergii Astakhov shows viewers "a new dance" in Oleg Mavromatti's 2014 *No Place for Fools* 124

12 Aleksandr and Tat'iana Platov pose for the press in Ol'ga Zhulina's *This Kiss Is Off the Record* (2008) 138

13 Rebel fighters posing with the flag of the Donetsk People's Republic during a beauty contest in Donetsk in March 2015 159

14 Diana poses as Nicole Kidman playing the role of Princess Grace of Monaco in Alina Rudnitskaya's 2019 documentary *School for Seduction* 161

15 Nastia Ivleeva and Kseniia Sobchak kiss in episode two of *Royal Cobras* (2021) 168

16 The knee-knocking dance in the official Eurovision video of Little Big's "Uno" (2020) 171

Preface

The path that brought me to this book has been anything but straight. I never planned to argue that Vladimir Putin's first two decades at the Russian Federation's helm were more about ironic style than political substance. Nor did I anticipate that putting Putin memes alongside drag queens would reveal a shift in the performativity of Russian citizenship during the 2000s and 2010s. On the contrary, writing this book has been an erratic zigzag through material that led me gradually to the realization that Russia's ideal citizen during the first two decades of the twenty-first century was a young, sexually available woman eager to shape herself in accordance with Putin's needs and desires.

My journey to writing *Russian Style* began with a series of detours I took when another book I thought I was writing hit a dead end. Having long been a fan of culture deemed "second rate" if not downright "bad," I originally planned to rescue forgotten works of early nineteenth-century Russian drama by showing how playwrights shaped gender back in their day. However, while I was making trips to theater archives in Russia, whose holdings from two hundred years ago turned out to be not just scant but thoroughly mined by those who came before me, Russian reality suddenly produced a bounty of stuff that seemed tailor-made for the gendered analysis that interested me: photographs of a topless Putin vacationing in Siberia, pop songs touting Russia's president as the ideal boyfriend, movies depicting the Soviet Union's war in Afghanistan as a failure of machismo, and self-help literature promising to teach Russian women how to become sexpot bitches, among other things. Rather than write about plays whose production history has been all but erased by the passage of time and whose Alexandrine verse felt worlds away, I began to play with campy spectacles and ironic performances happening in real time, which the internet delivered on an almost daily basis.

Equally intrigued by Putinism's questionable taste and its weird cultural output, colleagues began to invite me to present conference papers that explored topics like the dreadful presidential biopic *This Kiss Is Off the Record*, Russia's participation in the Eurovision Song Contest, the impact of the country's infamous 2013 ban on "gay propaganda," and the Russian adaptation of *Fifty Shades of Grey*. Some of these conference papers grew into articles, while others led to new and exciting collaborations, both of which, I was delighted to discover, aroused more interest among my students, other scholars, and even journalists than anything I had published before. I started to receive invitations to speak about gender and sexuality in Putin's Russia, and in the question-and-answer after these talks, those who brought me to their campus asked when the book they assumed I was writing would appear in print. Never one to ignore a good idea when it is handed to me on a platter, I decided to do precisely what my colleagues suggested. I accepted that my deep dive into Neoclassical and Sentimentalist drama had hit rock bottom and that the path I was now on, despite its many fits, starts, and eccentricities, had a clear direction and destination: between 2000 and 2020, Putinism *was* style, and that style fused heteronormativity, homophobia, and hypergender in a playful yet politically potent pastiche.

In other words, the path that led me to *Russian Style* has been queer from the get-go, even though the material examined in this book veers from the highly heteronormative to the gloriously gay. As a queer child brought up during the Cold War, I found that this approach and combination of material speak to me on a deeply personal level. Like the Russians I write about, I was schooled in the performance of acceptable gender as a child and have used cisgender drag many times and in many places, including the Soviet Union, the Russian Federation, and the Islamic Republic of Iran, to fit in where I truly do not belong. My Cold War girlhood sensitized me to the slightest deviation from feminine norms, shaming me when I fell shy of their mark. As distant as I now am from the Russian Federation, the points of contact linking my very American upbringing to Russians' experience of the first two decades of Putinism are many and have given me rich food for thought. Moreover, my linguistic and cultural queerness in relation to what I study in this book affords me a certain leverage when interpreting the gendered forms of citizenship that emerged between 2000 and 2020 in Russia. As someone who has spent almost three decades learning and teaching Russian language, literature, and culture but who will never be Russian herself, I am always, already defamiliarized from the object of my inquiry and well attuned not only to when art makes the stone stony but also to when it fails to do so, as well as when it makes something that is not even a rock look like a stone, to borrow from the Formalist critic Viktor Shklovskii.

It has taken me over a decade to accumulate the case studies on which this book rests, and I owe a profound debt of gratitude to the many people and institutions who have supported the work that led to *Russian Style*. I would like to thank those who invited me to speak and encouraged me to expand my talks into a monograph, including Magnús Bernhardsson, Evgenii Bershtein, Julie Buckler, Philip Bullock, Helena Goscilo, Maksim Hanukai, Dan Healey, Katya Hokanson, Tom Roberts, and Roman Utkin. I am also grateful to the people who read and provided feedback on early drafts of several chapters, namely Alexander Kondakov, Alexandra Novitskaya, and Yana Skorobogatov. Eliot Borenstein, Emily Johnson, Greg Mitchell, and Olga Shevchenko deserve even greater thanks for reading a first draft of the complete manuscript as part of the Manuscript Review Program at the Oakley Center for the Humanities and Social Sciences at Williams College. I am also deeply indebted to Amber Rose Cederström of the University of Wisconsin Press for her backing of this project, as well as to Eliot Borenstein (yes, again!) and Lilya Kaganovsky, who provided invaluable input as the Press's external readers. Kyle Sung has earned my undying thanks for the many hours he put into checking footnotes and converting them into bibliographic entries, while Sourena Parham helped to prepare the book's illustrations. To the brave students of Williams College who took different iterations of my course on gender and sexuality in post-Soviet space, I give thanks for their ceaseless curiosity and invaluable insights. Various stages of this project have been funded by Williams College, whose Dean of the Faculty and Oakley Center for the Humanities and Social Sciences provided particular support. On a more personal level, I am profoundly grateful for a writing retreat in Marfa, Texas, at the home of my dear friends David Egeland and Andy Friedman, as well as for the support and inspiration I have received over the years from my Slavist soulmate Emily Johnson and my beloved wife, Leyla Rouhi.

Several sections of *Russian Style* have already appeared in print. Material from "Glamazons *en travesti*: Drag Queens in Putin's Russia," which was first published in *Russian Performances: Word, Object, Action*, ed. Julie A. Buckler, Julie A. Cassiday, and Boris Wolfson (Madison: University of Wisconsin Press, 2018), appears in the introduction and chapter 3, which also contains part of my article "Vladislav Mamyshev-Monro, Frog-Princess of Neoacademism" from *The Russian Review* 78 (April 2019). Chapter 4 borrows from "Post-Soviet Pop Goes Gay: Russia's Trajectory to Eurovision Victory," an article initially published in *The Russian Review* 73 (January 2014), while chapter 5 draws on

"A World without Safe Words: Fifty Shades of Russian Grey" from the *Journal of Popular Romance Studies* (March 30, 2020) and "Sacrifice and Self in *Everybody Dies but Me*," which first appeared in *The "Other" Martyrs: Women and the Poetics of Sexuality, Sacrifice, and Death in World Literatures*, ed. Alireza Korangy and Leyla Rouhi (Wiesbaden: Harrassowitz Verlag, 2019). In all cases, I have received permission from the publisher to reuse this material in *Russian Style*. Finally, all translations from Russian are my own unless otherwise noted.

Russian Style

Introduction

In January 2018, a group of young men at the Ulianovsk Institute of Aeronautical Engineering decided to film themselves in the halls of their dormitory as they acted out their own version of Italian DJ Benny Benassi's 2002 music video "Satisfaction."[1] The original that inspired the fourteen air cadets shows scantily clad women in safety glasses using a series of tools—from simple saw to industrial jackhammer—in a campy send-up of how women's bodies are used to market everything from cars to power drills.[2] The Ulianovsk cadets' direct inspiration came from a 2013 video parody made by men in the British army, which transformed Benassi's bikini-clad women wielding belt sanders into Tom-of-Finland wannabes pushing brooms, vacuums, and irons.[3] The Russian video follows its British predecessor closely: the cadets wear improvised costumes that combine their own underwear with belts, ties, and caps from military uniforms, and they deliver a series of gyrating pelvic thrusts as they sweep, hammer, iron, and dust their way through their dorm. Using gestures that by 2018 represented clichés of gay male sexuality, such as fellating a half-peeled banana, the Ulianovsk cadets never imagined that their parody of a parody of a parody would go viral and lead to vague accusations of "gay propaganda," something the Russian Federation famously outlawed in 2013.

The cadets' two-minute parody placed them in the crosshairs of public scrutiny as Russian officials of various stripes debated the young men's supposed transgression and whether it merited punishment. While some called the video "a tragedy," others viewed it as an insult to the entire Ulianovsk region, as well as to Russian veterans, and "a scandal for aviation," comparing the cadets to the feminist punk protesters of Pussy Riot.[4] At the same time, a spate of new "Satisfaction" parodies began to appear on YouTube in support of the cadets, making what started as a single video into a viral movement that embraced groups of all types—students, swimmers, jockeys, dancers, and even

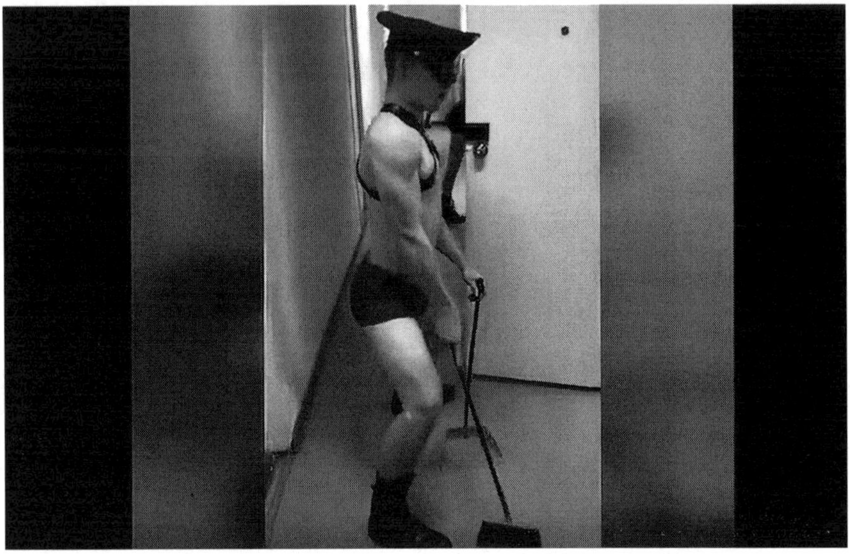

Figure 1. An Ulianovsk cadet twerks as he sweeps in the "Satisfaction" video from January 2018.

two retired women lip-syncing in the kitchen of their St. Petersburg communal apartment—in the parody of "Satisfaction."[5] By the time the scandal died down, the Ulianovsk cadets had become a cause célèbre, and the flood of "Satisfaction" parodies clearly demonstrated that these young men and their supporters were both willing and eager to create potential "gay propaganda" whether they were gay or not.[6]

At first glance, the 2018 "Satisfaction" videos seemed like another amusing episode in Russia's ongoing culture wars, to which Western readers and viewers could turn for a good laugh while bemoaning the growing illiberality of Vladimir Putin's Russia.[7] The videos of countless Russians twerking to Italian techno pop seemed right at home alongside photographs of a topless Putin on horseback from the late 2000s, coverage of the Pussy Riot affair in 2012, or news stories coming out of Russia about the 2013 ban on "gay propaganda," a 2014 embargo on women's lace panties for supposed "safety reasons," a regulation proposed in 2015 that would have prevented trans people from driving, and a 2017 judicial ruling that outlawed a meme of Putin as a "gay clown."[8] When taken together, these news stories reinforced long-standing stereotypes about Russia, where men are apparently manlier and women more feminine than in the West and the first two decades of Putin's rule led to a conservative backlash yet an overall upturn in the national capacity for self-irony.

At the same time that many in the West took pride in increasingly liberal policies like the legalization of same-sex marriage and the #MeToo movement, the Russian East seemed to have fallen victim to a rising tide of neonational neotraditionalism, whose alternating cycles of seriousness and irony were tough to read. Although such stereotypes contain a grain of truth, they fail to explain why gender and sexuality became so hotly contested in postsocialist Russia, as well as how they became Putin's go-to political weapons in the domestic arena between 2000 and 2020. Because these stereotypes define the Russian Other in relation to a Western self, they fail to recognize that two intertwined threads gave narrative coherence to news stories about young Russian women ripping their shirts open for Putin or government officials suggesting that gays be banned from blood donations.[9] Those threads were Russians' own performance of increasingly exaggerated gender roles during the two decades after Putin's rise to power and his regime's growing desire to police private sexual behavior.

Social scientists have touched on these trends in their analysis of Putin's first three terms as Russia's president and his brief stint as the country's prime minister. For example, anthropologists and sociologists have documented the emergence of gendered neotraditionalism in pronouncements from both the Russian government and the Russian Orthodox Church, while economists and political scientists debate the extent to which Russia adopted neoliberalism, with its emphasis on entrepreneurial individualism and self-regulation, during the reforms of the 1990s and the oil and gas boom of the 2000s.[10] Discussion of these trends has led the feminist scholars Valerie Sperling and Janet Elise Johnson to view gender and sexuality as tools of political legitimation used by both Putin's regime and its opposition.[11] At the same time, Andrey Makarychev and Sergei Medvedev have concluded that "a biopolitical turn has taken place in Russia, as exemplified by the application of a number of regulatory mechanisms for disciplining and constraining human bodies."[12] When taken together, the insights of social scientists provide a helpful lens for understanding Russian legislation and policy that appeared between 2000 and 2020 and focused on gender and sexuality. Eschewing any coherent ideology, the Putin regime made heteronormativity, with its concomitant homophobia, into an ideological proxy.

The net effect of the many policies and regulations that contributed to this biopolitical turn was to redefine citizenship in Russia during Putin's first two decades in power through the imperatives of compulsory heterosexuality and hypergender, that is, the embodiment of essentialized, polarized, and supposedly "traditional" forms of masculinity and femininity. After his rise to power in 1999, Putin's government made a concerted effort, through legislation, policy, and Putin's own public appearances, to alter the discourse of and the modes for performing citizenship in the Russian Federation, as seen in the country's popular culture. Whether we look to legislation and public policy or to popular music, literature, television, film, and the internet, we see that the Russian Federation's ideal citizen during the 2000s and 2010s had both a gender and a sexual orientation. The paradigmatic Russian who emerged from popular representations was not the country's hypermasculine leader, an oligarch, or even a man but a young, sexually available, heterosexual woman, who chose to shape her body, behavior, and desires in response to Vladimir Putin.

This book argues that the trends identified by social scientists took on a life of their own in Russia's popular culture, which between 2000 and 2020 generated everything from enthusiastic support for the "traditional values" advocated by the Kremlin to angry protests against the government's failed promises, corruption, and fraud. Despite more recent imposition of censorship that harkens back to Soviet days, Putin's regime initially exerted only limited control over much of the country's popular culture, which played a key role in propagating and interpreting the dual mandate to be an exemplary citizen of the Russian Federation and to bear children for the motherland. As the chapters that follow argue, popular culture offered a uniquely powerful means of transmitting the model of gendered and sexualized citizenship that emerged during Putin's first two decades in power, since the variegated universe of pop—spanning television, music, radio, podcasts, social media, advertising, and the like—made identity at the turn of the twenty-first century a matter of performance. Just as gender and sexuality represent performative constructs, so has citizenship shifted from ontological definitions, which focus on where we or our parents were born, to a more phenomenological understanding, which depends on embodied practices, like the languages we speak, the holidays and traditions we observe, the clothes we wear, what we eat and drink, as well as with whom we have sex and how. Popular culture's capacity to communicate the performative nature of identity via its contents, as well as the different media that constitute it, arguably made it the most important means of broadcasting the different modes in which post-Soviet citizenship could and should to be performed after Putin's rise to power, as well as a crucial arena where the performative demands of Russian citizenship could be resisted, negotiated, and even rejected.

This book's focus on popular culture arises largely from the recognition that in the course of any given day, each of us encounters and consumes countless instances of popular culture whether we intend to or not. Russians have a notorious penchant for their state-sponsored television, as well as a seemingly endless appetite for the internet, which makes it more likely that the average Russian surfing through YouTube in the 2010s would view the rapper Timati's 2015 homage to Putin titled "Best Friend" (whose official version has garnered more than fifteen million hits) or one of the many memes that recycle photos of the Russian president topless (whose hits are incalculable) than any of Putin's public speeches (whose hits range from the thousands to tens of thousands).[13] At the same time that the ubiquity of popular culture makes it an especially worthy object of scholarly analysis, its enormity and fecundity mean that any attempt to treat popular culture comprehensively is doomed to failure. As a result, the books, films, videos, websites, and performances examined in the pages that follow do not pretend to embrace the full scope of Russian pop cultural production between 2000 and 2020; rather, they represent especially vivid and paradigmatic examples that reveal the gendered and sexualized stakes of Putinism's biopolitical turn. In addition, they demonstrate pop culture's ability to spawn a broad range of simulacra of Russianness, which came neither from the ground up nor from the top down and became available to Russian speakers throughout post-Soviet space, regardless of ethnic, racial, religious, regional, or national differences, during Putin's first two decades in power.

My decision to focus on gender and sexuality means that the instances of Russian pop culture in the chapters that follow touch on other important shifts in the discourse of Putinism only occasionally and in passing. For example, the gradual ethnicization and racialization of the idea of Russianness between 2000 and 2020 is usually absent or only in the background of the videos, songs, and films examined in this book, precisely because Russian exceptionalism and ethnonational thinking became ever more prominent in political rhetoric during this time. Between 1999 and 2020, Putin increased the already existing semantic slippage between the words *russkii* (an adjective that describes the Russian ethnos, language, and many instances of culture) and *rossiiskii* (the adjectival form of the country Rossiia), using the resulting vagueness to articulate his by now infamous notion of the "Russian World."[14] Likewise, those marketing Russophone pop culture across post-Soviet space rarely adopted the clearly outlined nationalist platforms of someone like the political philosopher and strategist Aleksandr Dugin, who has been nicknamed "Putin's Brain."[15] Like Putin himself, they preferred to cite such platforms partially or obliquely, if at all, in effect leveraging the slippage not only between *russkii* and *rossiiskii* but also among the various nationalisms that came in and out of vogue during Putin's first two decades in power.

Throughout this book, I have chosen to use the English adjective "Russian," which conflates the semantic fields of *russkii* and *rossiiskii*, since it just happens to reflect the fluidity of terminology and thinking that Putin, along with many others, used to justify his empire building beginning with the 2014 seizure of Crimea. Whenever possible, I try to tease out the ethnic and racial undertones in pop cultural products by performers who did not identify as ethnically Russian or were not Russian citizens. However, I leave the complex and critical question of how the Russian Federation's many minorities—ethnic, racial, religious, regional, national, and sexual—actually fared in the rapidly changing 2010s and 2020s to those who study these minorities' lived experience, political struggles, and cultural expression.[16] Because pop culture deals in simulacra, even performers whose identity was in some way non-Russian contributed to the ersatz version of the "Russian World" that helped make Russianness increasingly white between 1999 and 2020 at the same time that they seemed to diversify Russophone pop.

When considered in parallel with changes implemented by the Kremlin, the popular texts that support this book's argument demonstrate that although new rhetoric about the "Russian World," "maternity capital," and "gay propaganda" created substantive changes in Russia's public discourse, the gendered and sexualized performance of Russian citizenship was a question not of substance but of style. In fact, popular culture's unrelenting attention to styles of speech, dress, comportment, interaction, and association allowed it to play a role in another important trend during this period, namely the substitution of content for style. For example, the rise of a distinctly Russian version of glamour in the 2000s showed that its obsession with glossy surfaces and stylistic flair could effectively block ideological content and political substance. Rather than pretend or even aspire to ideology, like Leninism and Stalinism in the twentieth century, Putinism of the early twenty-first century strove simply for style. Understanding the performativity of Russian citizenship during this time requires that we examine the different stylistic possibilities for performing gender and sexuality that emerged in post-Soviet Russia, as well as how they, like the ideological proxies of heteronormativity and homophobia, took the place of substantive political debate. As the country moved from perestroika and glasnost, through the roaring nineties and into Putin's presidency, the performative modes available to Russia's citizens evolved, shifting from notions viewed as uniquely Soviet or Russian, such as the difficult to define *poshlost'* and *stiob*, to others that appear more universal, such as charisma, camp, and kitsch.

Once we discern the overlapping modes of performance that became available to Russians in popular culture during Putin's first two decades in power, we can recognize that the Ulianovsk cadets' parody of "Satisfaction" represented more than an entertaining episode in Russia's culture wars. Whether they knew it or not, the cadets' and their supporters' parodies tapped into what Susan Sontag calls "the whole point of Camp": "to dethrone the serious. . . . One can be serious about the frivolous, frivolous about the serious."[17] As Eliot Borenstein aptly observes, the Ulianovsk cadets fought "for the right to be frivolous . . . in an atmosphere of pompous, self-righteously serious political and cultural pronouncements" at the same time that they showed "that Russians can still form horizontal connections, despite the state's monopoly on the public sphere," to quote Masha Gessen.[18] The frivolity and connectivity of the "Satisfaction" videos demonstrated the cadets' successful mastery of camp as a performative mode, as well as their ability to wrest control of this mode for performing gender, sexuality, and citizenship from the hands of the state. When we view the viral "Satisfaction" videos from this angle, we can see how their creators clearly understood and deftly manipulated the political substance that Putinism as style attempted to block.

Embodied Citizenship in the Soviet Union and in the Russian Federation

To understand how and why Russia's popular culture in the 2000s and 2010s came to represent young, reproductively inclined women as ideal citizens, we must take a brief excursion into the history of citizenship over the past century in Russia. In addition to exhibiting the same heteronormative underpinnings that characterize citizenship in modern states generally, the form of citizenship that initially developed under Putin shares several salient features with earlier versions from the Soviet and post-Soviet eras, as scholars have pointed out.[19] Interestingly, those studying gendered and sexual citizenship in Russia tend to separate these concepts even though gender and sexuality represent two sides of a single heteronormative coin. Feminist scholars writing about the different periods of gendered citizenship in the country's history focus understandably on the state's attempts to regulate women, while scholars investigating sexual citizenship analyze the state's exclusion of LGBTQ+ subjects, which, in the case of Russia, has meant writing about gay men.[20] However, grasping the full significance of the changes that Putinism wrought in Russian citizenship requires an approach that considers both sides of the heteronormative coin in its approach to citizenship as an embodied phenomenon.[21] Once we unite the insights of feminist and queer scholars, we realize that two types of citizens in the Soviet Union and in the Russian Federation have received the state's scrutiny and regulation over the past century: "normal" women, whose femininity is viewed as essential to the reproduction of the nation, and "abnormal" men, whose insufficient or deviant masculinity equates in the Russian imagination to homosexuality. Examining policies that have addressed women's reproductive labor on the one hand and men's flagging masculinity on the other reveals a series of pendulum swings in the discourse of embodied citizenship, which have taken the Soviet Union and the Russian Federation through multiple sexual revolutions in the last hundred years.

In addition to heralding the first of these sexual revolutions, the Bolsheviks' 1917 seizure of power led to a radical overhaul of the notion of citizenship itself. In their attempt to destroy preceding models of capitalist belonging, the Bolsheviks framed citizenship in the newly formed Soviet Union through the right to work, which functioned coercively to bring both men and women into the project of creating and maintaining the Soviet state.[22] With the Bolsheviks' monopoly on all forms of discourse, the early Soviet era (1918 through the early 1930s) saw dramatic changes in laws regulating both sex and the family, which were designed to allow Soviet citizens to enter the workforce and extended the state's reach into spheres relegated previously to church and family. Most significant, regulations that tackled the so-called women's question secularized marriage, eased divorce, and allowed abortion, which became legal in 1920. When taken together, these radical changes in social policy granted working women full rights as Soviet citizens and transformed motherhood from a private, personal, or familial matter into a civic duty. By creating communal institutions intended to shoulder the burden of childcare, the Bolshevik sexual revolution sought to make Soviet women into working mothers, who contributed to the building of socialism by both giving birth to future citizens, parented in part by the state, and producing goods and services.[23]

If early Soviet laws and regulations conceived of women as working mothers, they viewed men first and foremost as providers of military and industrial labor. The promise of communal kitchens, crèches, and housing not only allowed Russian women to enter the workforce but also freed Russian men from most parental duties, while new regulations governing alimony and child support suggested that fatherhood was little more than an economic matter. As part of the overall liberalization in sexual politics, the Bolshevik government also reaffirmed the decriminalization of sodomy that occurred in February 1917. Taken as a whole, the new policies governing women and same-sex relations between men ushered in an era of sexual permissiveness. However, we should be careful not to confuse the early Soviet sexual revolution with acceptance of either the "social ills" these regulations were intended to address or those who took part in them. A handful of Bolshevik thinkers, with Alexandra Kollontai at their head, celebrated the new sexual freedom, yet the vast majority of those who implemented Bolshevik laws governing sex had more pragmatic motivations. Vladimir Lenin considered "the sexual question" a potential diversion from revolutionary work, and the new sexual policies outlined earlier arose out of heated debates about how best to deal with the social chaos created by revolution and civil war. Dan Healey, for example, has shown that the decriminalization of sodomy arose not from any particular tolerance of homosexuality on the Bolsheviks' part but rather out of a contentious process that adapted pre-revolutionary legislative projects to the new country and left much of the work of defining sexual and gender deviance in the hands of doctors and the courts.[24] Broader discussion of sexuality in the early Soviet period viewed the human libido as something to be overcome and sublimated for the purposes of building the new socialist state.[25] In other words, although the Bolshevik sexual revolution boldly extended Soviet citizenship to women, the permissive laws and regulations addressing women and nonheterosexual men assumed that "normal" Soviet citizens of both sexes would use their sexuality not for personal gratification but for the country's demographic and economic needs.

Stalin's rise to power led to a sexual counterrevolution, which restricted or reversed many early Soviet policies in favor of bourgeois norms and values. At the same time, the years between 1936 and 1956 intensified several key features of the embodied citizenship instituted by the Bolsheviks, including the polarization of men's and women's roles and the state's growing reach into the private sphere. Most noticeable, the communalization of living space diminished the privacy of family life, which reverted to patriarchal practices when abortion became illegal in 1936 and divorce significantly harder to obtain in 1944. With maternity now a compulsory civic duty, Soviet women bore the double burden of family care and fulltime labor.[26] As part of the conservative backlash, sodomy was recriminalized in 1933–1934, at Stalin's personal urging, signaling "the birth of modern Russian political homophobia" as a means for distinguishing between those who can enjoy full rights as Soviet citizens and those who cannot.[27] The varied discussions of gender and sexuality that characterized the 1920s also came to a halt by the mid-1930s, contributing to a regime of sexual silence and queer invisibility.[28]

When viewed against its totalitarian backdrop, Stalin's sexophobic "great retreat" resulted in a scenario of citizenship that reinforced the femininity of Soviet women at the same time that it denied certain forms of masculinity to Soviet men. Stalin's cult of personality represented him metaphorically as the all-powerful father of the Soviet people and as a husband to Soviet women, whose duty to bear children for the great leader was supported by a variety of state benefits and institutions. Within this trope, Soviet men figured as Stalin's sons and were obliged to sacrifice themselves to the dangerous and often deadly projects of collectivization, industrialization, and national defense.[29] As a result, Stalinism's paradigm of citizenship reduced both men and women to their assumed physical capacities, asserting women's maternal duty and men's status as cannon fodder. In this context, the scapegoating of men who had sex with other men in antisodomy laws served a compensatory function by constructing an abject male Other, whose presence, both real and imagined, bolstered the depleted masculinity of heterosexual men. When taken with the actual demographic depletion of Soviet men due to migration, famine, collectivization, industrialization, the Great Purges, and World War II, the embodied citizenship of Stalinism contributed to a crisis of Russian masculinity with long-term effects.

After Stalin's death, in 1956, the Thaw began to reprivatize the everyday lives of Soviet citizens in a gradual process that extended to the end of the Soviet era and beyond. Key in this trend were the decriminalization of abortion in 1955, new policies in support of motherhood, and the 1968 family code, which simplified divorce. Nonetheless, the Soviet state continued efforts to compel women to bear children through a discourse of naturalized gender, which equated femininity with maternity and depicted motherhood as woman's biological destiny. Significantly, the housing boom of the 1960s led to greater privacy and the reemergence of the family as the basic social unit. When coupled with a loosening of sexual mores, the resurgence of the private sphere created space, in a very literal sense, for sexual practices and communities once deemed "deviant." Soviet queers, for example, not only congregated in private homes but increasingly gathered in public cruising spaces known as *pleshki*, taking part in the Soviet Union's second sexual revolution.[30] However, this partial liberalization continued Stalinism's silence about sex and failed to provide effective sex education and family planning to its burgeoning citizenry. Without other reliable forms of birth control, Soviet women turned to abortion, which became a mass phenomenon and functioned, because of a lack of trustworthy medical care, as a punitive measure for those women who refused to reproduce.[31] In addition, male homosexuality continued to represent a criminal offense that relegated all of the country's LGBTQ+ subjects to silence, to which social invisibility was added for Soviet lesbians, at the same time that a gay liberation movement took shape in the West.

While late-Soviet women struggled to balance work both inside and outside the home, Soviet men became the target of serious discussion when, in 1970, the crisis of masculinity first hit the Soviet press.[32] Alarmed by the country's falling birth rate, social scientists lamented the dire state of Soviet men, citing their lower numbers, shorter life spans, and higher morbidity rates in comparison to women. Writers of such pieces implicitly criticized the Soviet Union's unprecedented emancipation of women, as well as their country's socialized services, claiming that these achievements had effectively displaced men as household heads and breadwinners. Common concerns in the debate included the masculinization of women, the feminization of men, as well as men's passive victimization by their own biology and historical circumstance.

Adding to women's already onerous burden, commentators instructed the country's female citizens to save their male counterparts. Late-Soviet treatment of the crisis of masculinity tacitly acknowledged the emasculation and infantilization of Russian men, employing a patriarchal discourse of essentialized gender. Although a handful of new gender roles for men promised to recuperate their depleted manhood, the fact that Soviet men were denied the economic, political, and ideological freedom on which these roles relied placed them out of reach.

In short, both femininity and masculinity were considered to be in crisis by the late 1980s, as was the Soviet Union itself. The country's second sexual revolution failed to solve the perceived demographic crisis and instead exacerbated it by continuing to define men and women through their physical capacities. Despite a partial privatization of everyday life and more liberal sexual mores, the Soviet state never relinquished its control over the discourse governing citizens' gender and sexuality. This rhetoric focused obstinately on citizens' productive and reproductive duties, relegating non-procreative sex to the realm beyond citizenship. At the same time, the Soviet regime of embodied citizenship strove for a hegemony it never actually achieved, even under Stalin. Although overt dissent was not tolerated, the country's citizens developed a wide variety of adaptive strategies that allowed them to avoid the state's coercive call to citizenship. While late-Soviet gays rebelled by quietly occupying *pleshki* and lesbians might live queer lives unnoticed, women expressed their refusal to conform to the demands of citizenship through multiple abortions, and men could adopt a variety of dissident styles from the *stiliaga* (post–World War II fashionista) to the *fartsovshchik* (black marketeer) and socially disengaged boiler-room technician. In other words, despite laws and regulations designed to force citizen's active participation in building and populating socialism, the Soviet paradigm of embodied citizenship allowed for a variety of behaviors: while some fulfilled the state's demands to produce both labor and children, others resisted them by checking out and not reproducing.

With the demise of the Soviet Union in 1991, nonprocreative sex quickly became the media's hottest trend, signaling the third and final sexual revolution in twentieth-century Russia. The gradual liberalization of the post-Stalin era gave way to rampant deregulation, which led to a no-holds-barred attitude toward virtually all of the forms of gender expression and sexuality that qualified as "deviant" in the Soviet era. The state lost its monopoly over the discourse of sex and gender, and a variety of actors, including a newly free press, the Orthodox Church, aspiring politicians, and the capitalist marketplace, rushed to satisfy Russians' curiosity "about that."[33] Significantly, the Soviet-era statute banning voluntary sodomy was repealed in 1993 by president Boris Yeltsin in a bid to join the Council of Europe. However, as Alexander Kondakov has pointed out, the Russian Federation did not eliminate homophobia from its laws and regulations. In 1996, a separate clause outlawing homosexual rape was introduced into the country's criminal code, despite the fact that rape already represented a punishable offense, and, while accepting the World Health Organization's classification of illnesses in 1999, the Russian Ministry of Health saw fit to define "a disorder of sexual preference" as any divergence from consensual, adult, heterosexual pairing.[34] Nonetheless, the efflorescence of sexual discourse in the 1990s encouraged a few Russians to come out of the closet, briefly boosted the already extant gay-rights movement, and led to Russia's first gay journals, clubs, and cafes.[35] After more than seven decades of sexual silence, invisibility, and erasure, Russians' seemingly insatiable appetite for information about sex transformed the late Soviet era's passive resistance through nonreproduction into a very active consumption of television shows, books, magazines, and newspapers about sex and gender in all their permutations.

While the wholesale commodification of sex in the 1990s had its fans, it also found detractors. Many perceived the sexual freedom flooding into Russia as a sign of social chaos, and some interpreted the explosion of a free market for sexual discourse as an attack from the West. More specifically, the Soviet regime of queer invisibility led some Russians to believe that homosexuality was a post-Soviet invention or Western import.[36] Against the background of a falling birthrate and a precipitous drop in life expectancy, critics of the new sexual freedom began to lament, once again, the fragile and anxious state of Russian masculinity.[37] Although unprecedented economic and political opportunities launched a few lucky men into the ranks of "New Russians," the vast majority of the country's male population suffered from under- or unemployment and felt more emasculated than ever before. Pundits of different stripes began to voice nostalgia for Soviet-era paternalism with its essentialized gender roles, calling for the return of forms of gender and sexuality supposedly "traditional" to Russian culture.[38] Such neotraditionalism idealized gender roles that had not existed in Russia for well over a century, if at all, for example, men as sole breadwinners and women as full-time housewives. When taken together, the urgent crisis of masculinity and the neotraditional turn led many to view women, the demographic producers of the nation, as special citizens in need of the state's paternal care. Even though a larger cast of characters took part in the discussion of sex in the 1990s than during the Soviet era and the variety of available gender roles rapidly expanded, embodied citizenship of the 1990s represented a paradoxical blend of new and old. At the same time that the country's citizens took part in the boom in sexual discourse and commerce, which included sex work and sexual sponsorship among women's economic options, Russian gender roles were becoming more polarized and "traditional" than at any point during the Soviet era.[39]

When Putin became prime minister of the Russian Federation, in 1999, the pendulum of sexual revolution was poised for a backswing. After almost a decade of what some perceived as sexual anarchy, Putin's rise to power began the process of pushing the pendulum of sexual revolution to the right. Embodied citizenship in Russia continued to blend old and new by harking back to Soviet-era notions of citizens' duty to fulfill the state's demographic needs at the same time that it cast Russian men and women as neoliberal consumers and self-policing subjects. Although the Russian state no longer monopolized the discourse of gender and sexuality, it did its best to co-opt or silence competing voices during the 2000s and 2010s, for example, by strengthening ties with the Orthodox Church, closing independent media outlets, and imposing censorship laws and restrictions on internet access ostensibly to protect children. In addition, Putin's regime explained precisely what it meant by "traditional values" in policy papers that informed legislation intended to solve the country's demographic problems. One such document from 2013 defined "traditional family values" as the union of a man and a woman that results in the birth of three or more children and in which the family members respect parental authority and reside under a single roof.[40] Putin's government backed up such pronatal rhetoric with incentives for childbirth, such as the 2006 program of "maternity capital," which financially rewards women who bear two or more children.[41] Although "maternity capital" has gained little traction among those eligible for its benefits, the Putin-era swing to the right appears to have had broad support among the country's populace, which, as a whole, supported neither feminism nor LGBTQ+ rights in the early Putin years.[42]

While many of the state's policies during Putin's first two decades in power demonstrated the Soviet view that women's citizenship was first and foremost a demographic issue, a significant portion of the Kremlin's neoconservative rhetoric attempted to deal with the intractable crisis of masculinity. However, rather than trying to improve men's health and morale through costly programs that would ameliorate unemployment or substance abuse, the Kremlin created a compensatory masculine myth in the carefully constructed cult of Putin's personality, which initially functioned as the flip side of "maternity capital" and policies in support of Russia's children. A postmodern mash-up of the president's machismo, charisma, and political swagger, the cult of Putin that emerged in the 2000s depicted the Russian president as the ultimate *muzhik*, or real Russian man, contributing to the further polarization of gender norms in postsocialist Russia.[43] Numerous regulations played into Putinism's regime of compensatory hypermasculinity, yet the 2013 ban on propagating "nontraditional sexual relations" among minors mentioned earlier proved particularly paradigmatic. If Putin's hypermasculinity in the political sphere sought to justify Russia's resurgence as a land-grabbing superpower, then the "gay propaganda" law drew a line in the sand between the "normal" men and women who made up Russia's citizenry and the country's abject LGBTQ+ Others.[44] As Dan Healey argues, such homophobic policies fail to examine the responsibility of Russia's heterosexual men in the country's many woes. Instead, the myth of Russian hypermasculinity cultivated by Putin in the 2000s and 2010s transformed earlier rhetoric about male vulnerability and victimization into the unquestioned superiority and strength of straight Russian men.[45]

As much as the Putin-era backlash might remind us of Soviet scenarios of embodied citizenship, the return to "traditional values" during Putin's first two decades in power took place in a radically different domestic and geopolitical environment. Despite attempts to ignore sex education, limit abortions, and restrict women's reproductive rights to giving birth, the Russian state had less power to coerce its citizens to fulfill their supposed demographic duty than did its late-Soviet precursor.[46] The economic realities of Putinism's oxymoronic "sovereign democracy," which in the 2000s included freewheeling capitalism, an oil and gas boom, and rapid expansion of the internet throughout the country, created a distinctly Russian form of neoliberalism. Russians' newfound affluence gave them access to a marketplace with countless goods and services designed to help in the processes of self-maintenance and self-governance, signaling the shift of much of the burden of disciplining the country's citizenry from the state onto its subjects. In addition to placing responsibility for compliance with norms of gendered and sexual citizenship squarely on citizens' shoulders, the body's newfound significance made possible a variety of embodied political protests as seen in Pussy Riot, "living pain" performance artist Petr Pavlensky, and the mass protests against election fraud in 2011–2012. Rather than leading to any liberalization in the Russian government or its regime of citizenship, however, these actively protesting bodies contributed to a series of increasingly conservative policies implemented in years since.

The failure of such embodied protest underscores the overall passivity of the paradigm of citizenship enshrined by Putinism, which eschews active participation by the populace in the political process at the same time that it takes part in a global "transition in the role of the citizen from producer of work to consumer."[47] In Western states, this transition has led to what Lauren Berlant calls the privatization of citizenship, as well as "homonationalism," which, according to Jasbir Puar, constructs "U.S. sexual exceptionalism" in contrast to illiberal Eastern Others.[48] In the 2000s, the Kremlin gladly blurred the line between public and private, taking part in the privatization of citizenship Berlant describes. However, rather than joining the ranks of homonationalists, led by the United States and Western Europe, Putin's regime readily accepted the accusation of Eastern illiberality implicit in Puar's argument. By the 2010s, the Kremlin had constructed Russia's sexual exceptionalism on its supposedly "traditional values," making procreation, heteronormativity, and hypergender, a concept central to this book's argument, clear requirements for performing the country's privatized regime of citizenship. At the same time, Russia became a leader among those countries, from Indonesia to Uganda, that rejected homonationalism in favor of compensatory hypermasculinity and political homophobia. In other words, Putinism of the 2000s and 2010s used Russia's sexual exceptionalism to reconfigure citizenship in the domestic sphere and to draw new borders—both figuratively in the case of Syria and literally in that of Ukraine—between its "moral" allies and "immoral" enemies internationally.

Performing Citizenship in Putin's Russia

At the same time that the blend of old and new in Russia's regime of embodied citizenship began to sanction military aggression, the passivity of this regime shaped how citizenship could and should be performed by the country's citizens. On one hand, Putin cornered the market on public performances of political masculinity in the 2000s, as seen in Kremlin-sponsored photo shoots that show the Russian president working out in his judogi, playing ice hockey, or taming Siberian tigers with a tranquilizer gun. On the other hand, the average person on the street established belonging in the Russian nation through more private performances of the "traditional values" that the country's regime of citizenship sought to enshrine. Rather than claim rights or protest their erosion in the public sphere, an activity not just discouraged but punished by the illiberal Russian state, most Russians in the 2000s and 2010s negotiated the neotraditional versions of gender and sexuality that signified Russianness through countless quotidian performances, which either reproduced and reconstituted or reformulated and rejected heteronormative hypergender.

The passivity of this regime of citizenship means that the discussion of performativity in the chapters that follow differs in key respects from that of political scientists studying performative citizenship in Western liberal democracies. All analyses of performativity, that is, the idea that our actions, behaviors, and gestures are not caused by but are in fact the cause of our identities, owe an intellectual debt to J. L. Austin's analysis of performative utterances and Judith Butler's work on gender as a social construct, among others.[49] However, political scientists applying these ideas to citizenship in the West concentrate their attention on subjugated minorities' struggle for emancipation through public assembly, positing both the self-awareness and the agency of those who take part in such struggles.[50] According to these scholars, such reflexivity allows subjugated minorities to exercise "the *universal* right to claim rights" from states prepared to recognize and act on such claims.[51] As compelling as this scholarship is, its vocabulary of claiming rights and its supposition of a state willing to acknowledge rights claims have limited applicability in the Russian context. As described earlier, the terminology of citizens' rights has functioned in the Soviet Union and Russia largely as a euphemism for obligations to the state, which "is not necessarily perceived as a guarantor of individual freedoms and rights," since its repressive apparatus has historically interpreted rights claims as an existential threat.[52] The Russian case calls into question the presumed universality of the right to claim rights, and the very real risks to Russians who engage in what Charles Tilly has termed "contentious performances" of claiming rights in the public sphere help explain why this book devotes more space to the "small and big negotiations of everyday life . . . and even private actions that accumulate, sediment and accrue towards change" than to mass protests or rallies.[53]

Rather than limit Tilly's contentious performances to the relatively infrequent political protests that have taken place in postsocialist Russia, this book employs a broader notion of performative citizenship that recognizes but does not require the public activism, self-awareness, and agency to which political scientists typically attend. Instead, the performances of Russian citizenship discussed in the chapters that follow lie not only in Berlant's blurred public–private zone but also on the threshold between the country's passive regime of citizenship and overt activism, where reflex meets reflexivity and subjugation merges with agency. The Russian case calls for this wider understanding of performative citizenship since the growing illiberality and aggression of Putin's government have placed all the Russian Federation's citizens in a position not merely comparable to but arguably worse than that of subjugated minorities in Western liberal democracies, despite rights guaranteed in the Russian constitution. As with racial, ethnic, and religious minorities in the West, the presence of Russia's citizenry is tolerated and accepted as long as it performs some useful role. However, the precarity of Russia's citizens, both as a collection of individual bodies and as a collective body politic, immediately comes to light as soon as political, economic, or social winds change so that some segment of the populace is deemed abject, contagious, or disposable. Yet, unlike subjugated minorities in the West, who exercise their right to perform citizenship through free assembly, Russia's citizens risk becoming disposable if and when they dare to protest, as the poisoning and imprisonment of the anticorruption activist Aleksei Navalnyi vividly demonstrate. Putinism's passive regime of Russian citizenship is by and large a continuation of the Soviet state's ability to assert the precarity of all of its subjects, as the millions who perished due to collectivization, industrialization, the Great Purges, World War II, and the Gulag attest. Despite the fact that the Russian state under Putin has only recently, with its senseless war in Ukraine, begun to expend human life as immoderately as its Soviet precursor, it has nonetheless proven itself ready and able to ignore the law in its treatment of migrants, the disabled, and queers within Russia and to disenfranchise the country's electorate through blatant voting fraud. This normalization of precarity results from what Alexander Etkind calls "the deterioration of human capital" accompanying Russia's rise as "a petrostate," and it represents a constituent element of Putin-era citizenship that renders all citizens' performances potentially contentious, regardless of their location in public or private, their reflexivity, or their intent.[54]

Although the regime of citizenship that emerged during Putin's first two decades at Russia's helm shares this normalized precarity with its Soviet precursor, what and how individual bodies signify within this regime has undergone a noticeable shift. Not only did the role of Russia's citizens change "from producer of work to consumer," but the very mode of citizens' embodiment shifted from production to performance. During the Soviet era, the state policed the boundaries of citizenship by monitoring and rewarding what individual bodies produced, for example, through recognition of norm-breaking Stakhanovites or Mother-Heroes who bore ten or more children. This top-down control gave way in the post-Soviet era to a more diffuse expectation that the individual would successfully navigate the marketplace in order to regulate the body's surface, gestures, and attitudes and demonstrate adequacy as a heterosexual Russian man or woman. As the twentieth century gave way to the twenty-first, Russia's citizen-consumers learned to scrutinize the body's surface for suitable markers of gender and sexuality, to monitor its interior for appropriate physical and psychic processes, and to fashion its actions and movement in accordance with prevailing norms. As a result, the human body, which was treated largely as a fungible and disposable source of labor before the Soviet Union's demise, took on a commodified and instrumentalized life of its own, becoming the locus of post-Soviet performativity and citizenship.[55]

In both paradigms, however, productivity and performativity function not as a binary "either-or" opposition but rather as "indivisible and mutually productive" dimensions of embodiment, comparable to the distinction drawn by Alexei Yurchak between the constative (i.e., factual, descriptive) and the performative dimensions of late Soviet discourse.[56] We can fruitfully extend Yurchak's argument for a "performative shift," in which "it became increasingly important to participate in the reproduction of the *form* of [late-Soviet] ritualized acts of authoritative discourse than to engage with their constative meanings," to the politics of the body in post-Soviet Russia. The Soviet era's interest in bodies as a source of labor, which produced everything from coal, iron, and wheat to the next generation of citizens, gave way to the Putin era's interest in bodily affect and style, as seen in the president's own speeches and public appearances, as well as the glamour trend of the 2000s. Undeniably, the Russian state has expressed concern about what its citizens' bodies produce, as pronatal policies like maternity capital and restrictions on women's reproductive rights demonstrate, and the financial crisis of 2014–2017, along with economic sanctions levied in response to the annexation of Crimea and the invasion of Ukraine, have renewed the state's interest in what Russians make in the marketplace. Nonetheless, to paraphrase Yurchak, the replication of styles of gender and sexuality that were fixed and normalized in the 2000s became an end in itself by the 2010s, while the productive consequences of these styles remained relatively unimportant.[57]

"A Feminine Country That Wants to Be Manly"

The stylistic emphasis of performative citizenship under Putin has deep roots in Russian culture. At the very least, we can view the new stylishness that emerged during Putin's first two decades at Russia's helm as the remedy to a national lack of style, which the writer Viktor Erofeev diagnosed as symptomatic of Russian culture in the mid-1990s: "Without style, there's no person. Stylelessness is a terrible Russian scourge. . . . There isn't currently a Russian style, and this is a catastrophe. . . . The time is coming for a stylistic explosion. . . . A new generation of stylistically preoccupied Russians is beginning to appear. Who get high on style. Who get into style. The break will be painful, like everything in Russian history, but it's not only necessary. It's the Russian person's path to the self."[58] Although Erofeev includes both women and men in this short essay, the brunt of his critique falls on Russian men, as both the title, *Men*, of the book in which the essay appears and the similarity of the word "stylelessness" (*besstil'ie*) to that for "impotence" (*bessilie*) suggest.[59] After Erofeev diagnosed Russia's crisis of masculinity as a national lack of style, his prediction of a new generation of Russians intoxicated and even obsessed by style actually came true under Putin. However, the writer's belief that a revolution in Russian style would pave the way to the self is dubious at best. Erofeev fails to examine the connection between the national and the personal in his prediction, even though Russia's modern history richly illustrates the importance of questions of taste and style in the state's efforts to modernize and mobilize its populace, whether through Peter the Great's sartorial reforms or in Soviet debates over Socialist Realism.[60] Several scholars have even determined that the Russian intelligentsia, including Soviet dissidents and the protesters of 2011–2012, is first and foremost a stylistic phenomenon, a claim that requires that we consider how style drives the performative shift that took place after Putin became president. By linking modes of performativity that Russians themselves generated in the late Soviet era, for example, the *stiob* analyzed by Yurchak, to more universal modes that flooded the country's mediascape with the Soviet Union's demise, such as Sontag's camp, we can identify a continuum along which gender, sexuality, and citizenship have been performed by a wide variety of post-Soviet actors, from anti-Putin protestors to Putin himself. And despite Putinism's preference for style over substance, the mutually constitutive nature of productivity and performativity means that the right style could and did generate political substance, as both Putin's Kremlin-orchestrated photo ops and the Ulianovsk cadets' inadvertent foray into viral celebrity showed.

Despite Erofeev's accuracy in predicting a revolution in Russian style, he found its results less than satisfying some twenty years after the initial publication of *Men*. In an interview with the website *Kvir* from 2014, the author does not describe how the explosion of style led to an authentically Russian self, male or female. Instead, he laments that 2014's Russian man is feminized and formless: "We men are nonetheless defined by women. And in this regard, we've become hostages of the Other's gaze. . . . The secret of Russia is that it's a feminine country that wants to be manly. . . . Our reality only pretends that it's masculine: in fact, it's a woman disguised as a man. . . . The image of Russia as a transvestite haunts me. . . . Actually, she's fighting with her own sex. . . . We can see this change of clothes [when] unisex Soviet attire first appeared. In the 1920s and 1930s, everyone became uniformly sporty. And just a short while back our citizens—those who could allow themselves—changed into clothing from Italian boutiques. But notice that because of this we've lost our own style. We don't have one. [The Russian] man has turned into a wreck because he has no form."[61] Erofeev links his portrayal of the Russian man as a stylistic wreck enthralled by the Other to a national state of gender dysphoria, updating the terms of the crisis of masculinity for the twenty-first century, as well as visitors to one of Russia's largest gay web portals during the 2010s. Lest we think that comparing his country to a drag king or transman connotes some type of political correctness, we should bear in mind that this interview includes a lengthy yet specious argument about how men victimized by sexual assault suffer more than women do, as well as Erofeev's clichéd claim that one of his best friends is gay. By calling Russia trans, the writer revives fears of women's virility and men's emasculation, hinting that Putin's leadership bears responsibility for the country's mismatch between its biological sex and its gender identity.[62] Despite the pro-LGBTQ+ venue in which this queer metaphor appeared, it capitalizes on misogyny, homophobia, and transphobia, expressing a "male hysteria" that displaces the "anxieties and insecurities behind Putin's masculinity politics" on an array of Others.[63]

Erofeev's comparison of his country to a cross-dressed woman is curious, to say the least. In addition to blending time-honored tropes of Russia as either the motherland (*rodina-mat'*) or the fatherland (*otechestvo*), he sidesteps the assumption, widespread among many Russians, that all homosexuals are men and all gay men are transvestites in favor of cross-dressed women, who harken, as he himself remarks, back to the early Soviet vision of gender leveling. To understand why these gendered and temporal displacements worry Erofeev, as well as the larger phenomenon of male hysteria, we need to consider precisely how hypergender, the notion that male and female are not just "traditional" but natural and antithetical categories, does and does not work. As Erofeev's reference to Soviet unisex style hints, the regime of hypergender in Putin's Russia functions as a reaction against the utopian dream of gender equality that loomed over the Soviet Union throughout its existence. If we were to sketch a Venn diagram of this unrealized dream, it would contain two sets, one of men and another of women, whose attributes, attitudes, emotions, and actions would all lay on a single level plane and for the most part overlap. At the intersection of these two sets would be full-time employment, loyalty to the Communist Party, vigorous activity, and "sporty" clothing, while only a very limited number of traits would belong exclusively to women (e.g., childbearing) or men (e.g., fathering a child). In theory, the high degree of overlap in the Venn diagram of the Soviet gender utopia allowed individuals greater freedom to contribute to the Soviet cause and even acknowledged the social construction of gender, since both women and men had equal access to most socially sanctioned characteristics and activities. Fast forward to the twenty-first century, and the Venn diagram of Putin-era hypergender not only pulled the sets of masculinity and femininity apart entirely, eliminating any overlap, but also segregated these sets on hierarchically arranged planes, making femininity radically Other and fully subordinate to masculinity. This regime of hypergender rejected the Soviet legacy not only through its polarization and hierarchy but also in its denial of gender's social construction and assertion that biological sex in fact produces gender.

Needless to say, Putin's Russia has been no more successful in realizing the impossible dream of fully naturalized, polarized, and stratified gender than the Soviet Union was at entirely leveling it. Nonetheless, Erofeev's fear that Russia has become trans implicitly blames the Soviet dream of gender equity for the post-Soviet crisis of masculinity, since almost nothing—not even peeing standing up—was the exclusive domain of Soviet men. At the same time, Erofeev's complaint points to the inherent fragility of the gender regime that emerged in Russia after 1999. Like other instances of hypergender, Putinism's essentialized and stratified gender regime attempted to carve out exclusive domains for men and women. Yet in such regimes, the faintest hint of any attribute, feeling, or behavior seen as belonging exclusively to one gender has the power to sabotage and even invalidate the individual's inclusion in the other, leading to the misconception that any and everyone displaying traits from both genders must be trans. By falling into this misperception, Erofeev's lament that Russia has become trans calls attention to the fragility of Russian hypergender in the 2000s and 2010s, as well as Putinism's failure to address the crisis of masculinity in any meaningful way.

This particular instance of "male hysteria" on Erofeev's part suggests that the best way for Russian men to deflect accusations of not being manly enough is to blame those Others who hold men hostage in their gaze, be they female, homosexual, or trans, as those studying Putin's masculinity politics have noted.[64] Yet Erofeev's call for Russian men of the 2010s to get a form and find their own style opens the floodgates to new and more haunting displacements, since style really is nothing more than a means for the self to express identity by appropriating Otherness. During Putin's first two decades in power, this paradoxical call to blame Others yet adopt their style led to an increase in misogyny, homophobia, and transphobia, all of which have become "constitutive element[s] in the official and non-official performance of post-Soviet national identity."[65] In all three cases, hatred and fear of the Other deflects precarity and responsibility away from Russia's heterosexual men, with Putin at their forefront. While a romanticized female Other became the ideal citizen after Putin's rise to power, a demonized queer Other became the repository of abject citizenship. As the chapters that follow argue, both types of citizenship proved paradigmatic during the 2000s and 2010s. However, if the romantic paradigm of female citizenship stabilized Putinism's regime of hypergender, Russia's queer citizens threatened to topple this gender regime by unmasking its devices.

Against this backdrop, Russia's resurgent "power vertical" (*vertikal' vlasti*) in the 2000s begins to sound like a phallic metaphor that hoped to refute Erofeev's fear that Russia had become trans. However, the constant displacement of self onto Other inherent in Putinism's regime of hypergender ultimately erases any clear boundary separating Other from self, creating slippage between the country's heterosexual majority and its so-called sexual minorities, as well as among the different styles needed to perform masculinity, femininity, and citizenship. When viewed in this light, the discourse of contagion underlying the ban on "gay propaganda," which presumes that homosexuality "can be transmitted from one body to another," is simply one more metaphor for the phobia of self becoming Other and Other becoming self.[66] As this book argues, all of these metaphors operated as compensatory displacements, and all of them confirmed Erofeev's hunch that Russia became a country of cross-dressers after Putin's rise to power, since the performative regime of Russian citizenship that emerged during the 2000s and 2010s required all citizens, whether queer or not, to disguise whatever aspects of their person or life might appear "nontraditional" in more "traditional" clothing.

Once we attend to this slippage and unpack the discursive displacements in Russia's pop culture of the 2000s and 2010s, we can recognize Putin's own performance of hypermasculinity as a form of cisgender drag or *travesti*. After all, the Russian president is more than seventy years old, an age at which not even Botox injections and plastic surgery can maintain the youthful virility that made him the ultimate *muzhik* during his first two decades in power. The Kremlin's militaristic aggression in the 2010s, not to mention its devastating invasion of Ukraine in 2022, suggests that Putin's earlier performances of hypermasculinity have timed out and that nothing short of tanks, bombs, and missiles will disguise his own precarity and deflect his regime's vulnerability. Much as the late-Soviet performative shift analyzed by Yurchak ended with the Soviet Union's demise, so has its post-Soviet continuation come to a grim conclusion now that Putin's hypermasculine performances of the 2000s and 2010s have been depleted of what little substance they ever had. Rather than creating "gay propaganda," the Ulianovsk cadets' viral "Satisfaction" video exposed Putin's hypermasculinity as an instance of cisgender drag, and their young, twerking bodies revealed the outraged authorities' male hysteria, as well as the fragile masculinity that ultimately drives Putin's deadly forays into empire building.

Blazing the Trail to *Russian Style*

When taken together, the chapters that make up *Russian Style* argue that although Putin's regime initially promoted a form of embodied citizenship in which young, sexually available women represented the country's paradigmatic citizens, the different modes of performativity propagated in Russian popular culture during Putin's first two decades in power did not merely replicate and elaborate this schema. Just as important, these modes allowed Russian citizens to resist and even to protest the state's mandate of heteronormative hypergender. The forms of protest that emerged out of Putinism's paradigm of performative citizenship between 2000 and 2020 might accurately be labeled passive when viewed from the perspective of Western liberal democracies. However, this passivity, which views such protest as content-free due to its reliance on style, could and did morph into more active types of protest thanks to the *travesti* that became the ultimate destination for many performances of gender in Russian popular culture. And despite the apparent ability of Putinism to coopt the media and the means by which it disseminated its heteronormative project, the vastly varied products that appeared in Russia's mediascape during this period show that not all citizens fell passively into step with the mandate to be a "real" Russian man or woman, and some forged several steps ahead by contesting and rejecting the regime's performative demands for embodied citizenship.

My own path to writing this book has been decidedly eccentric, and the queer methodology that brought me to *Russian Style* and informs its argument has led me to a body of material that can only be described as eclectic. The pages that follow discuss everything from Putin memes to prison beauty pageants and internet questionnaires. Although I focus first and foremost on popular culture, from rap music to blockbuster cinema, I have found important and illuminating links between the truly popular and works typically considered either high culture, counterculture, or experimental. However, if we have learned anything in our post-post-Soviet and post-postmodern world, it is that no clear boundaries separate these esthetic categories, particularly when it comes to channeling or challenging the gendered zeitgeist of a resurgent Russia. I have chosen to put drag queens side by side with experimental documentary films precisely because this juxtaposition shows how all cultural products, esthetic categories, and styles are subject to slippage and change. As products of performance, both self-help literature for women and the Putin biopic gain their meaning not merely from the intent and agency of their performers but, just as important, from the eyes of their beholders.

The eclectic case studies presented in this book call for an equally varied method of analysis. In all cases, I begin with a close reading of the stylistic peculiarities of a given text or performance, so that I can support a central claim of this book, namely, that the primary function of style in Putin's Russia between 2000 and 2020 was to defer and deflect political substance. However, I occasionally reach into the toolkit of the social scientist when opportunity allows, for example, by asking real-life Russian drag queens their opinions of their fictional counterparts or corresponding with a romance writer about her authorial intent. Throughout, my goal is neither to slap a single stylistic label on the text or performance in question nor to delimit its meaning. Instead, I hope to show that the significance of the case studies I have chosen emerges only once we acknowledge and understand the complex stylistic overlays, drifts, and shifts that allow different readers, viewers, and listeners to slip and slide among a range of possible meanings.

My interpretations of the different media and materials that constitute *Russian Style* owe a profound debt to feminist and queer theory that originated in North America and Western Europe. Nonetheless, I am keenly aware of the problems that arise when paradigms generated in one culture are applied to another. For this reason, my use of notions like performative citizenship and queer performativity deliberately explores their limitations in the Russian context, as well as the ways in which Russians' unique experiences of gender and sexuality can productively augment ideas originally from the West. Including Russia in the conversation about how the global concepts of gender and sexuality can be experienced only locally promises to expand our understanding of the similarly local ways in which identity, as a performed construct, takes shape and evolves. At its most modest, this book aims to contribute to the growing connections among scholars and researchers interested in the performative dimensions of gender, sexuality, and identity in postsocialist culture. At its most ambitious, *Russian Style* hopes to inspire a performative shift away from the reductive stereotypes and Cold War binaries that have reared their heads since Russia's invasion of Ukraine and toward a more complex understanding of the role of hypergender and homophobia in constructing the type of "traditional values" on the rise not only in Russia but around the globe.

I

A Genealogy of Post-Soviet Pop Performativity

Viktor Erofeev's repeated accusation that Russians lost all sense of style in the post-Soviet era is clearly untrue for at least two reasons. First, he uses his own distinctive literary style, which combines slang with philosophy and lyricism with obscenity, to get his point across. Second, Erofeev's critique of his fellow countrymen's stylistic impotence begins with a vivid description of what he considers the worst faux pas of post-Soviet fashion, for example, the raspberry-colored blazers worn by New Russians and the tendency of Russian women to "all return from Germany as the spitting image of (and with their hair cut like) German women" in the 1990s.[1] Throughout his essays on the topic, Erofeev uses the word "style," which he never deigns to define, as a self-evident category that any truly stylish reader should already know, understand, and of course have. His own style of writing about style essentializes it as an esthetic category and even naturalizes it by claiming that style has its own "biology," which entails "general laws" of "development, growth, maturity, decrepitude, and dying."[2] All of Erofeev's stylistic decisions in these essays help to create a naturalized, hierarchical opposition between those who have style and those who do not, which sounds suspiciously similar to the essentialized gender regime that emerged in Russia during the 2000s and 2010s.

Erofeev is not alone in using the notion of style in a naturalizing and essentializing manner, and his essays on style continue a long tradition that juxtaposes style with substance, form with content, surface with depth, in an attempt to elucidate the binary opposition between *how* a text is written, an object seems, or a person speaks and *what* a text means, an object is, or a person says. Such debates about style go back to the ancients, among them Plato and Aristotle.[3] Those who have written about style in their wake, including Erofeev, more often than not develop prescriptive definitions that arrange different styles in a hierarchical manner, for example, Cicero's low, middle, and high styles, which Nicolas Boileau-Despréaux recycled some sixteen centuries later, or Northrop Frye's hieratic versus demotic styles.[4] As Erofeev's reproach to his supposedly style-free compatriots illustrates, such hierarchies are intended to help those producing and consuming culture of all types to negotiate its stratified world and, if they are successful, accrue cultural capital along the way.

Although these hierarchies play a role in the various Russian styles examined in this chapter, we should remember that the impulse toward hierarchical thinking typically arises from a desire to view style as a preexisting, ontologically stable category. Labeling a work of art baroque, rococo, or neoclassical or a song country-western, rock, or hip-hop often overlooks the inherent instability of all styles as products of performance. Rather than examine style as a biological, natural, essential, or ontological category, this book views it as a performative phenomenon and considers style a mode of performativity. By this definition, style is inherently unstable and refers to the different ways in which the self expresses identity through the appropriation of Otherness. In the context of pop culture, style allows performers of all types to construct and sell easily legible and reproducible simulacra of identity—be it gendered, sexual, ethnic, racial, religious, regional, or national—for mass consumption. The different media that constitute pop culture in the twenty-first century not only broadcast the varied styles in vogue at a given time but also promote the fluidity of these styles through their endless appetite for recycling past styles, reworking them for present needs, and adapting them to new performers and audiences.

By considering the different Russian styles that have come into fashion as the Soviet Union dissolved, the wild nineties raged, the aughts brought affluence, and the 2010s' austerity gave rise to prosperity, I hope to maintain the critical distance necessary to perceive the series of hierarchical distinctions that Erofeev glosses over and on which these styles depend. This chapter's discussion of seven different styles considers them as overlapping performative modes available to any and all seeking to perform Russian citizenship. The relative cultural isolation of the Soviet Union until the mid-1980s means that several of the styles examined here, for example *poshlost'* and *stiob*, have typically been viewed as unique to Russian culture, that is, as a product of Russia and the Soviet Union's exceptional historical and cultural development. Whether we subscribe to Russian exceptionalism or not, the opening up of glasnost and restructuring of perestroika in the 1980s brought these Russian styles into contact with performative modes seen either as global, such as charisma, or chiefly Western, as in the cases of camp, kitsch, glamour, and drag. My discussion of these terms assesses their differences and similarities, questioning the extent to which the designations of local and global, Eastern and Western, truly apply.

Moreover, this chapter does not pretend to exhaust the many and varied styles that have become available to Russians performing citizenship in the post-Soviet era, which span the Russian conspiracy theories studied by Eliot Borenstein and "Soviet retro" considered by Kevin Platt.[5] With one exception, my genealogy of Russian styles focuses on irony, whose rapid evolution at the end of the twentieth and the beginning of the twenty-first centuries characterized pop culture in Russia and more globally. The tendency of irony to draw attention away from depth and substance and toward surface and style means that the ultimate significance of any ironic style remains forever ambivalent. As irony's roots in "pretended ignorance" suggest, those performing ironically know something that they are either unable or unwilling to state directly, opening the door to multiple and often contradictory meanings. More often than not, such performers are faced with what Frederic Jameson calls "the increasing unavailability of the personal style," a postmodern dilemma that leads to pastiche, "blank irony . . . the random cannibalization of all the styles of the past, [and] the play of random stylistic allusion."[6]

The decision to analyze the seven styles included in this chapter as modes of performativity capable of generating Russianness has led me away from the traditional approach and scholarly canon associated with many of the terms treated in this chapter. As a result, readers anticipating an exploration of kitsch that begins with Clement Greenberg's 1939 essay "Avant-Garde and Kitsch" or a catalog of the scholarship inspired by Susan Sontag's 1964 "Notes on 'Camp'" will be disappointed.[7] Instead of this customary approach to style, which, I would argue, risks falling prey to hierarchical thinking even when it questions preexisting hierarchies, I have chosen to bare the hierarchical device by organizing my analysis around the gender and sexuality that Erofeev either elides or hysterically misconstrues. As foundational binary oppositions like self and Other, the distinctions between male and female, as well as heterosexual and queer, entail stratified judgment, and they play a pivotal role in shaping each of the performative modes discussed below. In addition, each mode displays its own temporal and affective tendencies, in which the performer's gaze is directed, in the case of the former, to past, present, or future and, for the latter, narcissistically inward at the self or empathically outward at the Other. Finally, some of these modes arose as pejorative labels, suggesting that performers' agency or lack thereof varies from style to style. Attending to each mode's gendered, sexual, temporal, affective, and agentic affinities allows us to discern the domain of a given mode, the common territory shared by different modes, and the slippage that inevitably occurs among all seven. Once we understand the hierarchical judgment encoded in each style by its specific affinities, we can grasp how the very distinction between substance and style—which is, after all, just one more binary opposition that maps back onto male–female and heterosexual–queer—ultimately obscures the political work these styles do for both performers and their audience.

Admittedly, the definition of style offered in this chapter lacks the hard edges and moral certainty of Erofeev's essays, since any definition relying on performativity leaves whatever it seeks to delineate open to slippage. Much as Eve Sedgwick defined "queer" in the 1990s as "the open mesh of possibilities, gaps, overlaps, dissonances and resonances, lapses and excesses of meaning," my own use of the concept of style acknowledges its open-ended and ever-evolving nature.[8] Moreover, any meaningful discussion of style in the realm of pop culture must consider not only the tricky question of pop performers' intent but also the equally difficult issue of how pop performances are received and understood by viewers around the globe. As ambitious as this might be, my hope is to show that the styles on offer in Russian pop culture between 2000 and 2020 circulated freely between the political sphere and everyday life, determining in large part the performative criteria for Russian citizenship during these years. Ultimately, tracing the genealogy of post-Soviet pop style allows us to understand how Putin's hypermasculinity both arose from and contributed to a performative shift, in which an ironic Russian style gave rise to political substance.

Charisma and the Putin Brand

Vladimir Putin's performance of hypermasculinity during his first three terms as Russia's president provides a convenient point of departure for the analysis of post-Soviet Russian style because of the familiarity of both domestic and global audiences with his clearly constructed, larger-than-life persona. A number of scholars, including Elena Gapova, Helena Goscilo, Oleg Riabov and Tatiana Riabova, Valerie Sperling, and Elizabeth Wood, have documented the masculinist agenda of the media campaign orchestrated by the Kremlin's political technologists after Putin's rise to power in 1999, which served to legitimate and popularize the Russian president.[9] This campaign generated countless images of Putin demonstrating his black belt in judo, shooting Siberian tigers with tranquilizer guns, piloting helicopters, swimming the butterfly stroke in Siberian rivers, and so on. The personage constructed in such photos oozed machismo and authority through their portrayal of Putin's athletic prowess, military might, subjugation of nature, and manly physique. While the Kremlin limited itself to depicting Russia's president as the possessor of what the father of sociology, Max Weber, called "specifically exceptional powers or qualities," Putin's fans went one step further by portraying him as "supernatural [and] superhuman" in comparison to previous leaders of the country, as the many memes that appeared between 2000 and 2020 of Putin astride bears, bald eagles, and unicorns, in locations from the wilds of Russia to outer space, suggest.[10] In addition, Putin's name, face, words, and gestures appeared in a stunning variety of locations far beyond Russia's state-sponsored television and the internet, including wall calendars, tooth flossers, refrigerator magnets, keychains, ax blades, action figures, and T-shirts.[11] Although the tremendous variety of such products makes it impossible to conduct a comprehensive survey of them, we can confidently state that the vast majority of the Putiniana generated between 2000 and 2020 stressed the Russian president's status as a real Russian man or *muzhik*. In other words, Putin's initial political celebrity—as manufactured by those inside the Kremlin and beyond—consistently styled his charisma as the upshot of his hypermasculinity.

Accordingly, the first performative mode we need to consider among the different styles at play in post-Soviet pop culture of the past two decades is charisma, which, in addition to exhibiting a clear affinity with heterosexual masculinity, has the capacity to morph into styles whose tendencies lie elsewhere. Before exploring the specific nature of Putin's charisma as he rose to political prominence, however, we should admit to the attenuated relationship between Weber's notion of charisma as the single most important quality conferring leadership and our application of this term to leadership of the Russian Federation in the twenty-first century. Although the analysis here relies on Weber for charisma's basic contours, charismatic leadership in post-Soviet Russia arose out of and has functioned in a vastly different environment than Weber imagined for at least two reasons. First and most obvious, Weber formulated his understanding of charisma more than a hundred years ago and turned to the premodern past for the majority of his examples. Applying his ideas to Putin's first two decades in the Kremlin requires that we acknowledge the vast differences between the political actors and spheres treated by Weber and those in Russia during the 2000s and 2010s. The intertwined networks of communication, media, and capitalism, which serve local purposes at the same time that they unite the globe, require that the successful twenty-first-century politician be more than an inspiring individual capable of galvanizing disciples. The basic requirements of charismatic leadership now include becoming a commodity suitable for circulation via all three global networks and establishing an identity not so much as an individual but more as a saleable brand.

The profusion of Putiniana in the 2000s vividly illustrates these postmodern desiderata for charismatic leadership. After Putin's hypermasculinity entered the

Russian mediascape and marketplace, it transformed the actual man Vladimir Putin into both a saleable product and a fashionable brand, so that clever entrepreneurs might turn a profit by naming hybrid tomatoes after the Russian president or writing James Bond-style action novels whose hero is a thinly veiled Putin.[12] As we would expect, figures less prominent than Putin himself often mobilized his brand by emphasizing their friendship with the Russian president and thereby basking in the aura of his masculinity. For instance, the actor, film director, and doyen of the arts Nikita Mikhalkov produced a half-hour-long televised birthday card on the occasion of Putin's fifty-fifth birthday, in 2007.[13] Laconically titled *55*, the documentary elicited comparisons with earlier Soviet films celebrating the great leader's birthday and demonstrated Mikhalkov's privileged, personal connection to Putin. In the realm of politics, the Chechen strongman Ramzan Kadyrov often styled himself as a Muslim satellite revolving around Putin's Russian Orthodox sun. Kadyrov's popular Instagram account had, until it was shut down in 2018, more than three million followers eager for images of him lifting weights, worshiping with friends, and praising Putin's latest public appearance.[14] And in popular music, the Tatar-Jewish rapper Timati created the video "Best Friend" to celebrate Putin's sixty-third birthday, in 2015.[15] Subsequent ventures by Timati's production company suggest that admiration and emulation of the Putin brand not only informed the rapper's hypermasculine and homophobic music videos but also inspired his production company Black Star's diverse line of products, including sportswear. As these examples show, Putin's charisma when he first rose to power had not only the followers and disciples described by Weber but also consumers, copycats, and fans.

The second factor we must keep in mind when taking Weber's notion of charisma as a point of departure for constructing a genealogy of post-Soviet style is the Soviet prehistory of charismatic leadership in the ideologically freighted phenomenon of the cult of personality. After Putin became Russia's president, pundits immediately began to liken the Kremlin's efforts to popularize him to the earlier cult of Stalin's personality, that is, to the state-sponsored campaign that deified perhaps the bloodiest dictator of the twentieth century and that Nikita Khrushchev debunked in his 1956 secret speech.[16] Such comparisons typically lamented Russians' nostalgia for the iron-fisted leadership of an earlier era, as well as the growing authoritarianism of Putin's regime. Although certain aspects of this comparison have sadly proven true, the postmodern landscape in which Putin rose to power undermined such parallels between the Russian Federation of the 2000s and its Soviet precursor. As Emily Johnson and I have argued elsewhere, the cult that took shape around Putin's personality did not originally function like its Soviet-style predecessors, which never would have allowed such uncontrolled forms of expression as the tooth flossers or action figures mentioned earlier. Nor did Putin's cult originally bond its followers to their leader exclusively through the "devotion," "hero worship," "absolute trust," or "duty" that Weber posited as "decisive for the validity of charisma."[17] In its early years, the cult of Putin was inherently multivalent, generating and accommodating responses from the sincere reverence evoked in some Soviet citizens by the cult of Stalin to the biting sarcasm that landed others in the Gulag. In addition, Putin's masculinity, unlike Stalin's, rarely took on the paternal dimensions that made Stalin "the father of all peoples." Instead, the many images depicting Putin as "a real man" focused initially on making him into an object of erotic arousal for the country's female population and sometimes its gay men, as the 2002 pop song "Someone Like Putin" vividly illustrated.[18] With lyrics by Aleksandr Elin, "Someone Like Putin" was performed by the nubile girl duo Singing Together and topped the Russian charts in 2002 by extolling the Russian president's virility, sobriety, desirability, and dependability when compared to other Russian men.[19] The widely divergent reactions to these cultic objects and texts distinguished the cult of Putin that took shape in the 2000s from its Soviet precursors, demonstrating the ambivalent role played by nostalgia in the construction of Putin's charisma and complicating any direct application of Weber's ideas to post-Soviet Russia.

The astonishingly wide variety of Putiniana generated between 2000 and 2020, when taken with the broad range of responses generated by Putin's manly figure, suggests that any consideration of Weber's concept of charisma in Russia's postmodern landscape must place it side by side with other performative modes into which charisma often morphs. In many of the examples of Putiniana mentioned earlier, Putin's virility straddled the threshold between Weber's notion of charisma and Sontag's definition of camp as an aesthetic sensibility. In fact, memes of Putin riding a unicorn over the rainbow or Putin portraits executed entirely in chocolate demonstrate that the Russian president's machismo tended to originate in charisma yet tipped over into camp, often ending up as kitsch. By approaching these performative modes as contiguous styles that bleed one into the other, we leave behind Weber's preference for the premodern and embrace the postmodern mediatization typical of political charisma in the twenty-first century. Placing charisma alongside camp and kitsch reveals their linkage in Putin's early performances of hypermasculinity, which represented a postmodern mash-up of multiple performative modes and functioned as the cornerstone of a gender order that paradoxically sought to naturalize the binary opposition between male and female through artifice and exaggeration.

Charisma, Camp, and Kitsch

Linking Weber's thoughts about charisma, a concept associated with the sincerity and earnestness of effective leadership, to terms like "camp" and "kitsch," which typically fall under the rubric of irony, represents a new approach to understanding the gendered nature of political celebrity. Although recent conversations in the academy and beyond have brought such concepts as "political masculinity" and "toxic masculinity" into vogue, they have yet to consider how Weber's notion of charisma, the alleged source of leaders' popularity and success, is inextricably linked to prevailing gender norms. Juxtaposing Weber's thoughts on charisma with Sontag's "Notes on 'Camp'" allows us to perceive the gendered underpinnings of charisma and to establish parameters for considering the different modes of performativity at play in the Russian mediasphere between 2000 and 2020. This juxtaposition also reveals a surprising complementarity between Weber's and Sontag's concepts.

Nowhere in his discussion of charisma does Weber address explicitly the differences between men and women as charismatic leaders, and Sontag likewise claims "that the Camp sensibility is disengaged, depoliticized—or at least apolitical" in her groundbreaking 1964 essay on the topic.[20] Despite Weber's oversight of gender and a claim that Sontag herself later recognized as wrong, the categories of gender, charisma, and camp overlap because of their shared performativity. Thanks to the work of scholars like Judith Butler and Sedgwick, we now accept the axiom that gender is a matter of performance, even if most gender expressions are designed to obscure their performativity so that they naturalize socially constructed behavior.[21] Charisma and camp both entail performances that mobilize binary gender as the means to bond performers to spectators and to create affective communities with the power to effect social change. Arguably, Weber's analysis of charisma bears a relation to Sontag's jottings on camp analogous to the relationship of masculinity to femininity. With this analogy in mind, we can productively use Weber's omission of gender as a corrective to Sontag's mistake of apoliticism and vice versa.

Needless to say, the charismatic leadership Weber describes can and has been applied to women. However, many of the twenty-first century's prominent female politicians, for example, Germany's Angela Merkel, the United States' Hillary Clinton, or Great Britain's Theresa May, have been found lacking in charisma when judged by Weber's initial paradigm, which focuses solely on men. When outlining the contours of charismatic leadership, Weber returns repeatedly to beserkers, warlords, chieftains, prophets, heroes, and kings, all of whom possess "specific gifts of the body and spirit [that] have been believed to be supernatural and not accessible to everybody."[22] Donald Trump's successful campaign for the presidency of the United States in 2016 laid bare the link between male potency and political charisma when he felt compelled to defend the size of his hands—and his penis—on Fox News.[23] Much like Trump's comments about his hands, Weber's original writings on charisma have steady recourse to terminology that we now recognize as thinly veiled code for masculinity. For example, Weber describes charisma as a universally recurring "category of domination-structure," adding, "Charisma knows only inner determination and inner restraint. The holder of charisma seizes the task that is adequate for him and demands obedience and a following by virtue of his mission. His success determines whether he finds them. His charismatic claim breaks down if his mission is not recognized by those to whom he feels he has been sent. If they recognize him, he is their master—so long as he knows how to maintain recognition through 'proving' himself."[24] This plainly sexist description of the charismatic leader demonstrates that despite Weber's pioneering demystification of the mechanism of charisma, he recognizes it only in men and behaviors that most cultures tag as masculine, thereby naturalizing the link between charismatic leadership and men. Because of the deep roots of this link in Weber's thought, it lives on in later treatments of charisma. For instance, Gregory Freidin's application of Weber's idea to the career of the poet Osip Mandelshtam asserts that "what distinguishes a charismatic figure, group, or institution from its ordinary counterpart in society is not . . . a particular program . . . but the difference in intensity of expression between the feebly electrified 'periphery' of a culture and the always steaming, awesome powerhouse of its 'center.'"[25]

The charismatic leader's ability to embody the "steaming, awesome powerhouse" of his culture and to command his followers' obedience from its center has not only a gendered but also temporal, affective, and agentic dimensions. Even though political leaders mobilize myths of the past and often rewrite history to suit their needs, they concentrate on what must be done in the present to realize a galvanizing vision of the future. This relentless focus on the future manifests itself several ways, from slogans that idealize the past, like Trump's "Make America Great Again," to the aspirational names of political parties, like Putin's "United Russia."[26] Convincing followers to buy into such visions of future greatness demands a healthy dose of narcissism from the effective leader, who asks followers to relinquish their worldview for his own. Effective leaders also exercise the ultimate agency, requiring followers to give up whatever hesitancy or ambivalence they might feel for black-and-white values that privilege one side of a binary opposition over another, such as masculinity versus femininity, heterosexuality versus queerness, good versus evil, and us versus them. When combined with charisma's inherent preference for masculinity, this forward-looking agency and narcissism mean that charisma typically places femininity, if not actual women, outside of the political realm.

Once we turn to Sontag's "Notes on 'Camp,'" we immediately recognize the flip side of Weber's charisma. Although camp, like charisma, arises out of a cult, its associations lie not with kings, the ability to command complete involvement and total obedience, or the awesome power of masculinity but with drag queens, a sense of underinvolvement or detachment, and the duplicitous seduction of effeminacy, which Sontag connects to "the epicene style" and "homosexuality."[27] In contrast to charisma's revolutionary earnestness, "The whole point of Camp is to dethrone the serious. . . . One can be serious about the frivolous, frivolous about the serious."[28] If charisma emanates from society's "steaming, awesome powerhouse," then camp arises on its "feebly electrified 'periphery'" with androgynes, in gay bars, and via pop culture.

As its predilection for androgyny suggests, camp embraces opposing elements in a binary opposition, turning charisma's black-and-white values into endless shades of gray. Moreover, rather than look to the future, like charisma, camp treasures the "old-fashioned, out-of-date, [and] démodé," as Sontag points out.[29] Camp brings the past into the present via nostalgia and stylistic recursion, and according to Sontag, "the process of aging or deterioration provides the necessary detachment—or arouses a necessary sympathy."[30] In addition to producing a distinctive historical dualism, camp's simultaneous detachment from and sympathy for the past results in an affective stance of pleasurable and even seductive ambivalence, as well as highly attenuated agency. Rather than narcissistically sweep followers up in their leader's vision, camp hovers between narcissism and empathy, offering a stylistic means to negotiate between now and then, here and there, self and Other without fully dissociating from one or merging with the other. At the beginning of her "Notes," Sontag confesses as much when she writes that she is "strongly drawn to Camp, and almost as strongly offended by it."[31] She also describes how speaking about camp "requires a deep sympathy modified by revulsion."[32] In other words, camp's distinctive mode of performativity seeks not to reconcile but rather to engender deeply divided emotions through "a complex system of inclusion/exclusion," and it uses this ambivalence "to assimilate and to exclude," creating communities of insiders or camp cognoscenti in the process.[33]

However, beyond these differences, charisma and camp share at least three features because of their shared performativity. First, both privilege form or style over content. Much as charisma is not about "a particular program," camp emphasizes "texture, sensuous surface, and style" to such an extent that, according to Sontag, "the lens of Camp . . . blocks out content."[34] Second, camp relishes not only the androgynous but also "the exaggeration of sexual characteristics and personality mannerisms," for example, "The corny flamboyant femaleness of Jayne Mansfield, Gina Lollobrigida, Jane Russell, Virginia Mayo; the exaggerated he-man-ness of Steve Reeves, Victor Mature," which sounds and looks strangely like Weber's "specific gifts of the body and spirit . . . not accessible to everybody."[35] In fact, camp and charisma converge in this "glorification of 'character,'" which, to quote Sontag, "is understood as a state of continual incandescence—a person being one very intense thing."[36] Perhaps the only difference between charisma and camp in their treatment of personal intensity is charisma's need to naturalize it as opposed to camp's revelation of its artificiality and excess.

Third and most important, charisma and camp both rely on a feedback loop between performer and audience in order to create, regulate, and disseminate their respective affects and effects. Both theorists are rather vague about how this feedback loop functions, but both agree, to quote Weber, that "It is recognition on the part of those subject to authority which is decisive for the validity of charisma."[37] Or, to quote Sontag, there is "a Camp vision, a Camp way of looking at things," but "[i]t's not *all* in the eye of the beholder."[38] The authority of either the charismatic leader or camp cognoscenti comes into being only when someone else recognizes it in a process whose inner workings sound uncannily like a Hegelian master-slave dialectic. However, if charisma conflates this authority with authenticity and masculinity, thereby masking the noncoincidence of all three, then camp grants authority to affectedness and denaturalized gender by exposing the fissures among them. As a result, charisma frequently functions as a heteronormative policing mechanism, while camp has become a potent instigator of global homonormativity in recent decades.

If the relationship between charisma and camp brings to mind a gendered binary opposition, then kitsch represents a third mode of performativity designed to disrupt the feedback loop on which both camp and charisma depend. It too privileges form and style over content; however, kitsch strives not to bond performers to their spectators but rather to distinguish those who hold the power to label an object or activity kitsch from those who end up unwittingly consuming or creating it. According to Sontag, camp is "generous," "a kind of love," "a tender feeling," and even "a mode of enjoyment, of appreciation—not judgment," whereas kitsch entails "an absence of love."[39] As Sedgwick elaborates in her *Epistemology of the Closet*, "Kitsch is a classification that redoubles the aggressive power of the epithet 'sentimental' by, on the one hand, claiming to exempt the speaker of the epithet from the contagion of the kitsch object, and, on the other, positing the existence of a true *kitsch consumer*. . . . Camp, on the other hand, seems to involve a gayer and more spacious angle of view. . . . Unlike kitsch-*attribution*, the sensibility of camp-*recognition* always sees that it is dealing in reader relations and projective fantasy (projective though not infrequently true) about the spaces and practices of cultural production."[40] Although Sedgwick and Sontag focus their attention on the fine line that divides camp from kitsch, the hostile process they describe, in which calling something kitsch places us outside and above the space of its production, allows us to perceive its distinctive temporal, affective, and agentic stance. Kitsch looks to the future and the past only insofar as they reinforce a hierarchical judgment made in the present. As such, kitsch represents a rejection of charismatic narcissism, as well as a refusal to empathize with the "true *kitsch consumer*." Thus, kitsch has little use for charisma's fetishization of masculinity or camp's attraction to androgyny. Instead, kitsch approaches binary oppositions, including those of gender and sexuality, as the means to restore the supposedly "correct" color to that which has been rendered black-and-white by charisma or as so many shades of gray by camp. Correspondingly, the process of kitsch-attribution described by Sedgwick denies agency to the hapless producers and consumers of kitsch at the same time that it grants it to those savvy enough to use the term.

For example, those who believe that Trump's orange hair, Barbie Doll wives, and allusions to his penis represent instances of kitsch look down their noses not only at Trump but also at those who find him charismatic and voted him into office. Yet, just like charisma and camp, kitsch does not go beyond the "sensuous surface" of whatever it judges, for example, by critiquing Trump's political platform or actions. In other words, whether a person, text, artifact, or image represents an instance of kitsch, camp, or charisma depends just as much on the perception of the viewer and the nature of the feedback loop as it does on the actual person or thing in question. Whether the Putin promulgated by the Kremlin in the 2000s and 2010s looked like Russia's charismatic leader, a campy shirt-free he-man, or the pistol-packing vigilante of contemporary Russian kitsch depended on our individual sensibilities, as well as the means by which a given instance of Putiniana made its way to us. Even those for whom Putin memes on the internet had already crossed over from camp into kitsch might have found the man charismatic if they met him in person.

However, few of us who paid attention to Putin's exploits when he first became Russia's president experienced him as the "steaming, awesome powerhouse" erecting the "power vertical" at Russia's center. Those of us outside the country stood on the distant periphery of Russian culture and politics and observed them increasingly through the feeble electrification of the internet. Despite greater proximity, those living in Russia occupied a similar position, since the Putin they saw on television or read about in the news was mediated either by Russia's sycophantic stated-sponsored media or by the more variegated world of the web. The inherent virtuality of the Putin seen by all, with the exception of a small circle of political insiders, allowed any given image of

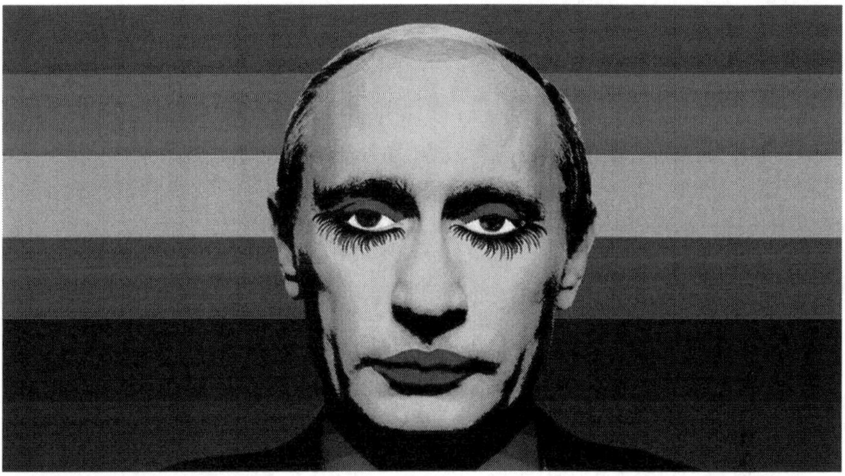

Figure 2. The meme of Putin as a gay clown banned as extremist material in 2017.

the Russian leader to slide almost effortlessly from charisma, through camp, and into kitsch, since the feedback loops of television, print journalism, and the internet allow very little actual feedback. The constant shifting among these three styles was not exclusive to representations of Putin during his first twenty years at Russia's helm, and it continues to characterize popular depictions of gendered behavior in Russia, the United States, and more broadly.

Given the ubiquity of such stylistic slippage in the twenty-first century, it is worth pausing to consider its ability to deliver a variety of political punches depending on its context. In the case of Trump, for example, memes like the Instagram post that transformed his official portrait from a black-suited head of state into a drag queen in the span of less than a minute functioned first and foremost to undermine whatever charisma he had through mockery and emasculation.[41] However, as Trump ably proved, such memes also kept him in the limelight and arguably increased his bandwidth and celebrity with the same gesture that sought to undermine them. Despite the origins of this type of stylistic slippage in global networks of communication, media, and capitalism, its double-edged power as a political weapon depends on the local context in which it operates. Unlike memes of Trump as a drag queen, which circulated on the web unchecked, those of Putin as a gay clown were banned as political extremism by a court in the city of Tver' in November 2017. This ban demonstrated both the Russian government's growing control over Putin's bandwidth within the country during the 2010s and the greater political potential of stylistic slippage in Russia when compared to the United States.[42]

Understanding the political differential of sliding from charisma into camp or kitsch requires that we consider not only the divergent political environments in the United States versus the Russian Federation but also the socioeconomic and cultural conditions deemed necessary by Sontag and others for the stylistic revolution that camp represents. Sontag's claim that camp exists "only in affluent societies, in societies or circles capable of experiencing the psychopathology of affluence," prevented many critics from perceiving camp in the cultures of both the Soviet Union and postsocialist Russia.[43] However, the very changes in American society that, as Andrew Ross outlines in "The Uses of Camp," led to the its development among American queers after World War II came to Russia in full force after the fall of the Soviet Union. As was true of Eisenhower's and Kennedy's America, Putin's Russia has undergone "a shift in the balance of *containment* of popular democracy"; "the reorganization of the capitalist bases of the culture industries, the new media technology and the new modes of distribution"; and "a wave of revivalist nostalgia."[44] In the 2010s, the Putin regime began to use an increasingly heavy hand to contain popular democracy, as the decision to outlaw the meme of Russia's president in drag demonstrates. The growing lists of what constituted "political extremism" and "gay propaganda" during Putin's first two decades in power were but two means that his regime used to manage the vast shifts in Russia's culture industry and mediascape, as well as the surge of nostalgia for the country's imperial and Soviet pasts. The rapid rise in Russia's gross domestic product during the 2000s also resulted in rampant consumerism, leading to colorful instances of the psychopathology of affluence. In other words, the "camp effect" described by Ross, which recycles outmoded cultural products and obsolete modes of production, allowing for "a rediscovery of history's waste [and] the *recreation of surplus value from forgotten forms of labor*," characterized Putin's Russia between 2000 and 2020 no less than it did Andy Warhol's New York.[45]

The socioeconomic and cultural conditions under which camp thrives help to explain the double-edged nature of the instances of stylistic slippage cited in this chapter. As postwar America demonstrated, camp arose as a tool for marginalized communities to negotiate shifts in the hegemony of cultural production, and, as Ross points out, "camp transforms, destabilizes, and subverts the existing balance of acceptance of sexual identity and sexual roles."[46] Camp's mode of performativity creates a cultural economy in which essentialist identities of all types come into question, and it allows those relegated to the fringe of cultural consumption, such as gays, lesbians, and trans folk, to play a key role in the production of cultural meanings and values, thereby repositioning outsider communities as cultural cognoscenti.[47] However, the very mobility of camp means that it "appears, on the one hand, to offer a transgressive vehicle yet, on the other hand, simultaneously invokes the specter of dominant ideology within its practices, appearing, in many instances, to . . . reinforce the dominant order."[48] Russia's entry into the global marketplace and webosphere after the demise of the Soviet Union transformed the country into a savvy producer of self-conscious camp and kitsch, both of which challenged Putin's increasingly authoritarian power vertical when wielded by horizontally connected communities of style cognoscenti in the 2010s.

What Style Is Your Protest?

To back up the argument that horizontal communities of style could and did exercise power during the 2010s, we need only consider the wave of political protests that swept over Russia in 2011 and 2012.[49] In the span of about two years, tens of thousands of Russians took to the streets of Moscow and other cities to protest "For Fair Elections" and against Putin's decision to run for a third term as president. Despite the involvement of outspoken opponents of the regime, including Aleksei Navalnyi, the protesters' political platform never went beyond a narrow set of demands, for example, freeing political prisoners and annulling fraudulent elections. The political substance of what some Western journalists called Russia's "Snow Revolution" seemed a bit thin; however, its style was anything but. As those studying political dissent in the post-Soviet era have shown, the style of the 2011–2012 protests was not just an accessory to some political platform but represented protesters' politics per se.[50] The roots of such protest via style reach back to late-Soviet practitioners of irony from Andrei Siniavskii to Dmitrii Prigov, who took for granted the "axiomatic opposition of power and style, power and culture, state authoritarianism and artistic autonomy."[51] However, 2011 and 2012's "irony-rich, but content-poor" protests used new and audacious forms of irony to denounce Putin's would-be charisma.[52]

In fact, protesters themselves labeled the connection they purposely fostered among themselves via social media their "horizontal," and they quickly proved their mastery in repurposing official utterances and images to question Putin's authority. Many of the viral quips intended to lay Putin's power vertical low converted Kremlin-generated slogans clearly intended to boost his charisma into campy nonsense. For example, one malapropism transformed the pro-Putin catchphrase "If not Putin, then who?" (*Esli ne Putin, to kto?*) into "If not Putin, then a cat" (*Esli ne Putin, to kot*), in effect demoting Putin from the ranks of humanity to a fuzzy domestic pet. Another popular protest slogan cleverly punned "*Vy nas dazhe ne predstavliaete*," whose English equivalent is either "You don't even represent us" or "You can't even imagine us." The

2011–2012 "protesters weaponized absurdity" with such bywords, whose political impact was sufficiently threatening that the Kremlin co-opted protesters' tactics and rhetoric in attempts to quash their movement.[53]

If the protesters' viral slogans sought to reduce Putin's charisma to campy absurdity, then the white ribbons that emerged as their symbol took these tactics one step further. By the 2010s, the phenomenon of colored awareness ribbons had spread from the United States around the world, and white ribbons signaling the Russian protesters' solidarity began to appear on their bodies, clothing, and cars.[54] Unsurprisingly, Putin spent a portion of his annual TV call-in show in December 2011 trying to discredit the protest movement, accusing those marching in the streets of doing so for pay, acting on behalf of the West, and trying to topple the Russian motherland. Yet his most noteworthy comment during the four-and-a-half-hour broadcast compared protesters' white ribbons to a form of contraception: "Frankly, when I saw on the [television] screen that some people had something hanging here on their chest, honestly, it's indecent, but I decided that it was propaganda in the fight against AIDS—that, excuse me, they had hung condoms [on themselves]."[55] Putin's attempt to beat protesters at their own game promptly backfired when a meme of him with an outsized condom wrapped over his head and around his neck popped up on the internet, went viral, and then became a poster brandished by those in the streets.[56] The meme of Putin draped in a condom redoubled his own attempt to besmirch protesters through association with HIV/AIDS and homosexuality. It also took his thinly veiled homophobic slur to its absurd conclusion by swathing the very person who embodied the country's phallic power vertical in an apparently used condom and placing him in a posture that made him look like a Russian granny donning her shawl. Whoever first created the meme of Putin draped in a condom transformed his light ironic touch, signaled by the filler words "frankly," "honestly," and "excuse me," into an image so dripping with irony that it pushed Putin's charisma from camp into kitsch.

Against this exchange of sexual aspersions, the rise of the feminist punk collective Pussy Riot to global prominence in early 2012 seems slightly less shocking than it truly was in its day.[57] Although the group produced its first raucous protest videos the preceding fall, "Putin Pissed Himself," which hit the internet in late January 2012 and instantly went viral, established Pussy Riot as a force to be reckoned with, since the group's performance denounced the sexism behind Putin's masculinist agenda in no uncertain terms.[58] The video shows eight women, disguised in a rainbow of second-hand dresses and balaclavas, atop the snowy platform of Moscow's Lobnoe mesto and against the background of St. Basil's Cathedral and the Kremlin. As they jump and

Figure 3. The meme of Putin draped in an oversized condom on a poster during the 2011–2012 protests. Used by permission of the Associated Press; photograph by Mikhail Menzel.

shake their fists, the song's lyrics champion the protesters occupying Russia's streets, urging them forward and praising their "protest charisma." However, the lyrics also strip Putin and his cronies of whatever charisma they had by calling them "a flock of bitches" (*staia suk*), accusing them of "male hysteria," and comparing Putin to a toddler who pees his pants in fear. In addition to showing a "brazen reclamation of public space from the state," the video of "Putin Pissed Himself" infantilized and feminized Putin to expose the gender disparity on which his regime rested.[59]

Pussy Riot's next video, "Punk Prayer: Mother of God Drive Putin Out," appeared one month later, creating the global sensation that led to the trial of three of its members and the imprisonment of two.[60] Once again, the group used a DIY punk aesthetic of thrift-store clothing and balaclavas to denounce the inherent sexism of Putin's regime, as well as its unholy alliance with the Russian Orthodox Church.[61] The video shows four members of Pussy Riot alternately praying and dancing in the Cathedral of Christ the Savior, which, in the words of Eliot Borenstein, represents "an architectural palimpsest of state power and the sacred."[62] The music of "Punk Prayer" alternates between pleas for the Mother of God to become a feminist and drive Putin out (sung like Russian liturgical music) and attempts to exorcise the "holy shit" responsible for exiling gay pride parades to Siberia (screamed to punk guitar riffs). As Pussy Riot's clearly rigged trial in the late summer 2012 demonstrated, "Punk Prayer" touched Putin's sore spot, and the group's reappropriation of the holy Mother of God for feminist purposes completely deflated the Russian president's repeated invocation of the sacred motherland for many viewers.

Pussy Riot received a tepid reception within Russia, and the disdain of most Russians for feminism of all stripes led them to view its members as naughty girls in need of a good spanking. Beyond Russia's borders, however, the members of Pussy Riot quickly became feminist everywomen, sparking a viral video campaign, in which people around the world donned their own, often homemade balaclavas and proclaimed, "I'm also Pussy Riot." Needless to say, the horizontal community of style that began in Russia but spanned the globe during the 2011–2012 protests failed to overturn the fraudulent elections, let alone topple Putin's regime. But it did make Putin sweat, as we see in the series of laws limiting free association, banning blasphemy, and outlawing "gay propaganda" that followed in the protests' wake.[63] The stylistically attuned protests that swept over Russia in the early 2010s exposed Putin's two worst domestic fears: mockery of his masculinist power vertical and horizontal connections formed outside the Russian state's control. By mobilizing the irony of camp and kitsch, protesters used the same stylistic weapons to dismantle Putin's charisma that the Kremlin's political technologists had used to build it up. Russia's president might joke about condoms and outlaw an image of himself as a gay clown, but he was powerless to delete the countless satirical memes of him that any denizen of the internet could enjoy thanks to a simple Google search.

Russia's Own Performative Categories

As this glance at the 2011–2012 protests shows, blending earnestness with irony generated real political substance for both Putin and those protesting against him. At the same time, any analysis of actions by protesters in the street or Pussy Riot opens the door to other modes of ironic performance typically viewed as exclusively Russian, whose boundaries are no less mobile and permeable than those delineating charisma, camp, and kitsch. The fact that the Russian terms *kharizma*, *kemp*, and *kitch* are clearly borrowed from Greek, English, and German has discouraged commentators, with a few notable exceptions, from considering them alongside such phenomena as *poshlost'*, *stiob*, or *glamur*.[64] Nonetheless, the history and usage of the latter three suggest that they lie in proximity to their foreign counterparts and that the effortless slide among charisma, camp, and kitsch might very well pass through or end up in *poshlost'*, *stiob*, or *glamur*. Unsurprisingly, each of these Russian modes of performativity has its own gendered, temporal, affective, and agentic affinities, which, while related and even similar to those that characterize charisma, camp, and kitsch, differ sufficiently from them to prevent us from subsuming the Russian terms into their foreign counterparts.

We can begin with *poshlost'* because of its clear similarity to kitsch, which several commentators have noted. *Poshlost'* has found its most succinct definition in Vladimir Nabokov's formulation of "the obviously trashy, the falsely important . . . the falsely beautiful, the falsely clever, the falsely attractive."[65] Svetlana Boym elaborates by calling *poshlost'* "the Russian version of banality, with a characteristic national flavoring of metaphysics and high morality, and a peculiar conjunction of the sexual and the spiritual [encompassing] triviality, vulgarity, sexual promiscuity, and lack of spirituality."[66] The bête noire of many a Russian writer, *poshlost'* appears repeatedly in the work of Anton Chekhov, who provides a vivid example in Anna Sergeevna, the title character of his short story "Lady with Lapdog" (1899). In the 1960 film adaptation, the director Iosif Heifits brings to life the blend of sex, trash, banality, and morality described by both Nabokov and Boym: immediately after her "fall," a dewy-eyed Anna Sergeevna laments her *poshlost'* in a *poshlyi* postcoital confession to the very man who just made her an adulteress.[67]

As Boym points out, the abstract noun *poshlost'* derives from the past tense of one of the Russian language's many versions of the verb "to go" (*poshlo*) and the associated adjective *poshlyi* initially referred to the traditional, old-fashioned, or ancient and not to the tacky, trashy, or tasteless, as it does today. This root points to the dual time frame of *poshlost'*, as well as to its nature "as a repetition gone sour [and] a convention turned into a worn-out cliché."[68] This characterization highlights both the similarity to and the difference from camp that make *poshlost'* appear, at first glance, to be the Russian equivalent of kitsch. The double time frame and the discursive duality of *poshlost'* work to establish a hostile hierarchy in which those in the know look down on those who unwittingly consume *poshlyi* objects and produce *poshlyi* sentiments. The notion of *poshlost'* grants agency to cultural elites, like Nabokov and Boym, establishing their preeminence in the realm of taste at the same time that it denies agency to those deemed *poshlyi*. Yet *poshlost'* differs from kitsch because of its feminine connotations, which arise not merely from the word's grammatical gender.[69] Like Chekhov's Anna Sergeevna, the clearest examples of *poshlost'* cited by the likes of Nabokov and Boym are maudlin and mawkish women or sentimental and effete men.

However, cultural elites like Nabokov and Boym have failed to notice one feature of *poshlost'* that the internet brings to the fore: its capacity to restore the agency of those who knowingly apply the label to themselves. Here again

Chekhov's "Lady with Lapdog" proves instructive. The melodramatic monolog in which Anna Sergeevna confesses her own *poshlost'* takes place while the story's protagonist, who just engineered her "fall," distractedly snacks on a watermelon. Yet, by declaring herself *poshlaia*, Anna Sergeevna gains enough individuality, authenticity, spiritual depth, and agency to warrant the protagonist's love, as well as the reader's compassion if not admiration. We find the post-Soviet version of Anna Sergeevna's ability to restore her agency via *poshlost'* in the dozens of tests on the RuNet offering to determine "How *poshlaia* are you?," all of which define *poshlost'* as a blend of the test-taker's attitudes toward sex and sexual peccadillos. One such test includes questions about the different sexual poses in the test-taker's repertoire, as well as, "What number do you find the most seductive?" (possible answers: 11, 69, or 02), and "What hangs and then stands, is cold and then hot?" (possible answers: "Are there really any other options? Of course, the [male] member," "I have no idea; I'm bad at riddles," and "The shower").[70] Although some of these tests claim to diagnose the *poshlost'* of "gals" and "guys," their contents, as well as the sites that house them, are pitched to a mostly female audience. The very fact that the heirs of Anna Sergeevna take such tests lets them take ownership of their *poshlost'*, and this self-awareness and self-irony restores at least a portion of the agency typically denied to those deemed *poshlaia*. In other words, the agentic affinity of *poshlost'*, as well as kitsch for that matter, is just as unstable as whatever lines divide the seven styles discussed in this chapter.

If *poshlost'* offers a close but inexact analogue to kitsch within Russian culture, then my second Russian term, *stiob*, functions more in opposition to than in accord with camp. Initially a slang term, *stiob* gained currency in scholarly circles through the work of the anthropologist Alexei Yurchak, whose 2006 book, *Everything Was Forever, Until It Was No More: The Last Soviet Generation*, explores this late-Soviet form of irony as evidence of a performative shift in post-Stalinist culture.[71] Yurchak defines *stiob* as "a peculiar form of irony that differ[s] from sarcasm, cynicism, derision, or any of the more familiar genres of absurd humor [since] [i]t require[s] such a degree of *overidentification* with the object, person, or idea at which this *stiob* [is] directed that it [is] often impossible to tell whether it [is] a form of sincere support, subtle ridicule, or a peculiar mixture of the two."[72] To illustrate Yurchak's definition, we need only think of the 1991 television appearance of the experimental artist Sergei Kurekhin, in which he gave an erudite hour-and-a-half lecture on several supposedly secret facts about Vladimir Ilych Lenin and the October Revolution. Kurekhin claimed, in dead earnest, that Lenin and his fellow revolutionaries were fans of hallucinogenic mushrooms, that their personalities had been displaced by the mushrooms they consumed, and, ultimately, "that Lenin was a mushroom."[73] Kurekhin's overidentification with official discourse about the Revolution's secret history allowed him to fool viewers, some of whom actually called the television station in search of verification and explanation.[74]

Interestingly, Yurchak's research with Dominic Boyer brings the notion of *stiob* out of the late Soviet context and argues for its relevance as "a portable analytics" in contemporary Western culture.[75] Citing American television programs like Comedy Central's *The Daily Show* and *The Colbert Report*, Yurchak and Boyer reveal a fundamental similarity between the discursive conditions of late socialism in the Soviet bloc and those of neoliberalism in the West, labeling *stiob* a means to expose "authoritative discourse's reliance on form" and "an alternative aesthetics and practice of political critique."[76] The double-voiced nature of *stiob*, its ability to resist authoritative discourse by reproducing it, its vacillation between seriousness and irony, all sound strikingly similar to the ambivalence of camp described earlier.

However, *stiob* differs from camp in at least three respects. First, the overidentification that serves as *stiob*'s central feature does not function empathically and fails to mediate between two equally valued and equally despised sentiments, styles, times, or genders. On the contrary, *stiob* functions as a form of aggressive narcissism, in which a subordinate subject, like Kurekhin, mirrors the dominant discourse back to those who created it with the aim of gutting it of any power.[77] Second, *stiob* requires an ambivalent agency that it simultaneously flaunts yet hides. For example, Kurekhin's seemingly effortless argument that Lenin was not a man but a fungus required both planning and effort, which his brilliant *stiob* performance subsequently disguised. Third, *stiob* has nothing to do with androgyny, the epicene style, or tender feelings. Rather, it functions as a passive-aggressive performative strategy, which, in most examples cited by academics, is used by men to beat other men in a race for cultural dominance, as the roots of *stiob* in the Russian verb "to whip or lash" confirm.[78] *Stiob* is not "good-natured" but "brutal" in its creation of a hierarchy in which those who "get it" mercilessly shame and subordinate those who don't.[79] The emergence of a neofascist *stiob* among ostensibly right-wing groups like Eduard Limonov's National Bolshevik Party and Petersburg Fundamentalists including Pavel Krusanov in the early 2000s, as well as the Russian state's appropriation of *stiob* in the 2010s, vividly illustrates this performative mode's temporal elasticity and masculinist aggression.[80] In other words, if camp typically creates a community of gender-bending cognoscenti through simultaneous exclusion and inclusion, *stiob* separates macho insiders from wimpy outsiders via mockery and shame, making *stiob* look like an ironic inversion of charisma.[81]

As a result, *stiob* has been an effective pin for pricking the bubble of charisma in Russian culture since the 1980s, as another episode from the 2011–2012 protests illustrates. Rabfak's video "Our Madhouse Votes for Putin" appeared at the start of the "Snow Revolution," and its viral popularity led to invitations from protest organizers for the group to perform at rallies, as well as a prize from Navalyni himself for the best music video to oppose United Russia.[82] The song's off-color words are, strangely enough, by Aleksandr Elin (the same lyricist who penned "Someone Like Putin"), and they convey a madman's pro-Putin worldview via *stiob.* By channeling the deranged beliefs of someone who can no longer tell the difference between the brutal treatment he gets in the madhouse and his country's politics, Rabfak transforms the song's professed support of Putin's campaign for a third term as president into the allegation that only a crazy person would vote for him, as the chorus makes evident: "Everything's so complicated, everything's so confused, / But brother, there's no time to figure it out, / Our madhouse votes for Putin, / Our madhouse is glad about Putin." Elin's brilliantly lame rhyme of *zaputano* (confused) with *za Putina* (for Putin) makes the link between Russia's president and political bedlam explicit, as does found footage in the video of men living with mental illness and dancing as they drunkenly disrobe. "Our Madhouse Votes for Putin" used the aggressive narcissism of *stiob* to show that Russian masculinity had run amok by the time of the fraudulent elections that triggered the 2011–2012 protests and to shame Putin for captaining a ship of fools.

Much like *poshlost'* and *stiob*, Putin-era *glamur* proves that these three Russian modes of performativity intersect yet do not fully overlap with their foreign counterparts. Unlike the previous two concepts, however, *glamur* figures as a very recent and obvious import into the Russian language, dating back only to the 1990s and operating as a key term in the rhetoric of excess in Russian culture of the 2000s and 2010s.[83] A product of Putin-era affluence, *glamur* was voted Russia's first "word of the year" in 2007, a mere three years after Condé Nast began publishing a Russian version of its *Glamour* magazine.[84] Much like camp, *glamur* downplays substance and depth in favor of eye-catching surfaces and glossy packaging, as its tie to another loan word, *glianets*, from the German for "shine," "luster," or "polish," suggests.[85] Helena Goscilo and Vlad Strukov have labeled *glamur* "the gaudy antipode" of *poshlost'* in their discussion of its role in Russian celebrity culture of the 2000s, which produced glamour fiction by Oksana Robski and whose poster child in the 2000s and 2010s was, according to many, Ksenia Sobchak.[86] TV personality, socialite, journalist, and then member of the political opposition, Sobchak was considered the Russian Paris Hilton in her younger days, and she did everything from hosting reality television to posing for the Russian *Playboy* before deciding to run in Russia's 2018 presidential elections. As Goscilo and Strukov contend and Sobchak illustrated in her youth, *glamur* operates via the "double-edged logic of 'anti-,'" signifying "The disjunction between fantasy and reality" and discouraging the type of political involvement that she eventually decided to pursue.[87]

Like *stiob* and *poshlost'*, *glamur* has a double valence in what it signifies, as well as its historical, affective, and agentic stances. While its conspicuous consumption remains out of reach for most Russians, who cannot afford to wear a Rolex, shop on the Champs-Élysées, or drive a Bentley, its mass-produced offshoots lie within the reach of all.[88] Suitably, *glamur* in Russia operates in dialog with two different imagined pasts: on one hand, the country's prerevolutionary splendor, opulence, and luxury, and, on the other hand, Soviet rationing, deficits, and lines.[89] Much like camp, *glamur* entails, in the words of Birgit Menzel, "a paradoxical mixture of exclusiveness and accessibility, aloofness and commonality, cynicism and compassion, artificial stimulation and authentic emotion."[90] And although true glamour requires agency in the form of large sums of money and the time to spend it, this agency seems significantly diluted, since truly glamorous people should look like they have always, already been that way.

Although these features sound closer to camp than either *poshlost'* or *stiob*, we run into the same problem as with these two Russian terms when we remember that *glamur* operates as a means of cultural exclusion, ruthlessly separating the haves from the have-nots.[91] In addition, "the glamourous being," to quote Tat'iana Tolstaia, "is young, thin, sinuous, and as a rule, of the female sex."[92] Tolstaia also notes that *glamur*, like charisma, is fundamentally "narcissistic. The basic condition of the glamorous woman is an erotic trance brought on by objects of luxury."[93] In other words, the feminine *glamur* exhibits an affective stance strikingly similar to that of the more masculine charisma. Yet, rather than galvanizing followers toward some aspirational future, *glamur* manifests what one critic has called "an aggressive passivity, insisting on the preservation of the already existing order of things and on ethical quietude."[94] Consequently, the "capacious empty form" of *glamur* functions in a manner diametrically opposed to charisma.[95] Rather than facilitate political action and social change, *glamur* represents "an extremely powerful instrument of dumbing-down, zombifying, [and] sabotaging intelligible efforts at resistance" either to itself or to the regime that enables it.[96]

Russian culture of the 2000s generated a deluge of glamour, for example, films like Andrei Konchalovskii's 2007 *Gloss*, television shows such as the TNT channel's *Sex with Anfisa Chekhova*, and Russia's first globally recognized designers of haute couture, moving some to speculate that Putinism's ideology might in fact be *glamur*. Yet the clearest example of *glamur*'s vapidity and mobility comes in yet another pop tune by Aleksandr Elin. "More Glamour" appeared in 2007, and the video by the girl group High Heels and the hairstylist (as well as plastic-surgery aficionado) Sergei Zverev contains a glut of gold lamé, rhinestones, ostrich feathers, fur, and black lace.[97] Both High Heels and Zverev change costume no fewer than four times, demonstrating their appetite for "More, more glamour! / More makeup and manicures! / More, more glamour! / A super face and a super figure." Perhaps the most arresting costume is Zverev's black-shirted white suit adorned with silver chains, as well as white angel wings sweeping the floor and white knee-high fur boots. Zverev's "rap" in this outfit tells the viewer "to find your own style. / Play down your minuses and play up your plusses. / Buy a real outfit in a boutique. / If you don't have money, get it on credit." The video's surfeit of glamorous clichés, as well as High Heels' sexually provocative moves, made many who saw "More Glamour" wonder whether the song represented an instance of *glamur* or of *poshlost'*, a question made only more pressing by the passage of time. In addition to modeling the relentless consumption and grooming necessary for the glamorous subject, "More Glamour" illustrates the slippage intrinsic not just to *glamur* but to any style tinged by irony.

As this brief genealogy demonstrates, *poshlost'*, *stiob*, and *glamur* represent modes of performativity related to yet distinct from charisma, camp, and kitsch. Positioning all six along a single stylistic continuum helps to expand our understanding of the tendency for all representations of hypergender in popular media to slide between and among different performative modes, depending on the viewer and the viewing context. The contiguity and complementarity of *poshlost'*, *stiob*, and *glamur* with charisma, camp, and kitsch prove that Russia was never excluded from the stylistic revolution described by Sontag in her "Notes on 'Camp.'" In fact, the word *poshlost'* was well established in the Russian lexicon as a term for banality, sentimentality, and vulgarity by the mid-nineteenth century, that is, decades before Weber's foundational writings on charisma, the emergence of the word "camp" in English, and the appearance of "kitsch" in German. As tempting as it is, I am not arguing for Russia's national preeminence as a purveyor of captivating vulgarity and enigmatic irony. Rather, the fact that all of these terms emerged at roughly the same historical moment and under comparable sociocultural circumstances should lead us to the realization, like Yurchak and Boyer's, that performative modes initially identified in one culture can and do function as "portable analytics" in another. By broadening the range of performative modes that contribute to ironic slippage, we more readily perceive not only the representational similarities shared by the meme of Putin as a gay clown and that of

Trump as a drag queen but also the important performative differences that produce a variety of political meanings in the contexts where these memes circulate.

Travesti and Drag

Given the global reach of ironic style in the age of the internet, my genealogy of post-Soviet pop performativity might benefit from including styles that originated outside the Anglo-American and Russian traditions discussed earlier, for example, Bollywood, K-Pop, or Hong Kong kung-fu. However, for the purposes of what lies ahead in this book, we need to consider a fourth and final ironic Russian style, which, I argue, became the meta-mode of performativity between 2000 and 2020: *travesti* or drag. In Russian, *travesti* has traditionally designated cross-dressing in the bounded spaces of the theater, cabaret, gay nightclub, television show, and cinema. Unlike *poshlost'*, *stiob*, and *glamur*, such cross-dressing actually embraces the androgyny, queerness, narcissism-cum-empathy, and recursive temporality that distinguish camp from the other performative modes already discussed, and *travesti* clearly involves Sontag's "epicene style" in its blending of male and female. The *travesti-artist*, or drag performer, typically wears the costume and plays the role of the opposite sex, serving up a blend of charisma, camp, kitsch, *poshlost'*, *stiob*, and *glamur*. However, *travesti* also grants its performer the agency of the professional actor, aligning it with charisma. Whether we look at the long tradition of women playing boys in Soviet children's theater or the rise of the Russian drag queen in post-Soviet Russia (discussed in more detail in chapter 3), the *travesti-artist* exhibits ambiguous gender and sexuality in spades and asks that audiences suspend their (dis)belief about prevailing notions of gender and sexuality in order to enjoy the spectacle of cross-dressing.

Another loan word brought into Russian, *travesti* derives from the Italian *travestire* (to disguise or to dress up), and its closest and most convenient translation into English is the word "drag." However, the loan word "*dreg*" entered the Russian language in the late 2010s as a synonym for *travesti* thanks to the popularity of *RuPaul's Drag Race*, the reality TV competition searching for America's next drag superstar since 2009. When used by drag practitioners and members of the LGBTQ+ community, the terms *travesti* and *dreg* exhibit an overlap comparable to that of the styles treated earlier, with the former referring to an older generation of theatrical professionals and the latter to a younger generation, whose cross-dressing, under the influence of RuPaul, represents not just a vocation but a lifestyle.[98] My own use of the words *travesti* and drag as synonyms acknowledges this distinction between career and lifestyle at the same time that it questions whether the boundary separating the stage from everyday life was as clear-cut before 2020 as those who use the word *dreg* imply.

Admittedly, *travesti* has traditionally been the province of professional actors in Russia, yet the Putin-era mandate that all Russians perform ever more essentialized, polarized, and "traditional" gender roles had the effect of liberating *travesti* from its professional confines and bringing it into the popular media and everyday life. Regardless of a person's perceived biological sex, gender identity, or sexual orientation, the successful performance of the heterosexual femininity or masculinity required of the country's citizens entailed cross-dressing as a "real" Russian woman or man, as Vladimir Putin himself richly illustrated in the 2000s and 2010s. Perhaps memes of Putin as a gay clown were outlawed because it takes little imagination, once we have seen Putin made up like a woman, to realize that the Kremlin's political technologists regularly cross-dressed him as a *muzhik* for photo ops in which he flew with endangered cranes, fished on the Yenisei River, or rode a Harley Davidson. As the country's fearless leader, Putin crafted a hypermasculinity that responded to and reiterated his regime's relentless call to hypergender, enabling *travesti* as the link connecting all of the stylistic modes already discussed. And, like Putin, Russian citizens could use *travesti* first to place themselves along the continuum of charisma and then to slip and slide among camp, kitsch, *poshlost'*, *stiob*, and *glamur*.

Since the next two chapters explore the emergence of cross-dressing as a performative mode in post-Soviet Russia, here I offer only two brief illustrations from popular music to show how *travesti* facilitated and intensified stylistic slippage during Putin's first three terms in office. The first involves an actual drag queen, Zaza Napoli, the creation of actor Vladim Kazantsev, singing her 2010 song "Lenin."[99] The video of "Lenin" begins with shots of the Kremlin's iconic towers and Red Square, location of the mausoleum of the Soviet Union's founder-father, and then cuts to a gaudily attired Napoli in the studio of the liberal radio station Echo of Moscow beside the journalist and blogger Aleksandr Pliushchev. Lip-synching to heavily synthesized Russian pop, Napoli sings the story of her undying love for Lenin instead of some latter-day thug, oligarch, or even "Vova" (nickname for Putin, to whose photograph she points). The song's chorus describes her inexplicable love:

> I love Lenin, Lenin, Lenin
> Because he's so dark-yellow and waxy.
> I love Lenin, Lenin, Lenin.
> Someone's going to tell me
> That I'm off my rocker.

I love Lenin, Lenin, Lenin
Because he's entirely Soviet and our own.
I really love Lenin, Lenin, Lenin.
What's my problem?[100]

The combination of tacky music, ludicrous lyrics, and video footage of Napoli in a glittering ball gown and then a Young Pioneer uniform results in a blend of all of the performative modes outlined earlier. In addition to leveraging the liberal charisma of Echo of Moscow and Pliushchev, Napoli generates campy nostalgia for the Soviet past, which tips over into kitsch once she appears in a Young Pioneer's red hat and scarf. Her plus-size drag straddles the line between *poshlost'* and *glamur*, while the entire tale of love for a political leader whose greatest virtue is an embalmed body that prevents him from cheating sounds like *stiob* of the pop tune "Someone Like Putin." Although Napoli's *travesti* places her squarely on the continuum of styles discussed in this chapter, she mobilizes a surfeit of performative modes, preventing any final determination of what her song actually means. On one hand, "Lenin" might be a scathing satire of Putin's cult, which in 2010 seemed like an inconsequential and incompetent latecomer in comparison to the cult of Lenin. On the other hand, "Lenin" might express the thwarted queer love of gender-nonconforming Russians for their hypermasculine president. In other words, Kazantsev's *travesti* allowed the character of Zaza Napoli to move among performative modes and to ignite a conflagration of Russian styles.

Lest we think that the meta-mode of *travesti* is limited to bodies of one gender that don the clothing of the other, my second example from the world of pop features Olia Poliakova, a Ukrainian singer costumed as "the superblond of all Rus'." Poliakova's 2012 music video "Russian Style" not only shows her at her platinum-blond and leggy best but also provides a hilarious send-up of Western stereotypes of post-Soviet women.[101] The title of Poliakova's song refers to the Korean mega-hit of the same year, "Gangnam Style," as do several musical and visual memes in "Russian Style." Within this global pop idiom, Poliakova, who usually sports a fanciful postmodern *kokoshnik* (traditional headdress of Slavic women), camps up the clichés of post-Soviet femininity in which global culture typically trades. The cheesy accordion music and deconstructed Soviet army uniforms, her backup dancers' ludicrously long braids and equally long legs, Poliakova's striptease appearance out of a barrel of red caviar before a group of hunky balalaika players, all come together in a stunning spectacle, demonstrating the global pop currency of the stereotype that assumes all post-Soviet women are "Russian." The song's lyrics, insofar as they say anything, describe the superblond, unlike her pop currency, as the sort of girl who refuses to sell

Figure 4. Zaza Napoli posing in her full feminine glamour. Used by permission of Vladim Kazantsev.

herself to the highest bidder. And the video's brief framing narrative locates Poliakova's pouty lips and gyrating hips in a Siberian log cabin, which houses the sole survivors of the apocalypse and in which one can take refuge only if wearing a *kokoshnik*. Looking like a Slavic Jayne Mansfield or Virginia Mayo, Poliakova provides a seemingly silly performance of hyperfemininity, whose deeper message appears to align with Putin-era neonationalism.

However, Poliakova's Ukrainian identity opens up other, perhaps more likely possibilities for how we might read "Russian Style." Although "Russian Style" (whose Russian lyrics continually repeat its English title) makes fun of Western stereotypes of post-Soviet femininity, Poliakova is in fact a Ukrainian woman, whose status as "the superblond of all Rus'" refers to the geographical and historical entity that Ukraine, Belarus, and Russia all claim as their ancestor. Is "Russian Style" a gesture toward pan-Slavic sisterhood? Or does Poliakova's *travesti* include not merely a woman cross-dressing as a superblond but, more significantly, a Ukrainian cross-dressing as Russian? The decision to record the song in Russian was probably pragmatic, since pop music sung in Russian enjoyed a considerably larger audience than its Ukrainian counterpart when "Russian Style" was released. Indeed, such a decision in 2012 was less fraught for a Ukrainian performer than it would become in 2014, that is, after

Figure 5. Olia Poliakova emerging from a barrel of caviar for the 2012 video "Russian Style."

Russia's seizure of Crimea, the outbreak of a separatist war in Donbas, the events of Euromaidan, and Russia's bloody invasion of Ukraine. In other words, Poliakova's linguistic and national *travesti* might very well have generated criticism of the very Putin-era neonationalism that "Russian Style" initially seemed to support.

As both these examples show, liberating *travesti* from its professional confines made cross-dressing of various types into the ultimate Russian style of Putin's first two decades in power. Unlike being trans, whose associations in Russian culture with homosexuality and pedophilia make donning the Other's clothes into the exposé of a shameful nonnormative self, *travesti* resembles camp since it maintains an ambivalent and often indecipherable distance between self and Other. Whether men like Kazantsev dressed up as women or Ukrainians like Poliakova as Russians, negotiating Russian style in the 2000s and 2010s required adopting the Other's clothing, gestures, and affect at the same time that it overlooked the actual relationship between self and Other. The aging Putin clearly embodied this aspect of *travesti*, as rumors of Botox treatments and plastic surgery in the 2010s were brushed under the carpet in favor of gossip about the Russian president's various mistresses and the babies they birthed in Swiss VIP clinics. Apparently, "the image of Russia as a transvestite" haunted not only Erofeev but also Putin himself, compelling the Russian president to craft his own hypermasculine drag.[102] And just as Putin's *travesti* of masculinity paved the way for multiple and sometimes mutually exclusive interpretations, so did the drag of gender and nation produced by more lowly figures, like Napoli and Poliakova, generate a gamut of possible meanings from complete capitulation to utter defiance before Putinism's imperative of heterosexual hypergender.

Conclusion

Although this book's performative definition of style emphasizes its inherent instability and mobility, juxtaposing the different ironic styles available in Russian pop culture during Putin's first two decades in power yields at least one steadfast conclusion: Putinism was more style than ideology between 2000 and 2020. Needless to say, the overarching Russian style that was Putinism during these two decades went beyond irony to embrace solemnity, sacrality, sincerity, and so on in the venues outside pop culture where Putin and his coterie appeared. However, by highlighting ironic modes of performance, this chapter exposes the dynamic relationship between self and Other at the heart of constructed Russianness, which more earnest styles, including charisma, elided. The different simulacra of Russian identity that arose in pop culture during the 2000s and 2010s all demonstrate that Russian citizenship required that the self appropriate and perform a hypergendered, heteronormative Otherness. While slipping and sliding among ironic styles, ranging from camp and kitsch to *poshlost'*, *stiob*, *glamur*, and *travesti*, such selves might accrue Russianness, cultural capital, and perhaps even charisma by copying the very gambit on which Putin's handlers banked during the initial phase of his cult.

The shifting boundaries that distinguish one ironic performative mode from another allowed for often subtle and sometimes abrupt shifts along a sliding scale of stylistic possibilities, while adopting *travesti* or drag intensified each style's effect and facilitated movement along this stylistic continuum. As the chapters that follow show, the dynamic possibilities of such *travesti*-driven ironic style contributed to a performative shift after Putin's rise to power, which was no less momentous than that analyzed by Yurchak in his study of late-Soviet society and culture. If, as Yurchak argues, the final decades of Soviet power witnessed a discursive shift, in which words lost their factual meanings to take on a newfound performative force, then the first two decades of the Putin era saw the shift of performativity itself from the realm of discourse to that of embodied performance. Rather than focusing on the production of words, widgets, or the next generation, Russian bodies began to generate a variety of styles that held the power to reinforce or contest Russian identity itself.

My decision to discuss charisma, camp, kitsch, *poshlost'*, *stiob*, *glamur*, and *travesti* in this particular order is not intended to imply a hierarchical relationship among these different styles. Rather, it is motivated by my suspicion that some of this book's English-speaking readers have greater familiarity with Anglo-American terminology than Russian. Moreover, by calling *travesti* a meta-mode, I do not mean to suggest that the performative cross-dressing this word describes somehow existed above or beyond the continuum of other styles during Putin's first three terms as president. On the contrary, the fact that *travesti* was no longer cordoned off on the professional stage made it an equal-opportunity style available to any and all Russians performing citizenship after 1999. The very nature of the performative shift from discursivity to embodiment prevented the styles discussed here from congealing into a stable hierarchy or durable list, making the genealogy this chapter offers both provisional and open-ended. At the very least, however, my genealogy demonstrates the central place of an ever-evolving irony, with its unstable meanings and ambivalent outcomes, in both Russian pop culture and more globally.

While such interpretive slipperiness might function as mere entertainment in an environment that permits free speech, the Russian government's growing control over free expression between 2000 and 2020 gave ironic performances greater political punch than they typically had in the United States or Western Europe. When used by the likes of Putin for topless photo ops, the slip and slide among different styles worked to essentialize heterosexual hypergender, contributing to the myth of Russia's sexual innocence and "natural" heterosexuality.[103] The Russian president's hypermasculine *travesti* pretended ignorance of the very artifice used to construct this myth and had the effect of insulating those in power from criticism and preventing the country's political opposition from posing any real threat to Putin's leadership. By shifting politics from the realm of ideas and actions to that of surface and style, Putin's own irony attempted to routinize the very opposite of what Weber and Sontag envisioned for both charisma and camp. Rather than challenging patriarchal power, as Weber outlines, or allowing for the integration of gays into society, as Sontag posits, Putin's own slide among charisma, camp, kitsch, *poshlost'*, *stiob*, *glamur*, and *travesti* did its best to naturalize the Russian president's hegemony with the same gesture that pretended ignorance of its nature as artifice.

However, when used by the likes of the 2011–2012 protesters, Pussy Riot, Napoli, Poliakova, or whoever first posted gay clown Putin on Tumblr in 2013, this stylistic slippage held the potential to unmask hypergender as the performance that it is and to expose the limitations placed on free expression in Russia as the product of male hysteria.[104] In other words, Putin was not alone in his clever use of the performativity that arises when charisma fuses with different, more ironic styles. The flexibility and mobility of these styles could and did lead to unanticipated consequences, as the story of the Ulianovsk cadets with which this book began aptly illustrates. The chapters that follow explore not only the origins of Putinism as style but, perhaps more interestingly, the ability of Russia's citizens to manipulate the actual political substance that Putinism's focus on surface and style attempted to block through their own *travesti*.

2

The Soviet Legacy of Traumatized Bodies

If drag or *travesti* brought charisma, camp, kitsch, *poshlost'*, *stiob*, and *glamur* together into a single Russian pop style during the 2000s and 2010s, then we have to wonder how and why a performative mode typically associated with androgyny and homosexuality became pop performativity's glue in Putin's Russia. Much as camp leverages the tantalizing distance between self and Other, *travesti* takes advantage of the gap between performers' bodies and what they put on. Yet as a form of irony, *travesti* pretends ignorance of the very gap that separates the performing self from its costume, inviting audiences to conflate performers *en travesti* with the Other they embody. Between 2000 and 2020, however, Russians' tendency to conflate cross-gender cross-dressing with male homosexuality made *travesti* within one's own sex and gender especially well suited for performing the homophobic hypergender required of Russian citizens. Regardless of biological sex, gender expression, and sexual preference, anyone—from Putin at the top of the power vertical down to the citizens at its bottom—could perform a drag version of the hypergender that aligned with one's biological sex. Such cisgender drag produced socially acceptable versions of masculinity and femininity without ever divulging whether the individual's performance sincerely expressed an authentic self or ironically caricatured the Other.

To understand why cisgender *travesti* became a central strategy for performing citizenship under Putin, we need look no farther than the sartorial regime that the Russian Federation inherited from the Soviet Union. The 1990s saw wave after wave of affordable clothing flood into Russia, whose vestiary style, according to Djurdja Bartlett, had become "a prisoner of time" after seventy years beyond the reach of global capitalism.[1] Beginning in the Stalin era, socialist fashion for women emphasized conservative garments, whose simplicity and modesty diverted attention from the female form and whose unavailability resulted in many Soviet women making their own clothing and wearing the same garments for years.[2] In contrast, the 1990s brought new fabrics, bold colors, and provocative trends into Russia, and the "fast fashion" on sale in stores and street markets allowed the country's women to express a greater degree of prepackaged femininity—and to display more of their curves and flesh—than ever before.[3] Simply put, the end of the Soviet Union transformed Russian women from producers and preservers of chaste wardrobes into consumers of disposable and revealing garments often made in Turkey or China.[4]

Despite dramatic changes in the clothes Russians wore during the 1990s, the sartorial regime of the 2000s and 2010s retained key features of its Soviet precursor. Given the growing emphasis on "traditional" gender norms, it comes as no surprise that dress and self-presentation were just as "emphatically gendered" after Putin's rise to power as they were before the Soviet Union's demise.[5] As Katerina Klingseis contended in 2011, "neither official Soviet texts nor present-day basic dress discourse allow for any gender ambiguities; with very few exceptions, traditional gender roles are largely adopted and reproduced without questioning."[6] This gender polarity dovetailed with the assumption (also inherited from the Soviet era) that good taste in clothing is not just an aesthetic but an ethical category that assesses any deviation from vestiary norms negatively.[7] Much like its Soviet predecessor, the "cult of clothing" that arose during Putin's first two decades in the Kremlin categorized individuals by clear-cut standards of gender, age, class, profession, ethnicity, and nationality, placing them in a moral hierarchy—all at a single glance.[8] Feminine fashion of the 2000s and 2010s combined the Soviet-era dictate that a woman's dress be tasteful and legible to all who see her with the post-Soviet sexualization of the female body.

The vestiary requirements of post-Soviet femininity explain the specifically Russian origins of the inevitably mixed message of cisgender *travesti* between 2000 and 2020. Russians' routine appraisal of the inner person on the basis of outer appearance aggressively policed the individual's performance of gender and sexuality, and Russian women predictably developed defensive strategies in response. Before 1991, Soviet women could wear garments that functioned as "armor," for example, "the coat for standing in lines," which protected its wearer from inclement weather, pushy shoppers, and unwanted judgment, and the *khalat* or housedress, which desexualized and infantilized whoever wore it.[9] After 1999, however, the suggestiveness of much feminine fashion weaponized the female body, proving that a woman's best defense was a good offense. The form-fitting designer dress, artfully applied makeup, and stiletto heels that many Russian women wore out of the house on a daily basis neither deflected nor discouraged the Other's gaze. Instead, their overt sex appeal drew attention in an attempt to determine the Other's judgment. Russian women who adopted a *travesti* of hyperfemininity as their workaday wear frustrated attempts at gender policing with strategies of self-presentation that looked like peremptory strikes in the fight over whether a book can be judged by its cover. At the same time that professional drag queens like Zaza Napoli used cross-gender *travesti* to violate the boundary between male and female and to earn a livelihood, Russian women used cisgender *travesti* to reinforce this boundary, ensuring the adequacy of their daily performance of hyperfemininity and their right to Russianness.

Once we consider the weaponized post-Soviet wardrobe within the larger regime of hypergender inaugurated by Putin's rise to power, we begin to recognize that women's cisgender drag served a purpose much greater than their own personal protection. By drawing a line in the sand between masculinity and femininity, stiletto- and Gucci-clad women not only thwarted aggressive gender policing but also helped to shore up the sagging masculinity of their male compatriots. This sartorial solution to the country's long-standing crisis of masculinity posited that women's emancipation in the USSR caused their masculinization, which in turn feminized Soviet men, and it also assumed that altering outer appearance holds the power to change not just the inner person but even the Other who gazes on and judges that person.[10] Perhaps post-Soviet men could regain the physical prowess, emotional maturity, independence, and self-control of which Soviet women had allegedly robbed them if post-Soviet women ceded these gendered attributes by donning debilitating footwear, plunging necklines, and girly makeup. Simplistic as this argument sounds, its logic explains both the prevalence and the final purpose of cisgender drag in Russia during the 2000s and 2010s, as well as the widespread belief that post-Soviet women bore responsibility for keeping their men tastefully dressed.[11] Moreover, this style-oriented fix for the crisis of masculinity literally covered up the fragile and traumatized bodies of Russian men, whose actual precarity became an internationally recognized fact when their life expectancy fell beneath age sixty in the 1990s.

Given the many factors that played into this drop in longevity, from rampant unemployment to high rates of alcoholism after 1991, it comes as no shock that Russian men's choice of clothing held little, if any, power to alleviate a very real demographic dilemma. On the contrary, attempts to reclothe Russian men in hypermasculine garb, from Italian suits to military uniforms, exacerbated the crisis, as we see in two films released in the mid-2000s. Fedor Bondarchuk's *9th Company* from 2005 and Aleksei Balabanov's *Cargo 200* from 2007 both look back to the Soviet Union's disastrous war in Afghanistan and depict the inability of cisgender *travesti* to construct or protect an unassailable masculine ideal.[12] As different as Bondarchuk's blockbuster is from Balabanov's dark farce, both films show the utter inability of uniforms, whether the paratrooper's or the policeman's, to cover the wounds that Soviet men had already endured, let alone deflect the bombs and bullets of live warfare. The protagonists in both movies weaponize cisgender drag to the fullest extent possible, yet most of their already scarred and broken bodies end up in a pile of corpses. By nostalgically gazing back at the Soviet Union's final military conflict, Bondarchuk and Balabanov locate the roots of the post-Soviet crisis of masculinity in late Soviet trauma, likening the sartorial solution of cisgender drag to a war that has already been lost.

The third film treated in this chapter, Sergei Loban's independently produced *Dust* from 2005, pushes this late Soviet genealogy of cisgender drag to its logical yet absurd conclusion.[13] Rather than tell the tale of Soviet soldiers or policemen, *Dust* plumbs the depths of masculine abjection in post-Soviet Russia by tracing the picaresque adventures of failed masculinity's most catastrophic incarnation, the emasculated man-baby. Like *9th Company* and *Cargo 200*, Loban's film lays bare the failure of cisgender *travesti* to cover up the traumatized and prematurely perishing male body and thereby protect Russian men from their own precarity. However, *Dust* transforms the unsettling knowledge that a book's cover never really tells its full story into an emancipatory opportunity when the cisgender drag of Loban's protagonist suddenly goes cross-gender. Taken together, these three films bring to light the Soviet legacy of traumatized bodies and draw our attention to the inscrutable gap between outer appearance and inner identity built into all forms of *travesti*. Despite the many differences in their films, Bondarchuk, Balabanov, and Loban all show that whatever trauma *travesti* represses can and does return at the drop of a hat, as well as how *travesti*'s inherent ambivalence prevents this meta-mode of Russian style from ever constructing hypermasculinity as an unassailable fortress and ever solving Russia's crisis of masculinity.

The Medals of a Nonexistent Power: *9th Company*

Without doubt, Bondarchuk's intent when making *9th Company* was not to expose the intergenerational trauma bequeathed to post-Soviet men but rather to look back at masculine heroism in the late Soviet era through the rose-colored glasses of nostalgia. The film's high production values, widescreen format, and running time of well over two hours invite comparison with Hollywood war epics, and its cinematography recycles well-worn tropes from films like Oliver Stone's 1986 *Platoon* and Stanley Kubrick's 1987 *Full Metal Jacket*, delivering a predictable story of patriotism and self-sacrifice.[14] Despite whatever intentions Bondarchuk had, *9th Company*'s painstaking reconstruction of the Soviet Union's ill-fated intervention in Afghanistan draws viewers' attention away from the movie's panoramic shots of the Hindu Kush mountains and spectacular special effects to reveal the inability of any uniform, even that of elite Soviet paratroopers, to armor its wearer. *9th Company* probably hoped to naturalize its characters' military drag by showing their willingness to give their lives in the heat of battle. However, Bondarchuk's film ultimately fails in this mission since its depiction of cisgender *travesti* gives rise to profound epistemological ambivalence.

Given Bondarchuk's decision to base *9th Company* on a real-life incident at the end of the Soviet Union's decade-long Afghan conflict, the film's message about the failure of soldiers' uniforms, equipment, and weaponry to shield them from death hardly comes as a surprise.[15] The first half of the movie tells the tale of a motley group of volunteers entering military service, undergoing the rigors of basic training, and emerging as a crack squadron of paratroopers destined for battle. In addition to leaving behind their civilian lives and clothes, the young men who eventually join "the valiant 9th Company" have their heads shaved and give up civilian names for military nicknames and ranks. Stripped of their previous identities, the young recruits endure further humiliation when their drill sergeant, a scarred veteran named Dygalo (Mikhail Porechenkov), calls them "clowns," "nobodies," and even "shit" that he will turn into "people." Dygalo then begins the process of transforming the individual boys we see in the film's opening shots into fighting men fit to wear blue berets and blue-and-white-striped tank tops, that is, the hypermasculine *travesti* by which both Soviet and Russian paratroopers are known.

9th Company's otherwise predictable story of male bonding takes two curious turns. The first happens when the recruits learn how to use plastic explosives. As the materiel is passed from soldier to soldier, one of our protagonists, whose artistic aspirations have earned him the nickname Gioconda (Konstantin Kriukov), fashions a life-sized penis out of the beige putty. When their nearsighted instructor removes his eyeglasses to lecture about the explosive's merits, his comments about its resemblance to modeling clay—a harmless toy that everyone had at home in childhood and with which it seemed entirely innocent to play—sound like an unwitting description of masturbation. The double entendre leads to suppressed laughter, as does Gioconda's decision to bend his sculpture back and forth from its initially erect shape. When the instructor grabs the flaccid explosive and shoves a detonator into its tip, open laughter erupts, causing him to put his glasses on and recognize Gioconda's handiwork for the phallus it is. Rather than punishment, however, Gioconda earns Dygalo's praise for his "lifelike" work, as well as a commission to paint the superior officer's portrait in a less than lifelike manner so that it glosses over the battle scars on his face. This openly comic episode in an otherwise humorless film reveals the illusory nature of the military masculinity taught in basic training, and it takes little imagination to perceive an inert explosive shaped like a flaccid penis and penetrated by a detonator as a metaphor for impotence and a harbinger of the physical trauma and psychic rape the men endure once deployed. Moreover, the instructor's myopia generates the scene's humor at the same time that it reflects the desire in evidence throughout *9th Company* that the cisgender drag of military masculinity remain forever out of focus.

Bondarchuk's film takes its second curious turn on the night before the newly minted soldiers leave for Afghanistan when they cement their identity as paratroopers in an orgy of shared pot, alcohol, and sex. The lone woman in the training camp goes by the nickname of Snow White (Irina Rakhmanova), and as we learn when the pale blond first appears on screen, each squadron completes basic training by spending the night before deployment with her. We learn that Snow White, unlike Gioconda's impotent plastic-explosive phallus, is "as reliable as a Kalashnikov," that "she comes like a machine gun," and that "You don't fuck her; she fucks you." The soon-to-be 9th Company finishes basic training by having sex, one after the other, with this women-cum-weapon, and as Fierce (Artur Smol'ianinov), the group's self-appointed leader, states, this is the final ritual that makes a boy into a war-ready *muzhik*. The sex the recruits share via Snow White climaxes when Gioconda compares her naked, sweat-covered body to that of Aphrodite rising out of the sea and proclaims her "a goddess of beauty." Gioconda's appeal to high-culture esthetics, as well as the scene's low-key lighting, glorifies the squadron's gangbang, distracting viewers from the obvious homoeroticism on screen. For example, when Fierce decides to teach the sexually naive Sparrow (Aleksei Chadov) how to "smoke like a gypsy" by deeply inhaling from a joint and blowing the smoke into his mouth as their lips touch, Sparrow declares his love to the group, which another soldier later exclaims as they all grovel at Snow White's feet. These open declarations of love, the shotgun kiss of shared pot smoke, and the sex they share through Snow White's machine-gun vagina all complete the young men's initiation as paratroopers and *muzhiki*, at the same time exposing their vulnerability and powerlessness.

These two episodes complicate the otherwise easy narrative of *9th Company* and prepare viewers for the out-and-out failure of the paratrooper's hypermasculine *travesti* in the second half of the film. Once in Afghanistan, our protagonists enter the theater of war, where they no longer rehearse maneuvers but perform the military masculinity into which basic training initiated them against real adversaries and with live ammunition. One by one, the young men fall victim to snipers and raids, and the film's final battle scene kills off the entire 9th Company with the exception of Fierce, who miraculously survives despite having been cut off from headquarters. Throughout, we witness the inability of even the toughest paratroopers to defend themselves from the bullets, mortars, and bayonets that rip into their bodies. When helicopters finally rescue Fierce, he learns that the battle was useless, since Soviet troops had already withdrawn from the region, and his traumatized reaction tells us that although his body is whole, his spirit is broken by the violence he has endured. The film is careful to show that Fierce's survival has nothing to do with his performance as a paratrooper: a good-luck amulet he was given when he arrived in Afghanistan has hung around his neck and protected him throughout his deployment, as we realize when Fierce rips the amulet from his neck, gazes up in horrified terror, and crumples to the ground in anguish.

Bondarchuk's film tries to represent the demise of its protagonists as a patriotic sacrifice that brings military glory. However, Fierce's final voice-over as he is demobilized conveys the confused state of knowing yet not knowing in which both he and the audience find themselves at the end of *9th Company*: "We left Afghanistan. We, the 9th Company, won our war. There was a lot we didn't know then. We didn't know that in two years the country we fought for would disappear and that wearing the medals of a nonexistent power would go out of style. . . . And a cruel new life made some of us princes and threw others into the gutter. We knew none of this then. We didn't even know that in the chaos of an enormous army's retreat we had simply been forgotten on that distant day. We left Afghanistan. We, the 9th Company, were victorious." Only a hopelessly naïve viewer could overlook the profound ambivalence in Fierce's speech, which seesaws between past and present, victory and defeat, knowing and not knowing, or the trauma he shares with the scarred Dygalo, who, we learn, signed up for another tour of duty only to die of a stroke. Ultimately, *9th Company* equates the futility of the hypermasculine *travesti* that turns boys into soldiers with the Soviet Union's humiliating defeat in Afghanistan, even though the film attempts to foreclose this unsettling knowledge with a parting shot of Fierce in his paratrooper's uniform and the very medals fated to go out of style on his chest.

Bondarchuk never succeeds in erasing the painful awareness that hypermasculine *travesti* requires earning and wearing the medals of a nonexistent power, whether in style or not. Nevertheless, *9th Company* succeeded in transforming its characters' performative failure into cinematic success by grossing an unprecedented $23.47 million in its first month at the box office.[16] Amid this commercial success, the movie was reproached for its inauthenticity by film critics, veterans of the Afghan war, and viewers alike due to the liberties that

Figure 6. Fierce wearing "the medals of a nonexistent power [that] would go out of style" in the final scene of Fedor Bondarchuk's *9th Company* (2005).

Bondarchuk took with the real-life events on which *9th Company* is based.[17] As it turns out, the actual 9th Company was neither abandoned nor cut off from headquarters, and only six of its thirty-nine soldiers perished in the battle that provides the film's climax. The mixed reception of *9th Company* echoes the ambivalence in Fierce's final voice-over, which laments the failure of cisgender *travesti* in the same breath that nostalgically lionizes it.[18]

A Lone Ruby Slipper: *Cargo 200*

My decision to place Bondarchuk's Hollywood-style blockbuster alongside Balabanov's *Cargo 200*, a movie that reviewers have compared to a punch in the face, might at first seem perverse.[19] Unlike *9th Company*, *Cargo 200* flies in the face of cinematic legibility, creating a viewing experience that one critic likened to "shock therapy," while another called the film "the only work of serious, modern social criticism in recent memory that actually made me want to puke."[20] By the same token, if *9th Company* aroused controversy after its release, then *Cargo 200* unleashed a firestorm when it first appeared in Russian movie theaters in 2007.[21] A bleak portrayal of the home front during the Afghan conflict, *Cargo 200* lacks the Hollywood clichés of *9th Company*, as well as any attempt at moral uplift. Instead, Balabanov bases his plot on improbable coincidence, stacking up a kidnapping, rape, three rotting corpses, and four murders by the movie's end. Although some critics praised *Cargo 200* as "Balabanov's strongest film," "Russian theater owners [were] reluctant to book it, and viewers . . . walked out of screenings in droves."[22] This mixed reception most probably arose from the film's extreme violence and the apparent about-face that Balabanov made in *Cargo 200*. Best known for the 1997 gangster film *Brother* and its 2000 sequel, *Brother 2*, Balabanov produced a number of films early in his career whose blatant nationalism contributed to their popularity.[23] In contrast, *Cargo 200* treats its story, characters, and setting with a cynicism that inoculates viewers from the easy patriotism of *9th Company*.[24] Accordingly, the depiction of late-Soviet *travesti* in *Cargo 200* picks up where Bondarchuk's film leaves off, demonstrating that everyone in the Soviet Union—from soldiers in Afghanistan to teenage girls at discotheques—wore armor more likely to kill than to protect its wearer.

This sobering assessment of the cisgender *travesti* needed to construct hypergender comes to light as soon as we consider the film's title, which is military jargon for the slain soldiers airlifted home from Afghanistan in zinc-lined coffins. As a code term, the phrase "cargo 200" both says and refuses to say precisely what it designates, much like Fierce's ambivalent closing monolog in *9th Company*. Yet Balabanov devotes his film to bringing such subliminal knowledge into full consciousness by transforming the metaphor of rape lurking in the background of *9th Company* into actual sexual assault in *Cargo 200*.[25] Once our teenager at the disco, the young and pretty Angelika (Agniia Kuznetsova), falls into the hands of a psychopathic police captain named Zhurov (Aleksei Poluian), he brings the corpse of her fiancé (a "very tough" paratrooper who served as a special operative in Afghanistan) into the room where she is handcuffed to a bed, opens the zinc casket, throws a handful of medals onto the corpse's uniformed chest, and then dumps her rotting fiancé onto the bed beside the terrified girl. The corpse in the middle of the film deciphers once and for all the code phrase "cargo 200," revealing the inevitable failure of even a "tough" paratrooper's cisgender drag to preserve his life. In addition, the grim union of Angelika—whom Zhurov has already raped once with a vodka bottle and will soon rape again through a prisoner-surrogate—with her fiancé-corpse constitutes the film's central erotic, or in this case anti-erotic, moment. In a gruesome parallel with the rape of the Sabine women and that of Lucretia, *Cargo 200* suggests that Zhurov's attempt to force Angelika to give up her dead fiancé for a psychopathic policeman is an apt foundational myth for post-Soviet Russia.[26]

As the description of Angelika's captivity and brutalization implies, her own cisgender *travesti* fails just as utterly as that of her dead fiancé. Critics have noted *Cargo 200*'s painstaking recreation of late-Soviet material culture, including sartorial norms intended to convey the individual's identity at a single glance. When we first see Angelika at the disco, she wears an outfit that immediately identifies her as the spoiled child of Party *nomenklatura*. She proudly stands out from her peers in a color-coordinated ensemble that includes a stylish red-and-white top, a piped and pocketed A-line skirt, matching beads and pendant earrings, and red patent-leather pumps. Angelika's clothing, skillfully applied makeup, and perky side ponytail confirm her refrain that she is the daughter of the local Communist Party secretary, and she uses her outfit to win the attention of Valera (Leonid Bichevin), a countercultural bad boy. However successful Angelika's weaponized attire is at the disco, it proves her undoing as soon as Valera takes her into the seedy underworld of illegal bootlegging. He quickly passes out in a drunken stupor, leaving Angelika vulnerable to the predatory Zhurov, who stalks the bootlegger's premises and is clearly drawn to her out-of-place attire. Although she tries to defend herself with a hunting rifle, Zhurov uses Angelika's would-be weapon to slay her last defender, and from this point on she becomes a terrified and ill-attired puppet in Zhurov's sadistic hands. In other words, the hyperfeminine drag that Angelika weaponized at the disco makes her an attractive and easy target for the psychopathic Zhurov.

The failure of Angelika's cisgender *travesti* becomes painfully clear at the movie's end when she has been stripped of everything except her beaded necklace and a single red pump. In another setting, such scanty attire would transform Angelika into an odalisque, but in Balabanov's film the lingering presence of a lone ruby slipper suggests a different comparison—to the 1939 *The Wizard of Oz*.[27] Throughout her abduction and brutalization, Angelika carefully holds on to her red patent-leather pumps, even asking her rapist to fetch them after he first assaults her. However, unlike the ruby slippers in *The Wizard of Oz*, which take Dorothy on a fantastic journey and then return her to Kansas as soon as she clicks her heels together and says, "There's no place like home," Angelika's pumps accompany her on a traumatic trip to hell from which *Cargo 200* shows no return. Dorothy's shoes enable her leap from danger back to safety, while Angelika's red pumps prove powerless to protect her from the danger that engulfs her or to return her to a safety that no longer exists.

Instead of Angelika returning home, the neatly uniformed Zhurov goes to her parents' apartment to retrieve her dead fiancé's love letters. In a final act of cruelty, Zhurov reads the letters aloud to Angelika, violating not only her person but also the language of love in which she took refuge. Clearly, the captain's uniform that Zhurov wears for most of the film functions not to reveal but to mask his true identity, allowing him not only to break the law flagrantly but also to use it for his own nefarious purposes. As his alcohol-addled mother (Valentina Andriukova) points out, Zhurov isn't exactly the paratrooper or *muzhik* a woman needs, and her limp-wristed gesture of doubt when she says as much confirms our suspicion that the psychopathic Zhurov is sexually impotent. The definitive wolf in sheep's clothing, Zhurov represents a powerless yet predatory masculinity that hides its utter lawlessness and lethal intent beneath the uniform of the law.

Although Angelika's rape is but one of Zhurov's many crimes in *Cargo 200*, it links the film's multiple plots together and demonstrates with crystal clarity the failure of cisgender *travesti* as an index of identity, means of personal protection, and guarantor of social relations. The final scene of *Cargo 200* drives this cheerless point home. After abandoning Angelika, Valera makes a new friend at a rock concert when another countercultural bad boy by the name of Slava (Dmitrii Kubasov) compliments his "cool T-shirt" emblazoned with the letters CCCP (USSR). The two young men, with matching shaggy hairstyles, blue jeans, and jackets, walk into the Leningrad dusk side by side as they devise a scheme to get more *babki*, slang for both money and women. Even though the image of a stripped and whimpering Angelika handcuffed to a bed in a corpse-littered room is indelibly imprinted in the viewer's mind, Valera and Slava are shockingly oblivious to the trauma in their wake, as well as the many crimes they will surely commit once the Soviet Union dissolves to give their *babki* scheme free reign. *Cargo 200* strikes a blow against such obliviousness by dredging up the repressed knowledge of both the individual and social traumas of the late Soviet era and placing them in full view for anyone brave enough to watch the film to its end.[28] As triggering as the viewing experience is for some, it eradicates the epistemological ambivalence of a phrase like "cargo 200," as well as a film like *9th Company*. Balabanov depicts in living color the many ways in which cisgender drag characterized performances of hypergender and identity more broadly during the final decade of Soviet power, leading to the realization that *travesti* sought yet failed to compensate for the country's wounded masculinity.[29] In addition, the telling detail of Valera's CCCP T-shirt—a garment that came into vogue only after 1991—connects the mercenary young men in the film's closing shot with their Putin-generation peers, offering a scathing critique of both post-Soviet nostalgia and the roots of Russia's current sartorial regime in the Soviet past.[30]

Once we view the costume and behavior of characters in *9th Company* and *Cargo 200* as cisgender *travesti*, Bondarchuk and Balabanov's films begin to look like post-Soviet drag renditions of the late Soviet era that provides their setting. Both create consciously campy depictions of the Soviet Union's war in Afghanistan, whether through their gory special effects, meticulous attention to late-Soviet material culture, or carefully curated musical soundtracks. And both reveal, regardless of their directors' intentions, the inherent fragility of all performances of hypergender, be they by individuals like Fierce and Angelika, groups from the family to the battalion, or even a country like the Soviet

Union as a whole. Moreover, *9th Company* and *Cargo 200* show the interdependence of these different social levels, since the failure of hypergendered *travesti* on any one has a cascading effect on the other two. Together, Bondarchuk and Balabanov's radically different films show that performing the cisgender drag required of hypergender was, for both men and women in the late Soviet era, an extremely dicey venture that became only more perilous after the Soviet Union's demise.

Secondhand T-Shirts: *Dust*

We see the many pitfalls of Putin-era cisgender drag in Loban's award-winning independent film *Dust*, which vividly depicts the impact on the first post-Soviet generation of the intergenerational masculine trauma whose genealogy Bondarchuk and Balabanov trace. If the late-Soviet sartorial regime shown in *9th Company* and *Cargo 200* failed to defend even elite paratroopers and entitled teenage girls, its post-Soviet successor could hardly be expected to protect the generation that saw its country go from global superpower to collapsed empire virtually overnight. Viktor Erofeev's castigation of his more affluent compatriots in the 1990s for wearing tasteless raspberry-colored blazers and cloning German fashion boded poorly for those Russians whose limited resources kept tailored suitcoats and foreign fashion beyond reach. In other words, Russia's humiliation as a nation after 1991 translated into the masculine abjection of post-Soviet men, which fell hardest on those who lacked the means, be they physical, emotional, or economic, to establish identity as a "real" Russian man or *muzhik*. *Dust* takes a deep dive into the linked sartorial and psychic challenges of such masculine abjection, presenting an anti-*muzhik* protagonist whose masculinity never aspires to rise, let alone rises, above anything but failure.

Although the failure to be a "real" Russian man can and has taken a variety of guises, its most catastrophic incarnation has always been the emasculated man-baby, as we see in Tat'iana Tolstaia's 1986 short story "Peters." Tolstaia paints a vivid portrait of masculine abjection, which the reversal of the "natural" hierarchy of the sexes supposedly brought about in the Soviet Union. Raised under the smothering care of an overprotective grandmother, the title character in Tolstaia's story has "flat feet and a woman's broad belly," "colorless hair," "flabby legs," and a "white hairless body sprinkled with tender red birthmarks."[31] Given his physical resemblance to both a woman and an overgrown infant, it comes as no surprise that Peters is ostracized by his childhood peers, who tease him with the nickname "tubby," as well as his adult co-workers, one of whom describes him as "a wimp. An endocrinological sissy."[32] The story chronicles Peters's utter defeat while pursuing the female objects of his desire, as he realizes, time and again, his complete humiliation. Even though the story ends with the faintest glimmer of hope, the reader understands that the passive Peters will never take the action necessary to become a "real" man or win a woman's love. When placed in the context of the late-Soviet crisis of masculinity, "Peters" reads like a cautionary tale about masculine abjection.

Dust's hero—the overweight, balding, and bespectacled Alyosha (Aleksei Podol'skii)—represents yet one more example of the impotent manfant, who continued as the nadir of Russian manhood after the Soviet Union's demise. Alyosha lives a mollycoddled life in his grandmother's shabby apartment, and he bears a striking resemblance to Tolstaia's Peters. Loban uses the film's opening scenes to establish Alyosha's masculine abjection, as his grandmother feeds him hotdogs and sugary tea for breakfast, insists he dress more warmly to avoid catching cold, warns him not to arrive late to work, and repeatedly calls the twenty-four-year-old man her "boy." Yet, unlike the passive Peters, Alyosha manages to break free from his docile submissiveness in *Dust*, whose plot pushes him out of his day-to-day rut and into a mysterious experiment concocted by the Federal Security Service (FSB). Although we never learn the state's goal in conducting the experiment, it functions for Alyosha as a deeply subversive moment of cisgender *travesti*, which first transforms his flabby, white body into the ripped physique of a bodybuilder and then replaces his passivity with action and even open aggression. His humiliation as a man melts away by the end of *Dust*, and the liberation through cross-gender *travesti* that Alyosha eventually experiences opens up new sartorial avenues for identity and self-expression.

We discover the role that cisgender drag plays in generating the shame of abject masculinity in *Dust*'s opening credits, during which Alyosha shops with his grandmother in a secondhand-clothing store. If the spectacle of a grown man compliantly letting his grandmother buy him used clothing fails to evoke our pity for Alyosha, then the barely suppressed laughter of the female sales clerks makes his pathetic status clear. His grandmother decides to buy Alyosha a T-shirt, which he suspects is women's clothing, but a sales clerk assures him it is "unisex, an all-purpose T-shirt." The oversized T-shirt with a cute kitty-cat on its front transforms Alyosha's shame as a man-baby into a bodily stigma that he wears for most of the film. Moreover, the salesclerk's snide description of the T-shirt as "all-purpose" (*universal'naia*) incorporates gay slang in Russian for a switch or verse (*universal*), that is, someone who enjoys active topping just as much as passive bottoming during sex. Although Alyosha looks like the stereotype of an effeminate bottom in this opening scene, he eventually learns how to top others and get what he wants by the film's end.

Alyosha's secondhand pussy T-shirt demonstrates his out-and-out failure to perform masculinity of any type at the start of *Dust*, and we can understand his clothing best by comparing it to the T-shirts worn by other men in the film. For example, Alyosha's buddy Misha wears a black T-shirt with the word "CANNABIS" on its front, while his companion at the gym is also in a black T-shirt with the slogan "KILL ALL DJ'S" surrounding the image of a gun. Although neither Misha nor the workout partner represents a masculine ideal, both manage to perform a version of masculinity that wards off the shame that taints Alyosha. However, other men in the film also wear secondhand T-shirts clearly imported from the United States, including one promoting "Prairie Pals Dairy 4-H Club" and another for "Pizza Oven Sioux City," allowing us to interpret all of this hand-me-down clothing as another instance of failed *travesti*. In his oversized kitten T-shirt, Alyosha has hit rock bottom for Russian manhood, but his peers in T-shirts touting a West that they had probably never visited betray the debased state of Russian masculinity as a whole in the early 2000s. In a classic instance of scapegoating, the other T-shirted men in the film project their own humiliation onto Alyosha by calling him emasculating epithets like "loser" and "faggot."

If the secondhand T-shirts in *Dust* represent the failure of Western garments to disguise the debased masculinity of the Russians who buy and wear them, then the shady experiment engineered by the FSB appears to reverse the very need for this type of cisgender drag. We first learn about the experiment early in the film, when Alyosha is taken away from the assembly line, where he puts together toy guns for a living, and is interviewed by FSB agents, who propose that he serve the motherland by participating in their secret project. The physical and mental tests that Alyosha takes during the interview—and promptly fails—suggest that the agents are seeking precisely the type of "cellulite grunt" (*salabon tselliulitnyi*) that Alyosha represents for others in the film. Once he arrives at the laboratory, Alyosha compliantly strips down to his underpants and enters a small, dark room with a mirror, even though he knows nothing about either the method or goal of the experiment. Then we, along with Alyosha, witness the miraculous transformation of his manboobs and flaccid arms into a bodybuilder's muscular torso and bulging biceps. Although the experiment lasts a mere two minutes, it entirely erases Alyosha's abjection by transforming his infantile and feminine reflection in the mirror into the *muzhik* ideal.

This brief transformation launches Alyosha on a quest to repeat the secret experiment so that he can take back the virile body that he now believes has been stolen from him. Ironically, each episode in this quest for ultimate manhood makes Alyosha act more and more like man while he looks more and more like a woman, revealing the profound psychic repercussions of the physical change, which, we later learn, is merely a side effect of the FSB experiment. The goodness, strength, and beauty that Alyosha says he experiences while in the darkened room appear to be the first positive sensations he has ever felt, and they foster new, unarticulated desires that thrust him out of his grandmother's apartment and into a variety of social institutions, each of which challenges him to adopt its distinctive mode of performativity. Loban's satire in the film comes to light during these episodes, which collectively demonstrate that all social institutions—from medicine to psychology, bodybuilding, clubbing, religion, and even political dissent—fail to understand and embrace Alyosha.

Typical in this regard is Alyosha's brief encounter in Moscow's Victory Park with a group of hearing-impaired people. Mistaking a young man in their midst for his stolen body, Alyosha lovingly caresses the stranger's muscular arm. The young man immediately chases Alyosha away in disgust, demonstrating that Alyosha's failed masculinity represents a greater social stigma than any disability. In the final such episode, a cross-dressed Alyosha, who dons makeup, blouse, skirt, and headscarf to evade the FSB, discovers that even the civil rights NGO Memorial fails to grasp his newfound desires, assuming he is one of Russia's "sexual minorities." Throughout his quest, the image of his stolen body haunts Alyosha, underscoring his humiliation and abjection.

However, two scenes disrupt the otherwise orderly unfolding of *Dust*'s satirical plot. The first of these takes place when Alyosha goes to the gym, where he lifts weights in the hopes of recreating the virile body he supposedly lost. His workout buddy introduces himself by describing the pussy T-shirt as "good" and asking Alyosha to teach him how to use the gym equipment. After a brief workout, in which Alyosha clumsily drops a barbell while his buddy almost dies of overzealousness, he asks Alyosha how he became "so buff" and whether he did so by working out on his own. Although the trainer at the gym sees the same girly T-shirt and flabby body we do, his workout buddy apparently perceives the goodness, strength, and beauty of Alyosha's body. This homoerotic response to Alyosha echoes his own reaction to the image he sees in the mirror during the experiment, and it defies easy explanation in a film whose verisimilitude and low budget shun special effects. Although *Dust* clearly pokes fun at the culture of bodybuilding in this episode, it is not clear what Alyosha's gym buddy sees in him that we, the film's viewers, do not.

The second episode to question *Dust*'s satire comes at the movie's climax, when the mastermind behind the FSB experiment, a gynecological specialist by the name of Professor Pushkar' (Petr Mamonov), delivers a twelve-minute-long monologue. After Alyosha bribes his way into the experiment for a second time, he pursues Pushkar' and ultimately finds him alone in the laboratory. The scientist then delivers a nihilistic diatribe, in which he calls Alyosha, as well as those like him, mere dust, a nothing, a dumb beast. However, Alyosha pays absolutely no attention to the onslaught of insults and existential angst; instead, he takes off the women's clothing he has worn for the last quarter of the film so that he can repeat the nefarious experiment for a third and final time. This time, however, Alyosha does not see the beautiful muscular body he so wants in the mirror. Nevertheless, he smiles and even laughs, dissolving as Pushkar' predicted he would. The film ends as the now happy but dematerialized Alyosha watches a kitschy TV comedy routine by Evgenii Petrosian alongside his grandmother.

Given the length of Pushkar's harangue, we might be tempted to take it for the film's philosophical message, a reading that certainly accords with the performance of Petr Mamonov, the only professional actor in *Dust*, as well as the film's title. However, Alyosha's complete indifference to Pushkar's speech suggests another interpretation.[33] Just as his buddy in the gym perceives the goodness, beauty, and strength in a body that everyone else views as shameful, so does Alyosha find something essential and authentic where Pushkar' claims there is nothing, something profoundly human where the professor sees only the bestial, something precious where he perceives only dust. By connecting these two atypical moments in Alyosha's quest, we recognize that the epistemological ambivalence of both cisgender and cross-gender drag in the film goes far beyond humiliation to an affective ambivalence that defies easy comprehension. Even though the FSB experiment appears to turn masculine abjection into ideal manhood, Alyosha has fulfilled his unspoken desires without retrieving the strong and beautiful body he believes he lost and after returning to his grandmother's apartment. Pushkar's philosophical rant becomes mere dust as we watch the quivering image of a blissed-out, nearly naked Alyosha in women's makeup on the other side of the experiment's looking-glass and realize that we have no idea of who Alyosha actually is, what he truly wants, and whether he is alive or dead.

Dust refuses to answer such conventional questions about its anti-*muzhik* hero. Instead of filling in the gaps of our knowledge about Alyosha, Loban delivers a postmodern *bildungsroman*, in which the trials and tribulations that should shape our hero lead not toward but away from any stable or coherent identity. Loban's decision to deprive viewers of the type of information they expect of the typical *bildungsroman* produces an unsettling effect, as one viewer's response to the film illustrates:

> A twofold, ambiguous feeling: on the one hand, it's a brilliantly apt satire, it's funny and conscientiously executed from a technical standpoint, but on the other hand . . . One feels sorry for the main hero and just, you know, even ashamed for

> him. For the whole film, Alyosha provokes my irritation, my disgust. . . . Until the end of the film, these feelings of shame, pity, and irritation haunted me. . . . I wonder who the person who played Alyosha is in real life? I'd like to know about his sensations during and after shooting . . . a month has already passed since I saw the film, but it's stuck with me! Later I dreamt about that terrible fat-and-meat-processing plant (I'm sure he stinks). Nasty dreams based on the film *Dust* haunted me for several nights in a row. Immediately after the film—[I had] a sensation of physical filth—I ran home at full speed to take a shower.[34]

This woman has little interest in exploring *Dust*'s social satire, since the film's epistemological and affective ambivalence have invaded her dreamlife. On one hand, she describes a lingering combination of pity, shame, and disgust, so visceral and repulsive that she tried to wash these feelings off her body after seeing the film. On the other hand, she expresses empathy for the actor Aleksei Podol'skii and curiosity about his affective state while playing Alyosha. Apparently, Podol'skii's performance of masculine abjection in *Dust* was so convincing that it infected this viewer with the very shame that Alyosha casts off when he undergoes the FSB experiment for the third and final time.[35]

By the end of *Dust*, Podol'skii's Alyosha offers a radical solution to Russia's crisis of masculinity. Having embraced the epistemological ambivalence of both cisgender and cross-gender *travesti*, Alyosha learns to ignore the repeated shaming of others in the film, and he achieves a stoic indifference to the social factors that first led to his humiliation, as seen in his affective ambivalence in the film's closing shots. Alyosha's ultimate imperviousness to his own abjection hardly comes as a surprise in a movie made by three former members of the 1990s performance art group zAiBi, whose Russian acronym comes from the phrase "For Anonymous and Free Art" but sounds like a command to "fuck off."[36] With an equally sarcastic disdain for the Putin regime coalescing in the early 2000s, Loban makes Alyosha into a post-Soviet everyman who learns that the only sure way to cast off masculine abjection is not to don the cisgender drag of hypermasculinity but simply not to care, inviting viewers to do the same.

Conclusion

Despite their radically different genres and styles, the three films examined in this chapter allow us to locate the roots of post-Soviet Russia's crisis of masculinity in the trauma that the late Soviet era inflicted on the male body. However, rather than acknowledging and attending to the wounds that Soviet men sustained, the post-Soviet era added to their traumatic inheritance by ignoring them, requiring that "real" Russian men hide the damage they endured beneath obsolete medals and secondhand T-shirts. When viewed from this angle, the infamous raspberry-colored blazers sported by New Russians, so loudly lamented by Erofeev, were just another vestiary strategy for coopting the Other's gaze and judgment, much like the sexy female apparel that flooded into Russia during the 1990s. These shocking-pink sport coats, as well as the glamorous Italian suits worn by New Russians' successors in the 2000s and 2010s, represented the masculine version of a peremptory strike in the battle over whether a book can be judged by its cover. Such weaponized garb was intended to distract not only the Other assessing their masculinity but also post-Soviet men themselves from knowledge of their own precarity. In short, the hypergendered drag required of Russian men after Putin's rise to power denied the first post-Soviet generation's many traumas by cloaking them in *travesti*'s epistemological ambivalence.

The bait and switch of men's cisgender drag after Putin's rise to power is nowhere more evident than in the Russian president's own sartorial swagger. In addition to the somber Kiton and Brioni suits he regularly dons, Putin reputedly has a collection of Swiss watches valued in the neighborhood of half a million dollars, as well as a Loro Piana jacket worth more than thirty times the average Russian's monthly wage.[37] When taken with the military uniforms, judogis, ski suits, scuba gear, hunting apparel, topless fishing togs, and crotch-hugging swimwear in which Kremlin photographers regularly caught him between 2000 and 2020, Putin's costly and largely Italian designer wardrobe amounts to a vestiary performance of hypermasculinity, whose unremitting grandiosity makes it look like a Freudian denial of *Dust*'s shameful pussy T-shirt. As different as their apparel is, both Putin and Alyosha dress their selves in an Other's clothing to cover up whatever shortcomings they might have as Russian men. As with all of the protagonists in *9th Company*, *Cargo 200*, and *Dust*, Putin's publicly performed and internationally broadcast drag banks on the slippage between self and Other intrinsic to *travesti*, which places Russian men performing cisgender drag along a single stylistic continuum connecting manfant to *muzhik*. And, like the slippage among charisma and the ironic pop styles on offer after 1999, that among the different sartorial options available to Russian men ultimately betrayed the fragility of the hypermasculine *muzhik*, proving that no man, not even Putin himself, could escape the taint of masculine abjection. Once seen in this light, the rising price tags of Putin's watches and suits clearly parallel his regime's growing aggression, which, when taken together, represent tacit admissions of both the man and his government's masculine fragility.

The failure of cisgender drag to offer any real solution to Russia's crisis of masculinity or protect Russian men from their own precarity helps explain the country's steadily escalating regime of hypergender during Putin's first three terms as president. In essence, the glamour craze of the 2000s was yet one more salvo in a growing gender war that began with Putin's 1999 ascension to power. Starting with early publicity that touted Russia's president as the ideal boyfriend, husband, or father, each successive attempt to construct masculinity and femininity as fully distinct and hierarchically arranged "natural" categories foretold its own defeat at the same time that it foreclosed other less totalizing strategies for performing gender and citizenship. As the chapters that follow show, this displacement of Russia's traumatized and fragile masculinity ever farther from its feminine counterpart led to progressively more polarized and essentialized myths of the "real" Russian man and woman, as well as increasingly extreme performances of the hypergender requisite to Russianness.

Regardless of their shared focus on cisgender drag, *9th Company*, *Cargo 200*, and *Dust* demonstrate an important attribute of *travesti* more broadly: the gap between self and Other leveraged by drag leads inevitably to the epistemological ambivalence of never really knowing what a book's cover has to do with its contents. Cisgender *travesti* might hope to naturalize socially constructed categories of gender, yet the slippage between self and Other, on which all forms of drag rely, prevents this hope from ever being realized. Moreover, cisgender drag has a curious tendency to segue into its cross-gender variant, as we see in Alyosha's queer costume change from secondhand T-shirt to skirt, scarf, and makeup in *Dust*. Clearly, the late-Soviet legacy of traumatized bodies had an impact not only Russia's straight men but also on its women and queers in the post-Soviet era. Understanding the full extent of this inheritance requires that we turn to cross-gender *travesti* and explore how it too aided in the construction of hypergender during Putin's first two decades at Russia's helm.

3

Travesti and the Post-Soviet Drag Queen

You're born naked. The rest is drag.
—RuPaul

When we turn our attention from cisgender drag to its cross-gender variant, we find the same stylistic slippage in the work of drag queens earning a living in Russia's entertainment industry between 2000 and 2020 as we did in *9th Company*, *Cargo 200*, and *Dust*. In all cases, however, the relative risks and effects of *travesti* depended more on the performer's own gender than on whether they dared to traverse the male–female divide. The performative shift that began after 1991 might have made a book's cover more important than its contents, but what lay beneath the individual's carefully dressed exterior was never irrelevant or ignored. Since all of the gendered strategies that added up to the Russian style that conferred citizenship after Putin's rise to power catered to the country's crisis of masculinity, men performing *en travesti* garnered more attention and greater approval than women, regardless of whether these men wore Italian suits or glittery ball gowns. The mere fact that this chapter on professional cross-dressing does not include drag kings, because I never found one working in Russia between 2000 and 2020, points to the gender-skewed intent and impact of Putin-era *travesti*.

Drag's gendered differential meant that Russian men who chose to wear women's clothing provided one option for deescalating, if not winning, the gender war that was gaining momentum after 2000, as *Dust*'s closing shots of a gaudily made-up and gleefully giggling Alyosha suggest. However, the fusion of gender and Russian citizenship during an era of resurgent nationalism led to most instances of cross-gender *travesti* in the country's arts and entertainment doing precisely the opposite. Rather than disarm the hypergendered norms by which "real" Russian men and women were judged in the 2000s and 2010s, Putin-era drag queens tended to mobilize and reinforce them. As a result, this chapter's examination of leading *travesti* artists reaches a conclusion oddly akin to the previous chapter's analysis of cisgender drag, suggesting that

RuPaul's maxim quoted earlier applied in Putin's Russia only in its negated form: nobody was born naked, because everyone was always already in drag.

To understand how this could possibly be the case, we must turn briefly to the history of professional drag in Russia and the Soviet Union, which takes us back to the imperial mandate that brought professional theater to the country in the eighteenth century. Unlike Ancient Greece or Shakespeare's England, Russia's first professional actors had no regulations banning women from the stage, yet a handful of men performed *en travesti* for comic purposes. By the end of the nineteenth century, "Cross-dressing and gender-bending routines became staples on vaudeville circuits."[1] Among these female impersonators or *transformatory* were Aleksandr Galinskii, one of whose shows "mimicked popular songstresses and actresses," and Nikolai Barabanov, who, in his stage persona of Ikar or Icarus, won acclaim through impersonations of Isadora Duncan in St. Petersburg's Crooked Mirror theater.[2] The advent of Soviet power brought such drag spectacles to a halt because of their association with bourgeois entertainment, and the practice of male comedians donning women's clothes appears to have resurfaced only in the Brezhnev era. In 1971, Vadim Tonkov and Boris Vladimirov began making regular appearances on Soviet television as the comic duo Veronika Mavrikievna and Avdot'ia Nikitichna, whose immediate forerunners were not pre-revolutionary *transformatory* but actresses in the *emploi* of *aktrisa-travesti*, who played boys from the 1930s on in Soviet children's theater.[3]

The demise of the Soviet Union brought about a drag renaissance in the Russian entertainment industry, which found avid advocates in both highbrow and popular venues. On one hand, prominent artists, such as the theater director Roman Viktiuk, the dancer-choreographer Valerii Mikhailovskii, and the artist Vladislav Mamyshev-Monro, gained renown by incorporating cross-gender drag into their work in the late 1980s and 1990s. Viktiuk's groundbreaking production of Jean Genet's *The Maids*, Mikhailovskii's St. Petersburg Male Ballet, and Mamyshev-Monro's impersonations of celebrities from Marilyn Monroe to Liubov' Orlova (treated in detail later in this chapter) helped relax the rigid gender binary enshrined by Soviet power and provided a gathering place for Russia's nascent gay community.[4] On the other hand, comedians like Igor' Kasilov and Sergei Chvanov of the New Russian Grannies (Novye Russkie Babki) achieved startling commercial success in Russia's popular media by wearing women's clothing. Clearly modeled on their Brezhnev-era predecessors, Kasilov and Chvanov's personae of Klavdia Ivanovna Tsvetochek and Matrena Ivanovna Nigmatullina made their first appearance on televised variety shows in 1999, becoming mainstays in this type of lowbrow entertainment. Similarly, the former Soviet Union's most famous drag queen, Verka

Serduchka (the creation of Andriy Danylko, to whom we return later), has recorded more than ten albums, hosted a TV talk show, and even represented Ukraine at the 2007 Eurovision Song Contest, where she took second place. If Viktiuk, Mikhailovskii, and Mamyshev-Monro brought drag back to Russia's high culture, then the New Russian Grannies and Serduchka revived the more popular tradition of the pantomime dame, best known through the Australian Barry Humphries's lavender-haired Dame Edna Everage. And while drag performers or *travesti-artisty* found new professional opportunities, a handful of male pop stars, most notably Boris Moiseev and Filipp Kirkorov, began to sport highly androgynous if not feminine garb.[5] In other words, the expansion of professional cross-gender *travesti* in Russia's arts and entertainment industry coincided with and contributed to the broader performative shift in post-Soviet culture that took place during the 1990s.

Although men earning a living through drag made a comeback after 1991, the 2017 ban on the meme of Putin as a gay clown suggests that there were limits beyond which performance *en travesti* led to scandal once Putin occupied the Kremlin. A vivid example of such scandal took place in 2013, when authorities seized paintings by the artists Konstantin Altunin and Vera Donskaia-Khil'ko in anticipation of the G20 summit held in Petersburg that year.[6] The most outrageous of Altunin's works, which bore the title "Travesti," depicts President Putin and Prime Minister Dmitrii Medvedev not merely in women's undergarments but in feminine *déshabillé* via the visual trope of the "woman at her toilet," whose history spans artists from Titian to Degas and Picasso. Also among Altunin's confiscated works were "Rainbow Milonov," which places the Petersburg politician and noted homophobe Vitalii Milonov against the backdrop of a gay pride flag; "Deputy Mizulina's Dreams," which shows the archconservative Duma representative Elena Mizulina performing fellatio; and "From a Confession," which imagines the nude torso of Patriarch Kirill of the Russian Orthodox Church covered by tattoos of Lenin and Stalin in imitation of Russian convicts.[7] As for Donskaia-Khil'ko, her seized work, named "Wrestling," places Putin and Barack Obama in a hypermasculine drag that includes multiple mammoth penises in lurid primary colors.[8] Apparently, the closer *travesti* came to the iconic Russian *muzhik* and the higher it climbed on the power vertical, the more it threatened to expose hypergender as the performance it is and the more transgressive were its effects.

The *travesti-artisty* on whom this chapter focuses fell on a much humbler level of Putin's power vertical, and even those who achieved star status, like Verka Serduchka, occupied only a small niche in Russia's sizeable arts and entertainment industry. Nonetheless, these men's professionally polished performances of femininity on the fringe of Russian culture reveal central strategies for coping with the crisis of masculinity during Putin's first twenty years in power. Regardless of their style of drag, all of these men demonstrate the hard work and sacrifice requisite for the self to don an Other's clothing, particularly when that Other wears the cosmetics, high heels, and tinseled finery of hyperfemininity. And regardless of the individual performer's motive—to heal his country's mutilated masculinity, to minister to its equally besieged femininity, or just to entertain—all of these *travesti-artisty* prove that the best qualified and most authoritative arbiter of Putin-era hyperfemininity was not a Russian woman but a cross-dressed Russian man.

The Salvational Drag of Vladislav Mamyshev-Monroe

To understand the hard work and sacrifice required by cross-gender *travesti*, as well as its potential for rescuing a traumatized post-Soviet body, we need only consider the artist widely hailed as the Soviet Union's first drag queen, Vladislav Mamyshev-Monro. Despite his familiarity with Brezhnev-era drag—including films like the 1971 *Gentlemen of Fortune* and 1975's *Hello! I'm Your Aunt*—Mamyshev-Monro deliberately distanced himself from his Soviet predecessors, all of whom preserved telltale markers, including dark five-o'clock shadows, of their biological sex. Instead, he traced his lineage back to Billy Wilder's 1959 Hollywood classic, *Some Like It Hot*, taking his last name not from the movie's cross-dressed leading actors but rather from its blond bombshell star, Marilyn Monroe. And unlike the male actors and the cross-dressing characters they played in both the Soviet film industry and in Hollywood, Mamyshev-Monro developed a form of *travesti* that went far beyond the pragmatic disguise or comic gag. Whether in the costume and makeup of Monroe, Adolf Hitler, Russia's mythical Snow Maiden, or Vladimir Putin, Mamyshev-Monro considered his cross-dressing an artistic and spiritual vocation, which only began by mimicking physical appearance but ultimately reanimated the psyche and soul of those whom he embodied. The quarter century Mamyshev-Monro devoted to the art of personified transformation offered one possible, albeit idiosyncratic path to solving Russia's crisis of masculinity through drag. By approaching cross-dressing as an exercise in vulnerability and empathy, Mamyshev-Monro claimed not only to reclothe the late-Soviet body in the Other's garments but, more important, to redress its trauma.[9]

A key member of Timur Novikov's New Academy of Fine Arts, Mamyshev-Monro was swept up by the movement's fascination with personal metamorphosis, classical beauty, artistic messianism, queerness, and *stiob*. His involvement in Neoacademism made him a fixture at exhibitions, raves, and performances in Leningrad's counterculture of the late 1980s and in post-Soviet Petersburg.[10] In all of these endeavors and particularly in his own artistic projects, Mamyshev-Monro's celebrity impersonations went far beyond those of other drag performers of his day by being the living embodiment of *stiob*. Whether playing Russia's empress of pop Alla Pugacheva or Osama Bin Laden, the artist pushed *stiob* beyond discourse into affect, using *stiob*'s overidentification with the Other to *become* the Other through his impersonation. As Mamyshev-Monro himself described, his art began by recreating the Other's external features with cosmetics, wigs, and clothing but ended only when the Other's essence penetrated his very soul: "When I embody one or another personality precisely—there's really nothing to hide—as a good artist, I draw an exact copy of that person on my face. And then everything he contains enters into me, all of his experiences, whatever complexities of character, fate, sexual complications—the whole broad spectrum of things comprising the person. It's the shortest path to getting the maximum amount of information."[11] Although his claim seems farfetched, many of Mamyshev-Monro's contemporaries corroborate that he actually became, if only for a moment, the people he impersonated. And as his *stiob*-inflected writings attest, he viewed his ability to embody a stunning range of cultural icons as a sacrificial duty, which made him into a latter-day Jesus and his art into Christ-like kenosis.

Mamyshev-Monro's own understanding of how his drag performances might save the world reads like a mystical response to Russia's crisis of masculinity. As he described in articles from the early 1990s, his mission was to bridge the gap that had developed over the course of human history between "Man and Woman, Evil and Good, Black and White, Horror and Beauty, Fire and Water, Devil and Angel, Mars and Venus" through his impersonations.[12] Mamyshev-Monro claimed a unique capacity to embody both Hitler, whom he considered the apex of toxic masculinity in the twentieth century, and Monroe, the quintessence of the century's seductive femininity. By using his own body as the receiver for their universal signals of "cruelty, inhumanity, and opportunism" on one hand and "love and beauty" on the other, Mamyshev-Monro would reintegrate the universe's deeply divided dualities and usher in a new era.[13] His "childlike [and] immediate perception of the Other as one's self and one's self as the Other" allowed his drag performances to unite and express the hypostases of hypergender within a single person, as he demonstrated in portraits and photographs that recreate Monroe's sexy skirts-up scene from Billy Wilder's 1955 *The Seven Year Itch* only to reveal male genitalia.[14] In addition to being diametrically opposed to Brezhnev-era *travesti*, Mamyshev-Monro's vision of drag as a profoundly empathic emptying of the self for the sake of all Others is intentionally ironic, self-consciously grandiose, and deliberately scandalous. Nonetheless, it provides the context for his ever-morphing self and helps explain the appeal of his work in the Russian art world of the 1990s and 2000s.

While any and all of Mamyshev-Monro's artworks illustrate the curative intent of his brand of *travesti*, the two that most clearly show what he had to offer once Putin rose to power focus on the Soviet Union's biggest movie star, Liubov' Orlova. The first, a photographic series from 2000 titled "Happy Love (Liubov' Orlova)," recreates her private life, while the second, from six years later, remakes Grigorii Aleksandrov's 1938 musical comedy *Volga-Volga* by digitally patching Mamyshev-Monro's cross-dressed head and falsetto voice over Orlova's. The two projects prove paradigmatic for our purposes because, in Mamyshev-Monro's opinion, Orlova's Soviet-era stardom expressed the universal signals of both Hitler and Monroe. Like Monroe, Orlova was a platinum blond movie idol, "an unfading Cinderella . . . the genuine, most passionate, and deified love of the entire [Soviet] people."[15] However, she also bore a resemblance to Hitler as one of the few to be "a colonel in the KGB [who] knew about people's executions, about the millions arrested in 1937 . . . and all the same she had the audacity to sing, 'I don't know any other country where a person can breathe so freely'—what cynicism."[16] In other words, Orlova offered Mamyshev-Monro an especially vivid example of the disparity between a book and its cover. When considered alongside the Orlova projects' twin time frame, which brings the Soviet past into the post-Soviet present, the movie star's inbuilt duality gave Mamyshev-Monro the ideal vehicle for exorcising post-Soviet nostalgia, rescuing the Putin era's "emphatically gendered" sartorial regime, and resolving the epistemological ambivalence of *travesti*.

As a photographic series, "Happy Love (Liubov' Orlova)" is highly representative of the work for which Mamyshev-Monroe is best known. Wearing different costumes and wigs, he creates a variety of Orlovas, whose breathtaking verisimilitude is captured in black and white, sepia, and color photographs depicting successive decades in her career.[17] Each images strives to convey the star's unique combination of charm and artifice as she smiles coyly at fans from under a veiled hat, talks on the phone in snow-white gloves, reclines in a silky négligée on the divan in her boudoir, or peers from the window of a first-class train cabin in a mink stole. Although these images show Orlova's private life, they bring to mind publicity shots because of Mamyshev-Monro's careful costuming and choreography. For example, the artist either wears gloves or hides his hands in each photo, since the aging star's mania for preserving her youth led to an obsession with "plastic surgery, creams, and beauty salons" and made it "forbidden to shoot Orlova's hands."[18] The final photo in "Liubov' Orlova" depicts the actress's funeral by showing Mamyshev-Monro—glamorously

Figure 7. Vladislav Mamyshev-Monro, photograph of actress Liubov' Orlova in her casket from the series "Happy Love (Liubov' Orlova)" (2000). Used by permission of the Vladislav Mamyshev-Monro Foundation.

costumed in a sparkling blue robe, matching turban, and blue velvet gloves—as he lies in state beneath a larger-than-life poster of the actual Orlova and a soignée fan admires her/his corpse. This photo doubles the image of Orlova, achieving two contradictory effects: the movie star's dead yet smiling eyes look out from the poster, locking the viewer in her gaze, at the same time that Mamyshev-Monro's closed yet living eyes refuse the gaze of the grieving fan. In addition to revealing Orlova's stardom as an instance of *travesti*, this final image of "Happy Love (Liubov' Orlova)" gives us the choice of maintaining Orlova's myth by meeting the poster's frozen gaze, grieving the myth's passage by staring at her corpse, or closing our own eyes as the artist himself does.

The necessity of choosing this final attitude, which refuses Orlova's seductive yet insidious *travesti*, comes to light once we turn to Mamyshev-Monroe's remake of *Volga-Volga*, which won the prestigious Kandinsky Prize in 2007.[19] Directed by Pavel Labazov and Andrei Sil'vestrov, the 2006 *Volga-Volga* trims Aleksandrov's 1938 original by about thirty minutes, compressing the story of how the letter carrier Arrow (Orlova/Mamyshev-Monro) travels from the backwater of Melkovodsk to Moscow's musical Olympiad and wins the grand prize. Although the dialog remains the same, the remake completely overhauls the soundtrack of Aleksandrov's musical comedy by transforming its very catchy and professionally polished songs into out-of-tune noise. In addition to singing in an off-pitch falsetto, Mamyshev-Monro presents a photoshopped head that never truly coincides with Orlova's, creating an uncanny effect, as the critic Mikhail Shiianov describes: "Putting Mamyshev-Monro in place of Orlova sharpens and strengthens the macabre essence of the film. It is not difficult to notice that the letter-carrier's head, which nonetheless talks, sings, and kisses as dictated by the script, is alien in relation to its body. It is disproportionate, clumsy, and at the same time capable of taking on positions entirely unnatural for a living creature. In other words, Arrow looks like a victim of a monstrous yet successful Stalinist experiment in grafting a man's head onto a woman."[20] When taken together, these digital manipulations disrupt the easy viewing experience that the original *Volga-Volga* has given Russian audiences since its release. Mamyshev-Monro's remake takes "the number one Soviet comedy," makes its characters sound like the amateur musicians they supposedly are, and invites his audience to consider the gruesome Stalinist reality lacquered over by Aleksandrov's slickly packaged musical.[21]

Several of the remake's more dramatic effects underscore the eerie humor described by Shiianov. In a handful of scenes, for example, anachronistic sound effects dispel any illusion that the film takes place in Stalin's Russia. When the local bureaucrat Comrade Byvalov (Il'ia Il'inskii) speaks on the telephone, a series of digital bleeps followed by the message, "This service is not available; please call back later" interrupts his call. In another scene, a door swings open, letting heavy-metal music spill out. And when Arrow dives from the deck of the yacht "Joseph Stalin," the iconic riff from the soundtrack of *Jaws* plays as she swims to shore. More significant, the remake's two climactic scenes feature Mamyshev-Monro's full body and color in an otherwise black-and-white film. First, the artist entirely reinterprets the scene in which Arrow debates whether to confess that she composed the song that wins the Olympiad: Orlova's aw-shucks monolog becomes a soul-searching soliloquy set against the bizarre background of swimming and nesting penguins. Second, when Arrow sings her winning song about the Volga at the film's end,

Mamyshev-Monro's almost atonal a capella is set against a garishly colored crest of the Soviet Union. Even without Mamyshev-Monro's crossed eyes and the final sour note, the remake's closing scene transforms Arrow's unabashed victory at the Olympiad into an emotionally fraught viewing experience that evokes just as much failure as triumph. In short, Mamyshev-Monro's remake turns a beloved Stalinist musical comedy into "a horror story about how terrifying it is to live in a happy Soviet country," revealing Orlova's performance in the role of Arrow as an instance of Stalinist drag.[22]

The *Volga-Volga* remake invites viewers to consider whether Aleksandrov's original, reputedly Stalin's favorite film, might itself be "a monstrous yet successful Stalinist experiment" continuing into the present day. The film's colorization in 2010 gave Aleksandrov's movie a new lease on life, and nostalgia for *Volga-Volga* has led to countless television screenings, as well as restaurants, hotels, movie theaters, and stores named in the film's honor. In addition to offering a brilliant parody, Mamyshev-Monro's remake "lets the viewer be located in two systems of time-space coordinates at once, identifying with neither of them [and allowing the viewer] to choose a critical position and unmask the rather weird absurdity of a life-affirming Soviet comedy."[23] This crucial third position—outside both the Stalinist utopia constructed by Aleksandrov's film and the Putinist reality under construction in 2006—represents a remedy, if not the cure, to Soviet-era dress-as-drag. By becoming Orlova in the role of Arrow, Mamyshev-Monro both maintains the Orlova myth by meeting her frozen gaze and grieves the myth's passage by resurrecting her corpse, allowing us, his viewers, to close our eyes at the remake's end and exit the systems of both Stalinism and Putinism if we so choose. Rather than sugarcoating the bitter pill of ideology or dressing the individual in ideological armor fated to fail, *travesti* as practiced by Mamyshev-Monro represents the very means to escape both of these scenarios. Even though his radical embodiments of such epistemological ambivalence eventually forced Mamyshev-Monro from Russia to Bali, where he died in 2013, his sacrificial drag invited viewers to consider new sartorial possibilities and new forms of drag.

Femininity as Profession: The Post-Soviet *Travesti-Artist*

Although Mamyshev-Monro's unique approach to *travesti* ushered in the post-Soviet drag renaissance, he distanced himself from pop performers who either flirted with androgyny (such as Moiseev, Kirkorov, or Sergei Penkin) or used full-on drag to earn a living in the country's entertainment industry. In his opinion, *travesti-artisty* of his day modeled themselves not on the quintessentially beautiful Marilyn Monroe but on "the woman-monster Alla Pugacheva," downgrading their impersonations from messianic art to mere craft.[24] When evaluated by the standards that moved Western scholars such as Judith Butler, Marjorie Garber, and Laurence Senelick to describe drag as potentially liberating in the 1990s, Mamyshev-Monro's negative assessment of Russian *travesti-artisty* seems remarkably accurate.[25] Although she appeared in all the places we might anticipate—nightclubs, cabarets, bars, television, movies, and the internet—the post-Soviet drag queen of the 1990s, 2000s, and early 2010s inhabited a different cultural niche than her counterparts in the West. Rather than expose gender as performance, most *travesti-artisty* working in Russia during this time naturalized the binary opposition between male and female that they parodied. The popularity of drag in the post-Soviet entertainment industry arose not from the subversive cross-dressing that has become an entertainment staple in the United States thanks to *RuPaul's Drag Race* but instead from the ability of the *travesti-artist* to bolster Russia's supposedly traditional heteronormativity through the performance of hyperfemininity. Professional drag performers met with success in Putin's Russia because they managed to create a fiction of femininity so natural that it could only be authored by a man.

Without doubt, the *travesti-artist* to enjoy the greatest professional success since the Soviet Union's demise is Verka Serduchka, the Ukrainian train conductress turned superstar created by Andriy Danylko. Serduchka proves the enduring popularity of the pantomime dame in Russophone pop culture, and her impressive list of achievements, in addition to those already mentioned, includes appearing in some fifteen films and twenty music videos, touring widely in the Former Soviet Union and abroad, and receiving numerous entertainment awards. Serduchka's performance of "Dancing Lasha Tumbai" on behalf of Ukraine at the 2007 Eurovision Song Contest in Helsinki made her an international pop sensation, reaching far beyond her already sizeable fan base to an estimated 106 million viewers around the world.[26] Her act in Helsinki raised eyebrows not only for its mastery of Eurovision's camp aesthetic but also and more importantly because of the similarity of the phrase "Lasha Tumbai" (which, the performer claimed, means "whipped cream" in Mongolian) to "Russia Goodbye."[27] This jab at Ukraine's neighbor to the north only two years after the Orange Revolution was a risky move at Eurovision, which bans all forms of political expression. Even so, Serduchka's version of the pantomime dame takes few if any risks with prevailing notions of gender in post-Soviet space despite its clear reliance on gender as a performative construct.

The actual target of Serduchka's brand of parody comes to light once we consider the relationship of the male actor to his female persona, as well as the type of femininity that pantomime dames like Serduchka choose to adopt

Figure 8. Verka Serduchka performing "Dancing Lasha Tumbai" on behalf of Ukraine at the 2007 Eurovision Song Contest. Used by permission of Getty Images; photograph by Johannes Simon.

more generally. As with Brezhnev-era drag and the New Russian Grannies, Danylko carefully distanced himself from the female persona of Serduchka, and when off stage he wore unambiguously masculine clothing and either avoided discussing his personal life altogether or mentioned past liaisons with women. On stage, Danylko embodied a femininity visibly past its prime and clearly from the lower social strata, which seduced the spectator (if at all) through the overidentification of *stiob* and strove for neither conventional beauty nor glamour but condescending *poshlost'*. Furthermore, none of these Soviet and post-Soviet pantomime dames entirely disguised their male bodies beneath the clothing and makeup of drag.[28] In addition to sporting five-o'clock shadows, Mavrikievna and Niktichna simply put headscarves and raincoats over the men's suits the actors wore on stage. Although the New Russian Grannies expanded this rural anti-chic from head to toe, they similarly eschewed the heavy makeup, wigs, and prosthetic curves for which drag queens are often known. Even Serduchka, who donned glitzy costumes, full drag makeup, and a prosthetic bosom in her heyday, made sure that her femininity missed the mark by typically omitting any suggestion of women's hair or hips and exaggerating her chest so that no one could miss its falsity. The outsider and abject femininity of Danylko's act went hand in hand with other indicators of subaltern status, such as Serduchka calling herself "the Ukrainian

Cinderella" and using surzhyk, a mixed sociolect of Ukrainian and Russian.[29] In short, Serduchka, like other pantomime dames, aimed not for gender camp, which creates community through fantasies of leveling and inclusion, but for gender kitsch, which discriminates between "us" and "them" via condescension and exclusion. Whatever subversive edge Serduchka's parody might have had was dulled by misogyny, ageism, classism, and chauvinism. This conservative form of gender parody appealed to viewers and the Russian Federation's state-sponsored media because it reinforced divisions of sex, age, class, and ethnic identity at the very time it appeared to erase them.[30]

Surprisingly, we find a similar pattern when we look to those *travesti-artisty* who did not make regular appearances on national television and whose embodiment of femininity aimed not for kitschy *poshlost'*, but for the height of Putin-era glamour. Given the low profile of most *travesti-artisty* in traditional media, the internet provided the best access to information about these Russian glamazons. A quick Google search in the early 2010s yielded more than 200,000 hits for the phrase "*travesti-artist*," which led me to identify more than one hundred Russian-speaking drag acts based in post-Soviet space at the time. The majority of these performers worked in live theater and nightclubs in a genre of performance called *estrada*, and they specialized in the drag queen's stock-in-trade of lip-synching and improvisational comedy, using extravagant makeup and costumes to embody the physical and affective attributes of femininity.[31] Despite the ostensible differences between these *travesti-artisty* and a pantomime dame like Serduchka, the Russian glamazon provided a striking example of how postfeminism was domesticated in Russia after Putin's rise to power: using the discourse of labor that Suvi Salmenniemi and Maria Adamson identified in self-help books pitched to Russian women, the Putin-era glamazon performed a clearly constructed and highly sexualized femininity, whose very pretense served to naturalize sexual difference and Russia's patriarchal gender hierarchy.[32]

This paradoxical transformation of artifice into nature arose from the Russian glamazon's peculiar discourse of labor, which describes femininity not simply as a matter of work but as the result of professional training and ultimately as an art. The original Russian glamazon, Sergei Zarubin, who performed as Lora Kolli, the reigning diva of the Moscow club scene in the 1990s, epitomized the blend of carefully cultivated theatrical talent and artistic inspiration that secured the drag queen's superiority to mere biological women and allowed her clearly conventional performance of hyperfemininity to be perceived as authentic.[33] Zarubin's biography in a book devoted to famous LGBTQ+ Russians stresses his decades of employment in the country's most prominent theaters, as well as the difference between a *travesti-artist* and "those for whom women's dress on stage is merely a realization of their own sexual complexes."[34] Zarubin describes his decision to perform in drag as a logical step in his development as an actor: "In the West there is no question of who or what you are . . . in the clubs there, ordinary gays come to work; they like to put on [fake] nails [and] to shave their legs and arms so that they look like a woman. There's some type of pathology in this. For me, Lora Kolli is an opportunity to prove myself professionally. Sexual orientation has nothing to do with it. It's just that sometimes actors, when they don't have any roles, start to direct or to write books. So, I created Lora Kolli and started to work, I think, rather successfully as a choreographer."[35] Zarubin's insistence that Lora Kolli was not "self-expression" but "work" effectively distanced the *travesti-artist* from Western drag queens by downplaying the link between drag and the LGBTQ+ community that often provides its most famous performers and ardent fans.[36] Zarubin's work in Viktiuk's production of *The Maids*, his long career in Moscow nightclubs, and his starring role in the original cast of *Ruckus in a Henhouse* (*Perepolokh v golubiatine*), a Russian stage adaptation of the 1978 French film *La Cage aux Folles*, all made him and Lora Kolli fixtures in post-Soviet gay culture. Nonetheless, his claim to an authentic performance of femininity rested on divorcing personal identity from stage persona, much like Danylko.

Zarubin's emphasis on artistic professionalism also distanced him from pantomime dames like Serduchka, and the most famous Russian glamazons of the 2000s and early 2010s, represented by Aleksandr Peskov, Zaza Napoli, and Anatolii Evdokimov, all echoed this sentiment. All three *estrada* performers transcended the gender kitsch of the pantomime dame, yet they deployed their male bodies in two distinct manners. While the older Peskov used his slim frame as a hanger on which to drape different feminine and masculine personae, Evdokimov and Napoli used the contours and expressive possibilities of their male bodies to naturalize the distinction between masculine and feminine that they violated, making them models of hyperfemininity for biological women.

As we might expect, Peskov touted his training in Soviet theater and circus schools, labeling himself a "parodist" and his specific style of parody "synchrobuffonery."[37] His debut in women's costume took place on the stage of Moscow's Estrada Theater in 1988, and he maintained a regular schedule of solo performances, on tour and in his own theater, including "The Many-Faced Peskov" (1995) or "Mask, I Know You" (1998), which featured impersonations of Russian celebrities as varied as Nikolai Baskov, Zemfira, Sofiia Rotaru, Verka Serduchka, and Zhanna Friske. A brief examination of one of these solo performances, called "Songs of the Year," from 2006, gives a sense of what made Peskov the self-proclaimed "king of parody."[38] In the span of less than two hours on stage, Peskov changes costume thirty-eight times, bringing to life thirty-seven different pop music personalities (Mamyshev-Monro's nemesis, Alla Pugacheva, appears more than once), including everyone from Liudmila Zykina to Valerii Leont'iev. Rather than building his parody on complexity, nuance, depth, or accuracy of imitation, Peskov diverts spectators' attention from the obvious lack of verisimilitude in his impersonations through their sheer number, and the bulk of his buffoonery arises from his ability to don the costume of just about any Russian celebrity—female or male—from the past half century.

The meaning of Peskov's quick changes into female pop stars becomes evident when two of the very women whose guise he adopts in "Songs of the Year" join him on stage. About two-thirds of the way through the show, Peskov appears in a light-blue satin dress and blond wig to sing the vaguely 'oriental' "La-La-Lei" by the Koryo-saram Anita Tsoi, who, we soon learn, sits at the front of the audience. Peskov's performance of "La-La-Lei" elicits smiles and laughter from Tsoi, and as the lip-synch comes to an end, Tsoi herself joins Peskov on stage, giving him an enormous cellophane-wrapped bouquet, and they perform the song's final chorus together. Just four costumes later, Peskov appears in a glittery minidress and short blond wig to lip-synch Katya Lel''s tune "My Marmalade Man," and we discover that, much like Tsoi, Lel' herself watches the impersonation with visible delight. Again, the number ends with Lel' mounting the stage to perform alongside Peskov, once she gives him the requisite bouquet, allowing spectators to compare the real woman and her drag simulacrum. Rather than outdo these women at their own game, the numbers featuring Tsoi and Lel' demonstrate that Peskov's drag, despite its high production values, does not pretend to naturalized or fully embodied femininity. Instead, much like the format of "Songs of the Year," which harkens back to Soviet-era television, Peskov's male physique nostalgically recreates femininity without fully embodying it, maintaining a visible gap between the stars he impersonates and his version of them. The constant repetition of Peskov's grammatically masculine name in promotional materials, as well as his status as parody's king and not its queen, underscores how "Songs of the Year" leaves the expression of actual femininity to biological women.

Once we shift our attention to a younger generation of glamazons led by Anatolii Evdokimov, we notice a different relationship between the *travesti-artist*'s body and the femininity he performed onstage.[39] Although Evdokimov, like Peskov, retained his grammatically masculine name in promotional materials for the Evdokimov Show, he distanced himself from Peskov by placing the older man's work in the past and confining its significance to Russia's home-grown variety theater.[40] Some fifteen years younger than Peskov, Evdokimov also took professional drag in Las Vegas and Thailand as his models, and he got his start, unlike Peskov, at an amateur night in the Moscow club where he tended bar in the 1990s. As headliner of his own drag show, Evdokimov not only toured across the former Soviet Union and Europe but also appeared in a 2002 music video by the pop duo Hands Up! (Ruki Vverkh!) titled "He Kisses You."[41] The video begins by cutting between images of what the viewer assumes is a romantic boy-girl couple and shots of Evdokimov applying makeup before a dressing-room mirror. After the none-too-shocking revelation that the woman in the romantic couple is, in fact, Evdokimov in drag, the video climaxes with the *travesti-artist*'s entrance on stage in full costume before a crowd of adoring fans that includes his boyfriend.

Evdokimov appeared in a wide variety of venues, including a 2010 advertising campaign for the Russian perfume and cosmetics chain L'Etoile, for which he offered master classes in facial care and makeup to the store's largely female clientele.[42] However, his fame came first and foremost from elaborate solo shows, such as the provocatively named "I've Done Everyone" or "Soundtrack," in which Evdokimov transformed himself into standard drag divas including Marilyn Monroe, Liza Minelli, Cher, and Madonna. Rather than emphasizing the inevitable quick changes necessary for this type of performance, Evdokimov cultivated a narrative about his body that concentrated on his good genes, athleticism, grueling workouts, ability to forgo plastic surgery, and abstinence from alcohol.[43] Unlike Peskov, Evdokimov strove for a femininity that allowed him to embody, to the fullest degree possible, the stars whose costumes he put on, and he stated in interviews that he wanted his viewers to believe that the real Madonna or Tina Turner stood on stage before them. Tricking spectators required relentless discipline in the form of physical training and rehearsal, as well as financial sacrifice: in one interview, Evdokimov stated that he had to deny himself a new Audi in order to pay for an elaborate Cleopatra costume.

The 2008 show "Evolution, or Woman Through the Eyes of Man" demonstrates the difference between Peskov's Soviet-style female impersonation and the glamazon's embodiment of an allegedly authentic femininity.[44] Mounted in honor of International Women's Day, "Evolution" depicts the development of woman from the garden of Eden to the drag diva. Three moments from the show allow us to trace its narrative arc and discern the place of Evdokimov's male body within it. The show begins with God's creation of woman at the request of man, which leads to Evdokimov's entrance on stage in a glittery, transparent bodysuit, curly blond tresses topped by a crown, and high-heeled shoes. This playful recreation of the biblical story of Eve's creation out of Adam's rib highlights Evdokimov's svelte, near-naked figure, as well as his ability to don the biological attributes and glamorous accessories of femininity. However, it does not fully mask his male anatomy, since, unlike many drag performers, Evdokimov chooses not to tuck his genitals, that is, not to mimic the most intimate contours of femininity. In a similarly untucked scene about halfway through "Evolution," Evdokimov lip-synchs to Mylène Farmer's song "Je t'aime mélancholie," dressed as a sex worker abused by her clients and pimp. In stark contrast to Farmer's video, which interprets the song as a victorious kickboxing match, Evdokimov's version ends with the sex worker's suicide, which appears as the ultimate sacrifice of female self to male desire. "Evolution" concludes with Evdokimov's rendition of Tina Turner's "Simply the Best," at the end of which he makes sure that the audience is not in the least tricked into thinking that the Tina Turner on stage is actually a woman. After impersonating Turner's iconic moves, Evdokimov removes his wig to the wild applause of spectators. This climactic unmasking assures that viewers understand woman's evolution both literally and figuratively through man, conveying a story in which femininity is born at man's behest, lives and dies to satisfy men's desires, and finds its ideal realization in a man's body.

Our final glamazon, Zaza Napoli, is the over-the-top, sequined-bedecked creation of the professionally trained actor Vladim Kazantsev.[45] Napoli, whose exotic stage name, like that of Lora Kolli, suggests foreign locales, debuted in Moscow's gay bars in 1997, quickly becoming a fixture in the club scene across Russia, with regular appearances in theater, television, and movies and on the internet. Unlike Peskov and Evdokimov, Napoli specializes in comedy improv, and we see vivid examples of her off-color, profanity-laden humor in the 2010 video of the song "Lenin" (discussed in chapter 1), as well as another video that spoofs the ballet superstar Anastasiia Volochkova.[46] Napoli brings to life a poetic lampoon of Volochkova by Orlusha (pseudonym of Andrei Orlov), embodying the not-so-fine line between glamour and *poshlost'*, camp and kitsch, masculinity and femininity.[47] Her XL tutu, copiously applied yet crudely contoured makeup, and generously proportioned bosom all mark Napoli as a woman. Yet her voice, which spouts a steady stream of throaty obscenities, and her figure, thick at the waist and lumpy through the legs, tell us that she is a man. As different as Napoli's style of drag is from that of Evdokimov, it nonetheless deploys the male body in an analogous manner: both preserve telltale markers of male identity, and both use the resulting mashup of femininity and masculinity to construct woman as a product of and subject to man. If Evdokimov aimed for awe-inspiring glamorous excess, then Napoli took glamour in the opposite direction to the very edge of bad taste. Napoli's stint in the mid-2000s as hostess of the television show *Sexual Revolution* on the TDK channel (Televizionnyi Damskii Klub, or Ladies' Television Club),

Figure 9. Anatolii Evdokimov *en travesti* as Eve, reenacting the creation of the world (2012).

as well as her time a few years later as the host of a similar show titled *Suk@ liubov'* (*Love Bitch*) on the NTV channel, demonstrated her expertise in "all aspects of family, personal, and intimate life" for these show's mostly female viewers.[48]

The tension between artifice and nature personified in the Russian glamazon helps to explain why even professionally polished drag queens like Kolli, Peskov, Evdokimov, and Napoli never fully impersonated women. Although all four sought the quintessence of feminine glamour—wearing sequined gowns, elaborate makeup and wigs, and sometimes even "Boobsforqueens," "the silicone breastplate that creates the illusion of real breasts"—they nonetheless maintained telltale masculine giveaways.[49] The glamazon of Putin's first two decades in power by far outstripped the pantomime dame in the completeness of her feminine embodiment, yet she avoided seeming "fishy," that is, being "a drag queen who looks extremely feminine, or one who convincingly resembles a cis woman," something that drag cultures in Thailand and the United States, among others, embrace.[50] The Russian glamazon's laborious and professionally crafted hyperfemininity granted her the authority to counsel biological women about wardrobe, makeup, romance, and sex, making the *travesti-artist* of the 2000s and early 2010s a model postfeminist subject, an idealized object of the male gaze, and proof of the male body's privilege to express authentic femininity.

Whether a pantomime dame like Verka Serduchka or a glamazon like Anatolii Evdokimov, the post-Soviet *travesti-artist* achieved something very different from Mamyshev-Monro's salvational drag. Even though the tools of the trade were essentially the same, performers like Danylko, Zarubin, and Kazantsev neither embodied nor encouraged the radical vulnerability and empathy that set Mamyshev-Monro apart from his peers. Rather than creating a third position from which to critique such binary oppositions as male/female, past/present, and self/Other, most professional drag performers of the 2000s into the 2010s used the epistemological ambivalence of *travesti* to preserve the hierarchical and heteronormative gender regime considered "traditional" and "natural" in Putin's Russia, proving the unique capacity of men to define and express femininity as a profession. The seeming paradox of male performers embodying hyperfemininity points to the double entanglement of professional drag after Putin's rise to power, as well as to its place in the country's larger postfeminist landscape, to which we return in chapter 4. Both pantomime dames and glamazons demonstrated that femininity was the bodily property of anyone willing to make themselves over through hard work, self-discipline, and the right beauty and fashion regimen. Most important, the femininity performed by all of these *travesti-artisty* asserted that women's appearance, autonomy, and desire existed strictly as a function of and in service to men, making any fix that these *travesti-artisty* offered for Russia's crisis of masculinity highly entertaining yet ultimately illusory.

The Drag Self in Feliks Mikhailov's *Jolly Fellows*

A final piece of evidence demonstrating the *travesti-artist*'s vocation not to challenge but to buttress Russia's supposedly natural and traditional gender binary comes from the 2009 film *Jolly Fellows*. The directing debut of Feliks Mikhailov, *Jolly Fellows* offers the only fictionalization of the drag queen to appear in Russian popular culture during Putin's first two decades in power.[51] The film incorporates elements of musical comedy (Danylko composed part of its score), psychological sketch, and road movie, and it looks, at first glance, like Russia's adaptation of the 1994 Australian movie *The Adventures of Priscilla, Queen of the Desert*, which Hollywood loosely paralleled in its 1995 *To Wong Foo, Thanks for Everything, Julie Newmar*. Much like these two English-language films, *Jolly Fellows* goes behind the scenes of a professional drag show to reveal the connection between LGBTQ+ performers' personal lives and their careers as female impersonators. The five drag queens in Mikhailov's film represent different generations and social backgrounds, and most of the film focuses on them as they tell the tale of how they first donned women's clothes. Despite differences, the drag queens' stories converge on three related points. First, performance in drag offers all five their sole refuge and only venue for self-realization in a homophobic society. Second, they all grew up in families that were in some way abnormal if not pathological. Third, "all cross-dressers are homosexuals, and all homosexuals are transvestites."[52]

The final scenes of *Jolly Fellows* bring the protagonists' cross-dressing out of the gay bar where they work and into real life, where they find themselves forced to defend their LGBTQ+ identities. All of this might sound familiar to those who have seen *Priscilla* or *To Wong Foo*, as well as earlier examples of the drag queen film, such as *La Cage aux Folles* and its 1996 Hollywood remake, *The Birdcage*. However, *Jolly Fellows* ends on a distinctly unfamiliar note for anyone who knows these earlier movies because all five of Mikhailov's protagonists fall victim to brutal gay bashings. The happy endings of the Western precursors to *Jolly Fellows* imply that the female impersonator's drag persona actually is her self, conflating acceptance by the Other of cross-dressing men with self-acceptance of nonbinary gender. On the contrary, *Jolly Fellows* depicts the pathology of and the real danger to any Russian man whose expression of femininity leaves the confines of professional theatrical performance and enters the realm of identity. The closing shots of *Jolly Fellows* depict a tragic battle in which the armor provided by hyperfeminine drag proves utterly incapable of protecting Mikhailov's drag-queen protagonists from Russia's ubiquitous homo- and transphobia.

The struggle in which Mikhailov's drag queens fight for their lives arises from two stories, linked through a bad cellphone connection and the film's crosscutting: that of the trans drag-show proprietor Roza (Ville Haapasala) and that of four *travesti-artisty* in her employ. Roza's story follows her home after the drag show as she meets a handsome stranger during a drenching storm. When the stranger sees Roza—dressed, coiffed, and glamorously made up—struggling with the hood of her car, he invites her into a nearby café, where she reads him an excerpt of her poetry. Roza eventually brings the flirtatious stranger home, where they share a glass of wine as he plays the piano. When her cellphone rings, Roza understands that her four friends are in trouble and excuses herself. As she turns her back on the stranger to leave, he picks up a heavy sculpture from the piano and bludgeons the unsuspecting Roza. He then surveys her fallen body, whispering his own tale in Roza's ear: "Once a poet just like you came up to a little boy on the playground and offered him some ice cream. The boy accepted. But the boy didn't like the tasty, sweet ice cream." This depersonalized excuse for the stranger's violence articulates the widespread assumption in post-Soviet Russia that homosexuality, cross-dressing, and pedophilia are inextricably linked, and it appears to justify the stranger's decision to dump Roza's unconscious body on a rainy street curb. Much like Angelika's cisgender drag in *Cargo 200*, the hyperfeminine *travesti* that expresses Roza's identity has made her an easy target for the broken and predatory stranger.

As Roza's sad story unwinds, her four friends on the other end of the spotty cell connection drive away in a car packed with provisions for a weekend in the country. When the car's driver, Fira (Aleksei Klimushkin), realizes she has missed a turnoff because of the rain, she sends the only passenger not in flamboyant drag, Lara (Pavel Briun), to ask directions from some drunken *muzhiki*. The men quickly discover Lara's three cross-dressed companions, forcing the four *travesti-artisty* to retreat into Fira's car and hastily drive away. When Fira decides to confront the drunken thugs, Lara replaces her masculine clothing with an elaborate feather headdress so that she is dressed to kill, just like her three friends. The four drag warriors confront their adversaries, and the film suddenly cuts from the ensuing fight to an idyllic pasture, in which Roza, now in an angelic white gown with flowing chiffon sleeves, joins the group so that all five can run in slow motion into the distance as the very song that the stranger played on Roza's piano crescendos and the camera pulls away. The wistfulness and sentimentality of *Jolly Fellows*' closing shots leave the viewer with a confusing message: Are we meant to mourn the demise of the film's protagonists or to celebrate the misty yet earnest vision of eternal drag sisterhood brought about by their deaths?

Given this ambivalent ending, we can hardly be surprised that reactions to *Jolly Fellows* in the Russian media ran the gamut. One reviewer trashed the movie as a "100-percent Soviet film . . . a tragicomedy of manners with a moral" that merely toys with political correctness, while another praised *Jolly Fellows* for its "authenticity" and avoidance of either melodrama or sentimentality, recommending screenings of "this new Russian film for all school children in upper grades, all parents of children, and all who in daily life and at work might encounter sexual minorities (that is, the majority of Russians)."[53] My own effort to make sense of these wildly disparate reactions to the lone story about drag queens in Russian popular culture inspired me to contact the real-life glamazons themselves. Since the internet produced dozens of sites with email addresses for *travesti-artisty*, I decided to ask performers like Zaza Napoli and Anatolii Evdokimov what they themselves think of Mikhailov's film.

From slightly more than one hundred email questionnaires, I received eleven responses representing performers in Moscow, Petersburg, Novosibirsk, Nizhnii Novgorod, and Minsk. Among those who answered me, one had full-time employment as a *travesti-artist*, nine worked part-time in the field, and one declined to state a profession. All had seen *Jolly Fellows*, and their opinions of Mikhailov's film were just as divided as the critics' reviews. Among those positively disposed, one performer wrote, "The film is fantastic, even super," while another described it as "Excellent, but the ending isn't the kind that one would like to see in this film," and yet another called it "the truth of life." However, others called *Jolly Fellows* "a horror," describing its protagonists as "Russia's most statistically mediocre drag artists." Although some seemed grateful simply to see *travesti-artisty* on the screen, others criticized the film's lack of verisimilitude and, more specifically, its suggestion that *travesti-artisty* wear women's clothing outside work. When asked how *Jolly Fellows* might have changed public opinion about the Russian glamazon, one performer reproached Mikhailov for showing "us as some kind of perverts who almost always wear women's clothes." Unsurprisingly, all who answered my survey chose to label their gender as male when given a choice among male, female, and other.

In short, the glamazons themselves appeared to share the negative attitude shown in Mikhailov's film toward men whose cross-dressing leaves the professional stage and enters real life. They also reproduced the same assumptions from popular discourse in Russia about homosexuality as the film, namely that all gays are transvestites, "AIDS is a gay disease, [and] pedophilia is a threat posed by gay men."[54] Although several of the *travesti-artisty* who responded to my survey revealed sympathy with and perhaps membership in

Russia's LGBTQ+ community, they ultimately—and wisely, in view of personal safety—divorced their identity and sexual choices offstage from their artistic vocation on stage. Both the fictional and the real-life Russian glamazons of the 2000s and early 2010s might have provoked an audience's laughter or tears in a staged spectacle of masculinity thinly disguised in feminine garb, yet they represented another instance of post-Soviet postfeminism or, as Helena Goscilo and Vlad Strukov describe it, "the odd post-Soviet conundrum of sexual liberation and gender enslavement."[55]

Mikhailov's film brings us back to the circumstances under which post-Soviet *travesti* leads to scandal. Although the leading characters in *Jolly Fellows* are by no means iconic Russian *muzhiki*, the actors who play them certainly are, as their earlier work in cinema and television demonstrates. The film does little to conceal Ville Haapasalo's chunky torso and lumbering gait or the broad shoulders, bulging biceps, and chest hair of Danila Kozlovskii in the role of Liusia. Yet *Jolly Fellows*' "statistically mediocre drag" avoids scandal by urging viewers to replicate the homophobia depicted in the film. The very mediocrity of Mikhailov's fictional *travesti-artisty* encourages the movie's Russian audience to reproduce Zarubin's disapproving assessment of Western drag queens: wearing women's clothing on stage is neither art nor profession for the film's protagonists but "some type of pathology" and "a realization of their own sexual complexes." *Jolly Fellow*'s earnest sentimentality collapses the gap between performer and costume on which *travesti* is premised in the post-Soviet context, diminishing its Russian audience's empathy for Roza and her drag sisters' miserable fate. By replacing *travesti*'s inherent ambivalence with the certain knowledge that the film's leading characters are queer, trans, and in at least one case HIV-positive, *Jolly Fellows* makes its protagonists appear just as absurd as the cross-dressed Putin and Medvedev in Altunin's "Travesti." However, if Altunin's painting critiques Putinism's penchant for hypergender by laying responsibility for the country's crisis of masculinity at Putin's feet, then Mikhailov's movie shifts the blame onto the country's gender-nonconforming men, avoiding both critique and scandal.

Conclusion

Despite their parodic humor and comic effects, the different instances of drag examined in this chapter all exhibit an intrinsic misogyny, leading to a single sobering conclusion. Rather than blur the line between masculinity and femininity, post-Soviet men performing cross-gender drag contributed to the separation of women's garb, behaviors, and attributes from those of men, as well as to the subordination of femininity to masculinity, which together created the regime of hypergender that governed Russian citizenship during the 2000s and 2010s. As the artist and drag queens treated in this chapter illustrate, attempts to cope with the trauma inherited from the Soviet past through a regime of hypergender only made its masculine and feminine extremes more fragile. Against the backdrop of Mamyshev-Monro's salvational drag, in which cross-gender and cisgender drag appear to cancel each other out, the effort to disguise post-Soviet Russia's wounded masculinity, whether with military uniforms or elegant dresses, does little more than bump the problem up the power vertical to Putin, who, in addition to costly Italian suits, regularly wore a cashmere-and-silk sweatsuit valued at more than three thousand dollars in the mid-2010s.[56]

The ultimate outcome of such efforts during Putin's first two decades in the Kremlin was male hysteria, as we see in Russian reactions to the most scandalous drag performer of the post-Soviet era: the bearded Conchita Wurst, whose "Rise Like a Phoenix" won Eurovision's Grand Prix for Austria in 2014. The creation of Thomas Neuwirth, Wurst became the poster child for LGBTQ+ tolerance in the European Union after her victory, eliciting reactions divided sharply between fans in Western Europe and detractors in the postsocialist East. Although "Rise Like a Phoenix" topped Russia's iTunes download chart in the wake of Eurovision, a variety of public figures expressed outrage at the bearded lady's victory, which, they opined, demonstrated the EU's decadence if not "the end of Europe," to quote the ultranationalist Vladimir Zhirinovskii.[57] Putin himself joined the tirade against Wurst, and a social media campaign took off featuring Russian men who shaved their beards off in protest.[58] As recently as 2017, the arch-homophobe Milonov continued the anti-Wurst invective by agitating for a lifelong ban on her entry into the Russian Federation.[59]

Wurst became a cause célèbre in Russia because her cross-gender drag appropriated the most important sartorial marker of Russian manhood: the beard. The history of facial hair in Russian culture reaches back to Kievan Rus', and it includes fines in medieval law for cutting off another man's beard (at a rate four times greater than for cutting off a finger), Peter the Great's forced shaving of his courtiers' beards and his beard tax of 1698 (both intended to Westernize and modernize his subjects), and the long-standing link in Russian Orthodoxy between a man's beard and his piety.[60] Although military service in Russia has required that men be clean shaven since the Soviet era, facial hair came back into fashion after the Soviet Union's demise, making it yet one more defensive sartorial strategy, like raspberry-colored blazers, Italian suits, and Swiss watches, available to Russian men.[61] Wurst's performance at Eurovision in a form-fitting golden gown and shoulder-length brunette mane while sporting a beard and mustache combined cross- and cisgender drag, much like images of Mamyshev-Monro as Marilyn Monroe in a windblown skirt. This type of gender-bending *travesti* led to scandal in Russia because it de-essentialized and de-naturalized the masculine–feminine binary. To paraphrase RuPaul's motto, drag artists like Mamyshev-Monro and Conchita Wurst prove that we really are born naked and the rest is drag.

My reading of Wurst's beard might seem to overstate the potential for facial hair to offend a Russian audience. Yet we only need to view the 2014 video "Beard," by the rappers Timati and MC Doni, to understand that "there's nothing better than a beard for [the Russian] man."[62] The video opens with shots of a bewhiskered and tattooed Doni cruising young women in downtown Moscow when he discovers, to his horror, that the enticing brunette he follows on the street is actually Conchita Wurst. We quickly learn that this is Doni's worst nightmare as he wakes up between two drowsy groupies and begins to explain that the only sure sign of masculinity is a beard. He then equates a man's beard with a woman's breasts as what decides the question of who leaves the club with whom. In the song's second verse, Timati ups the beard's ante by describing it as what unites Uzbeks like Doni and Jewish-Tatars like Timati with their ethnic Russian compatriots in post-Soviet brotherhood, as well as a marker of masculinity on par with the penis. The rapper exhorts listeners to:

> Preserve your tribe and wear a beard,
> Don't shave it for a dumb reason.
> The baton's passed on, you've shaved your beard (What?).
> Cut your member off, don't be like Conchita.

The video's action backs up the beard–penis parallel in multiple ways, for example, by showing a young hottie gauging a man's allure by measuring the length of his beard. Described as "the hymn of all bearded men" on YouTube, "Beard" had well over eighty million hits by the end of 2022, showing the importance of facial hair to Russian masculinity, as well as the threat posed by a bearded drag queen like Wurst, whose stage name combines Spanish and German slang for "vagina" and "penis."[63] When viewed in this light, the 2017 claim of Metropolitan Kornilii of Orthodox Old Believers that shaving off one's beard opens the flood gates to sodomy begins to make sense.[64]

As Doni, Timati, and their crew make explicit, Wurst's drag fell outside the norms of the *travesti* required for Russian citizenship between 2000 and 2020. Rather than reinforce a supposedly traditional and highly heteronormative gender binary, drag queens like Wurst and Mamyshev-Monro created a third possibility beyond male and female that critiqued any and all constraints placed on the expression of gender and sexual identity. Although the pantomime dames and glamazons discussed earlier avoided bending gender in this way, a new generation of queer drag performers, inspired largely by RuPaul's *Drag Race*, has emerged in response to the rise in homophobia sanctioned by Russia's 2013 law banning "gay propaganda."[65] For example, Lorina Rey (creation of Loran Kalustian) maintains a presence on multiple social media platforms and in Moscow's night life, describing herself as "a butch queen."[66] Her YouTube channel features fast-motion drag transformations that highlight Loran's ability to become women as varied as a drag queen elf and Jennifer Saunders in the role of Edina Monsoon from the British sit-com *Absolutely Fabulous*.[67] In Petersburg, Nedos, "the self-proclaimed empress of queer communism," describes herself as "the drag-thug, rapper-queen, queer-whore . . . the defender of social justice and the meta-modern, the strength of youth and the might of spring, the taste of free will, the genius, die-hard clitoris shot through with the blood of Yakutsk and the passion of Angela Davis, the personal vendetta of the tsar of straightdom Putin, the dominatrix of kitsch and phantasmagoria, and the madame of the total fucking annihilation of [white-hetero-cis-patriarchal-capitalist] global evil."[68] These young dragtivists represent "something new, political, and fierce" in the Russian mediasphere, and they, like other young queers in Putin's Russia, see makeup as "their armour, their joy, and a valuable weapon."[69]

Despite the obvious changes in Russians' sartorial style since the Soviet Union's demise, Putin's straightdom of the 2000s and 2010s retained key features of late-Soviet *travesti* that made it the single most important performative mode for expressing the heteronormative hypergender that permeated Russian citizenship. Not only films like *9th Company*, *Cargo 200*, and *Jolly Fellows* but also *travesti-artisty* earning their living in the Russian entertainment industry demonstrated that both cis- and cross-gender drag between 2000 and 2020 were indispensable because they propped up hypermasculinity, which would otherwise have collapsed under the weight of its own failure. However, *travesti*'s intrinsic ambivalence also has allowed a fictional character like *Dust*'s Alyosha, artists like Mamyshev-Monro, drag queens like Wurst, and a new generation of queer dragtivists like Lorina Rey and Nedos to protest the post-Soviet gender regime and to open up new sartorial possibilities, stylistic trends, and gender as well as sexual identities. These drag rebels signal the return of Russia's repressed and point to the country's masculinist power vertical with Putin at its pinnacle as the real culprit behind the ongoing crisis of masculinity. Those brave enough to queer the performative mode of *travesti* mobilize Russians' tendency to judge a book by its cover against itself and make their own peremptory strikes in the fight to reduce citizenship to heteronormativity after Putin's rise to power.

4

Queer Performativity in Putin's Russia

The Russophone entertainment industry experienced a minor revolution in 2020. January of that year saw the gay vlogger Karen Shainian launch his popular YouTube channel, which has more than 146,000 subscribers and documents LGBTQ+ life in Russia through series like *Straight Talk with Gay People* and *Queerography*.[1] In November, the first queer sitcom hit the RuNet: Fancy Production's nine-part *Here I Come*, which tells the coming-out story of Roma, a young college student who falls for the handsome Lyosha after a chance hookup.[2] And just a few months later, in fall 2021, the social-media star and television personality Nastia Ivleeva launched her six-part reality show, *Royal Cobras*, which pits Russian drag queens against each other in lip-sync battles modeled on *RuPaul's Drag Race*.[3] All three of these ventures presented brazenly queer subject matter in an emphatically positive light, flying just under the radar of the Russian Federation's 2013 ban on "gay propaganda" by describing their target audience as "18+." Unsurprisingly, all three also avoided Russia's tightly controlled, state-sponsored television, opting for broadcast via the considerably freer internet. Despite significant differences in their genres and aims, Shainian, Fancy Production, and Ivleeva proved that interest in LGBTQ+ content was on the rise among Russian speakers after the ban on "gay propaganda" seven years before.

The emergence of such queer-themed entertainment in the early 2020s begs two questions about Russia's notorious prohibition on "gay propaganda." First and most obvious, how did a censorship law like Article 6.21 of the Russian Administrative Code (officialese for the 2013 ban) give rise to media that fly in its face? Second, what impact did the law have not only on LGBTQ+ Russians but, more broadly, on the performance of heteronormativity that came to dominate citizenship during Putin's first two decades in power? Such openly queer projects as Shainian's YouTube channel, *Here I Come*, and *Royal*

Cobras suggest that by 2020, some Russians had grown weary of the heteronormative mandate that Article 6.21 upheld. To answer these questions more fully, we need to consider what queerness meant and whom it described in Russia between 2000 and 2020, so that we can discover how the different pop cultural styles examined in this book could result not only in the *travesti* that supported Putin's regime but also a queer performativity capable of challenging it.

As the previous chapter's drag queens illustrate, the hypergendered cross-dressing required of Russian citizens in the 2000s and 2010s had a troubled relationship to the country's LGBTQ+ citizens, as well as to queerness more broadly. Rather than challenge the country's neotraditional regime of heteronormativity, most performances *en travesti*, whether cross- or cisgender, reinforced it, and their cumulative effect was to shift blame for the country's ongoing crisis of masculinity away from gender-conforming Russian men and onto any and everyone else.[4] Only a handful of performances *en travesti* actually bent gender, celebrated same-sex desire, or expressed queerness, and these, like Conchita Wurst, inevitably provoked scandal. In other words, *travesti* entails neither queerness nor queer performativity. In fact, none of the individual styles discussed in this book demands that the performativity behind a given song, video, or text reject the status quo and embrace subversive queerness. Even camp's link to androgyny and homosexuality does not guarantee a queer message, since queer performativity results not from a given style's gendered, sexual, or agentic affinities but rather from its affective stance and temporal preference.

Instead of linking to either narcissism or empathy, queerness arises from shame, as Judith Butler and Eve Sedgwick contend. Moreover, the shame and stigma associated with queer performativity comes not just once but repeatedly across time from a reverberating chorus of homophobic Others.[5] This process has the power to form communities of both the shamers and the shamed, yet the humiliation of the label "queer" interrupts the feedback loop on which a shamed self relies to form and perform identity, forcing it to adopt "the protoform (eyes down, head averted) of this powerful affect."[6] Not only does shame disrupt the feedback loop that characterizes all of the Russian styles examined in this book, but its repetition across time also collapses these styles' range of temporal preferences into a single time-free present. Rather than charisma's aspiration for the future or camp's nostalgia for the past, queer performativity rejects the flow of time, operating instead in the anti-time created by the echoing epithet "queer." Although no single style requires queer performativity, introducing shame into any style can bring a queer performer into being, liberate them from the temporal, gendered, sexual, and agentic preferences of whatever styles they perform, and generate a performance that undermines hegemonic performativity itself, as Alyosha's fate in *Dust* illustrates.

Queer performativity may arise from an unlikely combination of shame and liberation, yet it leads to a range of feelings that go far beyond toxic humiliation. Much as *travesti* results in the epistemological ambivalence of knowing yet not knowing the inner person on the basis of outer appearance, so does queer performativity create an affective ambivalence composed of sharply conflicting emotions, such as love and hate, desire and disgust, courage and fear. When brought together in a queer performance by someone like Vladislav Mamyshev-Monro, these two types of ambivalence hold the power to dislodge and even shift the reigning paradigm of performativity in a given time and place. Admittedly, individual queer performances, like Mamyshev-Monro's drag remake of *Volga-Volga*, are a far cry from the all-encompassing performative shift in late-Soviet society analyzed by Alexei Yurchak.[7] Nonetheless, such performances represent micro-moments that accumulate to create macro-level social change, and they allowed any Russian whose identity formed around shame and stigma to make a queer contribution to the overall performative shift that took place during Putin's first three terms in office.

Needless to say, the mechanism of shame differs from person to person, as well as among cultures, periods, and political regimes.[8] Perhaps the most durable links connecting the different forms of identity politics that have emerged in North America and Western Europe over the past half century are, first, their shared belief that identity is a coherent and essentialized category and, second, their shared goal of reducing, if not eliminating, the shame and stigma that typically form minority identity. Whether focusing on race, ethnicity, religion, gender, sexuality, or disability, all of these movements have sought to make shame, which is "uniquely contagious from one person to another," less infectious, as we see in phenomena ranging from gay pride parades to #MeToo.[9] On the contrary, Putin's regime rejected the political correctness of Western identity politics, including the beliefs that LGBTQ+ are "born this way" and that they merit the civil rights and social visibility that come with de-shaming. The increasingly rigid norms of gender and sexuality in Putin's Russia instead made the humiliation that leads to queer performativity an equal-opportunity experience for all Russians regardless of whether they identified as LGBTQ+ or not.[10] At the same time that the opportunities for LGBTQ+ Russians to connect with their Western allies and each other rose dramatically thanks to the internet, the contagiousness of queer performativity was on the rise, and by the late 2000s, the homophobic chorus taunting "queer" became more numerous and vocal, as well as better organized.

By 2013, this chorus of homophobic Others was no longer just a metaphor. The "gay propaganda" law gave it concrete form and function, as well as the state's sanction to seek out the contagion of queerness and to shame those who dare infect anyone under the age of eighteen. Rather than criminalize homosexuality itself or those adults who engage in same-sex acts, Article 6.21 articulates its own peculiar performative utterance that institutionalized homophobic shaming as a social and cultural weapon. However, the "gay propaganda" law functions like any other performative utterance, which signifies not only as its authors intended, but also in spite of and sometimes even against their most precious intentions.[11] By weaponizing shame, the ban on "gay propaganda" reproduced the metaphor of shame as contagion and depicted homosexuality as a virulent infection, whose inevitable spread increased the number of queer performers, as well as the forms of queer performativity, contributing to the country's macro-level performative shift. The net result of the Putin regime's efforts to implement more rigid norms of gender and sexuality in the 2000s and 2010s was ultimately to broaden both the scope of queer performativity and the political significance of LGBTQ+ Russians. Thanks to the 2013 ban on "gay propaganda," the country's LGBTQ+ citizens provided the model for queering all of the Russian styles discussed in this book, as well as for resisting and undermining the heteronormative performativity Article 6.21 enshrined.

Although the notion of queer performativity outlined here comes from Western theorists on the crest of queer theory in the 1990s, their ideas help us make sense of both the sharp rise in homophobic discourse in the Russian Federation during the 2010s and the 2020s' boom in queer-themed entertainment. The texts examined in this chapter demonstrate that the institutionalization of state-sanctioned homophobia in Article 6.21 represented a pivot point not only for LGBTQ+ Russians but also for the range of styles used in pop cultural texts to examine queerness and to express queer performativity. If Russian pop performers played at being queer before 2013, then the years after saw an increase in documentary works devoted to Russia's LGBTQ+ community. However, the message of both fictions that strategically used and nonfictions that documented Russian queerness was one and the same: the experience of shame after the demise of the Soviet Union was so unrelenting that everyone in Russia ran the risk of being swept up in a rising tide of queer performativity and stigmatized as queer.

Going Gay at Eurovision: t.A.T.u. and Dima Bilan

Sergei Loban's *Dust* was not the only feature film coming out of Russia to flirt with queerness after the Soviet Union's demise. The post-Soviet buildup to the "gay propaganda" law also saw the release of Yurii Pavlov's *The Creation of Adam* in 1993, Sergei Livnev's *Hammer and Sickle* in 1994, Ol'ga Stolpovskaia and Dmitrii Troitskii's *I Love You* in 2004, Mikhailov's *Jolly Fellows* in 2009, and Sergei Tamaraev and Liubov' L'vova's *Winter Journey* in 2013.[12] However, whatever nonstraight content these films included was pitched first and foremost to a domestic audience, whose curiosity about LGBTQ+ identities and lifestyles did not usually go beyond the films' often oblique and sometimes homo- or transphobic treatment of their characters' nonnormative identities. We see a similar lack of daring to speak its own name in pop performances of Russian queerness before an international audience once we turn to the Eurovision Song Contest, the most widely watched annual event in television history.[13] Much like the hesitant and equivocal treatment of gayness in movies from the same time, Russia's participation in Eurovision during the years that led up to 2013 involved a highly stylized and easily deniable performance of queerness, which culminated in Russian victory at the contest in 2008.[14]

The Russian Federation first entered Eurovision in 1994, that is, at the depths of the country's abjection in the international arena, and the low scores that Russian entries initially received demonstrated that those selecting and vetting these acts understood neither the contest's widely debated camp esthetic nor how to leverage it to overcome Russia's humiliation as a deposed superpower.[15] Typical of this trend was the husband-and-wife team of Filipp Kirkorov (who came in seventeenth place in 1995) and Alla Pugacheva (who came in fifteenth in 1997). Despite their popularity at home, Kirkorov and Pugacheva were products of Russia's home-grown *estrada*, which looked like naive camp, if not out-and-out kitsch, to Eurovision cognoscenti. At the same time that Russians' tin ear placed them among Eurovision's vanquished, the contest's ever-evolving camp esthetic took a queer turn when the trans Dana International won the contest for Israel in 1998. In addition to bringing Eurovision's sizeable gay fandom out of the closet, Dana International's victory proved that performing queerness could lead to the contest's grand prix, as was also the case in 2007 for Serbia's Maria Šerifović and, in 2014, for Austria's Conchita Wurst. The contest's queer turn coincided roughly with groundwork laid by the European Union (in the 1999 Treaty of Amsterdam and the 2000 Charter of Fundamental Rights) for protection of its LGBTQ+ citizens. In other words, Eurovision entries performing queerness either openly (in the cases of Dana and Conchita) or seemingly (in the case of Šerifović) used a camped-up expression of European homonationalism to secure their winning edge, a strategy to which Russia turned in the early 2000s.

The ever-increasing gayness that Russia used to win Eurovision is most evident in the third-place performance of t.A.T.u. in 2003 and Dima Bilan's entries in 2006 (when he took second place) and 2008 (when he won the grand prix). The high marks that t.A.T.u. and Bilan received attest to the fact that Russians had finally mastered Eurovision's rules of engagement. However, the performance of queerness that led to their success was not the campy homonationalism of Dana International, Šerifović, Conchita Wurst, or even Verka Serduchka, who took second place on behalf of Ukraine in 2007, but rather a prime example of *stiob*.[16] By overidentifying with Europop homonationalism, t.A.T.u. and Bilan created double-voiced performances, which could be read, on one hand, as affirmations of LGBTQ+ identity by contest enthusiasts around the world and, on the other hand, as mockery of Europe's acceptance of nonnormative gender and sexuality by audiences in Russia. Transforming Eurovision camp into post-Soviet *stiob*, t.A.T.u. and Bilan not only wiped away the shame and stigma of past Russian losses but also hijacked a music contest widely considered gay for Putin's heteronormative national project.

The strategic *stiob* of all three of these Eurovision entries comes clearly into focus once we consider t.A.T.u.'s reception even before the duo represented Russia at Eurovision. As Dana Heller documents, t.A.T.u., whose acronym stands for "ta liubit tu" (this one loves that), was designed by manager Ivan Shapalov in response to Western stereotypes of the hot, young lesbian.[17] Lena Katina and Iuliia Volkova specialized in a slickly packaged faux lesbianism, as we see in their 2002 English-language hit, "All the Things She Said," the first Russian song to reach number one on the Media and Music Pan-European Singles Chart.[18] The song's lyrics describe the shame and confusion of girl-on-girl love, yet the video recycles well-worn visual tropes from heterosexual male porn, including rain-blurred close-ups of Katina and Volkova kissing and shots of the two singers in miniskirted school uniforms behind prison bars.[19] Their pseudo-lesbianism provoked scandal and attracted an avid following abroad, even though Katina and Volkova denied being gay at home and espoused "traditional" Russian values in statements such as, "Homosexuality is a kind of sickness, we are not homosexuals."[20] Well before their entry into Eurovision, t.A.T.u.'s "performance of lesbian desire [was] somewhere between the ostensible depth of longing and the parodic inversion of that longing," allowing them to construct a lucrative *stiob* of LGBTQ+ identity.[21]

Once t.A.T.u. was chosen to represent Russia at Eurovision, they simply continued this tactic, which delivered a message of Europop homonationalism to contest fans around the world at the same time that it asserted Russia's independence from European hegemony. The duo decided to sing the Russian-language "Don't Believe, Don't Fear, Don't Beg," and their performance in the contest finals reproduced the flesbian frisson that made them famous. Wearing blue jeans, cropped T-shirts, tennis shoes, a minimum of makeup, and tousled hair, Katina and Volkova moved almost carelessly around a circular stage flashing with lasers, and their performance climaxed as they held hands, fell to their knees, and looked as if they might deliver one of their on-stage kisses.[22] However, Russians watching "Don't Believe, Don't Fear, Don't Beg" could easily recognize the song's title as a prison aphorism popularized in Aleksandr Solzhenisyn's *The Gulag Archipelago* and understood this list of imperatives, which culminates in the command to "calm down" (*uspokoisia*) in the song's chorus.[23] In addition, the lyrics' depersonalized description of "someone like you [and] someone like me" urged listeners to identify with Katina and Volkova, whose capricious behavior throughout the contest and out-of-tune singing during the finals demonstrated that they certainly did not believe or fear Eurovision's rules of engagement or plan to beg for the grand prix. In other words, t.A.T.u.'s *stiob* allowed them to place third at Eurovision in 2003 by leveraging a global reputation as lesbians while singing a song whose Russian lyrics scoffed at Eurovision and the queer-friendly Europe it represented.

Unsurprisingly, t.A.T.u. continued to deliver a mixed message after performing at Eurovision. In the wake of their failure to win, for example, the avowedly straight Katina and Volkova rationalized their loss as the result of homophobia.[24] In more recent years, t.A.T.u. has even managed to sweep the duo's faux lesbianism under the rug, as was evident in their reprise of "Don't Believe, Don't Fear, Don't Beg" during the opening ceremonies for the 2009 Eurovision contest in Moscow.[25] Rather that costume themselves as teen-rebel rockers, the duo wore form-fitting satin cocktail dresses with high-heel shoes and carefully coiffed below-the-shoulder tresses, and the clumsiness of their momentary hug on stage gutted such gestures of the sex appeal they once had. Similarly, the song for which t.A.T.u. is best known in Russia, "Not Gonna Get Us" (Nas ne dogoniat), has morphed from a celebration of queer rebellion into an unofficial pop anthem since its release in 2001. The original video of "Not Gonna Get Us" begins with mug shots of Katina and Volkova, who flee the law atop a flaming, driverless tractor-trailer careening down a snow-driven Siberian highway in an apparently suicidal bid for the freedom to love each other.[26] However, all references to oppressed lesbians disappeared when t.A.T.u. performed "Not Gonna Get Us" at the 2009 Eurovision semifinals and then at the opening ceremony for the 2014 Winter Olympics in Sochi.[27] The Eurovision reprise included backup from the Red Army choir, a squad of energetic dancers in Russian national costume, and a Russian fighter jet poised for takeoff, while the rendition at Sochi featured Russian athletes in the country's official sweat suit jumping enthusiastically on stage. Now that the phrase "Not Gonna Get Us" appears on T-shirts with memes of Putin atop a horse or bear at tourist sites around Russia, the nationalist message lurking behind t.A.T.u.'s faux-lesbian *stiob* has come into full view.[28]

As satisfying as t.A.T.u.'s *stiob* at 2003's Eurovision was for Russian audiences, winning the contest required a more subtle performance of queerness, to which the pop star Dima Bilan gladly applied his talents as a singer and dancer in 2006.[29] Unlike t.A.T.u., Bilan performed the ballad "Never Let You Go" in Eurovision English, described by one journalist as "an exquisite tongue, spoken nowhere else, which raises the poetry of heartfelt but absolute nonsense to a level of which Lewis Carroll could only have dreamed."[30] By singing in the lingua franca of Eurovision, Bilan increased his comprehensibility to the contest's international audience at the same time that he presented an ambiguous spectacle that, despite references to heterosexual romance, could nonetheless be read as gay. The lyrics of "Never Let You Go" offer a confusing series of platitudes about lost love and eternal desire without ever stating explicitly the gender of the singer's beloved.[31] Those so inclined could interpret lines like "flesh of my flesh, bone of my bone . . . soul of my soul, blood of my blood" as a reference to same-sex desire. Bilan's appearance was similarly unclear: in a form-fitting white tank top, distressed blue jeans held up by a suggestively jutting belt, and white sneakers, his well-muscled, seemingly hairless body looked like that of both a teen idol and a gay centerfold. In addition, "Never Let You Go" included "a classic Eurovision *coup de théâtre*" that demonstrated Bilan's mastery of Eurovision camp.[32] As he earnestly made eye contact with the television camera, two tutu-clad ballerinas *en pointe* appeared behind the singer on stage. Bilan then mounted a white grand piano at the very moment when a third grease-painted ballerina emerged from the piano's rose-petal-strewn vulva. After leaping from piano to stage, Bilan fell to his knees while the grease-painted ballerina scattered rose petals into his open hand. When taken with the ambiguity of the song's lyrics and costume, Bilan's campy combination of high-culture ballet with low-culture pop allowed him to exploit his reputation in the 2000s as heterosexual but bi-curious and gay-friendly and to garner enough votes to take second place at the contest.[33]

When Bilan returned to the Eurovision stage in 2008, the calculated ambiguity of "Never Let You Go" was replaced by an all but explicit queerness in "Believe," the ballad of narcissistic self-adoration that finally won Eurovision for Russia. The lyrics, costuming, and staging of "Believe" abandoned the equivocal sexual stance of "Never Let You Go" for a flawless performance of metrosexuality.[34] Barefoot, clad in an immaculately white shirt and pants, and bowed over his microphone as he sat cross-legged, Bilan began "Believe" by beckoning the audience from the stage's apron in a variety of seductive postures, which deftly illustrated the journalist Mark Simpson's description of the metrosexual as "a desirable, smooth-skinned, buffed boy with a tarty grin" who "'queers' all the codes of official masculinity of the last hundred years or

Figure 10. Dima Bilan performing "Believe" with the composer Edvin Marton and the Olympic figure skater Evgenii Pliushchenko on behalf of Russia during the 2008 Eurovision finals. Used by permission of Getty Images; photograph by Andrej Isakovic.

so: It's passive where it should always be active, desired where it should always be desiring, looked at where it should always be looking."[35] After riveting the audience's gaze on himself, Bilan retreated to center stage, where he joined the composer Edvin Marton playing a Stradivarius violin and the Olympic figure skater Evgenii Pliushchenko describing elegant mini-circles on ice. As theatrical smoke swirled from beneath them, the three men abandoned their independent movements, fell to their knees in unison, and reached out to the audience. With his shirt ripped open to reveal a manscaped torso, Bilan crooned a final falsetto high. "Believe," which reputedly cost more than a million dollars to stage, contained no open declarations of same-sex desire; however, it united Bilan, Marton, and Pliushchenko in a self-consciously seductive spectacle of masculine virtuosity and vanity.

Much like "Never Let You Go," "Believe" allowed Bilan to perform queerness without committing to being gay. The unsure fusion of hetero- and homosexuality in 2006, which culminated in the weird metaphor of a piano-vagina, gave way in 2008 to metrosexuality, which, although it queers masculinity, typically refers to straight men. Bilan's winning performance sidestepped the issue of sexual preference by recycling the persistent stereotype of gay men as narcissists and replacing *inter*personal with *intra*personal desire. Echoing his performance on stage, the lyrics of "Believe" freely mix metaphors for the self's indomitability in a paean to solipsism:

> Even when the thunder and storm begins
> I'll be standing strong like a tree in the wind
> Nothing is gonna move this mountain or change my direction
> I'm falling off the sky and I'm all alone
> The courage that's inside is gonna break my fall
> Nothing is gonna dim my light within
> But if I keep going on it will never be impossible
> Not today.
> Cause I got something to believe in
> As long as I'm breathing
> There is not a limit to what I can dream
> Cause I got something to believe in
> Mission to keep climbing
> Nothing else can stop me if I just believe
> And I believe in me.

Although "Believe" forgoes all forms of romantic love, straight or otherwise, it nonetheless proclaims the ultimate homoeroticism in its passionate declaration of self-love. Lest such explicit narcissism alienate Eurovision's audience, Bilan judiciously altered the song's chorus during the televised finals, singing, "And we believe in you," while he, Marton, and Pliushchenko gestured to the audience. In short, Bilan's 2008 "Believe" achieved three linked aims: it perfected Russia's strategic performance of gayness at Eurovision, it took the grand prix, and it brought the competition to Moscow in 2009.

Unlike t.A.T.u., whose *stiob* of Europop homonationalism predated the duo's appearance at Eurovision, the double-voiced nature of Bilan's performance in "Believe" became evident only the next year. The overtly nationalistic spectacle hosted by Moscow in 2009 announced to the entire world that going gay had been no more than a strategic ploy, which Russia promptly replaced with its "traditional" heteronormativity once Eurovision took place on its own territory and terms.[36] As Emily Johnson has shown, Russia's official entry into the 2009 contest, Anastasia Prikhod'ko's "Mamo," traded Eurovision's dominant camp idiom for a Soviet-style performance of "the friendship of peoples."[37] And much like t.A.T.u.'s straightened-up version of "Don't Believe, Don't Fear, Don't Beg," Bilan's reprise of "Believe" during the contest's opening ceremonies enacted neither narcissistic self-love nor metrosexuality but rather a blatantly triumphant heterosexual fandom. After a lavish opening act by Cirque du Soleil, Bilan entered Moscow's Olimpiiskii stadium via the fly system, literally falling out of the sky to discover that he was anything but all alone. On the contrary, a team of women costumed as photo-snapping paparazzi helped him disentangle his trench coat from the wires attached to his back and strutted alongside him. Bilan then burst through three faux-brick walls before leaping back into the sky toward a Cirque du Soleil angel. Finally, the singer flew back down to the stage to sing "Believe" not with Marton and Pliushchenko as in 2008 but with a single female backup singer and a group of about ten white-clad violinists, as well as to the cheers of the twenty-five-thousand-person crowd.

If those watching the newly heterosexualized performances of Bilan and t.A.T.u failed to recognize Russia's rejection of the strategy of going gay, then events on the streets of Moscow during Eurovision 2009 delivered this message loud and clear. A small group of LGBTQ+ activists, including the gay rights activists Nikolai Alekseev and Peter Tatchell, decided to organize the first ever pan-Slavic Pride parade in hopes of capitalizing on the international media spotlight shining on Moscow. However, the city's mayor, Iurii Luzhkov, refused them permission to march on Pushkin Square, forcing the organizers to move their now illegal Slavic Pride parade to Sparrow Hills, where some thirty people held placards and chanted pro-LGBTQ+ slogans for about a minute before police arrested them.[38] Back at the city's center and with Luzhkov's approval, ultranationalist, Russian Orthodox, and white supremacist organizations held their own placards and chanted homophobic slogans, protesting a pride parade that had never really taken place and receiving just as much media attention as the demonstrators in Sparrow Hills. Unsurprisingly, the failed Slavic Pride parade aroused indignation among foreign press correspondents, while those within Russia took little notice of the abortive event and even called for LGBTQ+ Russians to go back into the closet.

When combined, the Slavic Pride scandal and Russian flag-waving at Eurovision 2009 made it abundantly clear that the strategy of going gay to win the contest had nothing to do with entering the European arena of accepting and protecting LGBTQ+ subjects and everything to do with restoring Russia's national pride and "traditional" heteronormativity. t.A.T.u. and Bilan used *stiob* to create a *travesti* of Europop homonationalism that delivered one message to Western European viewers and another to those in Russia. Although the decision to go gay at Eurovision in the 2000s effectively erased the shame and stigma of Russia's humiliation at the contest in the 1990s, neither t.A.T.u.'s nor Bilan's acts represented the queer performativity we might expect in the wake of such Eurovision abjection. Instead, the strategy of going gay allowed

Russia to colonize the contest, demonstrating that real Russian men and women do not limit themselves to performing masculine and feminine hypergender but are willing to take on queerness in defense of their country's greatness. Russia's ever gayer trajectory to a Eurovision win in the 2000s coopted the contest's rules of engagement and rewrote them for Putin's purposes. By doing so, the strategy of going gay in the realm of Europop sought to solve Russia's crisis of masculinity through a compensatory queerness that made Russia look LGBTQ+-friendly abroad at the same that the homophobic "gay propaganda" law gained momentum at home.

The Performative Contradiction of "Gay Propaganda"

Once we view Russia's 2008 Eurovision victory as an example of compensatory queerness, it takes little imagination to recognize the "gay propaganda" law as a counterpoised instance of compensatory straightness.[39] In the 2000s, the Russian Federation continued to suffer from a high death rate for Russian men, as well as a falling birthrate. When combined, these led to a shrinking population, which forced Putin's government to confront heterosexual Russians' failure to reproduce the nation.[40] In addition to creating incentives like "maternity capital," the Russian state once again turned to symbolic politics in hopes of boosting the country's population, as well as finding a scapegoat for the demographic and economic downturns of the late 2000s.[41] As Article 6.21 trickled up from cities in the Russian provinces like Riazan', Arkhangel'sk, and St. Petersburg to the federal level, it became clear that nonreproductive sexuality in the guise of Russia's so-called sexual minorities could serve as the country's internal enemy. The law's aim of protecting minors from "gay propaganda" cloaks yet one more attempt to prop up Russia's flagging masculinity, to reinvigorate reproductive heterosexuality, and to construct the country as categorically straight. When the Duma voted to approve Article 6.21 in the summer of 2013, the law's compensatory straightness transformed homophobia, which was already "a constitutive element in the official and non-official performance of post-Soviet national identity," into a state-sanctioned duty.[42]

Now that Article 6.21 has been in force for a decade, we have a clear understanding of its prehistory, as well as the real harm it has done to LGBTQ+ Russians.[43] However, the language of the "gay propaganda" law targets neither Russia's LGBTQ+ citizens nor the allegedly nonnormative sex practices in which they engage. Rather, Article 6.21 attempts to eradicate discourse about LGBTQ+ identities and lifestyles. In layman's terms, "Article 6.21. The Propaganda of Non-traditional Sexual Relations among Minors" prohibits describing or depicting anything associated with LGBTQ+ in anything but a negative light to anyone under the age of eighteen. To quote the law's cumbersome legalese, it penalizes those who foment "nontraditional sexual arrangements, the attractiveness of nontraditional sexual relations, a perverted conception of the social equality of traditional and nontraditional sexual relations," as well as those who impose "information about nontraditional sexual relations provoking interest in such relations" on minors. As a regulation in Russia's Administrative Code, the law does not address criminal liability, nor does its prosecution require that actual minors be exposed to or swayed by the "gay propaganda" in question. In other words, Article 6.21 is meant to censor all positive depictions of LGBTQ+ people, to limit Russians' freedom of expression, and to foster moral panic.[44]

Those researching Article 6.21 agree that the law signaled a fundamental shift in discourse about homosexuality in the Russian Federation.[45] According to Cai Wilkinson, the "discursive shift" enacted by the law "refutes the essentialization of sexual identity," moving "focus from individual to collective and from identity to behavior."[46] Alexander Kondakov, whose work offers the most sustained analysis of Article 6.21, expands this line of reasoning by pointing out that even the disciplines qualified to render expert opinion on homosexuality in Russia have changed in recent years from medicine and psychopathology to the social sciences.[47] More important, Kondakov argues that Article 6.21 has created a "shift in the law from physically isolating queer bodies to discursively isolating information about queerness," which signals a move "from regulating personal behavior to governing public appearances."[48] When taken together, these multiple discursive shifts not only contribute to the larger performative shift taking place in Russian society and culture under Putin but also suggest that the law represents a watershed in post-Soviet performativity.

To understand the far-reaching implications of Article 6.21, we need only consider how the law refutes essentialized sexual identity for queers and nonqueers alike. As scholars of sexuality in Russia contend, at no point in its history has the country fully subscribed to the idea that sexual preference or orientation is inborn.[49] The "gay propaganda" law continues this tradition by assuming that sexual identity is subject to change and vulnerable to forces outside the individual. As Kondakov points out, the law presumes that "children are inherently heterosexual but can change their sexual orientation if they are introduced to alternative sexualities" in the form of "gay propaganda."[50] In addition to articulating a surprisingly postmodern sexual fluidity, the discourse about queerness generated by Article 6.21 and in the Russian academy plays free and easy with two different types of sexual subjectivity: "This subject is split in two. One part rests on a person's essential truth about her or himself, the kind of sexuality with which they are born. Another part of the subject is performative and can be conditioned by environmental factors such as 'homosexual propaganda.' Importantly, constructivism is understood in Soviet social engineering terms. The point is not that notions are constructed and interpreted under the complicated intertwined influence of many different historical, social, and political factors; rather, persons are constructed within a short period of time by 'propaganda' through media such as newspapers, the law, and education."[51] This amalgam of essentialist and constructionist sexual identities leads Kondakov to conclude that the episteme of Russian sexuality is, in fact, queer, and he offers queer theory as a better paradigm for explaining Article 6.21's "anti-subjective discourse [which] does not generate subjectivity but opposes it directly through the multiplication of subjectivity options" than theories positing a coherent sexual subject.[52] Ultimately for Kondakov, Russian "sexuality is queer: people are not born in sexual boxes but constantly experience performative effects of social, historical, and political forces."[53] In other words, the discursive shifts ushered in by the "gay propaganda" law queer subjectivity itself, leading to a post-Soviet subject whose performativity focuses on behavior and appearance, in other words, on style.

Kondakov's realization that Russia's repressive "gay propaganda" law shares common territory with liberatory queer theory from the West is surprising, to say the least. Yet if we pursue this idea, we quickly see that many of the assumptions embedded in Article 6.21 represent a dumbing-down of the concept of performativity at the core of queer theory. Perhaps most obvious, the law's tedious repetition of the phrase "nontraditional sexual relations" reduces Butler's and Sedgwick's nuanced understanding of identity as a performative construct to a blunt presumption that the sex we have determines who we are.[54] This phrase, which the law itself never defines, depicts queerness not as an identity but as a grab bag of deviant sexual practices, leaving precisely what these practices entail to the imagination.[55] Moreover, by banning discourse about sex acts that the law refuses to name, it encourages Russians of all sexual orientations to cordon off their private lives, in which they can engage in and speak about the full gamut of sex acts, from their public lives, in which their behavior and appearance must demonstrate Russia's supposedly heterosexual, patriarchal, and reproductive sexual traditions.[56] This public–private divide encourages all Russians—gay and straight—to adopt a *travesti* not simply of hypergender but also of heterosexuality itself. Fittingly, the *travesti* of straightness fostered by Article 6.21 inverts a popular misreading of Butler's analysis of drag in *Gender Trouble* as "the paradigm of subversive action or, indeed, as a model for political agency."[57] If this simplification of Butler's argument views drag as a gender parody that necessarily disrupts and subverts heteronormativity, then the *travesti* inspired by the "gay propaganda" law inevitably buttresses norms of gender and reproductive sexuality, affirming them as "instruments of cultural hegemony."[58]

In addition to performativity, Article 6.21 also vulgarizes the concept of performative speech acts as first formulated by J. L. Austin.[59] The law's prohibition of "gay propaganda" assumes that any less-than-damning representation of homosexuality functions as a performative utterance, that is, a speech act with the power to change the social reality it describes. In fact, the law seems to take for granted "the smooth and 'happy' functioning" (what Austin termed the "felicity") of "gay propaganda" as a performative utterance.[60] Apparently, the "gay propaganda" banned by Article 6.21 was viewed by the Kremlin as the antithesis of much of the political discourse it generated before 2020, whose "infelicity" discouraged citizens from taking part in the political process. If Putin's annual addresses and TV call-in shows illustrated the numbing effect of many of Russia's political rituals before the invasion of Ukraine, in which the president repeated hollow performatives that failed to produce the changes they promised, then the "gay propaganda" banned by Article 6.21 restored the magical ability of doing things to words. In short, Article 6.21 posits that a simple slogan like "Gay Is Okay" has the power to turn any child or teenager who hears it into a homosexual.

Examining the performative assumptions embedded in the "gay propaganda" law ultimately leads to the realization that Article 6.21, like all legal statutes, is itself a performative utterance that seeks to change Russian society through words.[61] However, a censorship law like Article 6.21 inevitably suffers from what Butler calls "a performative contradiction," since it "*states what it does not want stated* [and] introduce[s] the censored speech into public discourse, thereby establishing it as a site of contestation, that is, as the scene of public utterance that it sought to preempt."[62] Thanks to this performative contradiction, Article 6.21 has not quashed all positive depictions of LGBTQ+ identities and lifestyles in Russia, nor has it restored the silence in which homosexuality was shrouded during the Soviet era. On the contrary, the law has propagated a great deal of discourse—good, bad, and ugly—about LGBTQ+ individuals and experiences. In addition to encouraging hate groups like Occupy Pedophilia and Occupy Gerontophilia the law has inspired a growing number of publications for those curious about precisely what Article 6.21 censors, the queer media boom of 2020, and a new generation of LGBTQ+ activists.[63] In addition, the law's prosecution requires that Russian courts enlist expert testimony to determine what is and is not "gay propaganda" in copious detail, generating more discourse about homosexuality in the Russian legal system than ever before.[64] If Article 6.21 aims to clamp down on discourse about LGBTQ+ identities and lifestyles, it clearly enjoys less felicity as a performative utterance than the "gay propaganda" it bans when viewed from the perspective of those who enacted it.

The performative contradiction embedded in Article 6.21 came fully into view in perhaps the most notorious case of the law's prosecution to make its way through Russia's courts, that of Lena Klimova, founder of Children-404, an online support network for LGBTQ+ adolescents.[65] A journalist in the city of Nizhnii Tagil, Klimova created Children-404 in early 2013, shortly before passage of the "gay propaganda" law, to address the dearth of information and support available to young Russians grappling with sexual and gender identity. The organization's pages on the social networks VKontakte and Facebook allow users to tell their story in their own words and images, to pose questions, and to seek support, not unlike The Trevor and It Gets Better Projects in the United States. After the law's passage, however, Klimova became embroiled in accusations of producing "gay propaganda" when Russia's arch-homophobe, the Petersburg politician Vitalii Milonov, sued to bring her to account. Local courts initially failed to find Klimova guilty, but when a member of the Young Guard wing of Putin's United Russia party picked up Milonov's cause, they finally rendered a guilty verdict in 2015, fining Klimova fifty thousand rubles. In addition, Roskomnadzor (Russia's Federal Service for Supervision of Communications, Information Technology, and Mass Media) banned Children-404's webpage on VKontakte, prompting the group to create a second page on the site that garnered more followers than the first.[66] As Klimova's case dragged on, it captured the attention of international media, gaining even more notoriety when the filmmakers Askold Kurov and Pavel Loparev released a documentary titled *Children-404*.[67] Throughout, Klimova continued her activism, authoring three books for and about LGBTQ+ youth and publishing the web project "Beautiful People and What They Say to Me," which chronicles the hate speech she has endured alongside images of those responsible for it.[68] In spite of the most precious intentions of those who authored Article 6.21, the attempt to silence Klimova under the law has produced more "gay propaganda," given Children-404 greater visibility, and made the journalist a recognized LGBTQ+ activist.

The overall infelicity of Article 6.21 as a legal performative is glaringly evident even without considering the law's prosecution. Shortly after its passage, Klimova asked the young people on Children-404 whether they believe in the existence of "gay propaganda," as well as whether they had ever encountered any. While the vast majority of her respondents answered "no," a few sarcastically said "yes":

> Kristina, age 16 (Samara): Our government is spreading propaganda. In my entire life, I haven't heard as much talk about "homosexuality" as I have in the past two years.
>
> Person from nowhere, age 14: Politicians themselves with their eternal conversations and arguments don't "protect against this illness" but on the contrary pay so much attention to it that people themselves begin to think about it against their will.
>
> Mariia, age 17 (Moscow): The biggest propaganda recently is the law itself. Before it, we lived in peace and quiet, and nobody breathed a word about it.
>
> Evgeniia, age 16 (Noril'sk): The only instance of propaganda that I've encountered in my young life is the uproar around the law. Moreover, an uproar raised by its advocates.[69]

These young people clearly perceive the performative contradiction embedded in Article 6.21 and do not appreciate its presumption that they are tabulae rasae on which others inscribe gender identities and sexual desires.[70] The postings on Children-404's webpages demonstrate the refusal of thousands of young Russians to agree with Article 6.21's many performative assumptions and submit to discursive demands whose claim to protect them denies their very existence.[71] Rather than view themselves as shameful social mistakes akin to the internet error message "404-page not found," those who submit problems and questions to Children-404 openly declare their queer identity with affirmations such as "We exist" and "We are not a mistake."

Thanks to its discursive shifts, its vulgarization of queer theory, and the contradictory assumptions that emerge from these two, the "gay propaganda" law marked a turning point for performative citizenship during Putin's first two decades in the Kremlin. Although the letter of the law prohibits what at first glance looks like a narrow range of discourse, the law's spirit makes multiple demands of all Russian citizens regardless of gender and sexual orientation. Even those in the country's "sexual majority" had to prove that they were real Russian men and women by performing a *travesti* of reproductive heterosexuality that included both hypergender and a vocal if not violent homophobia.[72] The higher incidence of hate crimes against LGBTQ+ people since the law's adoption, the hate speech Klimova records in "Beautiful People and What They Say to Me," the antigay purges in Chechnya where gay men have been detained, tortured, and extrajudicially killed since 2017, the "dramatic increase" in LGBTQ+ immigration from Russia in search of asylum, as well as the "victim-blaming and self-harassment" to which LGBTQ+ Russians subject themselves, all attest to the central role homophobia has played in felicitous performances of Russian citizenship since the law's passage in 2013.[73]

Those in Russia's "sexual minorities" face a difficult choice. Either they too adopt heteronormative *travesti* and live "a double life," which requires "self-control of behavior in public . . . so as not to look homosexual," or they, like those who post on Children-404, become de facto LGBTQ+ activists through their mere existence as visibly queer Russians.[74] However, anyone who chooses this second option in effect volunteers as the scapegoat for the compulsory homophobia of their heteronormative fellow citizens, a situation that become even more dire when Russia's Duma began expanding the "gay propaganda" law in 2022, so that "information about 'nontraditional lifestyles' or 'the rejection of family values' would be legally on a par with [promoting] pornography, promoting violence, or encouraging racial, ethnic, or religious enmity."[75] Clearly, the stoic indifference that Alyosha discovered in *Dust* was no longer an option for queer Russians in the 2010s as it was in the 2000s. Perhaps the law's greatest performative contradiction is that by turning all visible forms of queer existence into activism, Article 6.21 has done more to foster a coherent and even essentialized sexual identity for LGBTQ+ Russians than any other event in the country's history.

The Queer Archive versus Evil Naked Clowns in Suicide Belts

The de facto activism created by the "gay propaganda" law led LGBTQ+ Russians and their allies to alter their thinking about and approaches to sexual identity after the "gay propaganda" law went into effect. We see this most obviously in the Russian language's evolving lexicon for nonnormative sexuality. While euphemisms, such as *tema* ("the theme," which roughly translates as "in the life"), continued to have wide currency, much of the medical and legal terminology inherited from the Soviet era, such as *gomoseksualizm* and *gomoseksualist* ("homosexualism" and "homosexualist"), was replaced by loan words from English among Russian-speaking queers. As a result, many of the terms central to the discussion of sexual identity in the United States and Western Europe are now firmly ensconced in the Russian language, including *gei* (gay), *kvir* (queer), *kaming-aut* (coming out), and LGBT.[76] As with other languages, the influx of English terminology brought Russian speakers into the global exchange of ideas about gender and sexuality, including the beliefs that people are born gay and that sexuality represents a coherent category of identity. LGBTQ+ Russians' shift away from medico-legal terminology and toward the vocabulary of international gay rights contributed to the larger discursive shift in which Article 6.21 took part. At the same time, the ability of LGBTQ+ Russians and their allies to speak about queerness in increasingly precise and globally shared terms led to something that Article 6.21 was clearly intended to prevent: the rapid expansion of Russia's queer archive.

As is true elsewhere, Russia has long suffered from what Dan Healey describes as a stunted queer archive, and both mainstream media and most scholars developed the habit of "straightening up" the country's queer past long before passage of the "gay propaganda" law.[77] Predictably, Article 6.21 complicated this tendency, making, for example, any reference to the composer Pyotr Tchaikovsky's homosexuality politically fraught.[78] However, many LGBTQ+ Russians and their allies set out purposely to reverse the tendency to shroud homosexuality in silence by creating a wide variety of texts and projects that document queer experience in Russia and the Soviet Union. This documentary impulse seeks not only to recuperate the country's queer past but also to chronicle its queer present in hopes of creating a more inclusive future for all Russians.[79] Perhaps the clearest evidence of this trend is the online Museum of the History of LGBT in Russia created in 2014. Headed by an Expert Council that comprises academics and activists, the museum welcomes the submission of material and technical assistance from anyone willing to help, and it acts as an information portal for those seeking to document and learn about queerness in Russia.[80] Journalists have also joined the documentary trend, as seen, for example, in *Afisha*'s coverage "record[ing] the remarkable and not so [remarkable] events in the lives of the most diverse gays—from a plumber to a chief editor," Masha Gessen and Joseph Huff-Hannon's bilingual *Gay Propaganda: Russian Love Stories*, and *Inc.*'s reporting on the lives of gay entrepreneurs in Russia.[81] All of these projects rely on the internet, which, despite censorship regulations like Article 6.21, holds a vast repository of LGBTQ+ material on sites like Facebook, VKontakte, and LiveJournal.

Alongside these more conventional contributions to Russia's queer archive appeared creative projects that imagine LGBTQ+ existence in novel ways. Life writing in poetry and prose by Russian-speaking queer authors enjoys an avid audience on the internet, as well as in translation, while the émigré artists Slava Mogutin and Yevgeniy Fiks have devoted their careers to exploring queerness.[82] Mogutin's work includes texts and images inspired by his childhood in the Soviet Union and his youth in Yeltsin's Russia, while Fiks takes an explicitly archival approach in much of his work, for example, the book *Moscow*, which documents the city's Soviet-era cruising sites, or *Mother Tongue*, which creatively resurrects the slang of late-Soviet queers.[83] In the performing arts, Moscow's Teatr.doc has included Anastasia Patlay's *Coming Out of the Closet*, a verbatim play based on interviews with LGBTQ+ activists opposed to the "gay propaganda" law, in its repertoire since 2016.[84] The genre of the coming-out video has also become popular in Russia, inspiring both young queers to share their experience with a global viewership and the director Katia Mikheeva to animate real-life coming-out stories in several short films.[85] The examples provided here represent only a fraction of the material generated by the impulse to document Russian queerness, yet they provide clear proof that Article 6.21 has led some Russians to create a queer archive that goes directly against the most precious intentions of the law's authors.[86]

This burgeoning queer archive has had profound consequences for Putin-era performativity, many of which will come to light only in the post-Putin future. We get a glimpse of the changes in performativity, queer and otherwise, emerging in the wake of the "gay propaganda" law in two documentary films that blend the conventional and creative approaches to augmenting Russia's queer archive. At first glance, Alina Rudnitskaya's *Victory Day* from 2015 and Oleg Mavromatti's *No Place for Fools* from 2014 appear to have nothing in common.[87] On one hand, Rudnitskaya combines interviews she conducted in LGBTQ+ households with footage from St. Petersburg's annual Victory Day parade, showing how her subjects' everyday activism has led to the formation of a coherent queer identity. On the other hand, Mavromatti uses found footage to tell the story of the vlogger Sergii Astakhov, whose incoherent identity as a formerly gay disabled patriot and Russian Orthodox activist implodes in the course of the film. Despite these differences, both *Victory Day* and *No Place for Fools* depict the very real danger posed by the Russian state's call to nationalistic heteronormativity for not only queer but all Russians.

In many ways, Rudnitskaya's *Victory Day* resembles journalism that uses LGBTQ+ Russians' own words and images to document their lives. The film takes us into the St. Petersburg homes of six same-sex couples on Victory Day, the national holiday that has come to epitomize invented "tradition" since Putin's rise to power. The film's opening sequence crosscuts between the apartments where Rudnitskaya's subjects live and rows of tanks ready for the military parade celebrating the Soviet Union's victory over Nazi Germany. In the course of the film, the six couples answer questions about their lives as queer Russians, yet Rudnitskaya omits her own voice and presence so that her subjects' responses appear almost unprompted. The various scenes of each couple's domestic life—two women renovating their home, a man cutting his partner's hair, a family cooking in their kitchen—normalizes their lives, as do their at-home clothes, children, and pets. At several points, we see Rudnitskaya's subjects watching videos of infamous instances of homophobia. As they view diatribes from Milonov, Elena Mizulina, and the Putin-propagandist Dmitrii Kiselev, as well as a pride rally cut short by gay bashing, the couples describe the impact that Article 6.21 has had on them personally. We learn that one woman lost her job, one couple decided to come out, and others in the film anticipate a return to Soviet-era antiqueer hostility. The casual intimacy of Rudnitskaya's camera universalizes the experiences of her queer subjects, while the dual background of a military parade and homophobic ranting transforms her subjects' quotidian experience into political activism. *Victory Day* ends by once again crosscutting between Rudnitskaya's subjects and tanks in the street; however, just as the six couples pause in their daily routines to assume static poses for the camera, the previously immobile tanks begin to move through the city streets.

Rudnitskaya's thirty-minute documentary tells a seemingly simple story of LGBTQ+ Russians living openly queer lives without shame or regret. Unlike a number of Western documentaries made in the wake of the "gay propaganda" law, Rudnitskaya does not exoticize her subjects, nor does she express righteous indignation at the homophobia they endure.[88] Instead, she uses the images brought into the film from outside her subjects' homes to reverse the polarity of normal versus queer, questioning the very concept of victory in Putin's Russia. The stark contrast between the intimate interiors where Rudnitskaya's subjects live and the aggressively poised tanks and homophobic hostility just outside their windows forces us to see the Russian state as a threat to the humble domestic routines, if not the very existence, of all six couples.[89] As represented by the heavily armed military parade, as well as the likes of Milonov, Mizulina, and Kiselev, the state looks less like a defender of and more like an aggressor against its citizens. The final, immobile pose of each couple underscores the epistemological and affective stability of these LGBTQ+ Russians, as well as the coherence of their identities. In contrast, the rows of tanks and marchers shifting into noisy motion as the film ends take on the ambivalence and incoherence typically attributed to queerness. *Victory Day* portrays its LGBTQ+ subjects as the true victors in a battle to lead normal, stable, loving lives against a regime fueled by the hatred underlying "gay propaganda" and myths of a military triumph more than seventy-five years in the past.

Unlike *Victory Day*, whose subjects agreed to be filmed by Rudnitskaya, *No Place for Fools* uses the unsettling video blog of Sergii Astakhov to weave a deeply disturbing narrative that he himself neither imagined nor endorsed.[90] At the base of Mavromatti's film are more than 140 videos, uploaded to VKontakte and YouTube by Astakhov between 2013 and 2016, in which he styled himself a flag-waving Russian patriot and cross-kissing Orthodox believer. The vlog documents Astakhov's day-to-day life as a once gay disabled adult living in his mother's apartment, and individual posts touch on everything from his favorite Moscow shopping mall to time spent in a psychiatric hospital, love poems for his fiancée, Aniuta Bondarets, his favorite recipe for hot dogs, and his enthusiasm for gay porn and the Russian Orthodox Church. Although much of this content seems anodyne, the form of his posts is anything but, since Astakhov personifies the emasculated man-baby updated for

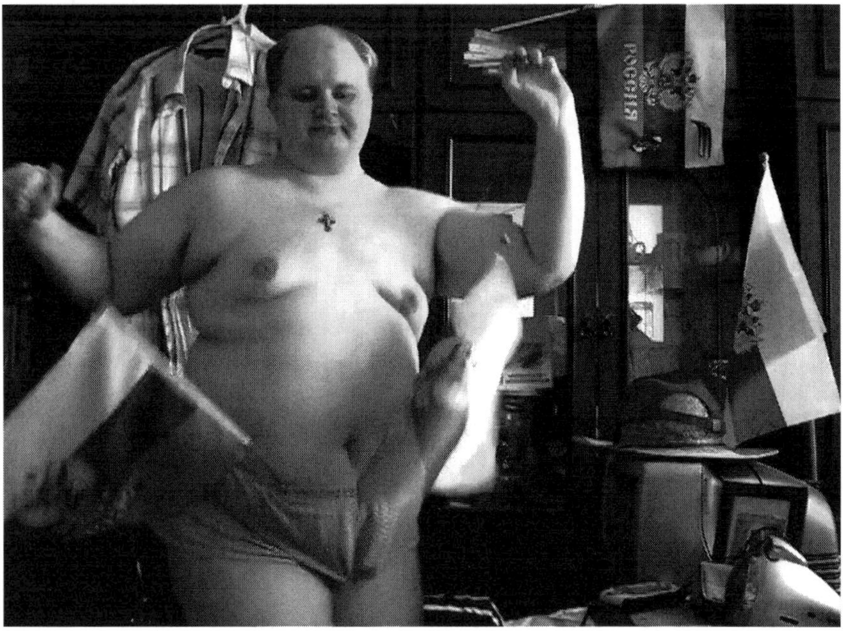

Figure 11. Sergii Astakhov shows viewers "a new dance" in Oleg Mavromatti's 2014 *No Place for Fools*. Used by permission of SUPERNOVA Film Union.

the 2010s. The videos in which he dances in only his underwear reveal a pudgy torso surrounded by folds of white flesh, while those in which he talks about his "traditional" values display a penchant for enumeration and repetition, giving the impression that higher-order language skills lie beyond his reach. In addition, Astakhov's rudimentary filming skills produce unnerving effects, for example, extreme close-ups shot from below the face that magnify nostrils, pimples, and dandruff and a camera so shaky that it can make viewers queasy. However, unlike Tolstaia's Peters and Loban's Alyosha, Astakhov appears to have little or no shame about his masculine abjection, which he eagerly parades for viewers.

Astakhov's bizarre blend of abject masculinity and incantations of Putinism's cherished tenets reveals a subjectivity just as shaky as his camera, and his vlog inspired not only Mavromatti's film but also Anatolii Ul'ianov's *My New Orthodox Video*.[91] Less ambitious that *No Place for Fools*, Ul'ianov's video splices together footage from Astakhov's originals so that the vlogger ends up performing a twenty-minute *stiob* of himself. Although *No Place for Fools* also repurposes Astakhov's posts, Mavromatti does so in a more complex manner, forcing viewers beyond any condescension we might feel as we watch Astakhov kiss the camera or drape himself in the Russian flag. Mavromatti alters Astakhov's vlog by desynchronizing image and sound, adding a musical soundtrack, inserting found footage from other sources, and running some of this found footage backwards.

The point of these manipulations becomes clear once we consider the relationship between Astakhov's own videos and the found footage played in reverse. Unlike the vast majority of Askhakov's posts, which are typically set in his mother's apartment if not his bedroom, all of the reversed footage in *No Place for Fools* occurs outdoors. Moreover, although the first segment played in reverse shows a dancing crowd early in the film, most of these clips appear at the end of *No Place for Fools*, and they show people, presumably suicides, unjumping from their deaths. Mavromatti couples the uncanny images of broken bodies returning to life with Beethoven's "Moonlight Sonata," as Astakhov recites a mesmerizing inventory of Bibles, sexualities, genders, and sexual perversions, all of which he calls "bullshit" (khuinia) before admitting to his utter loneliness. *No Place for Fools* ultimately likens Astakhov's incoherent subjectivity to these suicides played backwards. Rather than repeating Christ's miraculous return to life after crucifixion, the resurrection from masculine abjection that Astakhov apparently hoped to record in his vlog is shown to be a smoke-and-mirrors illusion that anyone who understands video editing can debunk.

Mavromatti has never commented on the questionable ethics of repurposing Astakhov's videos without his permission, not to mention reusing suicide videos ripped from the internet. However, the director implicitly acknowledged the highly triggering nature of not only Astakhov's original videos but also *No Place for Fools* when he described Astakhov's life as "a nightmarish schizophrenic birthday cake from which jumps out an evil naked clown with a suicide belt."[92] This gruesome metaphor aptly describes Astakhov's attempt to construct an identity that conforms with Putin-era mandates, only to have it implode. Despite his desire to be seen as a *muzhik*, a Russian patriot, and an Orthodox believer, viewers viscerally sense the epistemological unsteadiness and affective confusion, which make Astakhov genuinely queer and doom his efforts to construct a normative identity to failure. Just as the falling bodies, exploding cars, and burning buildings brought into *No Place for Fools* from viral videos cannot be restored by playing tapes of them backwards, so can Astakhov never erase his own queerness by repeating that he is "a Russian's Russian" (russkii rossiianin). In an eerie echo of Mavromatti's film, Astakhov died in 2017 from a heart attack at the age of thirty-two. As his country's definitive "meme man," Astakhov embodied a concentrated form of the queerness that infected all forms of subjectivity under Putin during the 2010s. Unlike Rudnitskaya's film, *No Place for Fools* suggests that the "gay propaganda" law did not simply reverse the polarity of normal vs. queer but erased any clear boundary between normativity and queerness, making Putin-era identity into a nightmarish schizophrenic birthday cake and those who adopt heteronormative *travesti* into evil naked clowns wearing suicide belts.

As *Victory Day* and *No Place for Fools* demonstrate, the queer archive emerging in the wake of the "gay propaganda" law neither describes nor prescribes a unitary queer identity for contemporary Russia. In addition to recording and affirming a queerness that Putin's regime would rather deny, the artifacts generated by this documentary impulse show how the attempt to eradicate the contagion of queerness has led to its infecting Russian identity and performativity more broadly. While Rudnitskaya's film shows the willingness of some LGBTQ+ Russians to abandon the heteronormative *travesti* required of compliant citizens, Mavromatti exposes the ultimate failure of such *travesti* for all who perform it, gay or straight. The political punch of Russia's burgeoning queer archive comes from its ability to show, even more clearly than opposition figures like Aleksei Navalny, the violence to the self that results from heeding the Putin regime's call to "traditional" Russian values.

Conclusion

At the same time that Russia's growing queer archive began to normalize LGBTQ+ existence, the chorus of those taunting "queer" became increasingly vocal in the wake of Article 6.21. Rather than adopt the English-influenced lexicon described earlier, supporters of the law and Putin-era neotraditionalism began to use the euphemism "nontraditional" to besmirch any and everything connected with queer life, from sexual relations and orientation to love itself. Moreover, a host of pejorative terms for queers, many derived from the word "pederast," became more permissible in everyday speech than ever before. Such antigay rhetoric, whether oblique or direct, sought to shame LGBTQ+ Russians as a whole and to drive those who chose to live openly queer lives back into the closet. Yet once we view terms like "nontraditional family," "pedik," or "pidor" as symptoms of the queerness infecting all forms of performativity in Putin's Russia, those who use them begin to sound as if they "doth protest too much." Article 6.21's attempt to inoculate Russians against "gay propaganda" had always already failed, and, instead of quarantining queerness in secrecy, the "gay propaganda" law infected Russian identity with a queerness that encompassed not only the country's shamed and stigmatized "sexual minorities" but also its shaming and shameless heterosexual majority.

Much as Article 6.21 propagated the very thing it aimed to censor, so did the law exacerbate the larger crisis of masculinity it was supposed to fix. By simultaneously scapegoating queers and blurring the line between normativity and queerness, the "gay propaganda" law raised the bar for meticulously performed hypergender and cast doubt on heteronormative *travesti*. As a result, Russian men hoping to avoid the shame of queerness had to craft their masculinity so painstakingly that they effaced its very nature as performance. We gain a clear sense of the problems that this particular performative contradiction can cause in Kirill Serebrennikov's 2017 film *The Student*.[93] The story of Venia, a teenager raised by a working mother, begins with his baffling refusal to swim during physical education at school. We quickly learn, however, that *The Student* depicts no ordinary adolescent rebellion. Venia has become a religious extremist and biblical literalist, who rejects not only casual flirting among boys and girls at the school swimming pool but also any attempt to teach them about contraception or evolution. The film offers no clear etiology for Venia's extremism, which demands utter purity and unswerving faith in his unmediated access to God's will. Nonetheless, Serebrennikov shows how others in the film—Venia's beleaguered mother, his biology teacher, the local Orthodox priest, the school's principal, and even his lone friend, Grisha—must be sacrificed to adolescent masculinity so that Venia can erase all traces of its performativity. Although he merely pushes away the bikini-clad girl who excites and seduces him, Venia brutally bludgeons Grisha to death when Grisha tentatively kisses him on the lips. The film ends after Venia engineers the biology teacher's dismissal from school, and we watch the police cover Grisha's slain body with a tarp. By the end of *The Student*, we recognize that the absolutely scrupulous and unmediated masculinity Venia tries to construct for himself is a myth whose maintenance damages everyone around him, as well as the larger society. If Astakhov's incoherent identity merely implodes in *No Place for Fools*, then Serebrennikov shows us how Venia's drive to embody a masculinity beyond performativity explodes like a bomb in *The Student*.

Once we expand our consideration of the impact of the "gay propaganda" law beyond Russia's domestic arena, we see that the law created a number of performative contradictions and complications internationally as well. Article 6.21's passage, in 2013, created an uproar in Western Europe and North America, where journalists and LGBTQ+ activists protested the law's homophobia. However, many depictions of LGBTQ+ Russians that appeared in Western media after the law's passage reduce queer Russians to their vulnerable and often white, male, wounded bodies.[94] Despite their best intentions, works like Ben Steele's two documentary films or Misha Friedman's photo essay *Lyudmila and Natasha: Russian Lives* condescend to their subjects and contribute to the ongoing polarization between Russian heterosexualism and Western homosexualism, in which each side claims political, social, and moral superiority.[95] At the same time that the European Union and United States leveraged their far from flawless sexual tolerance when negotiating internationally, Russia began to craft a new world alliance on the basis of its more "traditional" sexual exceptionalism.[96] The political homophobia enshrined in Article 6.21 allowed Russia to position itself as a civilization distinct from the United States and "Gayropa" and to pose as the global messiah of "traditional values" for postcolonial states looking to cast off Western influence.[97]

The global impact of the "gay propaganda" law has not been limited to bolstering Russia among competing world alliances. As we might expect, the queerness that Article 6.21 spread throughout the Russian Federation despite its authors' intentions has seeped beyond the country's borders and now contributes to discursive and performative shifts taking place globally. Although the Putin regime exerted untold energy to cast off the shame that stigmatized Russia in the 1990s, the compensatory heterosexuality that currently sets Russia's international brand apart is only as strong, stable, and coherent as the aging president who embodies it. As is the case for Russian men, maintaining the myth of Russia's hypermasculinity has required a series of exploits more violent and explosive than Venia's affirmation of masculine purity in *The Student*. During the past decade, Russia not only implemented the "gay propaganda" law in 2013 but also annexed Crimea in 2014, intervened in Syria's civil war in 2015, and initiated a conflict in Donbass that led to Russia's brutal invasion of Ukraine in 2022. Putin's aggressive tactics for maintaining his own as well as his country's image as a strongman might have temporarily silenced the international chorus taunting Russia in the 1990s and distracted citizens' discontent in the domestic sphere during the 2000s. Nonetheless, the shame to which all citizens of the Russian Federation have been vulnerable during the post-Soviet era sticks equally to Russia itself, which teetered between national abjection and civilizational greatness during Putin's first two decades in power. Article 6.21 has given the ongoing performative shift in post-Soviet Russia a distinctly queer fillip and subjected citizens, leaders, and the country itself to the unsettling epistemological and affective ambivalence associated with queerness. The ultimate performative contradiction of the "gay propaganda" law is, to quote Dan Healey, the fact that "Official homophobia has made Russian queerer—not straighter."[98]

5

Post-Soviet Postfeminism

The moral panic fostered by Russia's "gay propaganda" law was a product not simply of homophobia but, more specifically, of a homophobic obsession with gay men. Although all identities represented by the acronym LGBTQ+ were stigmatized as "nontraditional" thanks to Article 6.21, homosexual men posed a particular threat to the neotraditionalism on the rise after 1999. Gay men could easily perform a cisgender *travesti* of the hypermasculinity modeled by Putin yet refuse the demands of heteronormativity, making them dangerous reminders of the country's crisis of masculinity.[1] As a result, much of the homophobic rhetoric and violence instigated by Article 6.21 targeted homosexual men, who, like Grisha in Serebrennikov's film *The Student*, were sacrificed to shore up Russia's fragile masculinity. The antigay purges in Chechnya that first came to light in 2017 provided a frightening example of this type of scapegoating, as well as an opportunity for Putin's government to denounce such egregious antigay violence so that the rest of Russia looked like "a force of order and civilization" in comparison to its Muslim constituent republic.[2]

Russian women who refused the state's heteronormative mandate experienced less homophobic backlash than gay men, which suggests that unruly females represented a secondary target of the "gay propaganda" law. The Putin regime's efforts to discipline such women took the shape of either pronatal policies, such as the program of "maternity capital" instituted in 2007, or tacit approval of domestic abuse, as seen in the 2016 decriminalization of non-aggravated battery and the Duma's refusal to consider, let alone pass, a law against domestic violence, which takes the lives of an estimated fourteen thousand Russian women each year.[3] During Putin's first two decades in power, his regime apparently preferred not to police women's performance of gender publicly. Instead, the carrots and sticks that compelled women to fulfill their feminine duty to the state were wielded in private by intimate partners, family members, or women themselves. This privatization of gender policing relied on widespread stereotypes of Russian women as inherently maternal, long-suffering, self-sacrificing, and subservient to men, and it led many women to perform a highly compliant cisgender *travesti* with little if any prodding from outside.[4] Between 1999 and 2020, hyperfeminine women emerged as the ultimate neoliberal subjects in Russia and paradigmatic citizens in thrall to Putin, their hypermasculine leader.

Women's role as early adopters of cisgender *travesti* came to light in the short-lived viral celebrity of Putin's Army, a group of nubile college coeds whose YouTube campaign set the tone for Putin-mania in the early 2010s. In their most notorious video, a young woman named Diana rips open her white tank top, imprinted in lipstick with a kiss and the words "I rip for Putin," as the camera zooms in on her cleavage. She invites the video's presumably female viewers to compete for the prize of an iPad-2 by copying her and showing what they are willing to do for their leader.[5] Other videos show Putin's Army baring its support for Vladimir Vladimirovich by washing Russian-made cars in bikini tops, daisy dukes, and stilettos or baking him a birthday cake in nothing but baggy boyfriend shirts as members squirt whipped cream into their mouths.[6] Evidently, the passion these young women showed for Putin had nothing to do with his politics but rather grew out of their admiration of his status as a "stylish man," which, to quote Diana, made him a "worthy politician." As Valerie Sperling points out, the willingness of Putin's Army to perform a series of soft-porn clichés in support of their leader was part of a larger pattern in post-Soviet Russian politics, in which gender and sexuality either enhanced, as these young women did for Putin, or undermined politicians' perceived machismo.[7] Once we view Putin's Army as another instance of the slippage among charisma and ironic pop styles like camp, *poshlost'*, and *glamur*, we see that the young women's content-free enthusiasm for their leader modeled fandom for all of his followers by placing them in the position of busty but brainless Putin cheerleaders.

Phenomena like Putin's Army demonstrated the firm foothold of postfeminism on post-Soviet culture. Unlike actual feminism, which typically expresses a coherent ideology geared toward equality of the sexes, postfeminism represents a less coherent sensibility that blends core feminist ideas with antifeminist assumptions.[8] On one hand, this sensibility adopts the key feminist belief that women should be not merely objects of men's desires but also desiring subjects themselves, as well as feminism's emphasis on individualism, choice, and empowerment. On the other hand, postfeminism assumes several positions that most versions of feminism have fought hard to overturn, for example, that sexual difference is natural and femininity, the exclusive bodily property of women, who must constantly monitor and discipline themselves through a makeover paradigm. This incongruous mixture of gender essentialism and gender performativity not only reflects the split sexual subject presumed by Article 6.21 but also contributes to the overall commodification and pornification of twenty-first-century culture, in which individual identity is largely a matter of a sexualized bodily style and power has shifted "from an external, male judging gaze to a self-policing, narcissistic gaze."[9] The postfeminist sensibility expressed in media from women's magazines to chick flicks, self-help for women, popular romance, and reality TV shows urges women to become entrepreneurial, self-maximizing agents of their femininity, leading Rosalind Gill to conjecture that "neoliberalism is always already gendered, and that women are constructed as its ideal subjects."[10]

Social scientists studying Russian women have amply demonstrated their participation in the performative contradiction of postfeminism, as well as the ways in which its "gendered neoliberalism" became glocalized in the post-Soviet era.[11] For example, Suvi Salmenniemi and Maria Adamson studied the post-1991 boom in self-help literature, showing how the Soviet notion of labor was adapted to post-Soviet femininity.[12] Similarly, Sudha Rajagopalan has uncovered the postfeminist discourse generated by rape survivors on Russian television and in social media, while articles by Larissa Rudova and Andrea Lanoux on girls' literature reveal its basic makeover message.[13] Likewise, Holly Porteous's research on Russian women's magazines analyzes their postfeminist framework, which casts beauty labor as a duty for post-Soviet women.[14] These scholars ultimately describe the Putin-era's composite postfeminist subject as "a sexually empowered, maximizing and optimizing possessive individual who seeks to accrue value for herself through continuous labour, but whose autonomy and agency are firmly constrained by the prevailing gendered power structures."[15] In other words, Russian postfeminism during Putin's first two decades in the Kremlin played a game of bait and switch that promised female autonomy in return for the relentless work of becoming appropriately feminine, yet produced a feminine subject regulated and mediated by men.[16] Like its counterparts elsewhere, Putin-era postfeminism was remarkably "capitalism, neoliberalism and patriarchy-friendly," and it represented an efficient and effective means for privatizing the gender policing of Russian women.[17]

The myriad postfeminist messages circulating in the Russian media in the 2000s and 2010s helped to shift the burden of enforcing cisgender *travesti* from outside the individual, as in the case of gay men victimized by homophobia, to inside the bodies and psyches of Russian women. Postfeminism's incessant labor required that any woman who aspired to full femininity and Russianness scapegoat herself, so that the myths denying the country's crisis of masculinity remained unexamined and intact. Whether or not women decided to bear the two or more children required by the "maternity capital" program, a startlingly broad swath of the country's female population subscribed to the postfeminist dictate that they constantly make themselves over to become ideal feminine subjects and model Russian citizens.[18] As this chapter shows, the basic message that women's autonomy not only flows from but also leads back to men appeared after Putin's rise to power in the carefully crafted mythology surrounding Liudmila Putina, the presidential wife. This basic lesson in postfeminism was then adapted for ever wider and more diverse audiences, who gladly took up the different pop styles examined in this book. Whether we examine the self-help industry pitched at Russian women, popular romance novels, or the film director Valeriia Gai Germanika's depiction of adolescent angst, we see how Russian women of the 2000s and 2010s embraced the sensibility of postfeminism and donned the *travesti* of hypergender, so that their self-policing performance of femininity validated Putin's increasingly unpoliced and toxic masculinity.

Is This Kiss Really Off the Record?

I call Liudmila Putina "the presidential wife" and not the Russian Federation's first lady, since the institution of the first lady so beloved in American politics never took root in the Soviet Union or post-Soviet Russia. The spouses of Soviet and Russian leaders have played a negligible public role in comparison to their American counterparts, if they play one at all. Only a single leader's wife—Raisa Gorbacheva—tried to follow the example of American first ladies by reproducing the image of helpmate, confidante, and human-rights advocate familiar in the West. However, the majority of the Russian press and public found Gorbacheva's activism, as well as her presence by the side of her husband, Mikhail Gorbachev, off-putting and did not embrace her with the same affection as her American and European fans. On the other end of the spectrum, Naina Yeltsina attended so few events with the Russian Federation's first president that her most notable public appearance took place at his 2007 state funeral when Boris Yeltsin was already in his coffin. Yeltsina most significant contributions to the public sphere were her two tabloid-worthy daughters, and her refusal to continue Gorbacheva's attempt to emulate America's first ladies made Yeltsina more popular at home than abroad. In other words, much as Putin himself was a tabula rasa when he became president in 1999, so was the role of presidential spouse a more or less blank slate awaiting Liudmila Putina.

Moreover, journalists who tried, when the Putins first entered the presidential limelight, to dig up dirt about Liudmila's youth found that "her life before the inauguration had been 'removed' from the archives: documents were confiscated from where she had worked and studied."[19] In spite of the public's interest in the Putins, journalists discovered that they were all but sequestered from the media. Consequently, what little information we do have about Liudmila Putina has less to do with her actual person than the style of femininity that her husband's handlers decided would complement and enhance his own hypermasculine image. This information recycles well-worn stereotypes about Russian women, repackaging them so that Putina quickly became a feminine foil for Russia's black-belt, alpine-skiing, no-nonsense leader in the early 2000s. Whether in presidential biographies, journalism, or the fictionalized biopic *This Kiss Is Off the Record*, Putina's Kremlin-constructed image during her husband's first two terms as president provided a blueprint for acceptable femininity that also functioned as a thinly veiled allegory for exemplary citizenship.

Putina's official biography reads like a study in mundane clichés: A happy girl with an angelic demeanor, little Liuda was always at the top of her class in school, expressed her desire to start a family at an early age, and became an Aeroflot stewardess upon graduation. After an appropriately long courtship, she married a man whose successful career allowed her to become a housewife, bearing him two happy and adoring daughters. Putina's only forays into professional life came at her husband's behest, which led her into the suitably feminine career of teaching. Only three facts spice up Putina's otherwise bland biography. First, her husband's successful career was, after all, in the KGB, allowing them to live briefly abroad in East Germany. Second, she suffered a near-fatal car accident in her mid-forties, from which she was saved by her husband's undying love and highly placed medical connections. And third, her husband became the second president of the Russian Federation. These departures from an otherwise humdrum story depict Putina as a Russian everywoman swept off her feet by a knight in shining presidential armor, who transformed her into the Kremlin's fairy-tale princess.[20]

Perhaps more important, the rhetoric surrounding Putina in the early 2000s stressed that this Russian everywoman took more interest in home, hearth, and fashion than in her husband's career as his country's president. She was typically described as "very domestic. . . . A real woman, who can stay up all night and entertain guests, as well as tidy up the apartment and cook everything the next morning," not to mention a devoted wife and mother.[21] Putina's emblematic femininity excluded any interest whatsoever in her husband's work or in politics more generally. To one interviewer's question about the burden of being perpetually in the public eye, she answered, "As far as clothes are concerned, it's even nice. It's always nice for a woman to dress up. It's another thing altogether that politics themselves have never interested me. Now that's boring."[22] The interview continues to discuss Putina's choice of skirts over pants, clothing designers, hairdressers, and vacation spots, demonstrating the type of good taste that would eventually become Putin-era *glamur* and, at the same time, drawing a hard line between fitting feminine concerns and the masculine realm of politics. In addition to her preference for Escada over affairs of state, Putina plainly stated, "I am not a feminist, but I'd like for women to occupy a worthy place in the world."[23] Apparently, this "worthy place" is at home with children, since Putina also opined that "woman is intended by nature to give birth and to raise children. And as they say, you can't go against nature."[24] Although such declarations might have sounded downright antifeminist to audiences outside Russia, they conveyed the specifically post-Soviet contours of Russian postfeminism, which, in the 1990s, rejected women's labor outside the home as an unwanted legacy of the Soviet era's state-mandated gender parity.

Rather than balk, the Russian public that consumed Putina's postfeminist soundbites after 1999 found them reassuring, as a popular biographer of the presidential couple describes:

> when the details of [Putin's] personal life became known, we were relieved to learn that everything in his family life was just as it ought to be. His wife, an attractive woman with a typical Slavic appearance and figure, never interferes in her husband's affairs, doesn't try to influence state decisions, as Raisa [Gorbacheva] or members of the Yeltsin family once did. No, Liudmila Putina, unlike them, sits at home, creates domestic comfort and a safe refuge for her husband and raises their daughters. And she raises them excellently—their daughters study diligently, learn languages, and never find themselves in dubious situations, as the children of leaders of other countries and highly placed political figures often do.[25]

Putina's status as a "Slavic" woman served several purposes when her husband first rose to power. First, the reference to her "typical Slavic appearance and figure," which included blond hair and blue eyes, signaled the nascent racialization of citizenship in the Russian Federation, which gradually became more ethnically Russian and white in the coming years. Second, Putina's supposedly "Slavic" behavior placed the "natural" concerns and activities of women outside the masculine sphere of politics. Third and perhaps most important, the image of Putina as a stay-at-home wife and mother bolstered the Kremlin's pro-Russian, pro-family, and pronatalist policies.

The ultimate significance of Putina's tightly controlled image comes into even clearer focus once we shift from the presumed facts of her life to the only feature film to fictionalize the presidential couple. The director Ol'ga Zhulina's made-for-DVD movie *This Kiss Is Off the Record* was shot between 2001 and 2003 but premiered on Valentine's Day of 2008, two weeks before the national elections that placed Dmitrii Medvedev, Putin's handpicked successor, in the office of president.[26] The film's shoestring budget, cast of no-name, small-screen actors, and soundtrack, which imitated "an orchestral performance by a synthesizer," all place it squarely in the category of the B movie.[27] Although Zhulina and the producer Anatolii Voropaev denied that *This Kiss Is Off the Record* depicts Russia's first couple when the film appeared, anyone familiar with the presidential biography immediately identified its leading characters, Aleksandr and Tat'iana Platov, as Vladimir and Liudmila Putin, particularly since the fictional Platovs bear the surname Putin used when attending the KGB's espionage academy in the mid-1980s.[28] The claim of the film's creators to have adapted the genre of the fictional presidential biopic (e.g., Rob Reiner's 1995 *The American President*) seems equally disingenuous. As one critic stated, *The Kiss Is Off the Record* is more of a "fairy tale for women," that is, a chick flick, whose melodrama conveys the sacrifice, struggles, and joys of a woman who stands by her man.[29] The movie was universally panned by Russian critics, one of whom described it as "made of foam rubber," while Western journalists had a brief field day with the fact that the film made Putin into the Russian Federation's romantic lead.[30]

In addition to fictionalizing canned moments from the Putins' biography, *This Kiss Is Off the Record* forges an unexpected link between Tania Platova and one of nineteenth-century Russian literature's iconic female characters. The film begins as Platova drives her elder daughter home from school and listens as she complains about the poor grade she received on a school composition about Tat'iana Larina, the heroine of Alexander Pushkin's novel in verse *Evgenii Onegin*. As our Tania navigates the streets of St. Petersburg, she chastises her daughter for arguing that Pushkin's Tat'iana, contrary to the novel's plot, should have abandoned her much older husband for the young and handsome Onegin, her first love. The viewer learns that our Tania prefers the novel's actual ending, in which the heroine rejects Onegin, famously saying, "I've become another's wife—/and I'll be true to him, for life."[31] We then discover that our Tania has the tremendous luck, unlike Pushkin's, to have married her first love, and the conversation in the car is suddenly cut short as we witness a reenactment of the devastating car crash that almost crippled the real-life Liudmila Putina. By introducing Pushkin's Tat'iana in this opening scene, *This Kiss Is Off the Record* suggests a parallel between the presidential spouse, both fictional and real, and a literary heroine whom Dostoevsky famously called "the apotheosis of Russian womanhood."[32] Although the comparison among Liudmila Putina, Tania Platova, and Tat'iana Larina quickly breaks down, it nonetheless suggests that the job of the Russian Federation's presidential wife is to be a post-Soviet apotheosis of Russian womanhood, whose key psychological trait is self-denial of one's deepest desires for the sake of marital fidelity and social conformity.

Slightly later, *This Kiss Is Off the Record* returns to *Evgenii Onegin* to offer a bluntly literal interpretation of perhaps the novel's most elusive metaphor. Rather than explore the metaphysical and narrative implications of the trope of life's novel from *Evgenii Onegin*'s final stanza, the film depicts Pushkin's work as a sort of Russian bible, which all good citizens should memorize and use as a guide to behavior. We first encounter this lesson when our Tania, now teaching literature at a school in East Germany, encounters a willful student by the name of Uspenskii, who refuses to recite Tat'iana's letter to Onegin, claiming that this passage of the novel is "for girls" and that he, as a boy, should recite Onegin's letter to Tat'iana instead. Teacher Tania invites Uspensky to go ahead and do so, but he retorts that she did not assign this later section of the novel and asks whether any of the school's teachers have themselves memorized *Evgenii Onegin*. Without missing a beat, Tania calmly states that she knows the entire book by heart, and the doubting Uspensky challenges her to complete any passage he might quote. He begins with *Evgenii Onegin*'s famous opening quatrain, which Tania finishes without hesitation; however, she cleverly changes the title character's description of boredom by his uncle's sickbed into her own boredom with teaching lazy boys. At the very least, Tania's deep knowledge of *Evgenii Onegin* offers her a clever way to scold a cheeky student, and the scene ends when the chastened Uspenskii returns to his seat.

As it turns out, our Tania's lesson did not fall on deaf ears, and the willful Uspenskii resurfaces later in *This Kiss Is Off the Record* to confirm the ability of Pushkin's novel in verse not merely to guide but even to save the lives of those who internalize its precepts. Once the Platovs move to Moscow, Tania joins her husband on a holiday trip to visit troops in war-torn Chechnya, where she once again encounters Uspenskii. No longer the class clown but a senior lieutenant in the army, Uspenskii immediately recognizes his former teacher and tells her that he not only read but actually memorized *Evgenii Onegin* on her advice. Moreover, he taught the soldiers under his command to do the same, and Tania briefly reenacts the recitation competition first instigated by Uspensky in school with his troops in the theater of war. In addition to bringing the uniformed men and Tania together, the competition causes a short delay in the Platovs' journey to the next military encampment, preventing terrorists who mined their route from destroying the Platovs' entourage. Knowing *Evgenii Onegin* by heart saves the lives of the Russian soldiers, our heroine Tania, and her soon-to-be-president husband, illustrating the reward that comes to those who internalize Tat'iana Larina's lesson of self-sacrifice, loyalty, and obedience.

Like any chick flick, *This Kiss Is Off the Record* has many more scenes in which the film's characters are rewarded for sacrificing their own feelings and desires to those of husband, family, or country. Perhaps the most obvious of these occurs when Tania Platova miraculously walks for the first time after the fateful car accident. Having undergone a delicate operation and lain in hospital for months, Tania clearly suffers from both physical and psychological trauma. Neither her husband's pleas nor his imminent departure brings Tania to her feet. However, the moment she overhears the word "psychologist" in a conversation between her husband and doctor, Tania pulls herself from bed, lurches to her feet, and joins the two men so that she can assure them that "A psychologist isn't necessary." By denying her physical and psychological pain, Tania earns both the ability to walk and the approval of her husband and her doctor. This lesson of affirmation through denial takes on global significance in the film's penultimate scene, which also provides its title. Immediately after kissing Tania to thank her for speaking eloquently on his behalf at a press conference, now President Platov pronounces the phrase, "This kiss is off the record," as cameras flash and journalists record their kiss for a worldwide audience. As distant as this corny cinematic joke is from Tania's first troubled steps after the accident, both scenes capture the basic message that *This Kiss Is Off the Record* takes from *Evgenii Onegin*: the good wife, soldier, journalist, and citizen should sacrifice their desires and feelings for their president, who in turn promises to love and protect them.

Although this type of message is nothing new for movies on the Lifetime and Hallmark Channels, *This Kiss Is Off the Record* tells a slightly different story thanks to its Russian packaging, which combines post-Soviet presidential power with a reading of *Evgenii Onegin* so simplistic that it makes CliffNotes look sophisticated. Not only does this packaging deliver a specifically post-Soviet postfeminism for the film's Russian audience, but it also encourages viewers to understand the story of Tania's self-denial and affirmation more broadly as an allegory of how Russians should constitute their political selves. Viewers are invited to understand the Platov/Putin family through the longstanding analogy that maps the nuclear or "little family" onto the "great family" of the state. This trope has deep roots, as seen in the pre-Revolutionary term *tsar' batiushka* (tsar father) and the Soviet-era slogan that proclaimed Stalin *otets narodov* (the father of peoples). As such paternal terminology suggests, most studies of the Stalinist myth of the "great family" focus on filial ties between the head of state, figured as a father, and citizens, seen as sons.[33]

Figure 12. Aleksandr and Tat'iana Platov pose for the press in Ol'ga Zhulina's *This Kiss Is Off the Record* (2008).

However, *This Kiss Is Off the Record* shifts the link connecting the "little" and the "great" families from filial devotion between fathers and sons to conjugal fidelity between husband and wife.

Liudmila Putina herself made at least one remark, on the occasion of International Children's Day, linking the "little family" to the "great family" in Russia: "For a child, a good family is the same thing as good government."[34] With this connection in mind, we can interpret Putina's description of the presidential household, in which "the husband is the breadwinner and defender, [and] the wife is the preserver of the hearth," as well as her repeated references to her husband's "reliability" and her own "security," more broadly.[35] The sharp separation between masculine and feminine attributes, interests, activities, and even desires in the Putins' marriage described the Kremlin's vision of the relationship between Russia's leader and its citizens after Putin rose to power. While the president ventured into the public realm of politics to provide for and defend the country, citizens should occupy their "worthy place" by keeping Russia's home fires burning, rearing the next generation of children, and asking no questions in or of the political realm entrusted to Putin. When viewed from this perspective, many of Putina's statements about her husband sound like slogans from his election campaigns, for example, "with him it's possible to build a life together and not fear the consequences," or "I've always somehow believed in him."[36] In retrospect, the Russian media's remarks about the Putins' marital stability in the early 2000s were little more than a reassuring depiction, albeit on a smaller scale, of the much-vaunted economic stability, which, according to pollsters, kept Russian voters casting ballots for Putin and led them in 2020 to ratify changes in the Russian constitution with the effect of erasing term limits for his presidency. The rhetoric of Putina's public image in early presidential biographies and in *This Kiss Is Off the Record* allows us to recognize her refusal of political savvy in favor of tasteful feminine style as a call for Russia's citizens to abandon political activism and abrogate political agency in exchange for domestic stability.

Whether in the guise of Tania Platova or Liudmila Putina, the presidential wife represented the apotheosis not merely of Russian womanhood but, more disturbing, of Russian citizenship in the early 2000s. However, Putina's utility as the presidential wife had a short shelf life. In June 2013, a year after Putin began his third term in office, the presidential couple gave a clearly staged interview after attending a performance of the ballet *Esmerelda*, in which they announced their "civilized divorce."[37] In the years after, Putin bolstered his masculine image not by having a middle-aged wife standing faithfully by his side but rather through unconfirmed rumors of liaisons with significantly younger women. At the top of the list was the former Olympic gymnast Alina Kabaeva, who, according to the tabloids, gave Putin as many as four children.[38] Evidently, being cast aside by the man to whom she swore to be true for life represented the ultimate sacrifice required of Liudmila Putina's apotheosis of Russian womanhood and citizenship.

How to Become a Bitch

Even though the model of subservient femininity embodied by Liudmila Putina might have spoken to older Russian women reared in the Soviet Union, it held limited appeal for a younger generation brought up after 1991 and hoping to benefit from the economic boom of the 2000s. Rather than hearken back to Tat'iana Larina's nineteenth-century loyalty and self-sacrifice, many young women in Putin's Russia developed twenty-first-century desires for personal autonomy and economic independence. The country's burgeoning self-help industry did its best to support these aspirations, generating a glut of books, websites, and trainings that promised to teach women how to master their own lives and create their own happiness. Among the many trends instructing women in seduction, marriage, child-rearing, career-building, and female power, one stood out for its clear rejection of the "good girl" model represented by Putina: *stervologiia*, or bitchology. Whether in books or how-to lessons, bitchology touted an apotheosis of womanhood that was frankly self-centered, manipulative, and "bad." However, even though the bitch's own womanly yearnings came front and center, her femininity accommodated and internalized the needs of men.

The founder and evangelist of bitchology is Evgeniia Shatskaia, a pseudonym under which more than twenty-five books have appeared since 2002.[39] As Adamson and Salmenniemi point out in their study of how self-help literature domesticated postfeminism in Russia, Shatskaia's books illustrate "that the task of becoming a valuable feminine subject involves a large amount of labour" on one's personality, femininity, and sexuality.[40] Rather than catalog the myriad techniques needed to transform a plain Jane into a bitch—a task that promises, due to Shatskaia's hefty oeuvre, to be no less laborious than accruing value as a feminine subject—I prefer to focus on the word *sterva* or bitch, under which she gathers all of the clever advice and pithy aphorisms she has sold to Russian women for more than two decades. Luckily, discovering what this word means for Shatskaia does not require poring over the thousands of pages that she has published, since she happily includes such information in the free book teasers offered on websites hawking her wares.[41]

Like any good researcher, Shatskaia begins her explanation of what a bitch is with the word's etymology. She acknowledges that the Russian word *sterva* initially described carrion but quickly came to designate "a wife who perpetually nags her husband, tramples on his self-esteem, and humiliates him at the slightest opportunity."[42] She then notes a second semantic shift during the 1990s, which revealed that Russia's men were less adaptable than its women, who used any and all of their resources, including sex and lies, to get what they wanted. As Shatskaia explains, the 1990s marked a tipping point for femininity: "The character traits of women traditionally seen as positive—softness, kindness, modesty, etc.—suddenly turned out to be almost synonymous with 'stupidity' and an inability to stand up for oneself."[43] As a result, the word "bitch" lost its negative associations and came to represent a positive description of "a woman who uses everything nature has given her as a woman and acts like a real woman so that she achieves her goals assertively, or as we say, like a man."[44] More specifically, Shatskaia explains that a bitch is "any woman who follows (explicitly or implicitly, willingly or not) a masculine line of behavior based on struggle, competition, the need to dominate, and a marked desire to achieve one's set goal by whatever means necessary."[45] Shatskaia's bitch is little more than a postfeminist take on post-Soviet *travesti*, since the *sterva* hides desires traditionally considered masculine in a female body groomed and dressed to hyperfeminine perfection.

At times, Shatskaia's use of the term "bitch" hints at a nascent feminism, for example, when she claims, "all great women were bitches. How many nameless 'hens' have faded into oblivion simply as 'incubators' of healthy offspring. . . .

Is woman a mother or just a female? a full-fledged citizen or just a 'womb' for bearing new members of society?"[46] Shatskaia even admits the historical and cultural factors that shape our perception of "natural" sexual difference.[47] Yet, like so many Russian women, including Putina, Shatskaia rejects both feminism and women's emancipation, which, she concludes, was "artificially imposed" and led to "the masculinization of the fairer sex."[48] She then gives her own take on Russia's crisis of masculinity, as well as its solution: "I don't need men's rights and responsibilities. I want to remain a woman. It's good that we have equal rights with men. Equal, but not THE SAME. When we copy men, we make them infantile and like us; we switch roles with them, and then we ourselves blow smoke up to the ceiling, put our hands in our pant pockets, and reproach them for their weakness and being 'faggotized.' In my opinion, it's much more enticing to have a bitchy dish of strawberries and cream filled with 'male' brains (which are actually normal female brains)."[49] The homophobia and mixed metaphors in this passage effectively capture the incoherent fusion of gender essentialism and performativity that makes Shatskaia's bitch into a taming not of the shrew but of the femme fatale, whom theorists typically describe as a projection of male fantasies and fears.[50] Shatskaia herself admits as much when she describes bitches as "similar to men in their mindset," since they "have seen through men [and] begun to think like them."[51] However, Shatskaia's most provocative nod to the fact that the bitch's subjectivity is split—not only between essentialism and constructivism but also between male and female—comes in an epigraph that paraphrases Simone de Beauvoir yet claims to come from Syl'via Chiz, a supposed Belgian journalist who, as far as I can tell, exists only in the RuNet: "One is not born, but rather becomes, a bitch."[52]

The split subjectivity of the bitch, who for Shatskaia represents "the most biologically perfect species of the weaker sex," lays claim to a fully feminine desire whose unrelenting object is men.[53] Although Shatskaia urges her readers to begin their path to bitchiness by loving themselves, she acknowledges that self-love is not an end in and of itself but rather the means to learning "how to attract and hold on to the best men."[54] She celebrates the fact that "bitches are inseparable from men," as well as men's soul-felt knowledge that "the bitch is a result of a lengthy genetic mutation designed to conquer any man in any situation. The bitch is a cyborg or universal soldier (if we bring sci-fi to our aid) in whom all of the experience accumulated by women in the course of human history, all of their experience dealing with men, has been placed."[55] As Adamson and Salmenniemi point out, the "hard labor and work on oneself" that Shatsksaia prescribes for the aspiring bitch lead not to independence but rather to "a life mediated through men."[56]

To complement Shatskaia's guidance in print, a thriving industry of bitchology training emerged across the Russian Federation, as the filmmaker Alina Rudnitskaya documents in her 2008 short *How to Become a Bitch*.[57] Rather than merely describe, Rudnitskaya shows the techniques that turn a miserable, loveless girl into "a sexy, sly, strong woman who [can] influence men [and] manipulate them in order to get what she wants."[58] More specifically, *How to Become a Bitch* documents training sessions taught by the psychologist Vladimir Rakovskii, who, in addition to charging women about $100 per day for bitchology instruction in the late 2000s, also authored the 2018 self-help book *Women on the Brink* and runs training centers in Petersburg and Moscow. Rudnitskaya's film shows Rakovskii and his wife working in tandem to teach students skills like erotic dancing, taking on either *poshlost'* or *glamur* according to a man's taste, and wheedling money from a man. In one of the film's opening scenes, Rakovskii's students state their reasons for attending his training: they want to attract and seduce men, to marry a good man and preferably an oligarch, and even, as one says, to "rape" a man "without him realizing that he was raped."

As is the case with this unapologetic desire to sexually assault another person, several scenes in *How to Become a Bitch* make most viewers squirm in their seats. At multiple points in the film, Rakovskii's students strip down to black bras, panties, and thigh-high stockings, so that they can either practice an overtly *poshlyi* form of "dirty dancing" with each other or fellate a banana while Joe Cocker's "You Can Leave Your Hat On" plays in the background. However, even more squirm-inducing is Rakovskii's pedagogy of fear and humiliation, which strips down students' psyches so that they can be rebuilt as bitches. Rakovskii repeatedly singles out a vulnerable student, forces her to share her deepest fear, and then shames her before the group. The clearest example of this teaching method occurs early in the film, when Rakovskii asks a student named Lena to stop thinking and to free-associate with the word "sex." However, Lena fails to respond as her teacher wants and breaks down in tears. When he asks why she is crying, Lena whimpers, "I don't even know what I want, how I want [Rakovskii then prompts: and whether I want] and whether I want and whether I even need all of this." Having alienated Lena from her own desire, Rakovskii then states that a mother shouldn't tell her daughter to work hard and be a good girl but rather should instruct her to do whatever boys like so that she never has to work a day in her life. Rakovskii's inculcation of bitchology through shame quickly embeds Shatskaia's male mindset in Lena and the other students, and it also divests the film's many scenes of scantily clad women embracing and kissing each other of whatever homoerotism they might have. The closer his students' outward appearance and behavior come to the bitch's hyperfeminine ideal, the more deeply embedded in their psyches is masculine desire and a "self-policing, narcissistic gaze."

Those students who effectively replace their own desires with those of men earn Rakovskii's praise, as we see in one of the film's final scenes. After one woman, whose man demands that she adopt a punk-leather *poshlost'*, tells the tale of how she got money out of him for an expensive skirt, bent over as if to thank him with sex but ultimately left him high and dry, Rakovskii responds with an approving, "That's beautiful, beautiful. Do you see? In essence, we're teaching you how to control your men, and men more generally, so that they want, love, respect, and value you." However, the bitch academy's final lesson reveals that no amount of begging or bending over ever truly fools a man. After telling his students that the best place to find a man is on the job, Rakovskii warns them that "men are really not that stupid. And the biggest trick is that men understand everything, absolutely everything. And they'll guess about everything. Everything that you do to them they already know by heart. It's impossible to deceive men." In an interview about *How to Become a Bitch*, Rudnitskaya called the sexpot wiles taught during Rakovskii's training "a kind of Russian feminism."[59] More accurately, Shatskaia and Rakovskii's bitchology created a postfeminist *travesti* that not only transformed their students into shining examples of hypergendered charisma, camp, kitsch, *poshlost'*, and *glamur* all at the same time but also refurbished their psyches through a *stiob* of masculine desire.

The bitchology first preached by Shatskaia in the early 2000s spread in years after.[60] A spate of articles and books promising to transform their female readers into bitches came in Shatskaia's wake, and a number of life coaches like Rakovskii make their living instructing women in bitchology either in person or online. Shatskaia herself demonstrated the expansive potential of bitchology by branching into Orientalist pop sexology with *Geisha School: The Wisdom of the East for Today's Woman*, a 2006 book coauthored with Eliza Tanaka.[61] At the same time that bitchology became a cash cow for Russia's self-help industry, the word *sterva* gained common currency in popular culture. Once considered unspeakable in polite company, *Sterva* is now the name of a low-budget melodrama from 2009 and at least seven different pop songs released in the late 2010s and early 2020s.[62] In all of these examples, the bitch elicits just as much hate as love, driving men crazy with her sex appeal and bad behavior as these songs' penchant for rhyming the word *sterva* (bitch) with *nerv* (nerve) suggests. Now fixtures in Russia's popular imagination, the bitch and bitchology vividly illustrate postfeminism's false promise of unfettered feminine subjectivity, as well as the profound ambivalence provoked by women's desire even when mediated by men.

Fifty Shades of Russian Grey

While *stervologiia* preaches the benefits of becoming a bossy bitch, the virtues of becoming a submissive bottom come to light once we turn to popular romance published in the 2010s. Typically called "novels about love" or "women's novels" in Russian, the genre includes translations from English of bestselling authors like Nora Roberts and Danielle Steele, as well as original works by less lucrative local writers.[63] Perhaps the clearest example of postfeminism in popular romance appeared in a literary domestication penned by Alisa Klever (pseudonym of Tat'iana Vendenskaia) of E. L. James's internationally successful *Fifty Shades of Grey* trilogy.[64] On the covers of Klever's three books—titled *Two Months and Three Days*, *The Four Ends of the Earth*, and *The Fifteenth Paradise*—we discover that she has written "the Russian *Fifty Shades of Grey*," which "gives us the real Russian view of love in all of its manifestations."[65] Despite its obvious debt to James's BDSM publishing juggernaut, Klever's trilogy is a uniquely Russian product, whose smorgasbord of "nontraditional" sex practices intertwines bodies, emotions, consumption, and citizenship. In the end, the mild bondage, dominance, and submission in Klever's books provide yet one more iteration of the postfeminist sensibility, in which women's willing submission to a dominant man leads not only to their deeply satisfying orgasms but also to another way around Russia's crisis of masculinity.

Klever's adaptation of *Fifty Shades* to a Russian readership preserves key elements of E. L. James's original, such as its three-part structure, experimentation with BDSM, love between a fabulously wealthy man of the world and a virginal ingénue, and wedded, procreative bliss by the final page. Yet Klever takes liberties with the *Fifty Shades* formula, adding depth to her work in the process. In addition to replacing James's repetitive first-person narrator with selectively omniscient third-person narration, Klever creates a heroine whose name, identity, and experiences are unmistakably Russian. In place of James's Anastasia Steele, a senior English major who breaks into publishing with the help of her billionaire boyfriend, Klever's Arina Krylova is an aspiring veterinary student who lives on her own in Moscow, far away from the rural farm where she grew up. As *Two Months and Three Days* begins, Arina diligently studies veterinary science by day and works in an animal clinic by night, barely making ends meet.

In comparison to Anastasia Steele, Arina's vulnerability and loneliness prove especially striking once we consider her best friend and roommate, Nellie. Rather than provide expensive clothes, helpful dating advice, or a loving shoulder to cry on, "Nellie never liked Arina. There was something elusive that always infuriated Nellie, that provoked her desire to throw a glass at Arina."[66] As we discover in the course of Klever's trilogy, that elusive something is Arina's moral backbone, which represents a reproach to the mercenary *sterva* Nellie. In fact, Arina's best friend typically runs her out of the house whenever "boyfriends" show up looking for sex in exchange for gifts and money. In the most grueling depiction of sex in all three books, Nellie has a degrading ménage à trois with two such "boyfriends." In the process, Nellie realizes that "she is a prostitute. An utter prostitute," and shortly afterward she betrays Arina to the trilogy's villain, who subsequently tortures and rapes Nellie.[67] Arina's BFF is a far cry from the squeaky-clean Kate Kavanagh of *Fifty Shades*, whose only bad feelings toward Anastasia Steele take the form of briefly envying her billionaire boyfriend. Even though Klever's heroine has the same positive traits as James's—ambition, stick-to-itiveness, virginity, naïve beauty, and a belief in true love—Arina Krylova inhabits a lonelier and more dangerous environment than her *Fifty Shades* counterpart and has no real allies at the start of the Russian trilogy.

If Klever increases her heroine's independence and vulnerability, she decreases those of her hero, Maksim Korshunov, in comparison to *Fifty Shades*' Christian Grey. Like Christian, Maksim is a stunningly attractive, unfailingly erect "grey-eyed devil," ever attentive to his girlfriend's feelings, needs, and desires.[68] However, Maksim is not a self-made man but a professional photographer, whose edgy art and kinky lifestyle are financed by his oligarch father, Konstantin Korshunov, who as the novel's villain places multiple, life-threatening impediments in Maksim and Arina's way. Most of these obstacles arise from trauma inflicted on Maksim during childhood. In addition to hiring a surrogate to produce his heir and thereby depriving Maksim of a mother's love, the elder Korshunov scarred his young son by exposing him to actual sadism. Adding insult to injury, Konstantin Korshunov alienated his son from Russia by sending him to a posh British boarding school, where he all but forgot his native tongue, and virtually imprisoning him once he returned to Moscow: "[Maksim] lived [in Russia] from twelve to eighteen years old, but he spent these years beneath the scrutiny of his father's gaze, escorted to and from a private high school by two bodyguards. All that he saw in Russia were the malicious, unsmiling faces of servants and the insane things that his father clumsily hid from him and that Maksim preferred not to remember. Women screaming in pain. The loud sounds of music whose rhythm coincided with the sounds of a whip flying up and down."[69] This traumatic childhood deprives Maksim of both love and a homeland, representing a shift in the cause of the hero's emotional damage from *Fifty Shades*' crack-addicted mother to a psychopathic father. By making Maksim's father entirely responsible for both the child abandonment and sadism that James splits between Christian's mother and her pimp, Klever combines a Cinderella story with Beauty and the

Beast and introduces Russian overtones into the *Fifty Shades* formula. Much as Christian does for Anastasia, Maksim realizes all of Arina's fantasies: he gives her an overseas passport and her first orgasm, takes her virginity, finances her first trip abroad to experience the seductive perversions of the West, furnishes a luxurious apartment in Moscow for her, makes her pregnant, and proposes marriage. However, how Maksim does all of this, unlike his sexual advances, rubs Arina the wrong way, not only because he abridges her independence but also because where they end up and what he does feel distinctly un-Russian.

The national coloring of Klever's leading characters has profound implications for the basic plot she borrows from *Fifty Shades*. By bringing an authentically Russian girl from the provinces together with a man of dubious birthright, Klever separates the supposedly natural dominance of Russian men over women from forms of submission unnatural to Russia, as we see in the couple's first sexual encounters. Arina's lack of sophistication and naïveté attract the glamorous Maksim, encouraging him to imagine that this "real Russian beauty" is in fact a living, breathing Snow White.[70] The fairy-tale comparison motivates Maksim to arrange a photo shoot in which Arina enacts his BDSM fantasy inspired by the Disney heroine. In an impulse comparable to Nellie's desire "to throw a glass at Arina," Maksim tells her, "You have something elusive, something rare. I'd like to draw you. I'd like to possess you. To screw you."[71] Once Arina agrees, despite her better judgment, Maksim dictates every detail of the photo shoot, demanding her obedience to his every whim as both man and artist. In the process, "she became a woman, he made her a woman," and Arina discovers how "she truly liked the sensation of his power over her body," since Maksim "holds her in the sweetest captivity of which [she] could only dream."[72] The sex they have teaches Arina the joys of feminine submission, but the photo shoot does exactly the opposite. After costuming Arina as Snow White, Maksim throws her on the floor, covers her with blood, and then places her in a cage, making her the victim of his "somehow strange, crazy, and perverted sense of beauty."[73] As the shoot reaches its climax, Arina realizes that she has been forced to represent "annihilated innocence" and that the objectification of Maksim's camera lens, unlike his sexual objectification, has reduced her to "a thing."[74] Maksim's masculine dominance reads as natural and highly arousing in the bedroom. However, the same dominance appears perverse and dampens desire in the setting of the photo shoot, which places the Russian Arina inside a Hollywood interpretation of a German fairy tale that Maksim has recreated beyond the borders of Russia in Berlin.

In the wake of the photo shoot, Arina submits fully to Maksim's lust, yet she refuses any further victimization to his dark artistic vision and traumatic past.

When he tries to draw her deeper into the subculture of sexual dominance and submission by taking Arina to an exclusive British sex club, she recoils at the sight of a woman being auctioned as a slave and recognizes the narcotic potential of the sexual pleasure offered by BDSM.[75] At the end of the first book in Klever's trilogy, this revelation drives Arina to flee "Maksim Korshunov, son of an oligarch, photographer, the most handsome and most monstrous man in the world, who wants to own her like a thing."[76] Arina refuses the visible pleasure of the highly theatrical slave auction she witnesses. Instead, she opts for true love and self-determination, asserting, "I'm a free person with a free will."[77] Much as Anastasia Steele does with Christian Grey, Arina ultimately tames "the inhuman cruelty of the Korshunovs" in the second book of Klever's trilogy.[78] By rejecting Maksim's desire to dominate her and giving him the healing love he needs, Arina effectively repatriates him to Russia, which "had never been home for Maksim."[79] If he makes Arina "feel like a real woman," then she remedies his predicament of being "Russian by blood [but] a foreigner due to his alien essence," transforming Maksim into a real Russian man.[80] This ability to effect her lover's homecoming suggests that the provincial Arina possesses an authentically Russian soul, which Maksim, a pampered child of ill-gotten wealth, must repeatedly penetrate and impregnate to make his own.

The sometimes humorous clashes between our hero and our heroine's backgrounds support this interpretation of their evolving relationship. In one particularly funny scene, Maksim pursues Arina, who takes refuge at her parents' farm in the Russian countryside after the shocking slave auction. Convinced he cannot live without her, Maksim races toward Arina in his red Porsche Turbo, but his quest is slowed by a Moscow traffic jam and then grinds to a halt when he finds himself outside GPS range and spinning his car's wheels in a muddy field. The Russian provinces unman Maksim's German-made sports car, and their victory is attenuated only when Maksim finds Arina, brings her to multiple orgasms in her parents' barn, and then watches her help a mare give birth to a baby foal. In correspondence with me, Klever noted the serious message underlying this episode's humor: "for Russia, Moscow is a separate universe cut off from the rest of the country in many different ways. . . . The issue of 'the total rupture' between the elite and the real Russia is very widespread here among us."[81] As Klever's comment suggests, we can view the repatriation of the elite Muscovite Maksim through sex with Arina, an authentically Russian woman from the provinces, as a symbolic bridging of the socioeconomic gap that separates Russia's capital city from the countryside.

The patriotic undercurrent in Arina and Maksim's romance contributes to the dramatic difference in how and what BDSM signifies in Klever's trilogy when compared to *Fifty Shades*. Whereas James circumscribes her trilogy's "kinky fuckery" within a limited circle of bondage, spanking, and sex toys, Klever expands these by including a murder-mystery subplot that revolves around the genuinely sadistic Konstantin Korshunov. Rather than placing the psychopathic villain on the story's periphery as does James, Klever makes Maksim's father, whose cruel treatment of his son is matched by death-dealing sex practices, central to the drama around the two lovers. The nightmares that haunt Maksim from the very start of the trilogy represent traumatic memories of his father murdering a partner, whose refusal of a safe word and lack of "hard limits" in a BDSM scene led to her strangulation. In addition, these nightmares provide Arina with sufficient evidence to piece together the mystery of this woman's death, making Klever's subplot resemble Nordic noir detective fiction. The elder Korshunov's desire for control threatens the lives of all who come into contact with him, including Maksim, Arina, their unborn child, Arina's parents, and, most directly, Nellie. However, solving the mystery behind Maksim's nightmares allows Arina to draw a crucial distinction between her lover and his father: "If sadism for some is an impassioned, heady game, forbidden and enticing, but harmless and requiring mutual consent, then for [Konstantin] Korshunov, the entire point of the game was in making everything real."[82] Once she comes to this realization, Arina not only cures Maksim of his childhood trauma but also weans him of his more extreme BSDM practices in favor of gentler forms of sex.

The incorporation of a Nordic noir subplot represents Klever's most substantive innovation in the *Fifty Shades* formula, linking her trilogy to another work whose plot swirls around a sadistic psychopath: Balabanov's *Cargo 200*. Although Klever makes no explicit reference to the film, her trilogy picks up where Balabanov leaves off in its depiction of Konstantin Korshunov, a worthy companion for *Cargo 200*'s predatory Zhurov. True to the genre of romance, however, Klever's books argue that the intergenerational trauma depicted in Balanbanov's film can in fact be healed. Although Maksim seems likely to perpetuate his father's barbarous legacy in the first book of Klever's trilogy, the healing love offered by Arina in the second book, as well as her successful sleuthing in the third, brings the cycle of sadism to an end. The link connecting *Cargo 200* to Klever's books suggests that her BDSM, like the sadism in Balabanov's film, represents the larger violence that Putin's Russia inflicts on its own citizens and other countries. As Maksim asks himself, "Who needs handcuffs in the bedroom when the whole world fucks you 24/7 anyway?"[83]

This innovation in the *Fifty Shades* formula means that Arina and Maksim's BDSM repeatedly threatens to leave the sphere of safety for pain, addiction, and death, as was the case for the elder Korshunov and his murdered lover. To guarantee safety, Arina and Maksim try to separate their private BDSM from the larger social violence taking place in Russia's public sphere by domesticating their kinkier sex practices, as a scene from Klever's second book demonstrates. Maksim ties Arina up in the kitchen of their luxury condo as a prelude to sex, and he asks her whether she wants a safe word. She responds, "I don't need any kind of safe word," and Maksim then binds Arina's wrists with the ribbons that hold back the kitchen curtains, cuts her clothing off with kitchen shears, and covers her eyes with a dishtowel.[84] After some six pages of arousal, Arina finally loses control and in the moment of orgasm, "Arina cried out, and laughed, and writhed, restrained by the red ribbons, but in that very moment, she felt herself inexplicably free. As if the cage, in which she had sat her whole life suddenly fell to bits, allowing her to inhale with her whole chest. Lying in the arms of her powerful, strong man, Arina felt like a real woman. And it was wonderful."[85] Without Christian Grey's "red room of pain," Maksim and Arina use kitchen implements for their "kinky fuckery," finding eroticism in domesticity and freedom in constraint. Although Arina ran from the actual cage in which Maksim placed her for the photo shoot of Snow White, she discovers that submission during sex to "her powerful, strong man" frees her from the traumas of her own past, including her impoverished childhood in the countryside and her alcoholic father, which have held her in a psychic cage. In addition, her refusal of a safe word transforms Maksim and Arina's domesticated "kinky fuckery" into a form of edgeplay, whose blurring of hard limits of all types ultimately mirrors the lack of physical, psychological, and ethical boundaries in the Russian reality they seek to escape. After this scene, the phrase "no safe words" becomes the couple's loving refrain, and the trilogy ends with their sex life taking a final leap from BDSM, through the domestic, and into the virtual, when Maksim asks Arina to name her pleasure using a virtual reality headset as they fly off into the sunset on a private jet.[86]

Readers of Klever's trilogy ultimately reach a double-edged conclusion. On one hand, they learn, as Klever herself described in an email to me, that "in happiness and in love there aren't and can't be any 'norms.' Behind bedroom doors, all options are permissible as long as they make people happy."[87] On the other hand, the fictional world Arina and Maksim inhabit is modeled on Russian "society [that] imposes so-called traditional values rather harshly, not only in one's sex life, but in all other respects. . . . A conservative approach—that's Russia."[88] Although Klever's trilogy carves out space for Arina and Maksim's sexual autonomy, it depicts that space as highly circumscribed, largely protected by their exceptional wealth and *glamur*, and rapidly receding from reality into a virtual world constructed on board Maksim's private jet. The tension between these two readings suggests that Klever's trilogy presents another analogy for the feminine submission and masculine domination that characterize Putin's Russia. Although Arina preserves her free will, the most obvious lesson she learns is that "To be subject to [and] spread beneath the strong, powerful body of a man—this is a feeling that happens so rarely that you yearn for and want to experience again and again."[89] It takes little imagination to read Arina's statement as a description of the Russian populace's enthrallment with Vladimir Putin in the 2000s and 2010s or to see the sex that the dishtowel-bound Arina has with Maksim as what the nubile coeds of Putin's Army really wanted from their president. The postfeminist sensibility domesticated in Klever's trilogy not only reframes feminine desire as submission to a strong, powerful man but also claims to solve Russia's crisis of masculinity by revirilizing a generation of post-Soviet men deprived of their "natural" dominance.

Coming of Age in Putin's Russia

When taken together, Shatskaia's bitchology and Klever's kinky vision of feminine submission beg the question of how and when so many Russian women learned to subordinate their desires to those of men. One answer to this question lies in the different lessons that boys and girls learned as they came of age after Putin's rise to power. If Serebrennikov's *The Student* shows that others had to be martyred to turn boys into men, then we can see how girls became the necessary sacrificial lambs in Valeriia Gai Germanika's 2008 film *Everybody Dies but Me*.[90] The film depicts the point at which its three adolescent protagonists realize that girlhood's dreams of self-sufficiency and autonomy must yield to a woman's obligation to boyfriend, husband, and fatherland. Although Katia (Polina Filonenko), Zhanna (Agniia Kuznetsova), and Vika (Ol'ga Shuvalova) begin the film by rejecting traditional notions of feminine self-sacrifice, their path from childhood to the middle school disco leads to forms of loss that look suspiciously like martyrdom.[91] The three girls' futile stab at immortality in a world that threatens to kill them offers an achingly intimate account of female adolescence and exposes the incoherence of postfeminist subjectivity during Putin's first two decades as Russia's leader.

Everybody Dies but Me is a grueling watch that makes earlier cinematic depictions of Russian adolescence, for example, Stanislav Rostotskii's 1968 *We'll Live Til Monday* or Rolan Bykov's significantly bleaker *Scarecrow* from 1984, look like saccharine fables. Gai Germanika's film has roots in her 2005 documentary short, *Girls*, as well as a clear relation to her controversial 2010 television series, *School*.[92] The cinematography of all three works relies on the shaky closeups and unstable movement of a handheld camera, which gives *Everybody Dies but Me* such immediacy that few viewers can watch the film without empathizing with its protagonists. Critics discussing the film's coming-of-age story set in suburban Moscow typically comment on this vérité style, which makes "the border between authenticity and fiction almost indistinguishable."[93] Despite their agreement about the film's realism, those writing about *Everybody Dies but Me* do not agree on its meaning, claiming everything from hope springing eternal to utter hopelessness as the ultimate message of the film's grim story.[94]

Gai Germanika begins *Everybody Dies but Me* with a glimpse of the three girls' attempt to live in a world of their own making. Even before we read the film's title, we see the principal of Katia, Zhanna, and Vika's school announce the upcoming disco to their ninth-grade class. Immediately afterward, they meet in a field outside the school to bury the corpse of Zhanna's cat Tomik. Zhanna places the dead cat in a shallow grave and then pours two goldfish over the beloved pet, whom she hopes to "see again." The improvised funeral rite and ritual sacrifice convey the three girls' shared hopes and fears. The phrase "I want" initiates the conversation over Tomik's grave, articulating desires that are all either unrealized or unrealizable. Zhanna, for instance, wishes that Tomik's grave were deeper, that "the earth would sink and the soul fly away," and that "all grown-ups would die." The camera's tight focus on the girls' faces and interactions as they kneel by Tomik's resting place, hold one another, and playfully wrestle, conveys the trust of their three-way friendship. Their intimacy is reinforced when the girls get up and walk away, shoulder to shoulder, arm in arm, and Katia jokes, "We're just too small for this disco. Well, dammit, we'll die later."

In addition to preparing viewers for the film's title, the opening scene establishes the profound anxiety and ambivalence that Katia, Zhanna, and Vika share in the protected world they create. Their conversation careens from the reality of Tomik's death to aspirations for immortality, and although their gestures are aimed at one another, they direct their attention outward. Moreover, despite their obvious femininity—Zhanna has dyed streaks of her long brunette hair bright red; Vika wears a pink hoodie; and Katia sports gold earrings and a necklace—they display the traditionally masculine attributes of agency and autonomy within their universe. The uncertainty in the film's opening scene creates a palpable sense of the fragility of the private world constructed by the three girls, who repeatedly refer to Katia's abusive parents, Zhanna's indulgent mother, and the gang of brawling bullies in the background. As the camera cross-cuts between the girls' private ritual and the bullies' public fight, the burial of Tomik, a dead pussy, begins to look like a vain effort to deny the inevitable processes of puberty. Gai Germanika's initial depiction of adolescence as an androgynous and liminal state foreshadows the battleground of the disco, where the obligations of femininity, as well as the sacrifices of womanhood, vanquish childhood's hopes and dreams.

As much as the intimacy depicted in the opening scene of *Everybody Dies but Me* provides Katia, Zhanna, and Vika with support they lack elsewhere, their mutually constructed world contains the seeds of its own undoing. Shortly after the film's title, we see the girls back in school, as Zhanna struggles to solve a geometry problem on the blackboard. Rather than watch their friend's humiliation, Katia and Vika decide to help Zhanna: Katia writes the problem's solution on a slip of paper and then distracts the teacher so that Vika can roll the crumpled paper to Zhanna, who corrects her work on the board. Although the ruse allows Zhanna to earn an A on the assignment, Katia's inexplicable disruption prompts the teacher to fail her, causing her to storm out of the classroom. Not wanting to abandon their friend, Zhanna and Vika also leave the geometry class and join Katia in the stairwell, where they take an oath of loyalty. In addition to promising not to steal one another's boyfriends, they swear not to betray, to be faithful to, and to love each other, making them true friends "until we grow up."

The oath is tested that very evening when Katia sees the geometry teacher arrive at her parents' apartment, escapes through her bedroom window, and takes refuge with Zhanna. When Katia skips school the next day, Vika and Zhanna learn that they have become the talk of the school, since Katia's disappearance has forced their principal to cancel the disco. Although Katia, upon hearing the news, quietly returns to both her parents and school, she rightly intuits that Vika and Zhanna have placed their desire to go to the disco above her safety, violating their oath of the day before and driving a wedge into their friendship. Fearing Katia's status as a pariah, Zhanna and Vika decide to go to the disco without her, while the enraged Katia befriends another girl, whose homely appearance provides the cover she needs to escape her parents' hawkish watch, so that she too can go to the disco. In other words, the very desire to attend the school disco that initially strengthened the girls' bond becomes its undoing. Their oath of allegiance evaporates, as do their mutual love and support, and each girl now focuses not on their three-way friendship but on her own individual desire: Katia hopes to deceive her parents and hurt her former friends, Zhanna wants only to get drunk, and Vika fantasizes about stealing the bad-boy Aleks from his girlfriend, Nastia.

As a consequence, the three girls arrive at the disco with none of their initial strength and confidence but as vulnerable individuals. With their vow of loyalty shattered, each girl must now grow up on her own, and the remainder of Gai Germanika's film focuses on the sacrifice that each makes in this process. The loss initially represented by Tomik and the two goldfish shifts from outside to within the girls' developing bodies, and we witness how the unrelenting drive of each girl to pursue her own desire backfires for all three. Rather than realize the dream of exacting revenge on parents and friends, of being blissfully intoxicated for the first time, or of hearing Aleks say, "I love you," the disco deprives Katia, Zhanna, and Vika of these dreams, killing a vital part of their girlish selves as it transforms them into women.

Although comparing a school dance to war might seem extreme at first glance, the aptness of this metaphor for *Everyone Dies But Me* becomes clear once we consider the nature of the sacrifice that each girl makes when she arrives at the disco. Like venturing into battle, going to the disco requires that they don the armor of hyperfemininity by wearing a teen version of cisgender *travesti* that includes flounced skirts and pink pumps with matching headbands, jewelry, and sunglasses. The disco also brings Katia, Zhanna, and Vika into contact with hostile forces armed with a variety of weapons, and the ensuing struggle compels each girl to risk life and limb, inflicting physical and emotional wounds. The inherently gendered nature of war allows us to see the significance of the sacrifice each girl makes. War "is among the most consistently gendered of human activities. Every known society assigns war roles differentially by gender, with men as the primary fighters (and usually the only ones)."[95] In wartime, women typically do not fight on the front but provide support in the rear as mothers, nurses, and laborers. Yet the most feminized position in combat is not that of women providing support but that of the defeated enemy, who is often raped or killed. If Katia, Zhanna, and Vika arrive at the disco like young warriors dressed to kill in their adolescent *poshlost'*, then they leave humiliated and transformed into the feminized vanquished. Although each girl suffers defeat in a different manner, all three experience the disco as a battle in which, despite their most valiant efforts, they lose the androgyny fostered in the private world of their friendship, as well as their agency and independent desires.

The overarching pattern of venturing boldly into battle only to meet defeat first emerges in the story of Zhanna, whose dream of getting drunk for the first time goes hideously awry. She begins the evening of the disco by asking the man who drives her and Vika to the dance to buy them beer, which the two girls rapidly drink as they wait for the dance to start. After entering the school, the already tipsy Zhanna and Vika go to the girls' bathroom, where they find older girls drinking wine smuggled into the school through the window. When Vika fails to chug her wine, Zhanna shoos her off, telling her to search for her beloved Aleks on her own. From this point on, the tenth-grade girls egg Zhanna on as she consumes more and more red wine, even teaching her to take deep drags from a cigarette while drinking to increase her intoxication. Unsurprisingly, Zhanna never makes it to the dance floor, and when Vika returns to the girls' bathroom, she finds her friend slumped over in a stupor. Zhanna quickly pukes on her black-and-pink ensemble, passing out in a pool of her own vomit. The older girls have found themselves a willing victim, and, rather than accept Zhanna into their midst, they mock her as school officials carry her limp body away. Zhanna has clearly been conquered by the older girls, whose weapons of cigarettes, wine, and peer pressure have overpowered her. Rather than being accepted, Zhanna is both feminized and infantilized, as our parting shot of her suggests: Zhanna's father carries her, unconscious and in a fetal position, in his arms. The battle to grow up exacts a literally gut-wrenching toll on Zhanna, and the out-and-out humiliation she suffers at the hands of the tenth-grade girls will, we imagine, have repercussions long after the disco.

If the failure of Zhanna's dream of acceptance by more mature girls demonstrates her own immaturity, then Vika's attempt to grow up seems to meet with more success. After leaving Zhanna in the girls' bathroom, the naïve Vika goes in search of Aleks, around whom she has spun an elaborate romantic fantasy. However, Vika never declares her love to Aleks, since almost immediately she sees him leave with Katia, who, she believes, has broken their sworn loyalty by stealing her boyfriend. Vika then leaves the disco to find Aleks, but her search ends with a group of older boys partying on the street, who, much as the tenth-grade girls did with Zhanna, see a willing victim in Vika. The boys tease her about her romantic quest and then offer Vika some beer and a joint, which she reluctantly begins to smoke. This reluctance, however, turns into giggling compliance when the ringleader, Sasha, pays special attention to Vika, using a shotgun kiss of shared pot smoke to kiss her, much as the protagonists of Bondarchuk's *9th Company* do in their orgy with Snow White. The film's parting shot of Vika shows her and Sasha making out with reckless abandon, and, although we do not see the final outcome of Vika's decision to replace Aleks with another, the logical end of her story is sex with Sasha. Vika's sacrifice is certainly less brutal than Zhanna's. However, the narrative link of pot smoking to sex, for which the inexperienced Vika scarcely seems prepared, pushes her just as violently toward womanhood as Zhanna's binge drinking pushes her toward childhood.

In contrast to the incomplete stories of Vika and Zhanna, that of Katia traces each step of her sacrifice to its bitter end, replacing violation of the body through alcohol and drug abuse with actual physical violence. This abuse begins long before Katia arrives at the disco, since the film contains several scenes that show Katia's parents beating her in a futile attempt to curtail her adolescent rebellion. In these moments before the disintegration of the three girls' friendship, Katia cowers and whimpers when, for example, her father whips her with a towel. However, her utter defeat on the battleground of the disco leads, at the very least, to open defiance of her parents, including her refusal to submit to such beatings. This triumph mixed with defeat arrives in two stages, both of which arise out of Katia's readiness to trust the predatory Aleks. After Vika sees them leave the disco, Aleks takes Katia outside for a cigarette, flattering her with his attention. He lends an ear to Katia's woes, which she attributes to Tomik the cat giving her "the evil eye," and then Aleks tells her that his girlfriend, Nastia, means nothing to him. When Katia hears this, she aggressively kisses Aleks, emboldening his advances. Rather than return to the disco, as Katia proposes, he convinces her to go with him to the school basement, where he summarily undoes his own and Katia's pants and fucks her. After less than a minute of perfunctory pumping and grinding, Aleks pulls out of Katia and congratulates her, saying, in heavily accented English, "I am not a girl, not yet a woman." A visibly stunned Katia now tells Aleks that she was a virgin, and, although she willingly accompanied Aleks to the basement and put up no apparent protest, it is impossible to view the sex on screen as consensual.

The loss of Katia's virginity to the callous Aleks is undoubtedly a rape. However, the assault of her person escalates once Katia returns to the disco to find her mother with the principal. Her enraged mother grabs and then begins to beat Katia, who fights back for the first time. Aleks's imagined love allows her to stand up for herself, and Katia lunges toward him for protection. However, Aleks pushes Katia away, denying any knowledge of her before the menacing Nastia. An abashed Katia then leaves the disco with her mother, only to break free of her mother's grip, returning to the field outside the school where the film began. In a scene that eerily recreates the fight the three girls witnessed while burying Tomik the cat, Katia runs into the waiting Nastia, who brutally beats and kicks Katia until her bloodied body crumples to the ground. Rather than observe this clique's bullying from the outside as she did at the film's start, Katia is now the victim of their bullying as Aleks's cast-off.

After being raped by Aleks and beaten by his girlfriend, Katia initially lies on the ground and weeps. However, she soon makes her way home for the film's closing scene, which provides the title of Gai Germanika's film. Katia discovers her parents sitting at a table laden with food and drink in commemoration of the ninth day after her grandmother's death. When Katia's stunned parents express concern about the blood on her body, she defiantly tells them to fuck off, expressing her wish that everybody, including them, would die except her. A series of potent expletives is followed by Katia's threat to party again the very next night, as well as her denial of any love whatsoever for her parents. The tense exchange ends as Katia runs from the table and her parents plan to board up the window she uses to escape their watch. Lest we interpret Katia's defiance as a final victory built on the ashes of her defeat at the disco, Gai Germanika is careful to end this scene with a shot of Katia's beaten and bloodied body, shaken by sobs and huddled in a fetal position, on the floor of her bedroom. This closing shot repeats the same posture and sounds that accompanied Katia's first beating by her father, telling us that even though she has technically become a woman, the sacrifice she failed to anticipate has transformed her dream for the disco into a nightmare. Whatever elation or pleasure Katia awaited has been replaced by visceral pain and humiliation, in which she herself was complicit. Just as Zhanna and Vika entered the battle of the disco only to meet defeat, so does Katia find herself transformed from a hopeful young warrior into one of the vanquished, that is, into a woman.

When viewed as lost battles, the three girls' adventures at the school disco give us little hope at the end of *Everybody Dies but Me*. In addition to depicting the destruction of each girl's individual dream, Gai Germanika interweaves the girls' stories so that we can fill the gaps in the story of one with details from the other two. For example, Zhanna's over-the-top drinking makes us perceive Vika's pot smoking as a threatening violation of her body, while Katia's rape at the hands of Aleks suggests a similar negative outcome for Vika's heavy petting with Sasha. In addition, the film's vérité style, which includes amateur actors, real alcohol, and actual blows and blood during shooting, discourages us from reading Gai Germanika's realism as merely symbolic. Last, the film's circular plot eliminates whatever hope we might have for Katia, Zhanna, Vika, or any other Russian teenage girl for that matter. Not only does *Everybody Dies but Me* begin and end with brutal bullying, but both fights are also framed by the girls' futile desire to deny death. The sacrifices made by all three appear just as much to be steps backward to childhood as steps forward to womanhood. Zhanna's story proves paradigmatic in this regard: the micro-violence to the surface of her body early in the film, when she cuts herself to divert punishment for sacrificing the goldfish, is replaced at the disco by macro-violence to the interior of her body, in which she herself is complicit. Although all three girls are alive at the film's end, we know that their deaths have already begun and that the sacrifices they made at the disco have already moved them one step closer to the fate of Tomik the cat and Katia's grandmother, whose wake, we learn, no one even attended. The film's circular structure conveys the inevitability of the three girls' collective story, forcing their and our realization that when a girl becomes a woman, everybody survives but me.

Although *Everybody Dies but Me* begins by depicting its protagonists as an androgynous trinity empowered to create its own world, it ends with images of Katia, Zhanna, and Vika as isolated, subordinated, and fully feminized because of their initial womanly sacrifices. The film's narrative arc allows us to conjecture that all three girls probably had happy childhoods. Yet the trajectory we imagine after the closing credits leads to a string of similar, if not greater, feminine sacrifices that will eventually turn Katia, Zhanna, and Vika into the very women they wish dead: their shrewish geometry teacher, the school's authoritarian principal, Zhanna's powerless mother, and Katia's browbeaten and physically abusive mother. Katia, Zhanna, and Vika's entrance into womanhood provides a closeup of how Russian girls first encounter and absorb the lesson of feminine self-sacrifice that Pushkin's Tat'iana Larina, Ludmila Putina, the Putin-era bitch, and Klever's Arina Krylova all embody. *Everybody Dies but Me* also exposes how this lesson relies on a pedagogy that, like that of Rakovskii, uses fear and humiliation to strip down girls' psyches and rebuild them as women willing to scapegoat themselves so that the myths of Russian masculinity remain unquestioned and untouched.

Conclusion

In retrospect, we can see that all of the instances of postfeminism discussed in this chapter rely on the pedagogy of fear and humiliation that not only transforms Katia, Zhanna, and Vika into women in *Everybody Dies but Me* but also makes Rakovskii's livelihood at the bitch academy. Although this shame-based instruction is patently evident in Rudnitskaya's and Gai Germanika's films, the threat of social ostracism lies just beneath the surface of Tat'iana Larina and Liudmila Putina's undying loyalty if they should fail in their wifely duties, and it is Tania Platova's weapon of choice when teaching the upstart Uspenskii. More obviously, Klever's fictional BDSM universe transforms the pain and punishment occasioned by female misbehavior into sexual pleasure, which naturalizes Russia's "traditional" gender roles and makes men, like the Korshunov father and son, Rakovskii, Pushkin, Dostoevsky, and even the drag queens of chapter 3 into master teachers of femininity. In this regard, *Everybody Dies but Me* takes the additional step of showing how both men and women must instruct girls in the sacrifices required of womanhood. If Katia's abusive father and her rapist, Aleks, introduce her to the basic lesson of scapegoating herself, then her cowed mother and the bully Nastia drive home the larger message that girls become women by denying their own desires and replacing them with those of men. In other words, Putin-era postfeminism represented the perfect means for privatizing gender policing, since it taught women to use their own resources to monitor and make themselves over so that they secured and safeguarded the desires of men.

During Putin's first two decades at Russia's helm, Russian girls who mastered the lesson of obligatory self-sacrifice adopted a hyperfeminine *travesti* that marked them as "real" Russian women. At the same time, they performed a feminine version of the different pop styles, from charisma through *glamur*, adopted by their president, functioning as the yin to Putin's hypermasculine yang. Whether they sported baggy boyfriend shirts, donned tasteful Escada dresses, stripped down to sexy black undergarments, or dolled up for the school disco, those who embraced the post-Soviet postfeminist sensibility retooled their appearance and their psyche to satisfy male desire, which dictated their "worthy place" not only by a man's side but, more important, outside the public sphere and far from politics. As was true of Putin-era *travesti* more broadly, performing postfeminist hyperfemininity—whether as a bitchy dom or as a BDSM sub—gave rise to epistemological and affective ambivalence, which brings us back to the paradox of Russia's ever-expanding queerness. Despite the time, money, and effort spent on transforming themselves into feminine apotheoses of Russia's "traditional" heteronormativity, these women fell prey to the antisubjective discourse articulated in Article 6.21 and ended up crafting a subjectivity no more coherent than that of the man-baby Sergii Astakhov in *No Place for Fools*.

The incoherence of postfeminist subjectivity in Putin's Russia comes into sharp focus once we consider a beauty pageant, one of "traditional" femininity's cherished institutions, that took place in the Donetsk People's Republic in 2015.[96] Organized during the early days of the separatist conflict on the border between Ukraine and Russia that escalated into full-scale war in 2022, the beauty contest gave female soldiers eager for their region to join the Russian Federation the opportunity to model battle fatigues and evening gowns. In addition to celebrating International Women's Day, the pageant allowed one contestant to echo the sentiments of Putina and Shatskaia by telling journalists about her rejection of women's emancipation in favor of the "Slavic traditions" of cooking, bearing children, and caring for men.[97] The contest's judges did not choose a single winner but rather awarded prizes to all contestants, declaring them "flowers of the republic." Images from the pageant juxtapose army boots and platform stilettos, AK-47s and glittery gowns, revealing a grotesque attempt to shift attention away from a bloody armed conflict and onto feminine myths that war typically destroys. The Donetsk beauty contest showed how the postfeminist *travesti* of glamorous hyperfemininity could transform the heat of battle into tepid eroticism, as well as the incongruous lengths to which subservient Slavic woman would go in support of a political regime whose claim to power rests first and foremost on machismo.

While we might be tempted to discount the Donetsk beauty pageant as a one-off, the regularly scheduled beauty contests held in Russian penal colonies for women demonstrate the durability of their pedagogical intent.[98] Like the

Figure 13. Rebel fighters posing with the flag of the Donetsk People's Republic during a beauty contest in Donetsk in March 2015. Used by permission of Associated Press; photograph by Vadim Ghirda.

Donetsk pageant, those held in women's prisons are typically timed around International Women's Day, and they represent "the high point of the prison social calendar."[99] These prison pageants are judged by the very men tasked with punishing and patrolling female convicts, and inmates' participation not only breaks the numbing routine of prison life but can also lead to cash prizes and a positive mark on their criminal records. So popular that they garner support from commercial sponsors, NGOs, and civic organizations, Russian prison pageants "combine a beauty contest with demonstration of domestic abilities and traditional 'passive' feminine virtues," allowing inmates to switch drab prison uniforms for flounced dresses and chic up-dos.[100] The pageant's training in hyperfeminine *travesti* is meant "to rescript criminal women toward a predetermined 'ideal' of Russian womanhood" and to lead to their "refeminization."[101] Their penal setting recasts punitive shaming for female criminality as a holiday reward, calling into question the supposedly voluntary nature of these inmates' performance of feminine compliance.

As distant as such prison beauty pageants in the 2000s and 2010s were from a school disco in the Moscow suburbs or Rakovskii's bitch academy, the shame-based pedagogy on which all three relied goes back to Russia's creeping epidemic of queer performativity, yet ultimately led to a basic incoherence in the feminine subjectivities shaped under their auspices. By requiring women to sacrifice their own desires to those of men, all three inculcated a postfeminist sensibility that promised self-fulfillment yet delivered female subordination and compliance, as we see in Rudnitskaya's 2019 sequel to *How to Become a Bitch* titled *School of Seduction*.[102] The film follows three of Rakovskii's pupils during the decade after graduation from his bitch academy, documenting the small successes and larger failures of bitchology in action. Although the first student, Lida, successfully lands the husband and child she desperately wanted, she ends up repeating, in her own marriage, the same infidelity she used to steal her husband from his former wife. Vika, the second student, likewise achieves her fantasy of marrying and opening her own lingerie boutique, only to separate from her husband once pursuing these bitchy dreams drives her into psychotherapy.

For her third subject, Rudnitskaya follows Diana, the young woman who confessed her desire to rape men without their realizing it in *How to Become a Bitch*. Even though Diana scrupulously follows Rakovskii's lessons, we watch how her aspirations to *poshlyi* bitchiness become a never-ending spiral that lands her in a loveless marriage, as well as the Austrian Higher School for Ladies, a Petersburg charm school where she hopes to learn the *glamur* that Rakovskii never taught her. After watching Diana perform a drag version of Nicole Kidman in the title role of the 2014 film *Grace of Monaco*, we follow her to the real-life Monte Carlo, where she and her son gaze enviously at swank casinos, luxury yachts, and the wealthy who inhabit them. Throughout, Diana puts on her best performance of *glamur*, even as her son admits that she "tries to be elegant, but nature won't allow it." Rudnitskaya frames *School of Seduction* with footage from one of Russia's countless military holidays and a voice-over from one of Putin's many exhortations that women fulfill their feminine duty, linking the film's three stories of incoherent female subjectivity to the welfare of the Russian state. Rather than learning how to seduce and manipulate men, women like Lida, Vika, and Diana were themselves seduced and duped by postfeminism's false promise of female empowerment, only to find themselves serving the masculine desires on which Putin's Russia depends.

However, not all Russians were taken in by postfeminism's bait and switch during Putin's first two decades in the Kremlin, and some even used the same stylistic mash-up as bitch-academy graduates to critique the very skills taught there. The 2016 video of Leningrad's song "Exhibit" cleverly debunks postfeminism's makeover mandate by depicting a young woman's farcical attempt to follow the type of advice that Rakovksii and Shatskaia give for snagging Mr. Right.[103] Although the lyrics by Sergei "Shnur" Shnurov boast that the

Figure 14. Diana poses as Nicole Kidman playing the role of Princess Grace of Monaco in Alina Rudnitskaya's 2019 documentary *School for Seduction*.

song's female singer is "the main exhibit" wherever she goes, the video tells a different story that literally knocks the wind out of her bravado. "Exhibit" opens as an attractive young woman Skypes with an equally attractive young man, telling him that she has just left her father's home to discover herself through painting. When asked about the style of her art, she answers that she likes different styles and prefers "pastel'nye tona" (pastel tones), which the video's Russian subtitles sneakily render as the homograph "postel'nye tona" (bed tones), hinting at the singer's *poshlost'*. When Mr. Right suggests going to an art exhibition, the video's music and fun take off. The singer tries on one sexy outfit after another, ultimately deciding to copy a magazine illustration of Victoria Beckham hanging on the wall. Although the singer already has the pink jacket and skinny jeans for her Posh Spice *travesti*, she calls a friend to borrow some typically red-soled platform stilettos by the designer Christian Louboutin to complete the look.

While waiting for the costly Louboutins to arrive, the singer launches into a grueling grooming ritual, which includes facial mask, body waxing, hair curling, manicure, false eyelashes, and face paint so heavy that she looks uncannily like a drag queen. Once she begins to dress, however, the singer discovers that her jeans are just too skinny. She wraps her thighs in Saran Wrap and jumps on an exercise bike; she binges and purges *margantsovka* (a purple solution of potassium permanganate) in the effort to lose weight. Once the coveted Louboutins arrive, she gives their disappointingly non-red soles a thick coat of nail varnish and crams herself into her jeans. The singer then slides into the stilettos, hears the doorbell, and falls flat on her face since the nail varnish has glued her feet to the floor. Undaunted, she picks herself up, fixes the makeup on her bloodied face, and opens the door for Mr. Right as the song's chorus of "On Louboutins, nah, and in fucking awesome pants" swells in the background.

Unlike the song's lyrics, the video of "Exhibit" clearly mocks the beauty and weight-loss routines at the core of postfeminism's makeover paradigm. Moreover, according to Leningrad's female vocalist, "Exhibit" initially left the public cold until the video was released on YouTube, where it gained more than a hundred million hits in the span of a year.[104] "Exhibit" also hit number one on Russia's iTunes chart shortly after the video's release, winning the inaugural prize for best music video at the Russian National Music Awards, as well as the group's first Golden Gramophone, in 2016.[105] At the same time that Russia's music industry gave "Exhibit" its seal of approval, female fans started a copycat movement, in which they converted their own more affordable footwear, including house slippers and Uggs, into faux Louboutins by painting their soles red, and then posted photos of their handiwork on Instagram.[106] More ambitious fans made copycat videos in the thousands, parodying everything from men getting ready for a date to athletes preparing for tryouts.[107] In fact, Shnur enjoyed one parody by two Georgian men, who incorporated their country's traditional vocal polyphony into "Exhibit," so much that he posted it on Leningrad's official YouTube channel.[108] According to the web portal Yandex, "on Louboutins" was Russia's meme of the year in 2016, and the entire "on Louboutins" phenomenon inspired folklorists to document and unpack its virality.[109]

Some of the song's millions of fans might very well fail to notice its critique of postfeminism. However, recent comments below the official video for "Exhibit" suggest otherwise, for example, "When I was 12, I laughed at the heroine. Now I'm not laughing" and "This isn't a music video or a song—this is real life in Russia." Such comments bring into focus the song's *stiob* of postfeminism, demonstrating the ability of the stylistic slippage among charisma and adjacent ironic styles not only to build up but also to rip down postfeminism's precepts. The virality of the "on Louboutins" phenomenon in the mid-2010s demonstrated that it was just as easy for those who rejected the cisgender *travesti* of hypergender to use such stylistic slippage as it was for those who preached it, whether in the Kremlin, Rakovskii's Bitch Academy, a middle school disco, or a prison beauty pageant. The ideal Russian citizen between 2000 and 2020 may very well have been a young woman willing to put herself through the humiliating paces of postfeminism, but the same stylistic tools that created her could be used to form horizontal connections among those Russians who rejected everything she stood for, as well as the man she stood behind.

Conclusion

Now that Putin's first two decades in the Kremlin are receding into the past, Viktor Erofeev's accusation that Russian men of the 2010s were stylistic wrecks held hostage by the Other's gaze begins to make sense.[1] If we discount the writer's transphobic reaction to his motherland's cross-dressing, we can see that the Russian Federation under Putin's control suffered not from the national lack of style that Erofeev denounced in the 1990s but rather from a surfeit of styles, which quickly appeared and just as quickly morphed into new and different styles between 2000 and 2020.[2] However, rather than solve the country's persistent crisis of masculinity or offer its citizens respite from an ever more rigid regime of hypergendered heteronormativity, the slip and slide among charisma and ironic pop styles like camp, kitsch, *poshlost'*, *stiob*, *glamur*, and *travesti* made both of these problems worse. Appropriating Otherness through style might have promised to give citizens hoping to craft a fittingly Russian self in the 2000s and 2010s access to gendered norms of Russianness. However, the ease and speed with which these selves, from Vladimir Putin at the top of the country's "power vertical" to those at its base, adopted new styles turned the overabundance of Russian style into its opposite—a stylistic vacuum—in the course of just twenty years. The rapid-fire displacements of self and Other created by the stylistic slippage on offer in pop culture were so dizzying that in the end they exposed the masculine fragility and male hysteria lurking beneath the glossy surface of Putinism.

The clearest proof that such Russian style had reached the point of exhaustion comes from the simple fact that neither Putin's regime nor those who protested against it achieved their aims via the mash-up of charisma and irony that typified messaging on both sides of the political divide between 2000 and 2020. On one hand, the Russian state generated a spate of increasingly repressive laws and regulations in the course of the 2010s, implicitly acknowledging the refusal of many citizens to conform to the hypergendered standards of the country's purported "traditions." As the 2020s approached, the Duma continued to churn out laws against foreign agents, treason, political extremism, nongovernmental organizations, public assembly, and free speech. Likewise, Putin's anti-Western rhetoric reached fever pitch when he not only claimed that pedophilia represents a social norm in the West but also mocked the Anglican Church for entertaining "the idea of a gender-neutral God" in his 2023 state-of-the-state address.[3] Perhaps most telling, the Duma's overhaul of the "gay propaganda" law in November 2022 broadened it to Russians of all ages, increased fines for its violation, conflated "nontraditional sexual relations" with pedophilia, and singled out trans people with new verbiage about sexual "preference" and "sex change."[4] The growing need to elaborate and amplify the homo- and transphobia on which Putinism's hypergender has relied for well over two decades signals the state's failure to shape, let alone control, citizens' beliefs and behaviors through less coercive measures.

On the other hand, the swell in cultural protest, which included those who took to the streets in 2011–2012, Pussy Riot, and even musical groups like Rabfak and Leningrad, failed to budge the Kremlin's political will or to nudge that of fellow citizens in a more liberal direction.[5] A 2013 action titled "Fixation" by the pain artist Petr Pavlensky provides a vivid analogy for the impasse that both sides finally reached. On a chilly November day, Pavlensky nailed his scrotum to the cobblestones of Red Square, a gesture that came dangerously close to making the metaphorical castration of the Russian body politic literal.[6] Pavlensky's bare, tense, and silent body, with head hung and eyes locked on his shriveled penis and punctured scrotum, looked like a textbook illustration of the protoform of shame. In hindsight, we can see that "Fixation" represented another instance of masculine abjection, as well as the political deadlock and stylistic dead end in which both protesters and Putin would find themselves by the decade's close.

The luxury of hindsight also lets us discern two stages in the larger performative shift that began after Putin rose to power in 1999. During the first, his politics of machismo took their basic shape, since Putin's initial challenge as president was to inscribe himself on the nearly blank political slate created by Yeltsin's resignation. However, rather than fill this slate with any real content, Putin opted for fashioning an identity as Russia's *muzhik* in chief and romantic lead, a strategy that not only brought him attention from domestic and international audiences but also put him on the map as a world leader. The protests of 2011–2012 signaled the second phase, in which Putin's stylish performance of machismo had begun to lose its luster, inciting public outcry and open dissent at home. By the end of the 2000s and into the 2010s, many in

Russia no longer bought their leader's flashy yet virtually content-free speechifying about economic stability, Russia's civilizational greatness, or the need to protect their country's endangered "traditions," despite Putin's perennially high approval ratings. However, the ensuing waves of protest against his masculinity-driven politics led to successive crackdowns, making Russia's leading man a bully not simply in his own country but of international proportions. By no means does this rough periodization of the politics behind Putinism's style intend to diagnose the many factors that contributed to Russia's slow slide toward fascism between 2000 and 2020 or to lay blame for this trend anywhere other than on the Kremlin. Rather, my intention is to highlight that the political substance and agency of those Russians who leveraged their own Russian styles for protest proved so threatening to Putin's regime of toxic masculinity that he chose to poison, imprison, punish, and outlaw them.

Despite its uniquely post-Soviet contours and outcome, the performative shift that took place in Russia during Putin's first two decades in power was isolated in neither time nor space. The shift in embodied Russian citizenship from productivity to performance between 2000 and 2020 grew out of an earlier performative shift in which the ostensible meaning of words and utterances took a back seat to their performance in late-Soviet society.[7] Similarly, Putinism's preference for surface over depth gave rise to new styles for expressing the increasingly narrow constraints of Russia's "traditional" gender and sexuality, which not only led to another performative shift in the early 2020s but will continue to do so in a post-Putin future. If we look farther afield, we see that the stylistic slippage among charisma and ironic pop styles belongs not just to Putin's first two decades in power but, more broadly, to the globalized and mediatized space where the internet, popular culture, and politics meet in the twenty-first century. In other words, understanding Russian style under Putin gives us a better appreciation not just of the local history of performativity in Russia during the twenty-first century's first two decades but also of the transnational evolution of styles for expressing identity after the Cold War.

Even though the stylistic slippage that typified pop performativity in Russia between 2000 and 2020 was part of a global trend toward increasingly ironic expressions of identity, the events chronicled in this book stand out because of their neoconservative, neotraditional backdrop, as well as the stylistic gridlock that brought them to a close. Putinism's pervasive pedagogy of shame transformed the type of stylistic slippage, which usually leads to expanding participation in the political process in liberal democracies, into a powerful means to exclude more and more Russians from politics altogether. The incoherent subjectivity spelled out in the "gay propaganda" law made all citizens of the

Russian Federation vulnerable to an ever-expanding queerness, generating a performative precarity that led to a rising tide of misogyny, as well as xeno-, homo-, and transphobia, in the 2010s. To understand the stylistic stalemate that brought the Russian style this book considers to an end, we need only revisit Russia's drag renaissance and the Eurovision Song Contest.

Royal Cobras Bite Back

The post-Soviet rebirth of performance *en travesti*, which brought fame to glamazons like Zaza Napoli and Anatolii Evdokimov in the late 2000s, continued for well over a decade. Even after passage of the 2013 "gay propaganda" law, the number of drag queens performing in bars and clubs across the Russian Federation continued to grow, as did the public's curiosity about men whose work required the finery of hyperfeminine *glamur*. By 2020, articles about drag in Russia began popping up across the internet, for example, on *The Calvert Journal*, an English-language site devoted to postsocialist culture, and in *Wonderzine*, a Russian-language "online publication for contemporary women and their friends."[8] In 2020 Russia experienced even the publication of *Dragzina*, its first and only magazine devoted to the art of drag. Spearheaded by a group of openly queer dragtivists including Lorina Rey, *Dragzina* released its first and only issue in December of that year.[9] The uptick in publicity about the niche phenomenon of drag brought the attention of more mainstream media, inspiring the social media star and television personality Nastia Ivleeva to launch her own drag reality show. The first episode of *Royal Cobras* appeared on YouTube in late September of 2021, drawing hundreds of thousands of viewers, as well as the scrutiny of critics on both right and left.[10]

Although Ivleeva denied copying *RuPaul's Drag Race* (in Russian, *Korolevskie gonki RuPola*), the "lipsync battles" around which her show revolved owe a clear debt to its American predecessor, as does the name *Royal Cobras* (*Korolevskie kobry*). Each of the show's six episodes pitted six drag queens against each other to decide who would earn the right to advance to the show's finale. Ivleeva also invited a different celebrity guest, including the would-be politician Ksenia Sobchak and "Pussy Boy" Egor Krid, to host and judge the final lipsync battle of each episode alongside her. The premiere of *Royal Cobras* incited the ire of conservative viewers, provoking accusations of "gay propaganda" and outrage at Ivleeva's foul mouth. Never one to miss an opportunity for homophobia, the Petersburg politician Vitalii Milonov alleged that *Royal Cobras* propagated "nontraditional sexual relations," launching an ad hominem attack on Ivleeva and her queens: "Some sick girl is broadcasting shows in which sick perverts compete. Any man who dresses as a woman is a sick pervert unless he's Verka Serduchka. Ivleeva should go to prison. Let her organize competitions from there."[11] Milonov never explained how or why Verka Serduchka managed to avoid the illness and perversity that he perceived in Ivleeva's queens. Nor did he apparently notice the two "18+" warnings and the lengthy disclaimer at the start of each episode, in which Ivleeva's legal team stated in no uncertain terms the show's lack of intent to foment "nontraditional sexual relations."

Reactions to the show from liberal quarters ran the gamut. While the gay activist Nikolai Alekseev pointed out the absurdity of Milonov's homophobic diatribe, other members of the LGBTQ+ community noted that *Royal Cobras* "lack[ed] depth [and] removed all of the politicization of drag, leaving 'sequins and dancing freaks.'"[12] In their own ad hominem attack, a number of LGBTQ+ activists even questioned Ivleeva's right as a heterosexual to host a drag reality show, suggesting that she exploited her *travesti-artisty*, who allegedly performed free of charge, for her own gain.[13] The *Wonderzine* editor and reviewer Anton Danilov repeated the accusation that *Royal Cobras*'s host failed to check her straight privilege; however, he also expressed the hope that the show might "actively overcome homophobia and alleviate social stigma of all types."[14] Given that *Royal Cobras* copied neither the tragic formula of Mikhailov's *Jolly Fellows* nor the liberatory narrative of *RuPaul's Drag Race*, these ambivalent appraisals of the first Russian television show devoted to drag make sense, and the mix of disappointment, sympathy, and hope in Danilov's review shows just how difficult it was to figure out precisely what *Royal Cobras* achieved. As he pointed out, Ivleeva's show was hardly original, but Danilov's conclusion that it delivered "form without content" seems less like a damning critique and more like an insightful description of the work Ivleeva's show actually did.[15]

Those who watch more than one episode of *Royal Cobras* cannot help but notice its sometimes shoddy production values, Ivleeva's uneven enthusiasm and rapport with her celebrity co-hosts, not to mention the wildly varying abilities of the competing glamazons, who hailed from across post-Soviet space. In spite of the show's many shortcomings, the repeating form of the lipsync battle effectively normalized, over the course of six episodes, the idea that two men could and should dress up as glamorous sexpots and duke it out while mouthing the words to songs like Cream Soda's "I'm Crying to Techno" or Lady Gaga's "Applause." Moreover, the decision to put Ivleeva and her co-hosts through the paces of a lipsync battle created the show's most eye-popping moments. In one episode, the diminutive actor-comedian Denis Dorokhov ended up bumping and grinding with the much taller Ivleeva to Christina Aguilera's "Genie in a Bottle," eventually lifting his abashed co-host onto his hips in an impromptu lap dance.[16] Even more shocking was the lipsync battle

Figure 15. Nastia Ivleeva and Kseniia Sobchak kiss in episode two of *Royal Cobras* (2021).

with Sobchak, who stunned spectators by death-dropping into the splits, dirty-dancing with Ivleeva, and spanking her with a bright green feather boa, all to the tune of Ke$ha's "TiK-ToK."[17] Their performance culminated in a kiss so passionate that it took Ivleeva's breath away and forced both backstage to redo their smeared lipstick. The ensuing media kerfuffle included comments by Ivleeva on Sobchak's mastery of her tongue.[18] And of course, Milonov produced another gem in his own battle against "gay propaganda" when he fulminated that Ivleeva and Sobchak's kiss had turned Russian YouTube "into a circus of oral prostitution," whatever that is.[19]

Those reporting on Ivleeva and Sobchak's lip-lock speculated that it was just a PR stunt that copied a similar kiss Sobchak had received from the TV personality Tina Kandelaki at an awards show in 2007, which in turn copied Madonna's famous kiss with Britney Spears and Aguilera at the 2003 VMAs.[20] However, no one mentioned that Ivleeva and Sobchak had also ripped off t.A.T.u., whose girl-on-girl kisses were no less geared to titillation and PR. Not only does this chain of precedents prove that there really is nothing new under the sun, but they also point to the repetitive nature of the weird description of Ivleeva and Sobchak's kiss as "a circus of oral prostitution," which sounds like Russia's head homophobe in a lipsync battle with himself. Milonov's routine anti-LGBTQ+ tantrum was just as devoid of content and just as much a stylistic copycat as the kiss that inspired it. As liberal critics suspected, whatever support of or opposition to Russia's LGBTQ+ community came out of this particular tempest in a teapot was ultimately unintentional on the part of Ivleeva, Sobchak, and even Milonov, all of whom repeated the empty forms of their chosen styles to shine a spotlight on themselves.

The brouhaha created by Ivleeva and Sobchak's kiss, as well as *Royal Cobras* as a whole, suggests that the show's biggest achievement was not bringing greater awareness or sympathy to Russian drag artists or the country's LGBTQ+ community but rather delivering a form so utterly devoid of content that it could mix and match all of the Russian styles explored in this book. Ivleeva's fanciful costumes, penchant for profanity, and risqué hijinks created a glitzy jumble of camp, kitsch, *poshlost'*, and *glamur*, which her co-hosts infused with celebrity charisma, not to mention the *travesti* battles that gave *King Cobras* its raison d'être. This overload of Russian styles made Ivleeva's show into a low-budget *stiob* of its American predecessor, gutting *King Cobras* of whatever queerness viewers might have anticipated, as well as much of its entertainment value. In fact, the much-vaunted final episode, in which the winning drag queens would fight over a grand prize of a million rubles, never did drop on YouTube, suggesting that, unlike RuPaul's long-lived *Drag Race*, Ivleeva's stylistic mash-up burned out after just six episodes.

Eurovision Zombies and Cannibals

If *Royal Cobras* provides an example of the type of postmodern pastiche that comes from "the imitation of dead styles" and "random cannibalization of all styles of the past," the Eurovision Song Contest represents an engine for generating pop styles that live briefly precisely so that they can die and be cannibalized.[21] And as Dima Bilan's 2008 victory proved, winning Eurovision requires not merely pastiche but also recycling past styles with just enough novelty to occupy the contest's vanguard, something that Russian acts came close to doing three times during the 2010s. In 2012, the Buranovskie Babushki, a group of grandmothers from the Udmurt Republic, won viewers' hearts and second place with the song "Party for Everybody," which blended actual folk culture with Russian folk kitsch, as well as the Udmurt language and Eurovision English. Russia took second place again in 2015 with the aspirational rock ballad "A Million Voices," sung by Polina Gagarina, who imitated 1985's "We Are the World," as well as Marilyn Monroe's windblown white dress, which, rather than floating up, stretched down to the stage and pinned her in place. The only other Russian act that came close to winning Eurovision in the 2010s was Sergei Lazarev's third-place, fairy-tale love song, whose title, in a bizarre instance of personification, claimed that tears can "Scream." All three of these acts cleverly identified what was au courant at Eurovision, yet they failed to set a new trend and take the grand prix.

Russia tried a new strategy for its Eurovision entry in 2020: "Uno" by the rave band Little Big.[22] The songs that launched the group's fame in the mid-2010s, for example, "Give Me Your Money" and the viral dance hit "Skibidi," ruthlessly mock Russian stereotypes in a style that Maria Engström dubs "neocamp" but that could just as easily be labeled "East European kitsch."[23] For Eurovision, however, Little Big took a different approach by creating a faux-Latin song so loaded with clichés that they collapse under their own weight into a stylistic black hole. Although "Uno" begins like classic salsa, its syncopated clave rhythm is quickly overlaid with the group's signature electro-Europop sound. Moreover, the call-and-response lyrics deliver a stock Latinidad, which predictably rhymes "more than one margarita" with "my sweet señorita" and uses Spanish only when counting repeatedly from uno to seis. Those who listen to "Uno" without watching Little Big's official Eurovision video might very well mistake it for a techno cover of Sesame Street's "Spanish Counting Song."

The video of "Uno" pushes the song's potboiler Latinness over the edge by placing it on a retro disco stage stripped of any Latin references. Little Big's six performers all wear seventies-style bell bottoms, including two female singers in skintight blue lamé bodysuits with spangled hips. The group's deadpan faces match their equally deadpan dancing, in which they routinely stand still, arms akimbo, rapidly opening and closing their knees. The only person to break this repetitive pattern is the dancer Dima Krasilov (nicknamed "*pukhliash*" or "chubby" in Russian), who, in a XL baby-blue jumpsuit with matching sweatband, executes fast-paced moves that blend voguing and break dancing with a death drop. The video's robotic dancing, high-key lighting, and surplus of styles make the performers on stage look like cartoonish zombies who have cannibalized a random assortment of dead pop styles only to regurgitate them automatically. Little Big never performed "Uno" on the Eurovision stage since the Covid-19 pandemic forced organizers to cancel the contest in 2020. Nonetheless, the song's official video garnered more than 250 million hits and became the most watched video on Eurovision's YouTube channel, making the group that year's de facto winner. Evidently, Little Big's cannibalization of so many styles from the past proved that too much style was just enough to win fans' attention.

For Eurovision's next live broadcast, in 2021, Russia tried again to grab the world's attention yet failed to take the grand prix. The choice of the Russian-Tajik singer Manizha stirred controversy at home, and many of her compatriots expressed open hostility to the singer's ethnicity, feminism, advocacy of LGBTQ+ rights, and activism against xenophobia and domestic violence. Although Manizha placed ninth in Rotterdam, her "Russian Woman" received loud applause from those in attendance and even made it onto the top-100 chart in

Figure 16. The knee-knocking dance in the official Eurovision video of Little Big's song "Uno" (2020).

several Western European countries. In an official press release after her selection, Manizha described "Russian Woman" in patriotic terms, stating that the song depicts "the change in self-perception of the Russian woman over the past few centuries."[24] However, both the song's lyrics and Manizha's performance in the Eurovision finale showed the world that Russia was hardly "generous, open, bright, and unlike anywhere else" in its treatment of women.[25]

"Russian Woman" blended Eurovision's requisite camp with an open declaration of female independence, and Manizha's performance began with her standing inside an enormous "dress-manifesto," which looked like a huge tea cozy topped by a patchwork of fabrics representing Russia's different peoples.[26] Manizha's mother, who helped design the Natal'ia Goncharova-inspired costume, explained its function as "a symbol of the patriarchy, of the past," and a *travesti* "of all the baggage that has accumulated on the shoulders of Russian women."[27] Less than a minute into her performance, Manizha stepped out of the symbolically laden dress, revealing a second costume of red coveralls inscribed with the words "Rashn Wyman" on their back. As she went back and forth between Russian and English, folksong and rap, Manizha ventriloquized the sexist stereotypes her song debunks, from "You're over thirty, hello, where are your kids?" to the chorus's "Every Russian woman needs to know / You're strong enough to bounce against the wall." After motivational imperatives like "Be Strong" and "Be Creative" appeared on the wall behind her, the song's backdrop switched to a rapidly multiplying montage of actual Russian women of different ages, races, ethnicities, and gender identities, who sang along with Manizha to the song's end. Her performance at Eurovision urged Russian women to abandon their *travesti* of "traditional" Russian femininity for the clothing—be it Manizha's Rosie the Riveter coveralls or the drag queen's pink wig and the trans person's chest binder in the montage behind her—that lets them live as they want.

Given her earlier Instagram campaign against "beauty trauma," it hardly comes as a surprise that Manizha's "Russian Woman" casts off the heteronormative *travesti* to which Russian women are actually called.[28] Nor is it a surprise that the song won the 2021 Dana International Award for LGBTQ+ Equality as part of Eurovision's annual Vision Music Awards or that the love shown Manizha by feminists in the West translated into hatred for some at home.[29] As she prepared to perform in Rotterdam, Manizha found her Instagram account flooded with hate speech and bullying, while political figures in Russia suggested removing or even banning her from Eurovision.[30] A group of veterans filed a complaint that accused "Russian Woman" of aiming "to grossly insult and humiliate the human dignity of Russian women," while the Union of Orthodox Women charged the song with preaching "hatred toward men, which undermines the foundations of a traditional family."[31] The only thing truly surprising about Manizha's Eurovision performance was that an increasingly "traditional" Russia had sent someone so candidly "nontraditional" to represent it at the contest.

In essence, Russia's decision to send Manizha to Eurovision repeated the *stiob* that had brought both t.A.T.u. and Dima Bilan Eurovision success more than a decade before. However, rather than leverage a performance of lesbianism that the members of t.A.T.u. vehemently disavowed or Bilan's reputation in the 2000s as straight but bi-curious and gay-friendly, Manizha was a full-fledged feminist, who wrote, designed, and performed "Russian Woman" in earnest. Manizha's own style at Eurovision might have been alive and kicking, but from the perspective of her country it was already dead and ripe for cannibalization. The same gestures that Manizha used to cast off the *travesti* of "traditional" Russian femininity in "Russian Woman" created the much greater *travesti* of Russia impersonating a bastion of gender equality. Her lukewarm finish at Eurovision suggests that not all of the contest's fans fell for yet another bait and switch on Russia's part and that for many, "Russian Woman" looked like pussy without the riot. Despite Eurovision's desire to remain apolitical, the cannibalized styles of both Little Big and Manizha delivered plainly political messages about the stylistic catch-22 Russia had reached by 2020. Moreover, the European Broadcasting Union's exclusion of Russia from the contest a mere day after Putin invaded Ukraine in late February of 2022 belied any claim Eurovision might make about not engaging in politics.[32]

Ukrainophobia and the Russian Lack of Self

Putin's "special military operation" in Ukraine represents both a geopolitical and a stylistic watershed, signaling the Russian Federation's next performative shift in the twenty-first century. At first glance, the war in Ukraine might appear to undercut this book's argument about Putinism's preference for style over substance. Yet, as we search for the reasons behind Putin's war, we can and should locate his invasion of Ukraine in the stylistic evolution that has taken place since 1999 and consider how the stylistic impasse that Russia faced by 2020 might have contributed to an utterly unjustified invasion, which has killed thousands, displaced millions, and destroyed major Ukrainian cities, as well as the country's infrastructure. If the performative shift examined in this book saw the locus of meaning and signification drift from language to the body after Putin's rise to power, then the stylistic vacuum of Putin's masculinity politics in the late 2010s has given rise to another performative shift, in which macho political style has materialized in phallic weapons of war, like the Kinzhal and Iskandr missiles bombarding Ukraine. Putin's earlier manly political posturing and the bloody battle for Ukraine stand not in opposition but rather complement and mutually reinforce each other. In other words, the stylistic void that Putinism became by 2020 has been filled with the fatal stuff of war, transforming the now dead styles of irony that generated charisma for almost twenty years into a lethal seriousness that has taken the lives of Ukrainian citizens and that demands their country's annihilation.

Once we return to our definition of style as the self's means for expressing identity via the appropriation of Otherness, we also see that Russia's most recent performative shift adds Ukrainophobia to the growing list of fears that Putinism has manufactured in its struggle *not* to confront the country's crisis of masculinity. As Eliot Borenstein points out, Putin's Ukrainophobia has roots that reach back to the founding of Kieven Rus' more than a millennium ago, while his denial of Ukraine's sovereign legitimacy began in 2008, when he reputedly told U.S. president George W. Bush, "Ukraine is not even a state."[33] As Borenstein notes, however, Russians' "disbelief in Ukraine as a concept" does not simply dismiss the country, whose language, culture, history, and territory have all been subsumed in Russia's imperial project at multiple points in modern history. Rather, the Ukrainophobia that launched Putin's vicious invasion insists that "the Ukrainian Other is simply another variety of self," making any conflict between Russia and Ukraine into "a war between Russia and itself."[34]

At this point, we should recognize a repeating pattern: Ukraine represents yet one more Other holding Russia hostage in its gaze, and Putin's decision to invade Ukraine is another narcissistic refusal to distinguish fully between self and Other. Like Russian misogyny, transphobia, homophobia, and xenophobia more broadly, Putin's Ukrainophobia seeks to destroy an Other, whose own self and reality have already been erased through phobic projection and displacement. The vacuum of style that plagued Putinism by 2020 ultimately testifies to the absence of a coherent Russian self, as seen in the changing ideological proxies that Putin's apologists generated between 2000 and 2020. Whether in the guise of "sovereign democracy" or the "Russian World," or more recent diatribes against the West's alleged "new ethics" of political correctness, such faux ideologies cannibalize ideas from other times and places, creating an ideological pastiche that never truly articulates an intelligible "Russian idea" or self. Instead, the pastiche of ideology galvanizes support for Putin's regime by generating a righteous indignation that projects the faults of the incoherent Russian self onto despised Others.

We find a vivid example of this phenomenon in a 2021 manifesto written by the theater director Konstantin Bogomolov against the "new ethics," an umbrella term that has united Russian intellectuals on the right and left in their fight against a common adversary: Western civilization.[35] Bogomolov's attack focuses on the ways in which European culture supposedly inhibits a creature he calls "complex man." His vague description of what makes someone "complex" includes being both angel and devil, as well as the capacity not merely to love but, more important, to hate. Bogomolov contends that after World War II, Europe subjected "complex man" to liquidation, as well as "chemical castration and lobotomy," linking "new ethics" to Nazism by calling it a "new ethical Reich." Not content with this overdetermined historical parallel, he then describes "new ethics" as "nontraditional totalitarianism," following through on the homophobic slur in the adjective "nontraditional" by claiming that Europe has fallen prey to "queer socialism" as hatched by "queer activists, fem-fanatics, and eco-psychopaths." Bogomolov's overload of analogs leads him to juxtapose Hitler's hate-mongering Third Reich with "the New Ethical Reich [in which] a person is trained to love and deprived of the right to hate freely," leading the "complex man" to "self-castration."

As an award-winning theater director, Bogomolov dutifully trots out Anton Chekhov's *Cherry Orchard* to evoke the decadence of a bygone era in his manifesto. However, his most colorful comparison comes when he equates Europe's emasculated "complex man" to Alex, the juvenile delinquent protagonist of Stanley Kubrick's 1971 film *A Clockwork Orange*. Bogomolov's article even includes a still of the actor Malcolm McDowell in the role of Alex as he undergoes the eye-opening aversion therapy that ends his rampage of drug abuse, petty theft, sexual violence, and murder. However apt this comparison might be for what Bogomolov accuses "new ethics" of doing in the West, he forgets two important facts. First, Alex's aversion therapy is ultimately undone, allowing him to return to dreams of "ultra-violence" by the film's end. Second, Kubrick's movie, as well as the 1962 novel by Anthony Burgess from which the film is adapted, incorporates a slang called "Nadsat," which includes Russian words like "droog" (*drug* or friend) and "gulliver" (*golova* or head). In other words, Bogomolov's clearest illustration of the deleterious effects of "new ethics" has a Russian subtext of hatred and violence that his manifesto represses. With this in mind, we can view Bogomolov's fear of castration by the West's "new ethics" as a tacit admission of his own unconscious castration as a Russian man beholden to Vladimir Putin. Another theater director, Ivan Vyrypaev, who lives and works in the Europe that Bogomolov merely imagines, upholds this viewpoint in a response to Bogomolov's screed, which points out how he merely rationalizes narcissism in service to Putinism.[36] In addition to displacing responsibility for Russia's seemingly endless crisis of masculinity, his manifesto suggests that Russian accusations of Nazism, whether directed at European political correctness or at Ukrainian sovereignty, project the very real fascism that has come to characterize Russia under Putin's leadership onto a series of imaginary Others.

Rather than protect the "complex man," diminish fascism, or make a dent in the crisis of masculinity, Putin's war in Ukraine has done the opposite, for those in both Ukraine and the Russian Federation. In addition to the refugees who have flooded out of Ukraine, thousands have left Russia due to economic instability, the threat of conscription, and political crackdowns that include a new law that threatened anyone who dared to call Putin's "special military operation" a war with up to fifteen years in prison.[37] Such censorship has led to an exodus of journalists from Russia, as well as the demise of the country's independent media. Outside Russia's Orwellian mediasphere, Putin appears to have lost not only the battles to take Kyiv, Kharkhiv, and Kherson but also a war waged in macho memes with Ukraine's president, Volodymyr Zelenskyy. On one hand, Putin's public appearances after the invasion have shown Russia's bloated, seventy-year-old president wearing the same Italian suits and occupying the same Kremlin conference rooms in which the world has seen him for the past twenty years, as he chastens and humiliates various minions. On the other hand, Zelenskyy, who is Putin's junior by a full quarter century, has astutely used social media from Instagram to TikTok to broadcast images of himself in more varied clothing and daring settings, including full combat attire and on the battle front. This contrast has led to a glut of memes beyond the firewalls erected by Roskomnadzor, which size up the two presidents' virility and deem Zelenskyy the winner. Whether the meme shows two moons rising over an intergalactic horizon, the few features on earth visible from outer space, the heaviest object in the universe, or a supersized cargo plane as the only transport that can carry them, Zelenskyy's balls quickly became shorthand for his resolute leadership, and they even inspired a group of musicians headed by Les Claypool to record the song "Zelensky: The Man with the Iron Balls."[38] On the contrary, Putin found himself castigated once again with a condom, whose shiny red package reads, "Putin, for dicks that don't know when to pull out."

Although this battle of manly memes relies on the same techniques of political legitimation that, according to Valerie Sperling, have long typified politics in Russia, some of the images coming out of Ukraine since February 2022 tend not to embrace but to reject the limited terms of hypergender.[39] After the war's start, for example, a video of an almost topless Zelenskyy, doing booty drops to Beyoncé's "All the Single Ladies" in skin-tight black pants and platform stilettos, went viral on the internet.[40] Even though the video repurposed a parody from Ukrainian television already five years old of a song already ten years in the past, "All the Single Vlady's" garnered fan comments that ranged from "What CAN'T this incredible man do???" to "Never underestimate someone who can dance in five-inch heels."[41] While Zelenskyy blended Putin's topless antics from the late 2000s with the type of drag that mocked the Russian president in the "gay clown" meme banned in 2017, Ukrainian women showed their own willingness to cross the gender divide. Even before Russia's invasion, women composed about 23 percent of the Ukrainian military, which led to a series of photos featuring young, attractive, gun-toting female defenders of Ukraine once the war began.[42] One popular subgenre of this type of image shows combat-ready women holding cats, dogs, and children, making the amalgam of a masculine activity like war with a feminine attribute like nurturing all the more obvious. Other images in this vein include the former Miss Ukraine Anastasiia Lenna posing with an airsoft rifle, Ukrainian mothers carrying guns, grandmothers making Molotov cocktails, and, of course, the gutsy woman who cursed a Russian occupier, telling him to put sunflower seeds in his pocket so that they would grow on Ukrainian soil when he dies.[43] Given the life-and-death stakes of the war, these Ukrainian women do not appear to be donning any form of *travesti* or trying to craft an image of their motherland as trans. Instead, they are bravely expanding the Venn diagram of gender in their country, so that men and women share a greater number of life-saving attributes and activities, occupy the same level field of battle, and shoulder the burden of averting the existential threat to their families and country together.

Women in Russia have also done what they can to bring Putin's march through Ukraine to a halt. After the imposition of the new censorship law,

Marina Ovsiannikova, an editor at the state-controlled television Channel One, interrupted a live news broadcast while carrying a clearly visible placard on which was written "NO WAR. Stop the war; don't believe the propaganda; they're lying to you here."[44] Likewise, a group of Russian women has formed the Feminist Antiwar Resistance alliance, whose manifesto denounces the "'traditional values' includ[ing] gender inequality, exploitation of women, and state repression against those whose way of life, self-identification, and actions do not conform with narrow patriarchal norms," under whose banner Putin justifies the war.[45] In addition to organizing a protest on International Women's Day shortly after the conflict's start, the group maintains an active presence on Telegram so that they can share images from their protests, as well as guidelines and support for others hoping to combat the war. Like their Ukrainian counterparts fighting Russian troops, these women are Putin's worst nightmare, since they completely defy the postfeminist ideal of female citizenship in service to men, whether in the Russian Federation or elsewhere.

It is still too early for us to speculate about who or what Putinism's ideal Russian citizen will become in the wake of the monstrous war in Ukraine. However, we can state with confidence that this ideal will include neither the growing number of Russian women who refuse Putin's mandate of hypergender nor the millions of Ukrainians who reject his attempt to transform their country into a *travesti* of Russia. Perhaps Putinism's new dream of the ideal citizen lies in the two-hundred-seventy-thousand Russian troops, who, according to one estimate, perished on the battlefields of Mariupol', Lviv', and other Ukrainian cities during the first year of Putin's war.[46] Like the millions of Soviet soldiers who gave their lives in World War II and Afghanistan, the dead can no longer tell their own stories, making them fodder for the type of mythmaking we see in phenomena from the Immortal Regiment to films like Bondarchuk's *9th Company* and Russia's annual celebration of Victory Day. Putin's extravagant parade and bombastic speech marking this holiday in 2022—while both Ukrainian and Russian soldiers lost their lives in his reckless and senseless war—certainly confirms that the styles of gender and sexuality fostered by Putinism, which seemed all fun and games in the 2000s and took a turn for the worse in the 2010s, have always been dead serious.

Notes

Introduction

1. “Ul’ianovskie kursanty—Satisfaction,” YouTube, 20 January 2018, https://www.youtube.com/watch?v=k7y2ADtBhFc.

2. Benny Benassi, “‘Satisfaction’ (Official Video),” YouTube, 7 April 2012, https://www.youtube.com/watch?v=aZcSCT34H84.

3. johnnychs07, “army satisfaction,” YouTube, 9 February 2013, https://www.youtube.com/watch?v=ucOhx09ivg0.

4. Eliot Borenstein chronicles public reactions in “Boys Just Want to Have Fun: Just How Queer Are the ‘Satisfaction’ Videos?,” NYU Jordan Center, 27 February 2018, http://jordanrussiacenter.org/news/boys-just-want-fun-just-queer-satisfaction-videos/#.WtOzTtPwZ3m. See also Borenstein’s “Post-Soviet Masculinities: Sex, Power, and the Vanishing Subject,” in *The Routledge Handbook of Gender in Central-Eastern Europe and Eurasia*, ed. Katalin Fábián, Janet Elise Johnson, and Mara Lazda (London: Routledge, 2022), 82–83; and Borenstein, “Men at Twerk,” in *Meanwhile, in Russia: Russian Internet Memes and Viral Video* (London: Bloomsbury Academic, 2022), 93–95.

5. Masha Gessen, “How Russia’s Hilarious, Homoerotic ‘Satisfaction’ Became a Nationwide Meme of Solidarity,” *New Yorker*, 22 January 2018, https://www.newyorker.com/news/our-columnists/how-russias-hilarious-homoerotic-satisfaction-became-a-nationwide-meme-of-solidarity.

6. Borenstein argues that the Ulianovsk cadets’ group performance shields them from accusations of homosexuality, since “homosociality renders gayness all but unthinkable” in the Russian context (“Post-Soviet Masculinities,” 83). See also Alina Ryabovolova and Julie Hemment, “‘Je suis satisfaction’: Russian Politics in the Age of Hybrid Media,” *East European Politics* 36, no. 1 (2020): 9–26; and Galina Miazhevich, “An Innocent Provocation or Homoerotic Challenge? Mediations of the ‘*Satisfaction*’ Video Parody in the Russian Mediascape,” *Information, Communication & Society* 24, no. 8 (2020): 1123–39.

7. For an overview of Russia’s emergence as an antiliberal state, see Marlene Laruelle, “Russia as an Anti-liberal European Civilization,” in *The New Russian Nationalism: Imperialism, Ethnicity, and Authoritarianism, 2000–2015*, ed. Pål Kolstø and Helge Blakkisrud (Edinburgh: Edinburgh University Press, 2016), 275–97.

8. Ivana Kottasova, "Protests over Russia, Belarus and Kazakhstan 'Ban' on Lacy Underwear," *CNN*, 21 February 2014, https://www.cnn.com/2014/02/21/business/kazakhstan-lace-underwear-ban/index.html; Shaun Walker, "Transgender People in Russia Banned from Driving, Says Legal Amendment," *The Guardian*, 9 January 2015; Avi Selk and David Filipov, "It's Now Illegal in Russia to Share an Image of Putin as a Gay Clown," *Washington Post*, 5 April 2017.

9. ThePubliciti, "Putin's Army [English Subs]," YouTube, 19 July 2011, https://www.youtube.com/watch?v=klcyPNIA698; "Russia Gay Blood Donation Ban, Free Conversion Therapy Proposed by Moscow Mayoral Candidate," *HuffPost*, 2 February 2016, https://www.huffingtonpost.com/2013/08/26/russia-gay-blood-ban-_n_3816935.html.

10. For scholarship addressing these trends, see the work of Stephen J. Collier, Julie Hemment, Michele Rivkin-Fish, Jarrett Zigon, Anna Temkina and Elena Zdravomyslova, Ilya Matveev, and Peter Rutland.

11. Valerie Sperling, *Sex, Politics, Putin: Political Legitimacy in Russia* (New York: Oxford University Press, 2015), 29–79; Janet Elise Johnson, *The Gender of Informal Politics: Russia, Iceland, and Twenty-First Century Male Dominance* (Cham, Switzerland: Palgrave Macmillan, 2018).

12. Andrey Makarychev and Sergei Medvedev, "Biopolitics and Power in Putin's Russia," *Problems of Post-Communism* 62 (2015): 45.

13. Sasha Chest feat. Timati, "Luchshii drug (Prem'era klipa, 2015)," YouTube, 6 October 2015, https://www.youtube.com/watch?v=jp9pfvneKf4.

14. Pål Kolstø, "The Ethnification of Russian Nationalism," in *The New Russian Nationalism*, ed. Pål Kolstø and Helge Blakkisrud (Edinburgh: Edinburgh University Press, 2016), 18–45; Taras Kuzio, "Nationalism and Authoritarianism in Russia: Introduction to the Special Issue," *Communist and Post-Communist Studies* 49 (2016): 1–11; Marlene Laruelle, "Misinterpreting Nationalism: Why Russkii Is Not a Sign of Ethnonationalism," *PONARS Eurasia* (27 January 2016), https://www.ponarseurasia.org/misinterpreting-nationalism-why-russkii-is-not-a-sign-of-ethnonationalism; and Laruelle, *The "Russian World": Russia's Soft Power and Geopolitical Imagination* (Washington, DC: Center on Global Interests, 2015).

15. David von Drehle, "Opinion: The Man Known as 'Putin's Brain' Envisions the Splitting of Europe—and the Fall of China," *Washington Post* (22 March 2022). See also Marcin Skladanowski, "The Myth of Russian Exceptionalism: Russia as a Civilization and Its Uniqueness in Aleksandr G. Dugin's Thought," *Politics, Religion & Ideology* 20, no. 4 (2019): 423–46.

16. For such studies, see Helen Faller, *Nation, Language, Islam: Tatarstan's Sovereignty Movement* (New York: Central European University Press, 2011); Zvi Gitelman, *Jewish Identities in Postcommunist Russia and Ukraine: An Uncertain Ethnicity* (New York: Cambridge University Press, 2012); Iana Kirei-Sitnikova, *Politicheskie vzgliady trans* soobshchetva: Rezul'taty oprosa* (n.p.: Trans* Koallitsiia, 2015); Federic Prina, *National Minorities in Putin's Russia* (New York: Routledge, 2016); Dominic Rubin, *Russia's Muslim Heartlands: Islam in the Putin Era* (London: Hurst & Company, 2018).

17. Susan Sontag, "Notes on 'Camp,'" in *Against Interpretation and Other Essays* (New York: Farrar, Straus & Giroux, 1966), 288.

18. Borenstein, "Boys Just Want to Have Fun"; Gessen, "How Russia's Hilarious, Homoerotic 'Satisfaction' Became a Nationwide Meme."

19. For an overview of the "presumptively masculine and heteronormative subject" of citizenship in modern states, as well as contemporary paradigms of gendered, sexual, and queer citizenship, see Leti Volpp, "Feminist, Sexual, and Queer Citizenship," in *The Oxford Handbook of Citizenship*, ed. Ayelet Shachar, Rainer Bauböck, Irene Bloemraad, and Maarten Vink (New York: Oxford University Press, 2017).

20. The exception to this trend is Francesca Stella, whose work on lesbians and sexual citizenship interrogates Western paradigms and "emphasizes contingency and cultural difference rather than universality and sameness." Francesca Stella, "The Right to Be Different? Sexual Citizenship and Its Politics in Post-Soviet Russia," in *Gender, Equality and Difference during and after State Socialism*, ed. Rebecca Kay (Basingstoke: Palgrave Macmillan, 2007), 147; Francesca Stella, *Lesbian Lives in Soviet and Post-Soviet Russia: Post/Socialism and Gendered Sexualities* (New York: Palgrave Macmillan, 2015), 26–44; Francesca Stella and Nadya Nartova, "Sexual Citizenship, Nationalism, and Biopolitics in Putin's Russia," in *Sexuality, Citizenship and Belonging: Trans-National and Intersectional Perspectives*, ed. Francesca Stella et al. (New York: Routledge, 2016), 17–36. In addition to Stella and Nartova's work, the discussion of embodied citizenship in the Soviet Union and Russia that follows relies on E. A. Zdravomyslova and A. A. Temkina, "Transformatsiia gendernogo grazhdanstva v sovremennoi Rossii," in *Kuda prishla Rossiia? Itogi sotsietal'noi transformatsii*, ed. T. I. Zaslavskaia (Moscow: MVShSEN, 2003), 140–50; Elena Zdravomyslova, "Gendernoe grazhdanstvo i abortnaia kul'tura," in *Zdorov'e i doveria: gendernyi podkhod k reproduktivnoi meditsine*, ed. Elena Zdravomyslova and Anna Temkina (St. Petersburg: Izd. Evropeiskogo universiteta v Sankt-Peterburge, 2009), 108–35; Elena Zdravomyslova, "Gendered Citizenship in Soviet and Post-Soviet Societies," in *Nation and Gender in Contemporary Europe*, ed. Vera Tolz and Stephenie Booth (New York: Palgrave, 2005), 96–113; A. Temkina and A. Rotkirkh, "Sovetskie gendernye kontrakty i ikh transformatsiia v sovremennoi Rossii," *SotsIs* 11 (2002), http://www.isras.ru/files/File/Socis/2002-11/Tyomkina_Rotkirx.pdf; E. A. Zdravomyslova and A. A. Temkina, "Sovetskii etakraticheskii gendernyi poriadok," in *Sotsial'naia istoriia. Ezhegodnik, 2003. Zhenskaia i gendernaia istoriia*, ed. N. L. Pushkareva (Moscow: ROSSPEN, 2003), 463; Dan Healey, *Russian Homophobia from Stalin to Sochi* (London: Bloomsbury, 2018); Alexander Kondakov, "Rethinking the Sexual Citizenship from Queer and Post-Soviet Perspectives: Queer Urban Spaces and the Right to the Socialist City," *Sexualities* 1, no. 17 (2017): 1–17; Kondakov, "The Silenced Citizens of Russia: Exclusion of Non-heterosexual Subjects from Rights-Based Citizenship," *Social & Legal Studies* 23, no. 2 (2014): 151–74; Kondakov, "Pereopredelenie moral'nykh granits grazhdanstva v Rossii: Diskurs o gomoseksual'nosti posle raspada SSSR," in *XV aprel'skaia mezhdunarodnaia nauchnaia konferentsiia po problemam razvitiia ekonomiki i obshchestva*, vol. 3, ed. E. G. Iasin (Moscow: Izdatel'skii dom Vysshei shkoly ekonomiki, 2015), 43–51; Igor S. Kon, *The Sexual Revolution in Russia: From the Age of the Czars to Today*, trans. James Riordan (New York: Free Press, 1995); I. S. Kon, *Seksual'naia kul'tura v Rossii: Klubnichka na berezke* (Moscow: O.G.I., 1997).

21. The concept of embodied citizenship originated in disability studies and now includes not only gender and sexuality but also class, ethnicity, religion, and disability. For examples, see Emily Russell, *Reading Embodied Citizenship: Disability, Narrative, and the Body Politic* (New Brunswick, NJ: Rutgers University Press, 2011), and the

overview of the University of Nottingham's 2016 conference on embodied citizenship, https://embodiedcitizenshipblog.wordpress.com/.

22. Zdravomyslova and Temkina, "Gendered Citizenship," 96.

23. Temkina and Rotkirch, "Sovetskie gendernye kontrakty," 7. See also Eric Naiman, *Sex in Public: The Incarnation of Early Soviet Ideology* (Princeton, NJ: Princeton University Press, 1997); Gregory Carleton, *Sexual Revolution in Bolshevik Russia* (Pittsburgh: University of Pittsburgh Press, 2005).

24. Dan Healey, *Homosexual Desire in Revolutionary Russia: The Regulation of Sexual and Gender Dissent* (Chicago: University of Chicago Press, 2001) and *Bolshevik Sexual Forensics: Diagnosing Disorder in the Clinic and Courtroom, 1917–1939* (DeKalb: Northern Illinois University Press, 2009).

25. Frances Bernstein, *The Dictatorship of Sex: Lifestyle Advice for the Soviet Masses* (DeKalb: Northern Illinois University Press, 2007), 129–58.

26. Zdravomyslova, "Gendernoe grazhdanstvo," 113–20.

27. Healey, *Russian Homophobia*, xiv; see also 158–60. Irina Roldugina's archival research reveals that the recriminalization of sodomy in the Soviet Union happened at Stalin's personal behest. Irina Roldugina, "Vernacular Queer and Shifting Power in Russia: From the Late Imperial Era up to the 1930s" (PhD diss., Oxford University, 2021).

28. Kondakov, "The Silenced Citizens of Russia," 157. See also Brian James Baer, "Now You See It: Gay (In)visibility and the Performance of Post-Soviet Identity," in *Queer Visibility in Post-socialist Cultures*, ed. Nárcisz Fejes and Andrea P. Balogh (Bristol: Intellect Books, 2012), 37–39.

29. For discussion of Stalinism's castration of male subjectivity, see Lilya Kaganovsky, *How the Soviet Man Was Unmade: Cultural Fantasy and Male Subjectivity under Stalin* (Pittsburgh: University of Pittsburgh Press, 2008).

30. Healey, *Russian Homophobia*, 98–100. For a photographic homage to Moscow's Soviet-era *pleshki*, see Yevgeniy Fiks, *Moscow* (Brooklyn, NY: Ugly Duckling Presse, 2013).

31. Zdravomyslova, "Gendernoe grazhdanstvo," 120–33.

32. Elena Zdravomyslova and Anna Temkina, "Krizis maskulinnosti v pozdnesovetskom diskurse," in *O muzhe(n)stvennosti: Sbornik statei*, ed. S. Ushakin (Moscow: Novoe literaturnoe obozrenie, 2002), 432–51.

33. Eliot Borenstein, *Overkill: Sex and Violence in Contemporary Russian Popular Culture* (Ithaca, NY: Cornell University Press, 2008), 24–50.

34. Kondakov, "The Silenced Citizens of Russia," 162. See also Alexander Kondakov, "Resisting the Silence: The Use of Tolerance and Equality Arguments by Gay and Lesbian Activist Groups in Russia," *Canadian Journal of Law and Society* 28, no. 3 (2013): 403–24.

35. Healey, *Russian Homophobia*, 104–9. Russian gay culture of the 1990s is documented in Laurie Essig, *Queer in Russia: A Story of Sex, Self, and Other* (Durham, NC: Duke University Press, 1999); and David Tuller, *Cracks in the Iron Closet: Travels in Gay and Lesbian Russia* (Boston: Faber and Faber, 1996).

36. Baer, "Now You See It," 40.

37. Anna Rotkirch, *The Man Question: Loves and Lives in Late 20th Century Russia* (Helsinki: University of Helsinki—Department of Social Policy, 2000), 264–73. See also Viktor Erofeev, *Muzhchiny* (Moscow: Izdatel'skii Dom "Podkova," 1997).

38. Zdravomyslova and Temkina, "Transformatsiia gendernogo grazhdanstva," 141–42.

39. Anna Temkina and Elena Zdravomyslova, "The Sexual Scripts and Identity of Middle-Class Russian Women," *Sexuality & Culture* 19 (2015): 297–320.

40. E. B. Mizulina, "Kontseptsiia semeinoi politiki imeni Mizulinoi," *Advokat Anton Zharov*, accessed 1 November 2022, https://zharov.info/guestbook/koncepciya-semejnoj-politiki-imeni-mizulinoj.

41. Rivkin-Fish, "Pronatalism, Gender Politics, and the Renewal of Family Support in Russia: Toward a Feminist Anthropology of 'Maternity Capital,'" *Slavic Review* 69, no. 3 (October 2010): 701–24.

42. Ekaterina Borozdina et al., "Using Maternity Capital: Citizen Distrust of Russian Family Policy," *European Journal of Women's Studies* 23, no. 1 (2016): 60–75.

43. Sperling, *Sex, Politics, Putin*; Helena Goscilo, "Putin's Performance of Masculinity: The Action Hero and Macho Sex-Object," in *Putin as Celebrity and Cultural Icon* (London: Routledge, 2013), 180–207; Julie A. Cassiday and Emily D. Johnson, "A Personality Cult for the Postmodern Age: Reading Vladimir Putin's Public Persona," in *Putin as Celebrity and Cultural Icon*, ed. Helena Goscilo (London: Routledge, 2013), 37–64; Elizabeth A. Wood, "Hypermasculinity as a Scenario of Power," *International Feminist Journal of Politics* 18, no. 3 (2016): 329–50.

44. Kondakov, "The Silenced Citizens," 164.

45. Healey, *Russian Homophobia*, 138–47.

46. Stella and Nartova, "Sexual Citizenship, Nationalism, and Biopolitics," 27.

47. Volpp, "Feminist, Sexual, and Queer Citizenship."

48. Lauren Berlant, *The Queen of American Goes to Washington City: Essays on Sex and Citizenship* (Durham, NC: Duke University Press, 1997); Jasbir Puar, *Terrorist Assemblages: Homonationalism in Queer Times* (Durham, NC: Duke University Press, 2007), 2.

49. J. L. Austin, *How to Do Things with Words: The William James Lectures Delivered at Harvard University in 1955* (Oxford: Clarendon Press, 1962); Judith Butler, *Gender Trouble: Feminism and the Subversion of Identity* (New York: Routledge, 2007).

50. Shirin M. Rai, "The Dilemmas of Performative Citizenship," in *Gendered Citizenship: Manifestations and Performance*, ed. Bishnupriya Dutt, Janelle Reinelt, and Shrinkhla Sahai (Cham, Switzerland: Palgrave Macmillan, 2017), 25–26, 29, 32. See also Engin Isin, "Performative Citizenship," in *The Oxford Handbook of Citizenship*, ed. Ayelet Shachar, Rainer Bauböck, Irene Bloemraad, and Maarten Vink (New York: Oxford University Press, 2017), 500–523; Mary McThomas, *Performing Citizenship: Undocumented Migrants in the United States* (New York: Routledge, 2016). On the intersection of performance studies and political science, see Jenny Edkins and Adrian Kear, eds., *International Politics and Performance: Critical Aesthetics and Creative Practice* (London: Routledge, 2013); Shirin M. Rai and Janelle Reinelt, eds., *The Grammar of Politics and Performance* (London: Routledge, 2015).

51. Isin, "Performative Citizenship," 506.

52. Stella, "The Right to Be Different?," 162.

53. Charles Tilly, *Contentious Performances* (Cambridge: Cambridge University Press, 2008); Rai, "The Dilemmas of Performative Citizenship," 40. Stella's fieldwork among lesbians in Moscow and Ulianovsk confirms that some nonheterosexual Russians believe "'there are no rights in Russia'" and that "Western models of sexual citizenship predicated upon rights claims did not appeal to all [of her] interviewees." Stella, "The Right to Be Different?," 155, 158.

54. Alexander Etkind, "Introduction: Genres and Genders of Protest in Russia's Petrostate," in *Cultural Forms of Protest in Russia*, ed. Birgit Beumers, Alexander Etkind, Olga Gurova, and Sanna Turoma (London: Routledge, 2018), 6. See also Etkind's "The Decay of the Russian Public Sphere," *Current History* 114, no. 774 (October 2015): 278–81; and "Post-Soviet Russia: The Land of the Oil Curse, Pussy Riot, and Magical Historicism," *boundary 2* 41, no. 1 (2014): 153–70.

55. Helen Goscilo's analysis of glossy magazines of the 1990s describes the emergence of embodied style as a post-Soviet phenomenon. Helena Goscilo, "Style and S(t)imulation: Popular Magazines, or the Aestheticization of Postsoviet Russia," *Studies in 20th Century Literature* 24, no. 1 (2000): 15–50. Graham Roberts notes a similar shift from *homo faber* to *homo consumens* in "From Superman to the Invisible Man: Imagining the Male Body in Contemporary Russian Advertising," *Consumer Culture, Branding and Identity in the New Russia: From Five-Year Plan to 4×4* (London: Routledge, 2016), 79.

56. Alexei Yurchak, *Everything Was Forever, Until It Was No More: The Last Soviet Generation* (Princeton, NJ: Princeton University Press, 2013), 23.

57. Yurchak, *Everything Was Forever*, 26.

58. Viktor Erofeev, "Stil', stil', stil'," in *Muzhchiny* (Moscow: Izdatel'skii Dom Podkova, 1997), 10–12.

59. Erofeev, "Stil', stil', stil',"10.

60. Svetlana Boym, "Kitch i sotsialisticheskii realizm," *Novoe literaturnoe obozrenie* 15 (1996): 54–65.

61. Valerii Pecheikin, "Viktor Erofeev: Rossiia kak transvestit," *Kvir* 75 (1 June 2014), http://www.kvir.ru/articles/viktor-erofeev-rossiya.html.

62. Sergei Livnev's feature film *Hammer and Sickle* provides an intriguing backstory to the notion of Russia as trans (*Serp i molot*, Moscow: MMM-Studiia, 1994). The film tells the story of Evdokiia Kuznetsova, who undergoes the first ever gender-affirming surgery in Stalin's Russia, which is intended to address the deficit of men in the 1930s. As Kaganovsky points out in *How the Soviet Man Was Unmade*, Livnev depicts the newly crafted Evdokim Kuznetsov's masculinity as a matter of performance (156–69). As my students at Williams College have noted, the circumstances surrounding the gender-affirming surgery in the film are highly coercive, and we never learn whether Evdokiia was a willing participant in the experiment that transforms her into Evdokim.

63. Alexandra Novitskaya, "Patriotism, Sentiment, and Male Hysteria: Putin's Masculinity Politics and the Persecution of Non-heterosexual Russians," *NORMA: International Journal of Masculinity Studies* 12, nos. 3–4 (2017): 304.

64. Novitskaya, "Patriotism, Sentiment, and Male Hysteria," 307; Alexander Kondakov, "Crip Kinship: A Political Strategy of People Who Were Deemed Contagious by the Shirtless Putin," *Feminist Formations* 30, no. 1 (Spring 2018): 76.

65. Baer, "Now You See It," 39.

66. Kondakov, "Crip Kinship," 71.

Chapter 1. A Genealogy of Post-Soviet Pop Performativity

1. Viktor Erofeev, "Stil', stil', stil'," in *Muzhchiny* (Moscow: Izdatel'skii Dom Podkova, 1997), 12.

2. Viktor Erofeev, "Molodoi stil' (Na perekrestke mnenii. Zametki o biologii stilia)," in *Shchel'* (Moscow: RIPOL klassik, 2018), 315, 342.

3. Plato, *The Republic of Plato*, trans. Francis Macdonald Cornford (London: Oxford University Press, 1941), 81–85; Aristotle, *Aristotle's Poetics: A Translation and Commentary for Students of Literature*, trans. Leon Golden (Englewood Cliffs, NJ: Prentice Hall, 1968), 33–41; Aristotle, *On Rhetoric: A Theory of Civic Discourse*, 2nd ed., trans. George A. Kennedy (New York: Oxford University Press, 2007), 197–229. See also Catherine Steel, "Divisions of Speech," in *The Cambridge Companion in Ancient Rhetoric*, ed. Erik Gunderson (Cambridge: Cambridge University Press, 2009), 88–89.

4. Cicero, "Orator," *Cicero V, Loeb Classical Library*, trans. H. M. Hubbell, ed. Jeffery Henderson (Cambridge, MA: Harvard University Press, 1939), 356–57; Nicolas Boileau-Despréaux, *The Art of Poetry, Written in French by the Sieur de Boileau, Made English* (London: R. Bentley and S. Magnes, 1683); Northrop Frye, *The Well-Tempered Critic* (Bloomington: Indiana University Press, 1963), 94–108.

5. Eliot Borenstein, *Plots against Russia: Conspiracy and Fantasy after Socialism* (Ithaca, NY: Cornell University Press, 2019); Kevin M. F. Platt, "Russian Empire of Pop: Post-Socialist Nostalgia and Soviet Retro at the 'New Wave' Competition," *The Russian Review* 72 (July 2013): 447–69.

6. Fredric Jameson, *Postmodernism, or, The Cultural Logic of Late Capitalism* (Durham, NC: Duke University Press, 1991), 17–18.

7. Clement Greenberg, "Avant-Garde and Kitsch," in *Art and Culture: Critical Essays* (Boston: Beacon Press, 1961), 3–21; Susan Sontag, "Notes on 'Camp,'" in *Against Interpretation and Other Essays* (New York: Farrar, Straus & Giroux, 1966), 275–92.

8. Eve Kosofsky Sedgwick, *Tendencies* (Durham, NC: Duke University Press, 1993), 8.

9. Elena Gapova, "Polnyi Fuko: Telo kak pole vlasti," *Neprikosnovennyi zapas* 76, no. 2 (2011), https://magazines.gorky.media/nz/2011/2/polnyj-fuko-telo-kak-pole-vlasti.html; Helena Goscilo, "Putin's Performance of Masculinity: The Action Hero and Macho Sex-Object," in *Putin as Celebrity and Cultural Icon* (London: Routledge, 2013), 180–207; Oleg Riabov and Tatiana Riabova, "The 'Remasculinization' of Russia? Gender, Nationalism, and the Legitimation of Power under Vladimir Putin," *Problems of Post-Communism* 61, no. 2 (2014): 23–35; Oleg Riabov and Tatiana Riabov, "The Real Man of Politics in Russia (On Gender Discourse as a Resource for the Authority)," *Social Sciences* 42, no. 3 (2011): 58–71; Valerie Sperling, *Sex, Politics, and Putin: Political Legitimacy in Russia* (New York: Oxford University Press, 2015), 29–79; Elizabeth A. Wood, "Hypermasculinity as a Scenario of Power," *International Feminist Journal of Politics* 18, no. 3 (2016): 329–50.

10. Max Weber, *The Theory of Social and Economic Organization*, trans. A. M. Henderson and Talcott Parsons (Ithaca, NY: Cornell University Press, 1947), 358.

11. Goscilo, "Putin's Performance of Masculinity: The Action Hero and Macho Sex-Object"; Julie A. Cassiday and Emily Johnson, "A Personality Cult for the Postmodern Age: Reading Vladimir's Putin's Public Persona," in *Putin as Celebrity and Cultural Icon*, ed. Helena Goscilo (London: Routledge, 2013), 40–46.

12. For the Putin-inspired novel, see Aleksandr Ol'bik, *Prezident* (Donetsk: Izdatel'stvo "Stalker," 2002).

13. Nikita Mikhalkov, dir., "55. Dokumental'nyi fil'm o Vladimire Putine. Nikita Mikhalkov," YouTube, 22 September 2014, https://www.youtube.com/watch?v=afmYJULOkQc.

14. On Kadyrov's Instagram account, see RFE/RL's North Caucasus Service, "'Content Unavailable': Facebook Again Blocks Kadyrov's Instagram Account," *Radio Free Europe/Radio Liberty*, 14 May 2020, https://www.rferl.org/a/content-unavailable-facebook-again-blocks-kadyrov-s-instagram-account/30611740.html.

15. "Sasha Chest feat. Timati—Luchshii drug (Prem'era klipa, 2015)," YouTube, 6 October 2015, https://www.youtube.com/watch?v=jp9pfvneKf4.

16. For deeper analysis, see Cassiday and Johnson, "A Personality Cult for the Postmodern Age."

17. Weber, *The Theory of Social and Economic Organization*, 359.

18. Aleksandr Elin, "*Takogo kak Putin*/Someone Like Putin, English Subs," YouTube, 6 December 2008, https://www.youtube.com/watch?v=zk_VszbZa_s.

19. Cassiday and Johnson, "A Personality Cult for the Postmodern Age." For reporting on "Someone Like Putin," see Stephen Talbot, "Sound Tracks Pilot Episode," *PBS*, 25 January 2010, https://www.pbs.org/video/sound-tracks-sound-tracks-pilot-episode/.

20. Sontag, "Notes on 'Camp,'" 277.

21. Judith Butler, *Gender Trouble: Feminism and the Subversion of Identity* (New York: Routledge, 2007); Eve Kosofsky Sedgwick, *Touching, Feeling: Affect, Pedagogy, Performativity* (Durham, NC: Duke University Press, 2003).

22. Max Weber, "The Sociology of Charismatic Authority," in *From Max Weber: Essays in Sociology*, trans. H. H. Gerth and C. Wright Mills (New York: Oxford University Press, 1946), 245.

23. Gregory Krieg, "Donald Trump Defends Size of His Penis," *CNN Politics*, 4 March 2016, https://www.cnn.com/2016/03/03/politics/donald-trump-small-hands-marco-rubio/index.html.

24. Weber, "The Sociology of Charismatic Authority," 246.

25. Gregory Freidin, *A Coat of Many Colors: Osip Mandelshtam and His Mythologies of Self-Presentation* (Berkeley: University of California Press, 1987), 4.

26. As Eliot Borenstein describes when discussing post-Soviet political parties, "More than merely patriotic, these party names are *phatic*. And in some cases, they are also deliberately proleptic, as if they are trying to call into existence a desired state of affairs, as in an incantation or magic spell" (*Plots against Russia*, 111).

27. Sontag, "Notes on 'Camp,'" 280, 290.

28. Sontag, "Notes on 'Camp,'" 288.

29. Sontag, "Notes on 'Camp,'" 285.

30. Sontag, "Notes on 'Camp,'" 285.

31. Sontag, "Notes on 'Camp,'" 276.

32. Sontag, "Notes on 'Camp,'" 281.

33. Fabio Cleto, "Introduction: Queering the Camp," in *Camp: Queer Aesthetics and the Performing Subject: A Reader* (Ann Arbor: University of Michigan Press, 1999), 33, 31.

34. Sontag, "Notes on 'Camp,'" 278, 281.

35. Sontag, "Notes on 'Camp,'" 279.

36. Sontag, "Notes on 'Camp,'" 285–86.

37. Weber, *The Theory of Social and Economic Organization*, 359.

38. Sontag, "Notes on 'Camp,'" 277.

39. Sontag, "Notes on 'Camp,'" 291, 292, 278, 292.

40. Sedgwick, *Touching, Feeling*, 156.

41. This meme was created in 2015 by the Syrian artist Saint Hoax in their series "Fame Drags You Out." Sara Boboltz, "Here's Why Donald Trump Just Got a Drag Makeover," *HuffPost*, 25 August 2015, https://www.huffpost.com/entry/saint-hoax-celebrities-in-drag_n_55dc8da5e4b0a40aa3ac3758.

42. The ban on depicting Putin as a gay clown is item 4071 on "The Federal List of Extremist Materials" of the Ministry of Justice of the Russian Federation, "Ekstremistskie materialy," *Ministerstvo iustitsii Rossiiskoi Federatsii*, accessed 25 February 2022, https://minjust.gov.ru/ru/extremist-materials/. See also James E. Baker et al., "Putin as Gay Icon? Memes as a Tactic in Russian LGBT+ Activism," in *LGBTQ+ Activism in Central and Eastern Europe*, ed. R. Buyantueva and M. Shevtsova (New York: Palgrave Macmillan, 2020), 209–33; Eliot Borenstein, "'Putin Is a Dickhead,'" in *Meanwhile, in Russia: Russian Internet Memes and Viral Video* (London: Bloomsbury Academic, 2022), 60–63.

43. Sontag, "Notes on 'Camp,'" 289. Sontag considers Sergei Eisenstein's film *Ivan the Terrible* to be almost camp (284). Svetlana Boym echoes Sontag's opinion, asserting that the Soviet Union's lack of affluence precluded meaningful application of the term "camp" until the end of the 1980s. Svetlana Boym, *Common Places: Mythologies of Everyday Life in Russia* (Cambridge, MA: Harvard University Press, 1994), 19. For examples of Russian camp, see Maria Brock and Galina Miazhevich, "From High Camp to Post-modern Camp: Queering Post-Soviet Pop Music," *European Journal of Cultural Studies* 25, no. 4 (2021): 1–17; Maria Engström, "Little Big: Neo-camp and a New Generation of Russian Identity," *Riddle*, 20 May 2019, https://www.ridl.io/en/little-big-neo-camp-and-a-new-generation-of-russian-identity/; and the University of Pittsburgh's 2012 Russian Film Symposium, which was devoted to "Camp Cinema: Russian Style," accessed 2 November 2022, https://rusfilm.pitt.edu/2012-camp-cinema-russian-style/.

44. Andrew Ross, "Uses of Camp," in *Camp: Queer Aesthetics and the Performing Subject: A Reader* (Ann Arbor: University of Michigan Press, 1999), 310.

45. Ross, "Uses of Camp," 312, 320.

46. Ross, "Uses of Camp," 324.

47. Ross, "Uses of Camp," 326.

48. Moe Meyer, "Introduction: Reclaiming the Discourse of Camp," in *The Politics and Poetics of Camp* (London: Routledge, 1994), 11.

49. On the 2011–2012 protests, see Mischa Gabowitsch, *Protest in Putin's Russia* (Cambridge: Polity Press, 2016).

50. For examples, see Birgit Beumers et al., eds., *Cultural Forms of Protest in Russia* (London: Routledge, 2018); Lena Johnson, *Art and Protest in Putin's Russia* (London: Routledge, 2015); Lilya Kaganovsky, "*Vystuplenie i nakazanie*: Performing Political Protest in Putin's Russia (Voina, Pussy Riot, Pavlensky)," in *Russian Performances: Word, Object, Action*, ed. Julie A. Buckler, Julie A. Cassiday, and Boris Wolfson (Madison: University of Wisconsin Press, 2018); Alexandar Mihailovic, *The Mitki and the Art of Postmodern Protest in Russia* (Madison: University of Wisconsin Press, 2018).

51. Ilya Kalinin, "Why 'Two Russians' Are Less than 'United Russia': Cultural Distinctions and Political Similarities: Dialectics of Defeat," in Beumers et al., *Cultural Forms of Protest in Russia*, 49.

52. Eliot Borenstein, *Pussy Riot: Speaking Punk to Power* (London: Bloomsbury Academic, 2021), 42.

53. Borenstein, *Pussy Riot*, 5; Mihailovic, *The Mitki and the Art of Postmodern Protest in Russia*, 211–12.

54. For a brief history of such colored ribbons in relation to the St. George's ribbon, see Serguei Alex. Oushakine, "Performative Objects: How Things Do Things without Words," in *Russian Performances: Word, Object, Action*, ed. Julie A. Buckler, Julie A. Cassiday, and Boris Wolfson (Madison: University of Wisconsin Press, 2018), 62.

55. "Putin: itogi vyborov otrazhaiut real'nyi rasklad sil," *BBC News/Russkaia sluzhba*, 15 December 2011, https://www.bbc.com/russian/russia/2011/12/111215_putin_line_preview.

56. Miriam Elder, "Vladimir Putin Mocks Moscow's 'Condom-Wearing' Protesters," *The Guardian*, 15 December 2011.

57. On Pussy Riot, see Borenstein, *Pussy Riot*; Masha Gessen, *Words Will Break Cement: The Passion of Pussy Riot* (New York: Riverhead Books, 2013); Mike Lerner and Maxim Pozdorovkin, *Pussy Riot: A Punk Prayer* (UK: Docuramafilms and Cinedigm Entertainment, 2013).

58. Pussy Riot, "Pussy Riot's Action—Putin Has Pissed Himself!," YouTube, 18 January 2021, https://www.youtube.com/watch?v=5C4ZvODrazE.

59. Borenstein, *Pussy Riot*, 23.

60. Pussy Riot, "Pussy Riot—Punk Prayer 'Virgin Mary, Put Putin Away' (English Subtitles)," YouTube, 17 August 2012, https://www.youtube.com/watch?v=lPDkJbTQRCY.

61. Borenstein interprets Pussy Riot's balaclava and anti-fashion stance in *Pussy Riot*, 79–80.

62. Borenstein, *Pussy Riot*, 27.

63. Kalinin, "Why 'Two Russians' Are Less Than 'United Russia,'" 53.

64. For examples, see Susan Sontag [S'iuzan Zontag], "Zametki o kempe," *Photographer.ru*, accessed 2 November 2022, http://www.photographer.ru/forum/view_messages.htm?topic=10517; and B. V., "Kemp," *Entsiklopediia kul'turologii*, accessed 2 November 2022, http://dic.academic.ru/dic.nsf/enc_culture/1036/%D0%9A%D1%8D%D0%BC%D0%BF. Cleto boldly claims "that the word *camp* can*not* be adequately translated from English" (*Camp*, 10).

65. Vladimir Nabokov, *Nikolai Gogol* (New York: New Directions, 1961), 63, 70.

66. Boym, *Common Places*, 41.

67. Boym also cites this example (*Common Places*, 41).

68. Boym, *Common Places*, 46.

69. My use of the term *poshlost'* differs from that of Boym, who views it as the Russian translation of kitsch. Svetlana Boym, "Kitch i sotsialisticheskii realism," *Novoe literaturnoe obozrenie*, no. 15 (1995): 54–65. See also Theresa Sabonis-Chafee, "Communism as Kitsch: Soviet Symbols in Post-Soviet Society," in *Consuming Russia: Popular Culture, Sex, and Society since Gorbachev*, ed. Adele Marie Barker (Durham, NC: Duke University Press, 1999), 362–82.

70. Testometrika Team, "Naskol'ko ty poshlyi(aia)?," *Testometrika*, accessed 2 November 2022, https://testometrika.com/funny/how-vulgar-can-you/.

71. Alexei Yurchak, *Everything Was Forever, Until It Was No More: The Last Soviet Generation* (Princeton, NJ: Princeton University Press, 2006).

72. Yurchak, *Everything Was Forever*, 249–50.

73. Dominic Boyer and Alexei Yurchak, "American Stiob: Or, What Late Socialist Aesthetics of Parody Reveal about Contemporary Political Culture in the West," *Cultural Anthropology* 25, no. 2 (May 2010): 189.

74. Boyer and Yurchak, "American Stiob," 190.

75. Boyer and Yurchak, "American Stiob," 179–221. See also Boyer and Yurchak, "In Focus: Postsocialist Studies, Cultures of Parody and American Stiob," *Anthropology News*, November 2008, 9–10.

76. Boyer and Yurchak, "American Stiob," 212, 213.

77. B. V. Dubin, "Kruzhkovyi steb i massovye kommunikatsii: k sotsiologii kul'turnogo perekhoda," in *Slovo–pis'mo–literatura: Ocherki po sotsiologii sovremennoi kul'ture* (Moscow: NLO, 2001), 163–74.

78. Mark Yoffe, "The *Stiob* of Ages: Carnivalesque Traditions in Soviet Rock and Related Counterculture," *Russian Literature* 74 (2013): 208.

79. Yoffe, "The *Stiob* of Ages," 210.

80. Mischa Gabowitsch, "Fascism as Stiob," *kultura* 4 (December 2009): 3–8; Boris Noordenbos, "Imperial *Stiob*: The Aesthetics of Chauvinism," in *Post-Soviet Literature and the Search for a Russian Identity* (New York: Palgrave Macmillan, 2016), 111–43; Ania Aizman, "Stiob and the State," *NYU Jordan Center*, 6 February 2019, https://jordanrussiacenter.org/news/anna-aizman-on-stiob-feb-5/#.Yc8ywhNucwQ; Stephen Hutchings, *Projecting Russia in a Mediatized World: Recursive Nationhood* (London: Routledge, 2022). See also Natalia Roudakova, *Losing Pravda: Ethics and the Press in Post-Truth Russia* (Cambridge: Cambridge University Press, 2017), 181–87, 202–3.

81. On *stiob* in Timur Novikov's New Academy, see Julie A. Cassiday, Helena Goscilo, and Jonathan Brooks Platt, "Introduction: The Allure of Retro: Neoacademism after the Fall," *The Russian Review* 78 (April 2019): 190–92.

82. Rabfak, "Nash durdom (golosuet za putina)," YouTube, 13 October 2011, https://www.youtube.com/watch?v=zVxyBMCd4qY.

83. Helena Goscilo and Vlad Strukov, "Introduction," in *Celebrity and Glamour in Contemporary Russia: Shocking Chic* (London: Routledge, 2011), 2.

84. Mikhail Epshtein, "Vpervye v Rossii vybrany slova i antislova goda," *SpbTalk.ruRu*, 21 June 2008, https://www.spbtalk.com/threads/9713/. See also Maria Litovskaia and Olga Shaburova, "Russian Glamour and Its Representations in Post-Soviet Mass Media," in *Russian Mass Media and Changing Values*, ed. Arja Rosenholm et al. (London: Routledge, 2013), 193–208.

85. Goscilo and Strukov, "Introduction," 3.

86. Goscilo and Strukov, "Introduction," 3. In a 2007 survey about glamour in Russia, Sobchak was one of only four celebrities mentioned by respondents. Anna Petrova, "Nemnogo o glamure," *Baza dannykh FOM*, 13 September 2007, https://bd.fom.ru/report/map/d073724.

87. Goscilo and Strukov, "Introduction," 21. Rudova, "Uniting Russia in Glamour" (2–3); and Olga Mesropova, "I Choose Russia—I Choose Glamour" (12–14), *kultura* 6 (December 2008).

88. Vera Zvereva, "Pozyvnye glamura. Glamur: Kul'turnaia ekspansiia ili novaia ideologiia?," *Iskusstvo kino*, no. 11 (November 2006), http://old.kinoart.ru/archive/2006/11/n11-article3.

89. Goscilo and Strukov, "Introduction," 6.

90. Birgit Menzel, "Russian Discourse on Glamour," *kultura* 6 (December 2008): 4.

91. Menzel, "Russian Discourse on Glamour," 4.

92. Tat'iana Tolstaia, "Ia planov nashikh liubliu glamur'e," in *Den': lichnoe* (Moscow: Eksmo, 2012), 234. Survey results confirm the feminine associations of *glamur* and its perceived proximity to *poshlost'* and nonnormative sexual behavior (Petrova, "Nemnogo o glamure").

93. Tolstaia, "Ia planov nashikh liubliu glamur'e," 234. Zvereva, "Pozyvnye glamura," confirms this assertion by describing *glamur*'s predilection for "wonders, whim, and a pronounced narcissism."

94. Dmitrii Golynko-Vol'fson, "Agressivno-passivnyi glamur," *Khudozhestvennyi zhurnal* 60 (December 2005), https://moscowartmagazine.com/issue/35/article/668.

95. Zvereva, "Pozyvnye glamura."

96. Golynko-Vol'fson, "Agressivno-passivnyi glamur."

97. Shpil'ki and Sergei Zverev, "Bol'she glamura," YouTube, 4 February 2015, https://www.youtube.com/watch?v=AFJRbrXDxtk.

98. Anastasiia Folomeeva, "'U nas vse po Stanislavskomu': Dreg-artisty–o teatre, svobode i shizofrenii," *Teatralii*, 15 December 2020, https://teatralium.com/interviews/drag_queens/; "Dreg-artisty v Irkustske: O razorvannykh lifchikax, grudi s AliExpress i reaktsii okruzhaiushchykh," *The Village*, 5 June 2020, https://www.the-village.ru/people/people-city/384105-dragqueen; Zhenia Sozankova, "Dreg-artisty: Ob obraze, rabote, kosmetike i reaktsii okruzhaiushchykh," *The Village*, 21 February 2020, https://www.the-village.ru/people/people-city/374901-drag-artists.

99. *Zaza Napoli*, accessed 2 November 2022, http://www.zazanapoli.ru/; Zaza Napoli, "Zaza Napoli—Lenin/Ofitsial'noe video/Versiia 1," YouTube, 26 October 2010, https://www.youtube.com/watch?v=K8vJp1S2i0U.

100. "Tekst pesni Zaza Napoli—Lenin," *Lyricsonline.ru*, accessed 2 November 2022, https://lyricsonline.ru/45134-zaza-napoli-lenin.html.

101. Olia Poliakova, "Olia Poliakova—Russian Style (Full HD)," YouTube, 12 June 2014, https://www.youtube.com/watch?v=sK8dVWhUCqM.

102. Valerii Pecheikin, "Viktor Erofeev: Rossiia kak transvestit," *Kvir* 75 (1 June 2014), http://www.kvir.ru/articles/viktor-erofeev-rossiya.html.

103. Dan Healey, "'Untraditional Sex' and the 'Simple Russian': Nostalgia for Soviet Innocence and the Polemics of Diliia Enikeeva," in *What Is Soviet Now? Identities, Legacies, Memories*, ed. Thomas Lahusen and Peter H. Solomon (Berlin: Lit Verlag, 2008), 173–91.

104. "Gay Clown Putin," *Know Your Meme*, accessed 2 November 2022, https://knowyourmeme.com/memes/gay-clown-putin.

Chapter 2. The Soviet Legacy of Traumatized Bodies

1. Djurdja Bartlett, *FashionEast: The Spectre That Haunted Socialism* (Cambridge, MA: MIT Press, 2010), 172–80. See also Ol'ga Vainshtein, "Female Fashion, Soviet Style: Bodies of Ideology," trans. Helena Goscilo, in *Russia, Women, Culture*, ed. Helena Goscilo and Beth Holmgren (Bloomington: Indiana University Press, 1996), 64–93.

2. Bartlett, *FashionEast*, 70–71. See also Yulia Gradskova, *Soviet People with Female Bodies: Performing Beauty and Maternity in Soviet Russia in the mid-1930–1960s* (Stockholm: Stockholm University, 2007).

3. Olga Gurova, *Fashion and the Consumer Revolution in Contemporary Russia* (London: Routledge, 2015), 158.

4. Gurova, *Fashion and the Consumer Revolution in Contemporary Russia*, 77.

5. Katharina Klingseis, "The Power of Dress in Contemporary Russian Society: On Glamour Discourse and the Everyday Practice of Getting Dressed in Russian Cities," *Laboratorium* 3, no. 1 (2011): 96.

6. Klingseis, "The Power of Dress in Contemporary Russian Society," 102.

7. Klingseis, "The Power of Dress in Contemporary Russian Society," 97.

8. Gurova, *Fashion and the Consumer Revolution in Contemporary Russia*, 65, 100.

9. Vainshtein, "Female Fashion, Soviet Style," 67, 84–87.

10. Elena Zdravomyslova and Anna Temkina, "Krizis maskulinnosti v pozdnesovetskom diskurse," in *O muzhe(n)stvennosti: Sbornik statei*, ed. S. Ushakin (Moscow: Novoe literaturnoe obozrenie, 2002), 446–48.

11. Klingseis, "The Power of Dress in Contemporary Russian Society," 98, 102.

12. Fedor Bondarchuk, *9 rota* (Moscow: Art Pictures Group, 2005); Aleksei Balabanov, *Gruz 200* (St. Petersburg: STV Film Company, 2007). For the screenplay of *Cargo 200*, see Aleksei Balabanov, "Gruz 200," *Gruz 200* (St. Petersburg: "Seans," "Amfora," 2007), 433–74.

13. *Dust* was shot in 2001 but released in 2005. Sergei Loban, *Pyl'* (Moscow: SVOI-2000, 2005).

14. Dawn Seckler, "Fedor Bondarchuk: Company 9 (9-aia rota), 2005," *Kinokultura*, 26 April 2006, http://kinokultura.com/2006/12r-company9.shtml.

15. For treatment of *9th Company* as a war film, see Denise J. Youngblood, *Russian War Films: On the Cinema Front, 1914–2005* (Lawrence: University Press of Kansas, 2007), 206–9.

16. Seckler, "Fedor Bondarchuk."

17. Even Putin commented on the film's verisimilitude: "In my opinion, it's very close to real life on the basis of what I know." "Putin schitaet fil'm '9-aia rota' talantlivoi i udachnoi rabotoi," *RIA Novosti*, 7 November 2005, https://ria.ru/20051107/42016802.html.

18. Bondarchuk's movie inspired two video games in 2008: *9 rota*, accessed 27 July 2019, http://9rota-game.ru/, and *Pravda o deviatoi rote*, accessed 27 July 2019, http://pravdao9rote.ru/. Stephen M. Norris discusses these videogames and the controversy among veterans of the Afghan war in "Playing with History," in *Blockbuster History in the New Russia: Movies, Memory, and Patriotism* (Bloomington: Indiana University Press, 2012), 143–66.

19. Aleksei Medvedev, "Pro liudei i urodov. Kruglyi stol 'IK,'" *Iskusstvo kino*, no. 7 (June 2007), http://old.kinoart.ru/archive/2007/07/n7-article3.

20. Iuliia Liderman, "Balabanov snial 'tot' fil'm," *Iskusstvo kino*, no. 7 (2007), http://old.kinoart.ru/archive/2007/07/n7-article5; Karina Longworth, "Cargo 200 Review," *IMBd* (2 January 2009), https://www.imdb.com/news/ni0642080. On the controversy surrounding the film, see Andrew Osborn, "From Russia, without Love: New Movie Slams Soviet Union," *Wall Street Journal*, 21 June 2007.

21. Norris, "Playing with History," 189–207. For broader treatment of the film, see Nancy Condee, *The Imperial Trace: Recent Russian Cinema* (Oxford: Oxford University Press, 2009), 217–36.

22. Medvedev, "Pro liudei i urodov. Kruglyi stol 'IK'"; Tony Anemone, "Aleksei Balabanov: *Cargo 200* (*Gruz 200*, 2007)," *KinoKultura*, 2 October 2007, http://www.kinokultura.com/2007/18r-gruz.shtml.

23. On Balabanov's vigilante heroes in *Brother* and *Brother 2*, see Anthony Anemone, "About Killers, Freaks, and Real Men: The Vigilante Hero of Aleksei Balabanov's Films," in *Insiders and Outsiders in Russian Cinema*, ed. Stephen M. Norris and Zara M. Torlone (Bloomington: Indiana University Press, 2008), 126–40.

24. Osborn, "From Russia without Love"; Longworth, "Cargo 200 Review"; Medvedev, "Pro liudei i urodov. Kruglyi stol 'IK"; Lev Gudkov, "Raspolzaiushcheesia obshchestvo," *Iskusstvo kino*, no. 7 (June 2007): http://old.kinoart.ru/archive/2007/07/n7-article4; Evgenii Gusiatinskii, "Aleksei Balabanov: 'Vsegda zhivem v Rossii,'" *Iskusstvo kino*, no. 7 (June 2007), https://old.kinoart.ru/archive/2007/07/n7-article2.

25. Gregory Carleton also makes this point in "A Tale of Two Wars: Sex and Death in *9th Company* and *Cargo 200*," *Studies in Russian and Soviet Cinema* 3, no. 2 (2009): 215–28.

26. On rape as a foundational myth, see Susanne L. Wofford, "The Social Aesthetics of Rape: Closural Violence in Boccaccio and Botticelli," in *Creative Imitation: New Essays on Renaissance Literature in Honor of Thomas M. Greene*, ed. David Quint, Margaret W. Ferguson, G. W. Pigman III, and Wayne A. Rebhorn (Binghamton, NY: Medieval and Renaissance Texts and Studies, 1992), 189–239.

27. In Frank Baum's original story, the character of Dorothy had silver slippers; however, for the film she was given ruby-red slippers, with their concomitant erotic associations, to capitalize on the innovation of Technicolor.

28. Liderman, "Balabanov snial 'tot' fil'm."

29. Medvedev, "Pro liudei i urodov. Kruglyi stol 'IK.'"

30. Norris, "Playing with History," 195.

31. Tat'iana Tolstaia, "Peters," in *White Walls: Collected Stories*, trans. Antonina W. Bouis and Jamey Gambrell (New York: New York Review of Books, 2007), 175, 180, 183, 185. For the Russian original, see "Tat'iana Tolstaia. Noch', Peters," *Ark.ru*, 8 November 2016, https://ark.ru/zapoved/tigr/tatyana-tolstaya-noch-peters/2/.

32. Tolstaia, "Peters," 177, 182.

33. Critics also view Alyosha's indifference to Pushkar''s rant as key to interpreting the film. See Sergey Kuznetsov, "'Pyl" Sergeia Lobana, kak by retsenziia," *LiveJournal* (15 February 2007), https://skuzn.livejournal.com/398345.html; Elena Prokhorova, "Sergei Loban: *Dust (Pyl')*, 2005," *KinoKultura*, 14 January 2006, http://www.kinokultura.com/2006/11r-dust.shtml.

34. murrao, "Kommentarii," in Mikhail Trofimenkov, "'Pyl'': Zagrobnaia zhizn'—eto vechnyi prosmotr televizora s pripliasyvaiushchim Petrosianom," *KinoKafe* (no date), accessed 3 November 2022, https://www.kinocafe.ru/reviews/?rid=32573.

35. I have discovered, from teaching and speaking about *Dust*, that many find Podol'skii's acting so triggering that they cannot watch the film to its end.

36. On zAiBI and SVOI2000, see Aleksandra Obukhova, ed., *Performans v Rossii, 1910–2010: Kartografiia istorii, katalog* (Moscow: Tsentr sovremennoii kul'tury "Garazh," 2014), 152, 153, 214.

37. Ethan Singh, "From Russia with Glove: Despot Putin's Lavish Fashion Choices Include £10,000 Coat, £2,400 Roll-Neck—and Luxury Watch Collection," *The Sun*,

21 March 2022, https://www.thesun.co.uk/news/18023066/despot-putins-lavish-fashion-choices/.

Chapter 3. *Travesti* and the Post-Soviet Drag Queen

1. Louise McReynolds, *Russia at Play: Leisure Activities at the End of the Tsarist Era* (Ithaca, NY: Cornell University Press, 2003), 152.

2. McReynolds, *Russia at Play*; Nikolai Evreinov, *V shkole ostroumiia: Vospominaniia o teatre "Krivoe zerkalo"* (Moscow: Iskusstvo, 1998), 67–72.

3. Boris Wolfson, "Juggernaut in Drag: Theater for Stalin's Children," in *Russian Children's Literature and Culture*, ed. Marina Balina and Larissa Rudova (New York: Routledge, 2008), 186–89. See also Ol'ga Khoroshilova, *Russkie travesti v istorii, kul'ture i povsednevnosti* (Moscow: "Mann, Ivanov i Ferber," 2021).

4. Tim Scholl, "Queer Performance: 'Male Ballet,'" in *Consuming Russia: Popular Culture, Sex, and Society Since Gorbachev*, ed. Adele Marie Baker (Durham, NC: Duke University Press, 1999), 303–17.

5. Olga Khazan, "Why Homophobic Russia Loves Gender-Bending Pop Stars," *Atlantic*, 20 August 2013, http://www.theatlantic.com/international/archive/2013/08/why-homophobic-russia-loves-gender-bending-pop-stars/278833/.

6. Viktoriia Charochkina, "'Raduzhnyi Milonov' i drugie: Avtor iz"iatykh politsiei kartin predpochel pokinut' stranu," *The New Times*, 27 August 2013, http://newtimes.ru/articles/detail/70385/.

7. Amanda Scherker, "Artist of Painting Showing Putin in Lingerie Reportedly Flees Russia," *Huffington Post*, 28 August 2013, http://www.huffingtonpost.com/2013/08/28/artist-putin-in-lingerie_n_3830773.html.

8. Katherine Brooks, "Russian Police Nab Painting of Nude Vladimir Putin and Barack Obama (NSFW)," *HuffPost*, 6 December 2017, https://www.huffpost.com/entry/putin-obama-painting_n_3873023.

9. For more on Mamyshev-Monroe, see Julie A. Cassiday, "Vladislav Mamyshev-Monroe, Frog-Princess of Neoacademism," *The Russian Review* 78 (April 2019): 221–44.

10. Julie A. Cassiday, Helena Goscilo, and Jonathan Brooks Platt, "Introduction: The Allure of Retro: Neoacademism after the Fall," *The Russian Review* 78 (April 2019): 183–200.

11. "Voprosy i otvety: Otryvki iz razlichnykh interv'iu s Vladislavom Mamyshevym-Monro," in *Arkhiv M*, ed. Elena Selina and Antonio Dzheuza (Moscow: Artguide Editions, 2015), 322.

12. Vladislav Mamyshev-Monro, "Kuda ia popal? Gde moi veshchi? Stabil'naia mobil'nost' i mobil'naia stabil'nost' ob"ektivnogo sub"ektivizma Vladislava Mamysheva," in *Arkhiv M*, ed. Elena Selina and Antonio Dzheuza (Moscow: Artguide Editions, 2015), 56. See also Mamyshev-Monro, "Monrologiia: Prakticheskoe znachenie issledovaniia dlia udobstv i v silu deistviia na dannyi moment signala M.M., nazvannogo monrologiei," in *Arkhiv M*, ed. Elena Selina and Antonio Dzheuza (Moscow: Artguide Editions, 2015), 48–51.

13. Mamyshev-Monro, "Kuda ia popal?," 57.

14. Mamyshev-Monro, "Kuda ia popal?," 57.

15. "Liubov' ne umiraet: K vystavke v Galeree Marata Gel'mana," in *Arkhiv M*, ed. Elena Selina and Antonio Dzheuza (Moscow: Artguide Editions, 2015), 88.

16. "Voprosy i otvety," 322. In commentary for the 2002 exhibition "Snowgirl—New Art from Russia," Mamyshev-Monro called Orlova "the Western Snowgirl . . . of Stalin's epoch" in contrast to Monroe, whom he labeled "the Eastern Snowgirl . . . with the vividly pronounced physiognomy of Riazan' and the charisma of a Siberian woman." Vladislav Mamyshev-Monro, "Konets snezhnoi korolevy: Vladik Mamyshev-Monro dlia Eleny Selinoi i varshavskoi vystavki," in *Arkhiv M*, ed. Elena Selina and Antonio Dzheuza (Moscow: Artguide Editions, 2015), 91.

17. "Happy Love (Liubov' Orlova)" originally appeared in 2000–2001 in Marat Gel'man's galleries in Moscow and Kiev and then became limited-edition folders containing photographs with the artist's own framing and commentary. *Arkhiv M*, ed. Elena Selina and Antonio Dzheuza (Moscow: Artguide Editions, 2015), 130–35.

18. "Voprosy i otvety," 323.

19. Grigorii Aleksandrov, dir., *Volga-Volga* (Russia: Mosfil'm, 1938); Pavel Labazov and Andrei Sil'vestrov, dir., *Volga-Volga* (Russia: Studiia Videodom and Dom Sine Fantom, 2006) at "Volga-Volga (Vladislav Mamyshev-Monro)," *VK Video*, 11 March 2013, https://vk.com/video675122_164484549. On the original *Volga-Volga*, see Rimgaila Salys, "Chapter 3: *Volga-Volga*," in *The Musical Comedy Films of Grigorii Aleksandrov: Laughing Matters* (Bristol: Intellect, 2009), 203–80.

20. Mikhail Shiianov, "'Volga-Volga' Mamysheva-Monro: nedootsenennyi rimeik mrachnoi komedii," *RIA Novosti*, 23 April 2013, https://ria.ru/20130423/934067958.html.

21. Shiianov, "'Volga-Volga' Mamysheva-Monro."

22. Shiianov, "'Volga-Volga' Mamysheva-Monro."

23. Sergei Khachaturov, "Umom nash gender ne poniat': Sovremennoe izobrazitel'noe iskusstvo Rossii i problematika 'kvir,'" *Dialog iskusstv*, no. 4 (April 2013): 110.

24. Vladislav Mamyshev-Monro, "Transvestizm v traditsii russkogo messianstva," in *Arkhiv M*, ed. Elena Selina and Antonio Dzheuza (Moscow: Artguide Editions, 2015), 70.

25. Judith Butler, *Gender Trouble: Feminism and the Subversion of Identity* (New York: Routledge, 2007); Marjorie Garber, *Vested Interests: Cross-Dressing and Cultural Anxiety* (New York: Routledge, 1992); Laurence Senelick, *The Changing Room: Sex, Drag, and Theatre* (New York: Routledge, 2000).

26. Verka Serduchka, "Eurovision 2007 Final Ukraine Verka Serduchka Dancing," YouTube, 14 May 2007, http://www.youtube.com/watch?v=GP5YOhQZtlA; "Eurovision 2010 Ratings Follow Trend of 2007, 2008," Eurovision Song Contest, 8 July 2010, https://eurovision.tv/story/eurovision-2010-ratings-follow-trend-of-2007-2008.

27. Julie A. Cassiday, "Post-Soviet Pop Goes Gay: Russia's Trajectory to Eurovision Victory," *The Russian Review* 73 (January 2014): 6–7. In June 2022, Danylko changed the song to "Dancing Russian Goodbye" at a charity rally in support of Ukraine's war against Russia. Atlas Festival, "Verka Serduchka—Russia Goodbye & Make It Rain Champagne|Embrace Ukraine—#StrivingTogether," YouTube, 22 June 2022, https://www.youtube.com/watch?v=hvXUeHwDoRU. See also Jeremy Morris, "Elevating Verka Serdiuchka: A Star-Study in Excess Performativity," in *Celebrity and Glamour in Contemporary Russia: Shocking Chic*, ed. Helena Goscilo and Vlad Strukov (London: Routledge, 2011), 195–218; Peter Rehberg and Mikko Tuhkanen, "Danzing Time: Dissociative Camp and European Synchrony," *SQS* 2, no. 7 (2007): 51; Laada Bilaniuk,

Contested Tongues: Language Politics and Cultural Correction in Ukraine (Ithaca, NY: Cornell University Press, 2005), 165–72; Joseph James Crescente, "Performing Post-Sovietness: Verka Serduchka and the Hybridization of Post-Soviet Identity in Ukraine," *Ab Imperio* 2 (2007): 423–28; Serhy Yekelchyk, "What Is Ukrainian about Ukraine's Pop Culture? The Strange Case of Verka Serduchka," *Canadian-American Slavic Studies* 44 (2010): 228–30.

28. Morris discusses this briefly in relation to Serduchka in "Elevating Verka Serdiuchka," 206–7.

29. Morris, "Elevating Verka Serdiuchka," 212–13.

30. Performing in drag on Russian television still had its risks, as Danylko discovered in August 2013, when a rumor circulated that Verka Serduchka would be cut from the weekly variety show "Saturday Night" (Subbotnii vecher) due to the risk of "gay propaganda." "Rossiiskii telekanal otkazalsia pokazyvat' Verku Serduchku iz-za gei-propagandy," *LB.ua*, 13 August 2013, http://society.lb.ua/culture/2013/08/13/219488_rossiyskiy_telekanal_otkazalsya.html; "Telekanal 'Rossiia' poiasnil, pochemu Danilko ne vedet 'Subbotnii vecher,'" *RIA Novosti*, 13 August 2013, https://ria.ru/20130813/956036083.html.

31. For journalism on Russian drag queens, see Matthew Kupfer and Bradley Jardine, "Defying State Conservatism, Russia's Drag Queens Strut On: Despite Homophobic Laws, Declining Wages and the Threat of Physical Violence, a Distinctly Gay Art Form Perseveres," *The Moscow Times*, 17 February 2017, https://www.themoscowtimes.com/2017/02/17/russian-drag-queens-a57177.

32. Suvi Salmenniemi and Maria Adamson, "New Heroines of Labour: Domesticating Post-feminism and Neoliberal Capitalism in Russia," *Sociology* (13 January 2014): 1–18.

33. Vladimir Kirsanov, *69. Russkie gei, lesbiianki, biseksualy i transseksualy* (Tver': GanimeD, 2005), 439–446; Elena Milienko, "Sergei Zarubin: 'Lora—eto vsego lish' obraz!'" *Teatral*, 1 September 2008, http://www.teatral-online.ru/news/1668/; Sergei Sedov, "Sergei Zarubin: Lora Kolli sushchestvuet otdel'no ot menia," *xGay.ru*, 29 September 2005, http://www.gay.ru/people/view/zarubin2005.html.

34. Kirsanov, *69. Russkie gei, lesbiianki, biseksualy i transseksualy*, 442.

35. Kirsanov, *69. Russkie gei, lesbiianki, biseksualy i transseksualy*, 445–46.

36. Milienko, "Sergei Zarubin."

37. *Peskov Productions* (no date), accessed 4 November 2022, http://peskov-show.com.

38. "Aleksandr Peskov—Pesnia goda (Sol'noe shou)," YouTube, 12 May 2012, https://www.youtube.com/watch?v=hxuBO7B_G58.

39. *Evdokimov Show Theater* (no date), accessed 4 November 2022, https://www.evdokimov-show.com/.

40. Kira Sergeeva, "Anatolii Evdokimov: 'Travesti-shou—eto ne prosto muzhchiny v iubkakh," *Internet-Gazeta Newslab.ru*, 18 April 2011, http://newslab.ru/article/376381.

41. Ruki Vverkh, "Ruki Vverkh—On tebia tseluet (HQ)," YouTube, 7 May 2009, http://www.youtube.com/watch?v=Kkx8iqCuscc.

42. "Parodist stal litsom kompanii 'L'Etual,'" *Sostav.ru*, 11 August 2010, http://www.sostav.ru/news/2010/08/11/r5/.

43. Sergeeva, "Anatolii Evdokimov." See also Evdokimov Show, "Anatolii Evdokimov v programme 'Otkrytyi razgovor,'" YouTube, 2 November 2012, https://www

.youtube.com/watch?v=TFAX_gn_uO4; Evdokimov Show, "Pravda.ru—Anatolii Evdokimov v gostiakh u glavreda," YouTube, 21 March 2012, https://www.youtube.com/watch?v=mvu6VPv8N_8.

44. Evdokimov Show, "Evolution by Evdokimov Show Theater—DVD Concert," YouTube, 5 October 2012, https://www.youtube.com/watch?v=qFXOWWpCdVo.

45. *Zaza Napoli* (no date), accessed 4 November 2022, http://www.zazanapoli.ru/.

46. Zaza Napoli, "Zaza Napoli, Anastasiia Volochkova. Ispoved'. . . ," YouTube, 5 November 2010, https://www.youtube.com/watch?v=EUZjVjr4KA4.

47. For Orlusha reading his own poem, see "Orlusha, 'Pro Anastasiiu Volochkovu,'" YouTube, 14 December 2008, https://www.youtube.com/watch?v=-Jzy5LfrgSU.

48. Kirsanov, "Vladim Kazantsev i ego Zaza Napoli (14 aprelia 1973). Feia seksual'noi revoliutsii," in *69*, 547–52; "Raduzhnye novosti: Zaza Napoli ustraivaet 'Seksual'nuiu Revoliutsiiu' v priamom efire," *xGay.ru*, 11 October 2004, https://www.xgay.ru/news/rainbow/2004/10/11-4213.htm.

49. *BoobsForQueens* (no date), accessed 4 November 2022, http://boobsforqueens.com/index.html.

50. "fishy," *RuPaul's Drag Race Dictionary* (no date), accessed 4 November 2022, https://rupaulsdragrace.fandom.com/wiki/RuPaul's_Drag_Race_Dictionary.

51. Feliks Mikhailov, *Vesel'chaki* (Russia: Studio Timeline, Survive Entertainment, 2009). See also Marko Dumančić, "Feliks Mikhailov: *Jolly Fellows* (Vesel'chaki, 2009)," *KinoKultura* 29 (2010), 14 October 2009, http://www.kinokultura.com/2010/29r-veselchaki.shtml; "Jolly Fellows 2009," *Russian Film Symposium* (no date), accessed 4 November 2022, https://rusfilm.pitt.edu/jolly-fellows-2009/; Nina Tsirkun, "Transformatsiia kempa i retseptsiia kino," *Iskusstvo kino*, no. 1 (January 2013), https://old.kinoart.ru/archive/2013/01/transformatsiya-kempa-i-retseptsiya-kino.

52. A. A. Kondakov, "Poriadok diskurskov v formirovanii deviantnykh chert gomoseksual'noi sub"ektivnosti," *Paradigma* 16 (2011): 67.

53. Semen Kvasha, "Retsenziia na fil'm 'Vesel'chaki'. Razbitoe serdtse donny Rozy," *film.ru*, 13 October 2009, http://www.film.ru/articles/razbitoe-serdce-donny-rozy; Svetlana Stepnova, "O zhizni i liubvi (retsenziia na fil'm 'Vesel'chaki')," *Ruskino*, 25 October 2009, https://ruskino.ru/item/2009/10/25/o-zhizni-i-lubvi.

54. Kondakov, "Poriadok diskurskov v formirovanii deviantnykh chert gomoseksual'noi sub"ektivnosti," 73.

55. Helena Goscilo and Vlad Strukov, "Introduction," in *Celebrity and Glamour in Contemporary Russia: Shocking Chic* (London: Routledge, 2011), 10.

56. Emily Jane Fox, "Putin Works Out in a $3220 Sweatsuit as Only Putin Would," *Vanity Fair*, 2 September 2015, https://www.vanityfair.com/news/2015/09/putin-workout-gym-clothes.

57. "Conchita Wurst Tops Russian iTunes Chart," *PinkNews*, 12 May 2014, https://www.pinknews.co.uk/2014/05/12/conchita-wurst-tops-russian-itunes-chart/; zhirinovskii, "Zhirinovskii—Konchita Vurst eto konets dlia vsei Evropy. Evrovidenie 2014," YouTube, 12 May 2014, https://www.youtube.com/watch?v=8BtbuNCkFGU.

58. Joe Morgan, "Russians Shave Off Beards to Protest against Conchita Wurst," *GayStarNews*, 13 May 2014, https://web.archive.org/web/20150626234440/http://www.gaystarnews.com/article/russians-shave-beards-protest-against-conchita-wurst130514; Alan White, "Russians Are Shaving Their Beards In Reaction To Conchita Wurst's

Eurovision Win," *BuzzFeed*, 12 May 2014, https://www.buzzfeed.com/alanwhite/russians-are-shaving-their-beards-in-reaction-to-conchita-wu; James Edgar, "Putin Attacks Eurovision Drag Artist Conchita for Putting Her Lifestyle 'Up for Show,'" *The Telegraph*, 25 May 2014. See also Eliot Borenstein, "Post-Soviet Masculinities: Sex, Power, and the Vanishing Point," in *Routledge Handbook of Gender in Central-Eastern Europe and Eurasia*, ed. Katalin Fábián, Janet Elise Johnson, and Mara Lazda (London: Routledge, 2022), 82.

59. "Milonov potreboval vvesti pozhiznennyi zapret na v"ezd Konchity Vurst v RF," *Izvestiia*, 17 November 2017, https://iz.ru/672327/2017-11-17/milonov-potreboval-vvesti-pozhiznennyi-zapret-na-vezd-konchity-vurst-v-rf.

60. "Kratkaia Russkaia Pravda (po Akademicheskomu spisku poloviny XV v." *hist.msu.ru*, accessed 4 November 2022, http://www.hist.msu.ru/ER/Etext/RP/krp.htm; Zita Whalley, "The Controversial History of Russian Beards," *Culture Trip*, 30 March 2018, https://theculturetrip.com/europe/russia/articles/the-controversial-history-of-russian-beards/; Brian Boeck, "Beard Tax," in *Encyclopedia of Russian History*, ed. James R. Millar (New York: Macmillan, 2004), 133.

61. One interviewee in a 2017 article on bearded Russian men commented, "Sometimes, a beard works like a mask," suggesting a parallel with women's clothing that functions as "armor." Anastasiya Karagodina and Aizhan Kazak, "Why Russian Boys Dream of Having a Beard," *Russia Beyond*, 31 August 2017, https://www.rbth.com/multimedia/pictures/2017/08/31/why-russian-boys-dream-beard-831916.

62. Doni, "Doni ft Timati—Boroda (Prem'era klipa, 2014)," YouTube, 10 June 2013, https://www.youtube.com/watch?v=7mvqAEe58°M.

63. Emily Johnson highlights the role of homophobia in videos by Timati's production company Black Star Inc. in "Multiculturalism Timati-style: Ethnicity and Masculinity in Black Star Videos" (used by permission of the author).

64. "Rossiiskie staroobriadtsy sviazali gomoseksualizm s otsutsviem borody," *Natsional'naia Sluzhba Novostei*, 8 June 2017, https://nsn.fm/lenta-novostei/hots-rossiyskie-staroobryadcy-svyazali-gomoseksualizm-s-otsutstviem-borody.

65. Dimitry Kozachenko, "These LGBTQ Instagram Accounts Show That Queer Life in Russia Is Vibrant, Loving, and Defiant," *Calvert Journal*, 5 June 2019, https://www.calvertjournal.com/features/show/11212/lgbtq-instagram-russia-kozachenko; Ben Cohen, "RuPaul on the RuNet: 'Drag Race' Catches on in Russia," *Global Voices*, 28 March 2017, https://globalvoices.org/2017/03/28/rupaul-on-the-runet-drag-race-catches-on-in-russia/; Karen Shainian, "Russkii dreg, besstrashnyi i besposhchadnyi (18+)," YouTube, 10 December 2020, https://www.youtube.com/watch?v=X8qgovs45NU&t=51s.

66. "Lorina Rey," YouTube (no date), accessed 4 November 2022, https://www.youtube.com/channel/UCeV8tIxlRopIiRvBoBWYHbQ; see also Kozachenko, "These LGBTQ Instagram Accounts Show that Queer Life in Russia Is Vibrant, Loving, and Defiant."

67. Anastasiia Fedorova, "Queer Moscow: Dispatches from the Front Lines of Russia's LGBTQ Creative Revolution," *Calvert Journal*, 31 July 2019, https://www.calvertjournal.com/features/show/11285/queer-moscow-o-zine-lgbtq-revolution.

68. Anastasiia Fedorova, "Queer Petersburg: Dispatches from the Front Lines of Russia's LGBTQ Creative Revolution," *Calvert Journal*, 1 August 2019, https://www.calvertjournal.com/features/show/11287/queer-st-petersburg-o-zine-lgbtq-revolution.

69. Fedorova, "Queer Moscow"; Anastasiia Fedorova, "For These Queer Young Russians, Makeup Is Both Armour and a Weapon," *Calvert Journal*, 1 April 2019, https://www.calvertjournal.com/features/show/11099/genderless-makeup-russia-miliyollie.

Chapter 4. Queer Performativity in Putin's Russia

1. Karen Shainian, YouTube, no date, accessed 5 November 2022, https://www.youtube.com/c/KarenS.

2. Fensi prodakshen, "Ia idu iskat' | veb-serial | pervyi sezon," YouTube, last updated 13 August 2021, https://www.youtube.com/playlist?list=PLX_ysH5jGc2GjLUHmfHBl6nHwMSYvDbnY.

3. Nastia Ivleeva, "Drag–shou Koroloveskie kobry," YouTube, last updated 13 January 2022, https://www.youtube.com/playlist?list=PLn2SiPuzV6DtYLeVyCaiuyLZS12-bCbcq.

4. Dan Healey, *Russian Homophobia from Stalin to Sochi* (London: Bloomsbury, 2018), 138.

5. Judith Butler, "Critically Queer," in *The Routledge Queer Studies Reader*, ed. Donald E. Hall and Annmarie Jagose (London: Routledge, 2013), 19; Eve Kosofsky Sedgwick, "Shame, Theatricality, and Queer Performativity: Henry James's *The Art of the Novel*," in *Touching Feeling: Affect, Pedagogy, Performativity* (Durham, NC: Duke University Press, 2003), 61.

6. Sedgwick, "Shame, Theatricality, and Queer Performativity," 36; David M. Halperin and Valerie Traub, "Beyond Gay Pride," in *Gay Shame* (Chicago: Chicago University Press, 2009), 20, 23. See also Judith Halberstam, "Shame and White Gay Masculinity," *Social Text* 23, nos. 3–4 (Winter 2005): 219–33; Elspeth Probyn, *Blush: Faces of Shame* (Minneapolis: University of Minnesota Press, 2005).

7. Alexei Yurchak, *Everything Was Forever, Until It Was No More: The Last Soviet Generation* (Princeton, NJ: Princeton University Press, 2013).

8. Sedgwick, "Shame, Theatricality, and Queer Performativity," 63.

9. Sedgwick, "Shame, Theatricality, and Queer Performativity," 64.

10. Sedgwick points out that the queerness that emerges from her definition of queer performativity is not limited to LGBTQ+ subjects (63).

11. Butler, "Critically Queer," 28–29.

12. Yurii Pavlov, dir., *Sotvorenie Adama* (Russia: Lenfil'm, 1993); Sergei Livnev, dir., *Serp i molot* (Russia: MMM-Studiia, 1994); Ol'ga Stolpovskaia and Dmitrii Troitskii, *Ia liubliu tebia* (Russia: Malevich Prodakshnz, 2004); Feliks Mikhailov, dir., *Vesel'chaki* (Russia: Studio Timeline, Survive Entertainment, 2009); Sergei Tamaraev and Liubov' L'vova, *Zimnii put'* (Russia: Mika Film, 2013).

13. On Eurovision, see Philip V. Bohlman, *The Music of European Nationalism: Cultural Identity and Modern History* (Santa Barbara: ABC-CLIO, 2004), 1–31, 339–43; Philippe Le Guern, "From Global Kitsch to National Pride: The Eurovision Song Contest," *The Web Journal of French Media Studies* 3 October 2000, accessed 15 August 2013, http://wjfms.ncl.ac.uk/leguWJ.htm; John Kennedy O'Connor, *The Eurovision Song Contest: The Official History* (London: Carlton Publishing, 2007); *Eurovision Song Contest* (no date), accessed 5 November 2022, http://www.eurovision.tv/. On Eurovision and queerness, see *SQS: Journal of Queer Studies in Finland* 2, no. 7 (2007).

14. On Russia's participation in Eurovision before 2008, see Julie A. Cassiday, "Post-Soviet Pop Goes Gay: Russia's Trajectory to Eurovision Victory," *The Russian Review* 73, no. 1 (January 2014): 1–23.

15. On Russian participation in Eurovision, see Yana Meerzon and Dmitri Priven, "Back to the Future: Imagining a New Russia at the Eurovision Song Contest," in *Performing the 'New' Europe: Identities, Feelings and Politics in the Eurovision Song Contest*, ed. K. Fricker et al. (London: Palgrave Macmillan, 2013), 111–24; Galina Miazhevich, "Sexual Excess in Russia's Eurovision Performances as a Nation Branding Tool," *Russian Journal of Communication* 3, nos. 3 and 4 (Summer/Fall 2010): 248–64; Emily Johnson, "A New Song for a New Motherland: Eurovision and the Rhetoric of Post-Soviet National Identity," *The Russian Review* 73, no. 1 (January 2014): 24–46.

16. Miazhevich briefly discusses *stiob* in relation to "sexual excess" as a national branding tool (7–9, 14–15).

17. Dana Heller, "t.A.T.u. You! Russia, the Global Politics of Eurovision, and Lesbian Pop," *Popular Music* 26, no. 2 (May 2007): 195–210.

18. Heller, "t.A.T.u. You!" 196–97.

19. T.A.T.u., "t.A.T.u.—All The Things She Said (Official Music Video)," YouTube, 24 December 2009, https://www.youtube.com/watch?v=8mGBaXPlri8.

20. Mossopp, "tATu Flame Out! ("Face" Magazine—UK)," *Tatysite.net*, 9 December 2003, http://eng.tatysite.net/press/press.php?id=%201168_0_7_0_M.

21. Heller, "t.A.T.u. You!," 207.

22. T.A.T.u., "TaTu Eurovision 2003," YouTube, 21 November 2006, at http://www.youtube.com/watch?v=94FYrYJF16E.

23. Miazhevich, "Sexual Excess in Russia's Eurovision Performances," 256.

24. Heller, "t.A.T.u. You!," 203; Miazhevich, "Sexual Excess in Russia's Eurovision Performances," 257–58.

25. T.A.T.u., "t.A.T.u. Ne ver', ne boisia Eurovision 2009," YouTube, 11 May 2009, https://www.youtube.com/watch?v=dtdA2-YRv78.

26. T.A.T.u., "Tatu—Nas Ne Dogoniat," YouTube, 29 July 2010, https://www.youtube.com/watch?v=Oe4Wp8DQRYo.

27. T.A.T.u., "t.A.T.u. Not Gonna Get Us Eurovision 2009 Semifinal 1," YouTube, 12 May 2009, https://www.youtube.com/watch?v=TypdkNGoYvo; t.A.T.u., "t.A.T.u.—'Nas Ne Dogoniat' Live @ Winter Olympics Games 2014," YouTube, 5 March 2014, https://www.youtube.com/watch?v=iNrvmHPDOic&t=212s.

28. By 2020, "Not Gonna Get Us" was so far removed from t.A.T.u.'s performance of lesbianism that it featured in the Russian blockbuster *Ice 2* as a duet sung by a hockey-playing father and his figure-skating daughter. T.A.T.u., "t.A.T.u.—Nas ne dogoniat fil'm LED 2,'" YouTube, 27 February 2020, https://www.youtube.com/watch?v=qdzmzkzwOfg.

29. For a different reading of Bilan's performance, see Stephen Amico, *Roll Over, Tchaikovsky! Russian Popular Music and Post-Soviet Homosexuality* (Urbana: University of Illinois Press, 2014), 122–34.

30. Anthony Lane, "Letter from Oslo. Only Mr. God Knows Why. The Meaning of the Eurovision Song Contest," *New Yorker*, 28 June 2010: 41.

31. According to Heiko Motschenbacher, such gender ambiguity is commonly used to construct sexual identity at Eurovision. Motschenbacher, "The Discursive Interface

of National, European and Sexual Identities: Preliminary Evidence from the Eurovision Song Contest," in *Intercultural Europe: Arenas of Difference, Communication and Mediation*, ed. Barbara Lewandowska-Tomaszczyk (Stuttgart: Ibidem-Verlag, 2010), 92–93.

32. Karen Fricker, Elena Moreo, and Brian Singleton, "Part of the Show: The Global Networking of Irish Eurovision Song Contest Fans," in *Performing Global Networks*, ed. Karen Fricker and Roni Lentin (Newcastle: Cambridge Scholars Publishing, 2007), 159. Dima Bilan, "Dima Bilan—Never Let You Go (Eurovision 2006 Russia)," YouTube, 19 September 2007, http://www.youtube.com/watch?v=HMyKo018ECo.

33. Singleton, Fricker, and Mareo read Bilan's 2006 performance as "a mainstream spectacle sure to appeal to young female viewers [with] a high-camp flourish which clearly seemed aimed at the queer gaze of gay spectators" (21). Fourteen years later, Bilan, whose sexual orientation generated rumors for years, was outed by the gay blogger Anton Suvorkin. Anton Suvorkin, "MAKEEVA I KVANTOVYI RAZBOR ALEKSA KURS ZA ODIN RUBL'. TAINY VDOVY GRADSKOGO DETALI PARNIA DIMY BILANA," YouTube, 28 January 2022, https://www.youtube.com/watch?v=cZulSDHWjok.

34. Miazhevich, "Sexual Excess in Russia's Eurovision Performances," discusses the sexual dimension of Bilan's 2008 performance on 259–60.

35. Mark Simpson, "MetroDaddy Speaks!," *Salon.com*, 5 January 2004, http://www.salon.com/2004/01/05/metrosexual_ii/. See also David Coad, *The Metrosexual: Gender, Sexuality, and Sport* (Albany: SUNY Press, 2008), 18–36.

36. Eurovision Song Contest: Moscow 2009 (Moscow: "M'iuzik Tried," 2009).

37. Johnson, "A New Song for a New Motherland"; Anastasia Prikhod'ko, "Anastasia Prikhodko—Mamo (Russia)—Eurovision 2009 (The Final)," YouTube, 17 May 2009, http://www.youtube.com/watch?v=K5kKOVoO55g.

38. hgwb2009, "Slavic Pride 2009: 40 Arrested," YouTube, 16 May 2009, http://www.youtube.com/watch?v=HGmEayo8ZK4.

39. Alexander Sasha Kondakov and Evgeny Shtorn reach a similar conclusion in "Sex, Alcohol, and Soul: Violent Reactions to Coming Out after the 'Gay Propaganda' Law in Russia," *The Russian Review* 80 (January 2021): 37–55.

40. Robert Coalson, "Echoes of War and Collapse: Russia's Demographic Decline as Small 1990s Generation Comes of Age," *RadioFreeEurope/RadioLiberty*, 12 January 2020, https://www.rferl.org/a/russia-demographic-data-dip-as-small-1990s-generation-comes-of-age/30373049.html.

41. Healey, *Russian Homophobia from Stalin to Sochi*, 6.

42. Brian Baer, "Now You See It: Gay (In)Visibility and the Performance of Post-Soviet Identity," in *Queer Visibility in Post-Socialist Cultures*, ed. Nárcisz Fejes and Andrea P. Balogh (Bristol: Intellect Books Ltd., 2013), 39.

43. On the genesis of the "gay propaganda" law, as well as its basic functioning, see Emil Edenborg, "'Homosexual Propaganda': Regulating Queer Visibility," in *Politics of Visibility and Belonging: From Russia's 'Homosexual Propaganda' Laws to the Ukraine War* (London: Routledge, 2017), 76–105; Healey, *Russian Homophobia from Stalin to Sochi*, 1–19 and 131–147; Dan Healey, "Russian Gay Propaganda Law," in *Global Encyclopedia of Lesbian, Gay, Bisexual, Transgender, and Queer (LGBTQ) History*, vol. 3., ed. Howard Chiang et al. (New York: Gale, 2019), 1400–1403; Alexander Kondakov, "The

Censorship 'Propaganda' Legislation in Russia," in *State Sponsored Homophobia 2019*, ed. Lucas Ramón Mendos (Geneva: ILGA, 2019), 213–15; Roman Utkin, "Introduction. Illegal Queerness: Russian Culture and Society in the Age of the 'Gay Propaganda' Law," *The Russian Review* 80 (January 2021): 7–16. On the increase in homophobic hate crimes in the wake of the law, see Alexander Kondakov, "The Influence of the 'Gay-propaganda' Law on Violence against LGBTIQ people in Russia: Evidence from Criminal Court Rulings," *European Journal of Criminology* (2019): 1–20; Aleksandr Kondakov, *Prestuplenie na pochve nenavisti protiv LGBT v Rossii: Otchet* (St. Petersburg: Tsentr nezavisimykh sotsiologicheskikh issledovanii, 2017); *Laboratoriia issledovanii seksual'nosti* (LIS) (no date), accessed 5 November 2022, https://lgbtrightsinrussia.wordpress.com/; and *Violent Affections: Queer Sexuality, Techniques of Power, and Law in Russia* (London: UCL Press, 2022). Lena Klimova describes the law's negative impact on LGBTQ+ Russians in *Stranitsa naidena* (n.p.: Izdatel'skie resheniia, 2017), 121–34.

44. Kondakov, "The Censorship 'Propaganda' Law in Russia," 213–15.

45. On differing views of sexual subjectivity, see Richard C. Mole, "Constructing Soviet and Post-Soviet sexualities," in *Soviet and Post-Soviet Sexualities* (London: Routledge, 2019), 1–15; Laurie Essig, "'Bury Their Hearts': Some Thoughts on the Specter of Homosexuality Haunting Russia," *QED* 1, no. 3 (Fall 2014): 39–58.

46. Cai Wilkinson, "Putting 'Traditional Values' into Practice: The Rise and Contestation of Anti-Homopropaganda Laws in Russia," *Journal of Human Rights* 13 (2014): 363–79 (363, 370).

47. Alexander Kondakov, "The Queer Epistemologies: Challenges to the Modes of Knowing about Sexuality in Russia," in *The Sage Handbook of Global Sexualities*, vol.1, ed. Zowie Davy et al. (Los Angeles: Sage Publications Ltd., 2020), 82–98.

48. Alexander Kondakov, "Regulating Desire in Russia," in *Research Handbook on Gender, Sexuality and the Law*, ed. Chris Ashford and Alexander Main (Cheltenham: Edward Elgar Publishing Limited, 2020), 396–408 (397, 403). See also James E. Baker and Kelly Clancy, "Putin as Gay Icon? Memes as a Tactic in Russian LGBT+ Activism," in *LGBTQ+ Activism in Central and Eastern Europe*, ed. R. Buyantueva and M. Shevtsova (New York: Palgrave Macmillan, 2020), 210–11.

49. Essig, "'Bury Their Hearts'"; Kondakov, "The Queer Epistemologies." Kevin Moss notes that scholarship on homosexuality in Putin's Russia supports "the universalizing view of homosexuality—the view that anyone can become lesbian or gay." Kevin Moss, "Russia's Queer Science, or How Anti-LGBT Scholarship Is Made," *The Russian Review* 80 (January 2021): 18.

50. Kondakov, "The Queer Epistemologies," 90.

51. Kondakov, "The Queer Epistemologies," 95.

52. Kondakov, "Eksperty v oblasti netraditsionnykh seksual'nykh otnoshenii: Sudebnaia nauka o gomoseksual'nosti posle priniatii zakona o 'propaganda,'" used with the permission of the author, 20.

53. Kondakov, "The Queer Epistemologies," 95.

54. On the terminology for traditional values and nontraditional relations, see Marianna Murav'eva, "'(Ne)traditsionnye seksual'nye otnosheniia kak iuridicheskaiia kategoriia istoriko-pravovoi analiz," in *Na perepute: Metodologiia, teoriia i praktika LGBT i kvir-issledovanii*, ed. A. A. Kondakov (St. Petersburg: Tsentr nezavisimikh sotsiologicheskikh

issledovanii, 2014), 68–85; Nikolai Gorbachev, "Proizvodstvo normativnosti v diskurse zapreta 'propagandy gomoseksualizma,'" *Na pereput'e*, 86–100.

55. Essig, "'Bury Their Hearts,'" 51–52; Kondakov, "Regulating Desire in Russia," 404.

56. For an articulation of these "traditions," see E. B. Mizulina, "Kontseptsiia semeinoi politiki imeni Mizulinoi," *Advokat Anton Zharov* (no date), accessed 1 November 2022, https://zharov.info/guestbook/koncepciya-semejnoj-politiki-imeni-mizulinoj.

57. Butler, "Preface (1999)," in *Gender Trouble: Feminism and the Subversion of Identity* (New York: Routledge, 2007), xxiii.

58. Butler, *Gender Trouble*, 189.

59. J. L. Austin, *How to Do Things with Words: The William James Lectures Delivered at Harvard University in 1955* (Oxford: Clarendon Press, 1962).

60. Austin, *How to Do Things with Words*, 14.

61. Lorenzo Fiorito, "On Performatives in Legal Discourse," *Metalogicon* (2006) 19, no. 2: 101–12.

62. Butler, "Implicit Censorship and Discursive Agency," in *Excitable Speech: A Politics of the Performative* (New York: Routledge, 1997), 130. Kondakov similarly notes, "the text of the law and its real effects can differ from one another in a fundamental manner." A. A. Kondakov, "Konfiguratsiia prava: Kak deistvuet zakon o 'propagande' v shkolakh," *Zhurnal sotsiologii i sotsial'noi antropologii* 20, no. 5 (2017): 201.

63. Kondakov, "Konfiguratsii prava," 187–88; Kondakov, "Eksperty v oblasti netraditsionnykh seksual'nykh otnoshenii," 4; Radzhana Buyantueva, "LGBT Rights Activism and Homophobia in Russia," *Journal of Homosexuality* 65, no. 4 (2018): 456–83.

64. Kondakov, "The Censorship 'Propaganda' Legislation in Russia," 214.

65. Klimova lists twelve instances of prosecuting Article 6.21 in *Stranitsa naidena*, 118–20.

66. Dmitrii Kurkin, "'Deti-404': Kak ia sozdala gruppu poderzhki LGBT-podrostkov," *Wonder*, 6 March 2018, https://www.wonderzine.com/wonderzine/life/experience/233597-404; "'Dolzhna byt' zakryta, unichtozhena, sterta navsegda': Kak osnovatelia proekta 'Deti-404' nakazali za 'gei-propagandu,'" *Meduza*, 26 January 2015, https://meduza.io/feature/2015/01/26/dolzhna-byt-zakryta-unichtozhena-sterta-navsegda; Aleksandra Savina, "Roskomnadzor zapretil piat' LGBT pablikov," *Wonder*, 21 September 2015, https://www.wonderzine.com/wonderzine/life/news/215229-deti-404; Klimova, *Stranitsa naidena*, 6–7.

67. Askold Kurov and Pavel Loparev, *Children-404* (Berlin: Rise and Shine, 2014).

68. Klimova's books include *Stranitsa naidena*, *Nastoiashchaia devchonka: Kniga o tebe* (Izdatel'stvo "Samokat," 2019), and *Vyzhit' i zhit': Dolgo i schastlivo* (n.p.: Izdatel'skie resheniia, 2020). For more on "Beautiful People," see Tetyana Lokot, "Affective Resistance against Online Misogyny and Homophobia on the RuNet," in *Gender Hate Online*, ed. D. Ging et al. (Cham: Springer International Publishing, 2019), 213–32.

69. Klimova, *Stranitsa naidena*, 129.

70. As Klimova states in *Stranitsa naidena*, Article 6.21 gives "the impression that people are clearly divided into adults and children while children and adolescents before the age of majority lack a sexual orientation or are strictly heterosexual" (7).

71. Klimova, *Stranitsa naidena*, 7.

72. As Jennifer Suchland demonstrates, Article 6.21's homophobia takes part in a larger ethno-national project in post-Soviet Russia. "The LGBT Specter in Russia: Refusing Queerness, Claiming 'Whiteness,'" *Gender, Place & Culture* 25, no. 7 (2018): 1073–88.

73. Kondakov, *Prestuplenie na pochve nenavisti*; Emil Edenborg, "Homophobia as Geopolitics: 'Traditional Values' and the Negotiation of Russia's Place in the World," in *Gendering Nationalism: Intersections of Nation, Gender and Sexuality*, ed. Jon Mulholland et al. (Cham, Switzerland: Palgrave Macmillan, 2018), 67–87; Alexandra Novitskaya, "Sexual Citizens in Exile: State-Sponsored Homophobia and Post-Soviet LGBTQI+ Migration," *The Russian Review* 80 (January 2021): 66; Irina V. Soboleva and Yaroslav A. Bakhmetjev, "Political Awareness and Self-Blame in the Explanatory Narratives of LGBT People amid the Anti-LGBT Campaign in Russia," *Sexuality & Culture* 19 (2015): 293.

74. A. Kondakov, "Pereopredolenie moral'nykh granits: Diskurs o gomoseksual'nosti posle raspada SSSR," in *XV aprel'skaia mezhdunarodnaia konferentsiia po problemam razvitiia ekonomiki i obshshestva*, vol. 3, ed. E. G. Iasin (Moscow: Izdatel'skii dom Vysshei shkoly ekonomiki, 2015), 48. See also Kondakov, "Regulating Desire in Russia," 408.

75. RFE/RL's Russian Service, "Russian Lawmakers Approve First Reading of Amendments to Tighten 'Gay Propaganda' Law," *RadioFreeEurope/RadioLiberty*, 27 October 2022, https://www.rferl.org/a/russia-gay-propaganda-amendments-duma-approved/32103685.html.

76. On Russian terminology for nonnormative sexuality after 2013, see Utkin, "Introduction. Illegal Queerness: Russian Culture and Society in the Age of the 'Gay Propaganda' Law," 14–15. On Russian vocabulary for LGBTQ+, see "Kvir ot A do Ia: Spetsial'nyi proekt BURO. i 'Otkrytky,'" *BURO*, 16 December 2019, https://www.buro247.ru/lifestyle/obshcestvo/16-dec-2019-queer-abc-by-ozine.html; "LGBT—poleznye terminy," *Nuntiare et Recreare* (no date), accessed 5 November 2019, https://www.nuntiare.org/%D0%BE-%D0%BD%D0%B0%D1%81/%D0%BD%D0%B0%D1%88%D0%B8-%D0%BC%D0%B0%D1%82%D0%B5%D1%80%D0%B8%D0%B0%D0%BB%D1%8B/%D0%BB%D0%B3%D0%B1%D1%82-%D0%BF%D0%BE%D0%BB%D0%B5%D0%B7%D0%BD%D1%8B%D0%B5-%D1%82%D0%B5%D1%80%D0%BC%D0%B8%D0%BD%D1%8B/; "Ob"iasniaem: kak korrektno govorit' o LGBT," *Maiak* (5 February 2019) at https://mayak.org.ua/news/objasnjaem-kak-korrektno-govorit-ob-lgbt/.

77. Healey, *Russian Homophobia*, 177–94, 201–9.

78. Philip Ross Bullock, "'That's Not the Only Reason We Love Him': Chaikovsky Reception in Post-Soviet Russia," in *Soviet and Post-Soviet Sexualities*, ed. Richard C. M. Mole, 103–28. (London: Routledge, 2019), 203–28.

79. Aleksandr Kondakov, "Kvir-arkhiv, LGBT-muzei i poteriannye mal'chiki: dve versii istorii seksual'nosti," in *Politika affekta: Muzei kak prostranstvo publichnoi istorii*, ed. A. Zavadskii et al. (Moscow: Novoe literaturnoe obozrenie, 2019), 123–47. Dan Healey mentions several such projects in *Russian Homophobia from Stalin to Sochi*, 205–7.

80. *Muzei istorii LGBT v Rossii* (no date), accessed 5 November 2022, http://lgbtru.com.

81. "'Ia mogu vstat' i skazat': tak bol'she ne budet': 27 istorii iz zhizni rossiiskikh geev," *Afisha*, 22 February 2013, https://daily.afisha.ru/archive/gorod/archive/gay-issue/; Masha Gessen and Joseph Huff-Hannon, ed., *Gay Propaganda: Russian Love Stories* (New York: OR Books, 2014); Nikita Kamitdinov, "'Esli styditsia orentatsii, liudi uvidiat slaboe mesto i budut pol'zovat'sia.': Monologi LGBT-predprinimatelei o gomofobii, 'gei-lobbi' i vykhode iz shkafa," *Inc.*, 25 February 2020, accessed 13 March 2022, https://incrussia.ru/understand/lgbt-entrepreneurs/.

82. For queer Russian writing in English, see Margarita Meklina and Anne O. Fisher, eds., "Life Stories, Death Sentences," *InTranslation*, June 2019, accessed 13 March 2022, https://intranslation.brooklynrail.org/2019/06/.

83. Slava Mogutin, *Food Chain* (New York: ITNA Press, 2014); Yevgeniy Fiks, *Moscow* (Brooklyn: Ugly Duckling Presse, 2013) and *Mother Tongue* (Pleshka Press, 2018).

84. "Vyiti iz shkafa," *Teatr.doc* (no date), accessed 5 November 2022, https://teatrdoc.ru/events.php?id=186. See also Anastasia Patlay, "In Search of Complexities: Documentary Theatre in Today's Russia," *Extended Play*, 7 July 2020, https://extendedplay.thecivilians.org/in-search-of-complexities-documentary-theatre-in-todays-russia-7720/.

85. Clinton Glenn, "'IA GEI! (I Am Gay!)': Russian Coming Out Video Narratives on YouTube," *Digital Icons: Studies in Russian, Eurasian and Central European New Media* 21 (2021): 131–47; Illuminator x Katia Mikheeva, ""Pogovorim? Shall We Talk?," Private account, accessed 5 November 2022, https://www.youtube.com/watch?v=xAbq22gS-RM&feature=emb_logo.

86. Galina Miazhevich and Maria Brock demonstrate the expansion of LGBTQ+ discourse since 2013 in Russian media at "Quiet Revolution: Discursive Representations of Non-Heteronormative Sexualities in Post-Soviet Russia" (2018), accessed 5 November 2022, https://www.quiet-revolution.org/.

87. Alina Rudnitskaya, *Den' pobedy* (Russia: 317-Film, 2014); Oleg Mavromatti, *Durakam zdes' ne mesto* (Russia/Bulgaria: Supernova, 2015).

88. For documentaries about Russian homophobia that express Western homonationalist assumptions, see Ben Steele, *Cold Fear: Gay Life in Russia* (London: BBC Worldwide, 2014) and *Hunted: The War against Gays in Russia* (England: Blakeway Productions, 2014), as well as Vice New's five-part series "Young and Gay in Putin's Russia" from 2014; Vice Video's 2019 "Inside the Chechen Prison Where Gay Men Say They Were Tortured"; and David France, *Welcome to Chechnya* (Music Box Films, 2020). On this genre of film, see Clinton Glenn, "Мы не ошибка (We Are Not an Error): Documentary Film and LGBT Activism against the Russian Anti-'Gay Propaganda' Campaign," in *LGBTQ+ Activism in Central and Eastern Europe: Resistance, Representation and Identity*, ed. Radzhana Buyantueva and Maryna Shevtsova (Cham, Switzerland: Palgrave Macmillan, 2020), 77–100.

89. For discussion of the tanks as the film's "conceptual frame," see Aleksei Artamonov, "'Den' pobedy': Tanki, 'topolia' i LGBT v novom doke Aliny Rudnitskoi," *Colta*, 16 December 2014, https://www.colta.ru/articles/cinema/5722-den-pobedy.

90. Sergii Astakhov, "Astakhov Sergii," YouTube (no date), accessed 5 November 2022, https://www.youtube.com/channel/UCba4jRsoLIOklXXd6ZAyzNA. See also Eliot Borenstein, *Plots against Russia: Conspiracy and Fantasy after Socialism* (Ithaca, NY: Cornell University Press, 2019), 196–99.

91. Anatolii Ulianov, "My New Orthodox Video/Moe novoe pravoslavnoe video (2013)," YouTube, 31 October 2013, https://www.youtube.com/watch?v=OX27UrIvrLQ.

92. Oleg Mavromatti, "Director's Statement," *Oleg Mavromatti*, 2014, accessed 5 November 2022, https://olegmavromatti.com/sample-page/.

93. The Russian title of the drama on which Serebrennikov based his film was *(M)uchenik*, a play on the words *uchenik* (student, disciple) and *muchenik* (martyr). Kirill Serebrennikov, *Uchenik* (Russia: Hype Film, 2016).

94. Katharina Weidlack, "*Quantum Leap* 2.0 or the Western Gaze on Russian Homophobia," *Adeptus* 11 (2018): 1–20; M. Katharina Weidlack, "Gays vs. Russia: Media Representations, Vulnerable Bodies and the Construction of a (Post)Modern West," *European Journal of English Studies* 21, no. 3 (2017): 241–57. See also Michele Rivkin-Fish and Cassandra Hartblay, "When Global LGBTQ Advocacy Became Entangled with New Cold War Sentiment: A Call for Examining Russian Queer Experience," *Brown Journal of World Affairs* 21, no. 1 (Fall/Winter 2014): 95–111.

95. Misha Friedman, *Lyudmila and Natasha: Russian Lives* (New York: New Press, 2014); Laurie Essig and Alexander Kondakov, "A Cold War for the Twenty-first Century: Homosexualism vs. Heterosexualism," *Soviet and Post-Soviet Sexualities*, 79–102 (80). See also Aleksandr A. Kondakov, "Mezhdunarodnye diskussii o gomoseksual'nosti: effekty bumeranga v potokakh vlasti," *Sotsiologiia vlasti* 30, no. 1 (2018): 14–32. Although the terms "homosexualism" and "heterosexualism" gesture toward Puar's concept of homonationalism, they avoid the problems that arise when homonationalism is applied to countries in Central and Eastern Europe. Roman Leksikov and Dafna Rachok, "Beyond Western Theories: On the Use and Abuse of 'Homonationalism' in Eastern Europe," in *LGBTQ+ Activism in Central and Eastern Europe*, ed. R. Buyantueva and M. Shevtsova (New York: Palgrave Macmillan, 2020), 25–49.

96. Baer, "Now You See It"; Emil Persson, "Banning 'Homosexual Propaganda': Belonging and Visibility in Contemporary Russian Media," *Sexuality & Culture* 19, no. 2 (June 2015): 256–74; Nikita Sleptcov, "Political Homophobia as a State Strategy in Russia," *Journal of Global Initiatives* 132, no. 1 (2017): 140–61.

97. Healey, *Russian Homophobia*, 7. On the neologism "Gayropa," see Oleg Riabov and Tatiana Riabova, "The Decline of Gayropa? How Russia Intends to Save the World," *Eurozine*, 5 February 2014, https://www.eurozine.com/the-decline-of-gayropa/. See also Kevin Moss, "Russia as the Saviour of European Civilization: Gender and the Geopolitics of Traditional Values," in *Anti-Gender Campaigns in Europe: Mobilizing against Equality*, ed. Roman Kuhar and David Patternotte (London: Rowman & Littlefield, 2017), 195–214.

98. Healey, *Russian Homophobia from Stalin to Sochi*, 209.

Chapter 5. Post-Soviet Postfeminism

1. Brian James Baer, "Now You See It: Gay (In)Visibility and the Performance of Post-Soviet Identity," *Queer Visibility in Post-Socialist Cultures*, ed. Nárcisz Fejes and Andrea P. Balogh (Bristol: Intellect Books, 2013), 37–55.

2. Emil Edenborg, "Homophobia as Geopolitics: 'Traditional Values' and the Negotiation of Russia's Place in the World," in *Gendering Nationalism: Intersections of Nation, Gender and Sexuality*, ed. Jon Mulholland et al. (Cham: Springer International Publishing AG, 2018), 82.

3. Nerses Isajanyan, "Russia: Decriminalization of Domestic Violence," *Library of Congress Law* (June 2017) at https://permanent.fdlp.gov/gpo87191/russia-decriminalization-domestic-violence.pdf; Alexey Yurtaev, "Inside the fight over Russia's Domestic Violence Law," *openDemocracy*, 17 February 2020, https://www.opendemocracy.net/en/odr/russia-domestic-violence-law/; Yulia Gorbunova, "The Chilling Inaction on Domestic Violence in Russia Is Endangering Women's Lives," *euronews*, 29 July 2019, https://www.euronews.com/2019/07/29/the-chilling-inaction-on-domestic-violence-in-russia-is-endangering-women-s-lives-view?utm_medium=Social&utm_source=Twitter#Echobox=1564419588. See also "Domestic violence in Russia," *Wikipedia*, accessed 6 November 2022, https://en.wikipedia.org/wiki/Domestic_violence_in_Russia#The_data_on_annual_deaths_of_14,000_women.

4. On Russian women's self-policing, see Elena Gapova, "Polnyi Fuko: Telo kak pole vlasti," *Neprikosnovennyi zapas* 76, no. 2 (2011), *ZhZ*, accessed 2 November 2022, https://magazines.gorky.media/nz/2011/2/polnyj-fuko-telo-kak-pole-vlasti.html.

5. ThePubliciti, "Putin's Army [English Subs]," YouTube, 19 July 2011, https://www.youtube.com/watch?v=klcyPNIA698.

6. "Scantily-clad Girls in Putin's 'Army' Wash Russian-made Cars," YouTube, 21 July 2011, accessed 13 June 2021, https://www.youtube.com/watch?v=aOe4JRry5j8; ArmiaPutina, "Tortik dlia Putina! Chocolate cake!," YouTube, 7 October 2011, https://www.youtube.com/watch?v=rVCiwYqX18o.

7. Valerie Sperling, *Sex, Politics, and Putin: Political Legitimacy in Russia* (New York: Oxford University Press, 2015). On Putin's Army, see 97–100.

8. Rosalind Gill, "Postfeminist Media Culture: Elements of a Sensibility," *European Journal of Cultural Studies* 10 (2007): 147–66; and Gill, "The Affective, Cultural and Psychic Life of Postfeminism: A Postfeminist Sensibility 10 Years On," *European Journal of Cultural Studies*, 20, no. 6 (2017): 606–26.

9. Gill, "Postfeminist Media Culture," 151.

10. Gill, "Postfeminist Media Culture," 164.

11. Gill, "The Affective, Cultural and Psychic Life of Postfeminism," 609.

12. Maria Adamson and Suvi Salmenniemi, "New Heroines of Labour: Domesticating Post-feminism and Neoliberal Capitalism in Russia," *Sociology* 49, no. 1 (2015): 88–105; and Adamson and Salmenniemi, "'The Bottom Line Is That the Problem Is You': Aesthetic Labour, Postfeminism and Subjectivity in Russian Self-Help Literature," in *Aesthetic Labour: Rethinking Beauty Politics in Neoliberalism*, ed. A. S. Elias et al. (London: Palgrave Macmillan, 2017), 301–16. See also Salmenniemi, "In Search of a 'New Wo(Man)': Gender and Sexuality in Contemporary Russian Self-help Literature," in *Russian Mass Media and Changing Values*, ed. A. Rosenholm et al. (London: Routledge, 2013), 134–53.

13. Sudha Rajagopalan, "Misogyny, Solidarity and Postfeminism on Social Media: The Work of Being Diana Shurygina, Survivor-celebrity," *European Journal of Cultural Studies* 22, nos. 5–6 (2019): 739–62; Larissa Rudova, "'Who's the Fairest of Them All?' Beauty and Femininity in Contemporary Russian Adolescent Girl Fiction," *The Russian Review* 73, no. 3 (2014): 389–403; Andrea Lanoux, "Laundry, Potatoes, and the Everlasting Soul: Russian Advice Literature for Girls after Communism," *The Russian Review* 73, no. 3 (2014): 404–26.

14. Holly Porteous, "'There Are No Ugly Women, Only Lazy Ones': The Duty of Beauty Labour in Contemporary Russian Women's Magazines," in *Körper—Geschlecht—Wahrnehmung. Geistes- Und Sozialwissenschaftliche Beiträge Zur Genderforschung*, ed. Helle Ehlers et al. (Berlin: Lit Verlag, 2013), 133–56; Porteous, "From Barbie to the Oligarch's Wife: Reading Fantasy Femininity and Globalisation in Post-Soviet Russian Women's Magazines," *European Journal of Cultural Studies* 20, no. 2 (2017): 180–98; Porteous, "'A Woman Isn't a Woman When She's Not Concerned about the Way She Looks': Beauty Labour and Femininity in Post-Soviet Russia," in *The Palgrave Handbook of Women and Gender in Twentieth-Century Russia and the Soviet Union*, ed. M. Ilic (London: Palgrave Macmillan, 2018), 413–28.

15. Salmenniemi and Adamson, "New Heroines of Labour," 3.

16. Salmenniemi and Adamson, "New Heroines of Labour," 14.

17. Gill, "The Affective, Cultural and Psychic Life of Postfeminism," 618.

18. On the outcomes of "maternity capital," see Ekaterina Borozdina et al., "Using Maternity Capital: Citizen Distrust of Russian Family Policy," *European Journal of Women's Studies* 23, no. 1 (2016): 60–75.

19. Mariia Chernitsyna, "Ledi pod grifom 'Sekretno': 'MK' raskryvaet semeinye tainy Liudmily Putinoi," *Kompromat.ru*, 9 September 2005, http://www.compromat.ru/page_17355.htm.

20. Nelli Goreslavskaia explicitly compares Putina's life to a fairy tale in a chapter subheading: "Once upon a time there was a little girl . . ." Goreslavskaia, "Zhila-byla devochka . . . ," in *Vladimir Putin i Liudmila Putina: Vne politiki* (Moscow: Algoritm, 2007, 2008), 62.

21. N. Gevorkian, A. Kolesnikov, and N. Timakova, *Ot pervogo litsa: Razgovory s Vladimirom Putinym* (Moscow: Vagrius, 2000), 58.

22. Gevorkian et al., *Ot pervogo litsa*, 151.

23. Gevorkian et al., *Ot pervogo litsa*, 140.

24. Elena Novoselova et al., "Roditel'skoe sobranie s Liudmiloi Putinoi," *RGRU*, 6 January 2006, http://www.rg.ru/2006/06/01/lyudmila-putina.html.

25. Goreslavskaia, *Vladimir Putin i Liudmila Putina*, 233.

26. Ol'ga Zhulina, dir., *Potselui ne dlia pressy* (Russia: Prodiuserskaia kompaniia Anatoliia Voropaeva, 2008); Grigorii Zaslavskii, "Valentinka: Fil'm o iunykh godakh prezidenta mozhno budet uvidet' tol'ko pri bol'shom zhelanii," *Nezavisimaia gazeta*, 13 February 2008, https://www.ng.ru/culture/2008-02-13/16_valentinka.html.

27. Sergei Grigorashenko, "Retsenziia na fil'm *Potselui ne dlia pressy*," *MirSovetov* (no date), accessed 5 December 2008, http://mirsovetov.ru/a/miscellaneous/movies/kiss-no-press.html.

28. Gevorkian et al., *Ot pervogo litsa*, 48.

29. Svetlana Stepnova, "Zhenskoe schast'e—byl by milyi riadom . . . ," *Ruskino* (15 February 2008) at https://ruskino.ru/item/2008/2/15/zhenskoe-schaste-byl-by-milyj-ryadom. See also Zaslavskii.

30. Grigorashenko; Nataliia Rostova, "Pervoe litso—na prokat," *Novaia Gazeta*, 13 February 2008, https://novayagazeta.ru/articles/2008/02/14/39327-pervoe-litso-na-prokat. For Western reporting, see Sophia Kishkovsky, "A Love Letter to Putin (but It's Not Addressed to Him)," *New York Times*, 6 February 2008; Yuri Zakharovich, "A Movie

Valentine for Putin," *Time*, 13 February 2008, http://content.time.com/time/arts/article/0,8599,1712848,00.html.

31. Alexander Pushkin, *Eugene Onegin*, trans. Charles Johnston (New York: Penguin Books, 1977), 231.

32. Fyodor Dostoevsky, "Pushkin (A Sketch)," in *A Writer's Diary*, vol. 20 (1877–1881), trans. Kenneth Lantz (Evanston, IL: Northwestern University Press, 1994), 1285.

33. Katerina Clark, "The Stalinist Myth of the 'Great Family,'" in *The Soviet Novel: History as Ritual*, 3rd ed. (Bloomington: Indiana, 2000), 114–24. Hans Günther discusses the mother within this myth in "Wise Father Stalin and His Family in Soviet Cinema," in *Socialist Realism Without Shores*, ed. Thomas Lahusen and Evgeny Dobrenko (Durham, NC: Duke University Press, 1997), 178–90.

34. Novoselova et al., "Roditel'skoe sobranie s Liudmiloi Putinoi."

35. Goreslavskaia, "Zhila-byla devochka . . . ," 113, 83.

36. Oleg Blotskii, *Vladimir Putin: Doroga k vlasti. Kniga vtoraia* (Moscow: Osmos Press, 2002), 22; Gevorkian et al., *Ot pervogo litsa*, 145. Putina's statements echo a sex-charged campaign ad for Putin before his 2012 return to office. perviirazpolubvi, "Otkrovenie devushki pro ee pervyi raz," YouTube, 20 February 2012, https://www.youtube.com/watch?v=MbIzj21XotU.

37. "Liudmila Putina: Nash brak s Vladimirom Putinym zavershen," *RT na russkom*, 6 June 2013, accessed 30 June 2021, https://www.youtube.com/watch?v=3zhdJnKEvJU. See also Anastasia Denisova, "How Vladimir Putin's Divorce Story Was Constructed and Received, or When the President Divorced His Wife and Married the Country Instead," *M/C Journal* 17, no. 3 (June 2014), https://journal.media-culture.org.au/index.php/mcjournal/article/view/813.

38. Callie Patteson, "Who Is Alina Kabaeva, Putin's Alleged Lover and Mother of His Secret Twins?," *New York Post*, 20 April 2022, https://nypost.com/article/who-is-alina-kabaeva-putin-alleged-lover/; Patrick Knox, "First Mistress? Who is Vladimir Putin's Rumored Girlfriend Alina Kabaeva?," *The U.S. Sun*, 22 February 2022, https://www.the-sun.com/news/1601251/alina-kabaeva-vladimir-putin-rumoured-girlfriend-wedding-gymnast/; "Alina Kabaeva rodila dvoiniu: chto izvestno ob otnosheniiakh sportsmenki s Putinym," *24 Lifestyle*, 13 May 2019, https://lifestyle.24tv.ua/ru/alina_kabaeva_rodila_ot_putina_vse_ob_otnoshenijah_kabayevoj_i_putina_n1152510.

39. For Shatskaia's biography, see "Evgeniia Shatskaia. Ob avtore," *LitRes* (no date), https://www.litres.ru/evgeniya-shackaya/ob-avtore/. LitRes lists Shatkaia's books at https://www.litres.ru/evgeniya-shackaya/ (both accessed 6 November 2022).

40. Adamson and Salmenniemi, "New Heroines of Labour," 5.

41. The book teasers quoted in the following paragraphs are on the LitRes website under the "Chitat' fragment" buttons at https://www.litres.ru/evgeniya-shackaya/stervologiya-kratkiy-kurs-dlya-zanyatoy-stervy/chitat-onlayn/ for *Stervologiia: Kratkii kurs dlia znatnoi stervy* (1000 Bestsellerov, 2010) and https://www.litres.ru/evgeniya-shackaya/bibliya-stervy-kratkiy-kurs/chitat-onlayn/ for *Bibliia Stervy: Kratkii kurs* (1000 Bestsellerov, 2012) (both accessed 6 November 2022).

42. Shatskaia, *Stervologiia*, 8.

43. Shatskaia, *Stervologiia*, 8.

44. Shatskaia, *Stervologiia*, 9.

45. Shatskaia, *Stervologiia*, 8.

46. Shatskaia, *Bibliia stervy*, 6.

47. Shatskaia, *Bibliia stervy*, 16.

48. Shatskaia, *Bibliia stervy*, 6; Shatskaia, *Stervologiia*, 6; Shatskaia, *Bibliia stervy*, 47.

49. Shatskaia, *Stervologiia*, 6. Slightly later on the same page, Shatskaia generates more homophobic rhetoric when she compares advanced and beginning bitches to "gays and pederasts. The essence is the same, but there are nuances."

50. Virginia M. Allen, *The Femme Fatale: Erotic Icon* (Troy, NY: The Whitston Publishing Company, 1983), 7 and 195; Mary Ann Doane, *Femmes Fatales: Feminism, Film Theory, Psychoanalysis* (New York: Routledge, 1991), 2–3.

51. Shatskaia, *Bibliia stervy*, 23, 6.

52. Shatskaia, *Bibliia stervy*, 8. Simone de Beauvoir's original reads, "One is not born, but rather becomes, woman." *The Second Sex*, trans. Constance Borde and Sheila Malovany-Chevallier (New York: Alfred A. Knopf, 2010), 283. As for Syl'via Chiz, all my efforts to find this alleged Belgian journalist led to Russian quotation-compiling websites like citaty.info and citaty.su.

53. Shatskaia, *Bibliia stervy*, 17.

54. Shatskaia, *Stervologiia*, 5.

55. Shatskaia, *Bibliia stervy*, 8.

56. Shatskaia, *Bibliia stervy*, 15; Salmenniemi and Adamson, "New Heroines of Labour," 7.

57. Alina Rudnitskaya, "Kak stat' stervoi (2008)," YouTube, 5 March 2017, https://www.youtube.com/watch?v=jYPmdRBvAsQ. The film is available as *Bitch Academy* in the collection *Wholphin, No. 11, DVD Magazine of Rare and Unseen Short Films* (San Francisco: McSweeney's, 2010).

58. "Bitch Academy. An Interview with the Filmmaker," np. This interview appears in the booklet that accompanies *Wholphin, No. 11*, cited in note 57.

59. "Bitch Academy," n.p.

60. Temkina and Zdravomyslova argue that bitchology takes part in the instrumentalization of feminine identity management and gender polarization in the post-Soviet era. Anna Temkina and Elena Zdravomyslova, "The Sexual Scripts and Identity of Middle-Class Russian Women," *Sexuality and Culture* 19 (2015): 314–16.

61. Evgeniia Shatskaia and Eliza Tanaka, *Shkola geishi: Mudrost' vostoka dlia sovremennoi zhenshchiny* (Moscow: Eksmo, 2006).

62. Vladimir Shevel'kov, *Sterva* (Ukraine and Russia: Kinokompaniia "Shpil'," 2009). The seven pop songs titled "Sterva" are by Misha Marvan and Kan (2016), Arnol'd (2017), Lesha Svik (2019), Fogel' (2020), Asia (2020), Vania Dmitrienko (2021), and Aslan Kiatov (2021).

63. On popular romance in Russia, see Emily Johnson, "Exploring His/Her Library: Reading and Books in Russian Romance," *Journal of Popular Romance Studies* 9 (30 March 2020), http://www.jprstudies.org/2020/03/exploring-his-her-library-reading-and-books-in-russian-romance/.

64. E. L. James, *Fifty Shades of Grey* (New York: Vintage Books, 2011), *Fifty Shades Darker* (New York: Vintage Books 2011), *Fifty Shades Freed* (New York: Vintage Books, 2012).

65. Alisa Klever, *Dva mesiatsa i tri dnia: Roman* (Moscow: Eksmo, 2015), *Chetyre storony sveta i odna zhenshchina: Roman* (Moscow: Eksmo, 2015), and *Piatnadtsatyi rai: Roman* (Moscow: Eksmo, 2015). See also Julie A. Cassiday, "A World without Safe

Words: Fifty Shades of Russian Grey," *Journal of Popular Romance Studies* 9 (30 March 2020) at http://www.jprstudies.org/2020/03/a-world-without-safe-words-fifty-shades-of-russian-grey/.

66. Klever, *Piatnadtsatyi rai*, 184.

67. Klever, *Chetyre storony sveta*, 30.

68. Klever, *Dva mesiatsa i tri dnia*, 64.

69. Klever, *Chetyre storony sveta*, 51.

70. Klever, *Dva mesiatsa i tri dnia*, 242.

71. Klever, *Dva mesiatsa i tri dnia*, 91.

72. Klever, *Dva mesiatsa i tri dnia*, 161, 160, 162.

73. Klever, *Dva mesiatsa i tri dnia*, 186.

74. Klever, *Dva mesiatsa i tri dnia*, 181, 183.

75. Klever, *Dva mesiatsa i tri dnia*, 298.

76. Klever, *Dva mesiatsa i tri dnia*, 305.

77. Klever, *Chetyre storony sveta*, 110.

78. Klever, *Chetyre storony sveta*, 116.

79. Klever, *Piatnadtsatyi rai*, 296.

80. Klever, *Chetyre storony sveta*, 205, 49.

81. Alisa Klever, email, 29 July 2016.

82. Klever, *Piatnadtsatyi rai*, 256.

83. Klever, *Chetyre storony sveta*, 52.

84. Klever, *Chetyre storony sveta*, 198.

85. Klever, *Chetyre storony sveta*, 205.

86. Klever, *Piatnadtsatyi rai*, 339.

87. Klever, email, 29 July 2016. Arina echoes this sentiment in the trilogy's third book: "*As long as the two of us are here together in the twilight of our bedroom, who'll dare to judge us for what we do with our bodies?*" Klever, *Piatnadtsatyi rai*, 50 (italics in original).

88. Klever, email, 29 July 2016.

89. Klever, *Piatnadtsatyi rai*, 328.

90. Valeriia Gai Germanika, *Vse umrut, a ia ostanus'* (Russia: Profit, 2008). See also Julie A. Cassiday, "Sacrifice and Self in *Everybody Dies but Me*," in *The "Other" Martyrs: Women and the Poetics of Sexuality, Sacrifice, and Death in World Literatures*, ed. Alireza Korangy and Leyla Rouhi (Wiesbaden: Harrassowitz Verlag, 2019), 23–37.

91. On martyrdom and sacrifice in Russian culture, see Yuliya Minkova, *Making Martyrs: The Language of Sacrifice in Russian Culture from Stalin to Putin* (Rochester: University of Rochester Press, 2018).

92. Valeriia Gai Germanika, *Devochki* (Russia: Kinoteatr.doc, 2005); *Shkola* (Russia: Profit and Russia's Channel One, 2010). For *School*'s impact on social opinion, see Stephen Hutchings, "Serializing National Cohesion: Channel 1's 'Shkola' and the Contradictions of Post-Soviet 'Consensus Management,'" *The Russian Review* 72 (July 2013): 470–91. For optimistic readings of both *School* and *Everybody Dies but Me*, see Julia Vassilieva, "'Becoming-Girl' in the New Russian Cinema: Youth and Valeria Gai Germanika's Films and Television," *Camera Obscura* 29, no. 1 (2014): 59–79.

93. Aleksandr Kolbovskii, "Valeriia Gai-Germanika: *Everybody Dies but Me* (Vse umrut, a ia ostanus', 2008)," *KinoKultura*, 15 October 2008, http://www.kinokultura.com/2008/22r-vseumrut.shtml.

94. For the former, see Kolbovskii, "Valeriia Gai-Germanika"; for the latter, see Elena Fanailova, "Nikto iz nas ne vyidet otsiuda zhivym," *Seans* 37/38 (8 July 2010), https://seance.ru/articles/nikto-iz-nas-ne-vyiydet-otsyuda-zhivyim/.

95. Joshua S. Goldstein, "War and Gender," in *Encyclopedia of Sex and Gender*, ed. Carol R. Ember and Melvin Ember, vol. 1, *Topics and Cultures A-K* (New York: Kluwer Academic/Plenum Publishers, 2003), 107–16. See also Goldstein, *War and Gender: How Gender Shapes the War System and Vice Versa* (New York: Cambridge University Press, 2001).

96. Alan Taylor, "Beauty in the Ceasefire: A Pageant in Donetsk," *Atlantic*, 9 March 2015, http://www.theatlantic.com/photo/2015/03/beauty-in-the-ceasefire-a-pageant-in-donetsk/387247/?utm_source=Russian+Life&utm_campaign=adedbe3616-Russia_File_Mar_19&utm_medium=email&utm_term=0_2e99ba62b2-adedbe3616-84240921&mc_cid=adedbe3616&mc_eid=424dc42cda#. On beauty pageants in the Soviet Union, see Melanie Ilic, "Women and Competition in State Socialist Societies: Soviet Beauty Contests," in *Competition in Socialist Society*, ed. Katalin Miklóssy and Melanie Ilic (New York: Routledge, 2014), 159–75; Elizabeth Waters, "Soviet Beauty Contests," in *Sex and Russian Society*, ed. Igor Kon and James Riordan (London: Pluto, 1993), 116–34.

97. Vice News, "A Rebel Beauty Pageant: Russian Roulette (Dispatch 98)," YouTube, 9 March 2015, https://www.youtube.com/watch?v=_9glPPNLQyg.

98. Dominique Moran, Judith Pallot, and Laura Piacentini, "Lipstick, Lace, and Longing: Constructions of Femininity inside a Russian Prison," *Environment and Planning D: Society and Space* 27 (2009): 700–20. For photographs from a 2013 prison beauty pageant, see pene4ka, "Konkurs krasoty v zhenskoi kolonii (28 foto)," *Bugaga*, 6 December 2013, http://www.bugaga.ru/interesting/1146741638-konkurs-krasoty-v-zhenskoy-kolonii.html.

99. Moran et al., "Lipstick, Lace, and Longing," 710.

100. Moran et al., "Lipstick, Lace, and Longing," 709.

101. Moran et al., "Lipstick, Lace, and Longing," 700, 701.

102. Alina Rudnitskaya, *School of Seduction: Three Stories from Russia* (Denmark: Danish Documentary, 2019).

103. Leningrad, "Leningrad–Exhibit (aka Louboutins)," YouTube, 13 January 2016, https://www.youtube.com/watch?v=et281UHNoOU.

104. Aleksandr Gorbachev, ed., *Ne nado stesniat'sia: Istoriia postsovetskoi pop-muzyki v 169 pesniakh (1991–2021)* (Moscow: Institut muzykal'nykh initsiativ, 2021), 744–45.

105. "Novyi trek 'Leningrada' vozglavil charty rossiiskogo iTunes," *Lenta.ru*, 25 January 2016, https://lenta.ru/news/2016/01/25/leningrad/.

106. El'vira Egorova, "Rossianki nachali krasit' tufli 'pod labuteny' kak v klipe gruppy 'Leningrad,'" *Metro*, 20 January 2016, https://www.metronews.ru/novosti/russia/reviews/rossiyanki-nachali-krasit-tufli-pod-labuteny-kak-v-klipe-gruppy-leningrad-1182887/.

107. A Google search for videos using the term "parodiia" with "labuteny," "na labutenax," or "Eksponat" yields from three to ten thousand hits.

108. Leningrad, "Tumany (თუმანი)—Na labutenakh, Vakh!," YouTube, 6 February 2016, https://www.youtube.com/watch?v=WAX4r-gH8ao.

109. Aleksandra Arkhipova et al., "Fol'klor 'na labutenax': Kak 'labuteny' iz pesni Shnura 'Eksponat' zashagali po seti i po zhizni," *Colta.ru*, 5 March 2016, https://www.colta.ru/articles/society/10975-folklor-na-labutenah.

Conclusion

1. Valerii Pecheikin, "Viktor Erofeev: Rossiia kak transvestit," *Kvir* 75 (1 June 2014), http://www.kvir.ru/articles/viktor-erofeev-rossiya.html.

2. Viktor Erofeev, "Stil', stil', stil'," *Muzhchiny* (Moscow: Izdatel'skii Dom Podkova, 1997), 10–12.

3. For a video of this part of Putin's address, see *The Telegraph*, "Putin Attacks Church of England for Considering Gender-Neutral God," YouTube, 21 February 2023, https://www.youtube.com/watch?v=I-FjJnFpuwQ.

4. "KoAP RF Stat'ia 6.21. Propoganda netraditsionnykh seksual'nykh otnoshenii i (ili) predpochtenii, smeny pola," Konsul'tantPlius, 14 April 2023, https://www.consultant.ru/document/cons_doc_LAW_34661/d4344568bd586d541d39273855ba64ba9d18e84a/.

5. On cultural protest in the 2010s, see Mischa Gabowitsch, *Protest in Putin's Russia* (Cambridge: Polity Press, 2016); Birgit Beumers et al., eds., *Cultural Forms of Protest in Russia* (London: Routledge, 2018); Lena Johnson, *Art and Protest in Putin's Russia* (London: Routledge, 2015); and Alexandar Mihailovic, *The Mitki and the Art of Postmodern Protest in Russia* (Madison: University of Wisconsin Press, 2018).

6. Jonathan Brooks Platt, "Hysteria or Enjoyment? Recent Russian Actionism," in *Cultural Forms of Protest in Russia*, 141–59. See also Marina Galperina, "An Interview with Petr Pavlensky: Anarchist Artist Nails His Balls to Red Square, So You Don't Have To," *Animal*, 18 November 2013, accessed 11 February 2022, http://animalnewyork.com/2013/interview-petr-pavlensky-anarchist-artist-nailed-balls-red-square-dont/.

7. Alexei Yurchak, *Everything Was Forever, Until It Was No More: The Last Soviet Generation* (Princeton, NJ: Princeton University Press, 2013).

8. "O saite," *Wonderzine* (no date), accessed 7 November 2022, https://www.wonderzine.com/pages/about.

9. Polina Kriukova, "Pevyi rossiiskii zhurnal o drege: Dragzina," *Blueprint*, 30 November 2020, https://theblueprint.ru/fashion/magazines/dragzina; Anastasiia Fedorova, "Dragzina: Join the Queer Artists Claiming Russia's Summer Houses as Their Own," *Calvert Journal*, 22 September 2020, https://www.calvertjournal.com/features/show/12154/dragzina-dacha-russia-z.

10. Nastia Ivleeva, "Drag–shou Koroloveskie kobry," YouTube, last updated 13 January 2022, https://www.youtube.com/playlist?list=PLn2SiPuzV6DtYLeVyCaiuyLZS12-bCbcq.

11. Zarina Dzagoeva, "'Korolevskie kobry' Ivleevoi: chto za shou i pochemu o nem gudit ves' internet," *News.ru*, 1 October 2021, https://news.ru/culture/korolevskie-kobry-ivleevoj-chto-za-shou-i-pochemu-o-nyom-gudit-ves-internet/.

12. Shura Guliaeva, "'Dreg kak protest v Rossii nikomu ne nuzhen': 4 problemy predstoiashchego shou Anastasii Ivleevoi. Ob"iasniaiut aktivisty i feministskaia issledovatel'nitsa," *The Village*, 27 September 2021, https://www.the-village.ru/weekend/opinions/kobry.

13. Guliaeva, "'Dreg kak protest v Rossii nikomu ne nuzhen'."

14. Anton Danilov, "Kakim poluchilsia pervyi vypusk dreg-shou 'Korolevskie kobry Nasti Ivleevoi': shantay you stay ili sashay away?" *Wonderzine*, 29 September 2021,

https://www.wonderzine.com/wonderzine/entertainment/entertainment-opinion/259157-ivleeva-and-drag.

15. Danilov, "Kakim poluchilsia pervyi vypusk dreg-shou 'Korolevskie kobry Nasti Ivleevoi'."

16. Nastia Ivleeva, "Korolevskie kobry x Denis Dorokhov," YouTube, 14 January 2022, https://www.youtube.com/watch?v=ZWDaJbZZoeo.

17. Nastia Ivleeva, "Korolevskie kobry x Kseniia Sobchak," YouTube, 19 October 2021, https://www.youtube.com/watch?v=HypuZjaut3g.

18. Elena Ivanova, "'Ona otlichno vladeet iazykom': Ivleeva rasskazala, ponravilsia li ei potselui s Sobchak," *Radio Komsomol'skaia Pravda*, 22 October 2021, https://radiokp.ru/znamenitosti/ona-otlichno-vladeet-yazykom-ivleeva-rasskazala-ponravilsya-li-ey-poceluy-s-sobchak_nid492065_au37688au.

19. Anastasiia Pavlenko and Svetlana Medvedeva, "'Devochki prikalivaiutsia': mogut li nakazat' Sobchak i Ivleevu za strastnyi potselui," *Moskva24*, 20 October 2021, https://www.m24.ru/articles/kultura/20102021/158747.

20. For Sobchak and Kandelaki's kiss, see Dmitrii Komel'kov, "Potselui Kandelaki i Sobchak," YouTube, 7 February 2012, https://www.youtube.com/watch?v=9XWYPvsrimM; for Madonna kissing Spears and Aguilera, see BitchVEVo, "Madonna, Britney Spears & Christina Aguilera Kiss!!! HD," YouTube, 24 July 2012, https://www.youtube.com/watch?v=MAy-NtCQCB8.

21. Fredric Jameson, *Postmodernism, or, The Cultural Logic of Late Capitalism* (Durham, NC: Duke University Press, 1991), 18.

22. Little Big, "Little Big—Uno—Russia—Official Music Video—Eurovision 2020," YouTube, 12 March 2020, https://www.youtube.com/watch?v=L_dWvTCdDQ4.

23. Maria Engström, "Little Big: Neo-camp and a New Generation of Russian Identity," *Riddle*, 20 May 2019, https://www.ridl.io/en/little-big-neo-camp-and-a-new-generation-of-russian-identity/.

24. "Pevitsa Manizha predstavliaet Rossiiu na 'Evrovidenie-2021': Ona ispolnit pesniu 'Russkaia zhenshchina,'" *TASS*, 8 March 2021, https://tass.ru/kultura/10857225.

25. "Pevitsa Manizha predstavliaet Rossiiu na 'Evrovidenie-2021'."

26. Manizha, "Manizha–Russian Woman–LIVE–Russia–Grand Final–Eurovision 2021," *dailymotion*, accessed 11 February 2022, https://www.dailymotion.com/video/x81g3nx; Nastia Sotnik, "Istoriia odnogo plat'ia: plat'e Manizha na 'Evrovidenii-2021,'" *Blueprint*, 18 May 2021, https://theblueprint.ru/fashion/industry/istoriya-odnogo-platya-manizha.

27. Sotnik, "Istoriia odnogo plat'ia."

28. Sasha Raspopina, "Beauty Trauma: Tajik Singer Manizha Starts Campaign against Toxic Beauty Standards," *Calvert Journal*, 26 September 2017, https://www.calvertjournal.com/articles/show/9035/beauty-trauma-tajik-singer-starts-campaign-against-toxic-beauty-standards.

29. Oliver Adams, "A Russian Woman for the People! Russia's Manizha Wins the Dana International Award for LGBTQ+ Equality 2021," *wiwibloggs: Eurovision News with an Attitude*, 8 August 2021, https://wiwibloggs.com/2021/08/08/vision-music-awards-2021-russia-manizha-wins-the-dana-international-award-for-lgbtq-equality/265658/; Mark Simon, "Why Manizha's 2021 Eurovision Entry Touched a Raw Nerve

in Russia," *ZOIS*, 12 May 2021, https://en.zois-berlin.de/publications/why-manizhas-2021-eurovision-entry-touched-a-raw-nerve-in-russia.

30. Andrew Roth, "'I Won't Allow Myself to Be Broken': Russia's Eurovision Candidate Manizha Takes on 'the Haters,'" *The Guardian*, 9 April 2021.

31. Dzhumaguly Annayev, "Tajik-born 'Russian Woman' Singer Endures Racist, Chauvinist Taunts Online," *Caravanserai*, 25 March 2021, https://central.asia-news.com/en_GB/articles/cnmi_ca/features/2021/03/25/feature-01.

32. "Eurovision: Russia Banned from Competing at 2022 Song Contest," *BBC News*, 25 February 2022, https://www.bbc.com/news/entertainment-arts-60530513.

33. Eliot Borenstein, *Plots against Russia: Conspiracy and Fantasy after Socialism* (Ithaca, NY: Cornell University Press, 2019), 205.

34. Borenstein, *Plots Against Russia*, 212, 213, 227.

35. Konstantin Bogomolov, "Pokhishchenie Evropy 2.0: Manifest rezhissera," *Novaia gazeta*, 10 February 2021, https://novayagazeta.ru/articles/2021/02/10/89120-pohischenie-evropy-2-0. On the emergence of the phrase "new ethics," see Ella Rossman, "Kak pridumali 'novuiu etiku': fragment iz istorii poniatii," *syg.ma*, 27 September 2020, https://syg.ma/@ella-rossman/kak-pridumali-novuiu-etiku-fraghmient-iz-istorii-poniatii.

36. Ivan Vyrypaev, "Vozvrashchenie 'pokhishchennogo' Zapada: Otvet na stat'iu Konstantina Bogomolova 'Pokhishchenie Evropy 2.0,'" *Novaia gazeta*, 11 February 2021, https://novayagazeta.ru/articles/2021/02/11/89158-vozvraschenie-pohischennogo-zapada.

37. Tiffany Hsu and Michael Greenbaum, "'Minute-to-Minute Triage': Weighing News against Safety in Russia," *New York Times*, 15 March 2022.

38. Les Claypool, Stewart Copeland, Eugene Hütz, Sean Lennon, Sergey Ryabstev, and Billy Strings, "Claypool, Hütz, Copeland, Lennon, Ryabtsev, & Strings—'Zelensky: The Man with the Iron Balls,'" YouTube, 20 April 2022, https://www.youtube.com/watch?v=BowjATQloVA.

39. Valerie Sperling, *Sex, Politics, and Putin: Political Legitimacy in Russia* (New York: Oxford University Press, 2015).

40. "ALL THE SINGLE VLADY'S | Volodymyr Zelenskyy Dancing to Beyonce In women's heels | WW3," The Last Trump, YouTube, 1 March 2022, https://www.youtube.com/watch?v=PKHGp1XPv48.

41. Ruth Waytz and jane goodall, "ALL THE SINGLE VLADY's." See also Rebecca Flood, "Resurfaced Clip of Volodymyr Zelensky Dancing in High Heels Goes Viral," *Newsweek*, 4 March 2022, https://www.newsweek.com/volodymyr-zelensky-dancing-high-heels-viral-resurfaced-viral-clip-ukraine-russia-war-1684820.

42. Stefan Weichert and Emil Filtenborg, "For Ukraine's Female Soldiers, Armed Conflict Is Not the Only Danger," *euronews*, 11 May 2021, https://www.euronews.com/my-europe/2021/05/07/for-ukraine-s-female-soldiers-armed-conflict-is-not-the-only-danger.

43. "Ukrainian Woman Offers Seeds to Russian Soldiers So 'Sunflowers Grow When They Die'—Video," *The Guardian*, 25 February 2022.

44. "Ukraine War: Editor Interrupts Russian TV News Show," *BBC*, 14 March 2022, https://www.bbc.com/news/world-europe-60744605.

45. Feminist Anti-War Resistance, "Russia's Feminists Are in the Streets Protesting Putin's War," trans. Anastasia Kalk and Jan Surman, *Jacobin*, 27 February 2022, https://jacobinmag.com/2022/02/russian-feminist-antiwar-resistance-ukraine-putin.

46. David Axe, "It's Possible 270,000 Russians Have Been Killed Or Wounded In Ukraine," *Forbes*, 7 February 2023, https://www.forbes.com/sites/davidaxe/2023/02/07/its-possible-270000-russians-have-been-killed-or-wounded-in-ukraine/?sh=635234092eec.

Bibliography

Adams, Oliver. "A Russian Woman for the People! Russia's Manizha Wins the Dana International Award for LGBTQ+ Equality 2021." *wiwibloggs: Eurovision News with an Attitude*, 8 August 2021. https://wiwibloggs.com/2021/08/08/vision-music-awards-2021-russia-manizha-wins-the-dana-international-award-for-lgbtq-equality/265658/.

Adamson, Maria, and Suvi Salmenniemi. "'The Bottom Line Is That the Problem Is You': Aesthetic Labour, Postfeminism and Subjectivity in Russian Self-Help Literature." In *Aesthetic Labour: Rethinking Beauty Politics in Neoliberalism*, edited by Rosalind Gill, Christina Scharff, and Ana Sofia Elias, 301–16. London: Palgrave Macmillan, 2017.

———. "New Heroines of Labour: Domesticating Post-feminism and Neoliberal Capitalism in Russia." *Sociology* 49, no. 1 (2015): 88–105.

Aizman, Ania. "Stiob and the State." NYU Jordan Center, 6 February 2019. https://jordanrussiacenter.org/news/anna-aizman-on-stiob-feb-5/#.Yc8ywhNucwQ.

"Alina Kabaeva rodila dvoiniu: chto izvestno ob otnosheniiakh sportsmenki s Putinym." *24 Lifestyle*, 13 May 2019. https://lifestyle.24tv.ua/ru/alina_kabaeva_rodila_ot_putina_vse_ob_otnoshenijah_kabayevoj_i_putina_n1152510.

Allen, Virginia M. *The Femme Fatale: Erotic Icon*. Troy, NY: Whitston Publishing Company, 1983.

Amico, Stephen. *Roll Over, Tchaikovsky! Russian Popular Music and Post-Soviet Homosexuality*. Urbana: University of Illinois Press, 2014.

Anemone, Anthony. "About Killers, Freaks, and Real Men: The Vigilante Hero of Aleksei Balabanov's Films." In *Insiders and Outsiders in Russian Cinema*, edited by Stephen M. Norris and Zara M. Torlone, 126–40. Bloomington: Indiana University Press, 2008.

———. "Aleksei Balabanov: Cargo 200 (Gruz 200, 2007)." *KinoKultura*, 2 October 2007. http://www.kinokultura.com/2007/18r-gruz.shtml.

Annayev, Dzhumaguly. "Tajik-born 'Russian Woman' Singer Endures Racist, Chauvinist Taunts Online." *Caravanserai*, 25 March 2021. https://central.asia-news.com/en_GB/articles/cnmi_ca/features/2021/03/25/feature-01.

Aristotle. *Aristotle's Poetics: A Translation and Commentary for Students of Literature*. Translated by Leon Golden. Englewood Cliffs, NJ: Prentice Hall, 1968.

———. *On Rhetoric: A Theory of Civic Discourse*. 2nd ed. Translated by George A. Kennedy. New York: Oxford University Press, 2007.

Arkhipova, Aleksandra, Maria Volkova, and Danila Rygovskii. "Fol'klor 'na labutenax': Kak 'labuteny' iz pesni Shnura 'Eksponat' zashagali po seti i po zhizni." *Colta.ru*, 5 March 2016. https://www.colta.ru/articles/society/10975-folklor-na-labutenah.

Artamonov, Aleksei. "'Den' pobedy': Tanki, 'topolia' i LGBT v novom doke Aliny Rudnitskoi." *Colta*, 16 December 2014. https://www.colta.ru/articles/cinema/5722-den-pobedy.

Austin, J. L. *How to Do Things with Words: The William James Lectures Delivered at Harvard University in 1955*. Oxford: Clarendon Press, 1962.

Axe, David. "It's Possible 270,000 Russians Have Been Killed Or Wounded In Ukraine." *Forbes*, 7 February 2023. https://www.forbes.com/sites/davidaxe/2023/02/07/its-possible-270000-russians-have-been-killed-or-wounded-in-ukraine/?sh=635234092eec.

B. V. "Kemp." In *Entsiklopediia kul'turologii: Akademik*. Accessed 2 November 2022. http://dic.academic.ru/dic.nsf/enc_culture/1036/%D0%9A%D1%8D%D0%BC%D0%BF.

Baer, Brian James. "Now You See It: Gay (In)Visibility and the Performance of Post-Soviet Identity." In *Queer Visibility in Post-socialist Cultures*, edited by Nárcisz Fejes and Andrea P. Balogh, 35–56. Bristol: Intellect Books, 2012.

Baker, James E., and Kelly Clancy. "Putin as Gay Icon? Memes as a Tactic in Russian LGBT+ Activism." In *LGBTQ+ Activism in Central and Eastern Europe*, edited by R. Buyantueva and M. Shevtsova, 209–33. New York: Palgrave Macmillan, 2020.

Balabanov, Aleksei. *Gruz 200*. St. Petersburg: "Seans," "Amfora," 2007.

Bartlett, Djurdja. *FashionEast: The Spectre That Haunted Socialism*. Cambridge, MA: MIT Press, 2010.

Berlant, Lauren. *The Queen of American Goes to Washington City: Essays on Sex and Citizenship*. Durham, NC: Duke University Press, 1997.

Bernstein, Frances. *The Dictatorship of Sex: Lifestyle Advice for the Soviet Masses*. DeKalb: Northern Illinois University Press, 2007.

Beumers, Birgit, Alexander Etkind, Olga Gurova, and Sanna Turoma, eds. *Cultural Forms of Protest in Russia*. London: Routledge, 2018.

Bilaniuk, Laada. *Contested Tongues: Language Politics and Cultural Correction in Ukraine*. Ithaca, NY: Cornell University Press, 2005.

Blotskii, Oleg. *Vladimir Putin: Doroga k vlasti. Kniga vtoraia*. Moscow: Osmos Press, 2002.

Boboltz, Sara. "Here's Why Donald Trump Just Got a Drag Makeover." *HuffPost*, 25 August 2015. https://www.huffpost.com/entry/saint-hoax-celebrities-in-drag_n_55dc8da5e4b0a40aa3ac3758.

Boeck, Brian. "Beard Tax." In *Encyclopedia of Russian History*, edited by James R. Millar, 133. New York: Macmillan, 2004.

Bogomolov, Konstantin. "Pokhishchenie Evropy 2.0: Manifest rezhissera." *Novaia gazeta*, 10 February 2021. https://novayagazeta.ru/articles/2021/02/10/89120-pohischenie-evropy-2-0.

Bohlman, Philip V. *The Music of European Nationalism: Cultural Identity and Modern History*. Santa Barbara, CA: ABC-CLIO, 2004.

Boileau-Despréaux, Nicolas. *The Art of Poetry, Written in French by the Sieur de Boileau, Made English*. London: R. Bentley and S. Magnes, 1683.

BoobsForQueens. Accessed 4 November 2022. http://boobsforqueens.com/index.html.

Borenstein, Eliot. "Boys Just Want to Have Fun: Just How Queer Are the 'Satisfaction' Videos?" NYU Jordan Center, 27 February 2018. http://jordanrussiacenter.org/news/boys-just-want-fun-just-queer-satisfaction-videos/#.WtOzTtPwZ3m.

———. *Meanwhile, in Russia: Russian Internet Memes and Viral Video*. London: Bloomsbury Academic, 2022.

———. *Overkill: Sex and Violence in Contemporary Russian Popular Culture*. Ithaca, NY: Cornell University Press, 2008.

———. *Plots against Russia: Conspiracy and Fantasy after Socialism*. Ithaca, NY: Cornell University Press, 2019.

———. "Post-Soviet Masculinities: Sex, Power, and the Vanishing Subject." In *The Routledge Handbook of Gender in Central-Eastern Europe and Eurasia*, edited by Katalin Fábián, Janet Elise Johnson, and Mara Lazda, 80–88. London: Routledge, 2022.

———. *Pussy Riot: Speaking Punk to Power*. London: Bloomsbury Academic, 2021.

Borozdina, Ekaterina, Anna Rotkirch, Anna Temkina, and Elena Zdravomyslova. "Using Maternity Capital: Citizen Distrust of Russian Family Policy." *European Journal of Women's Studies* 23, no. 1 (2016): 60–75.

Boyer, Dominic, and Alexei Yurchak. "American Stiob: Or, What Late Socialist Aesthetics of Parody Reveal about Contemporary Political Culture in the West." *Cultural Anthropology* 25, no. 2 (May 2010): 179–221.

———. "In Focus: Postsocialist Studies, Cultures of Parody and American Stiob." *Anthropology News*, November 2008, 9–10.

Boym, Svetlana. *Common Places: Mythologies of Everyday Life in Russia*. Cambridge, MA: Harvard University Press, 1994.

———. "Kitch i sotsialisticheskii realism." *Novoe literaturnoe obozrenie*, no. 15 (1995): 54–65.

Brock, Maria, and Galina Miazhevich. "From High Camp to Post-modern Camp: Queering Post-Soviet Pop Music." *European Journal of Cultural Studies* 25, no. 4 (2021): 1–17.

Brooks, Katherine. "Russian Police Nab Painting of Nude Vladimir Putin and Barack Obama (NSFW)." *HuffPost*, 6 December 2017. https://www.huffpost.com/entry/putin-obama-painting_n_3873023.

Buckler, Julie A., Julie A. Cassiday, and Boris Wolfson, eds. *Russian Performances: Word, Object, Action*. Madison: University of Wisconsin Press, 2018.

Bullock, Philip Ross. "'That's Not the Only Reason We Love Him': Chaikovsky Reception in Post-Soviet Russia." In *Soviet and Post-Soviet Sexualities*, edited by Richard C. M. Mole, 103–28. London: Routledge, 2019.

Butler, Judith. "Critically Queer." In *The Routledge Queer Studies Reader*, edited by Donald E. Hall and Annmarie Jagose, 18–31. London: Routledge, 2013.

———. *Gender Trouble: Feminism and the Subversion of Identity*. New York: Routledge, 2007.

———. "Implicit Censorship and Discursive Agency." In *Excitable Speech: A Politics of the Performative*. New York: Routledge, 1997.

Buyantueva, Radzhana. "LGBT Rights Activism and Homophobia in Russia." *Journal of Homosexuality* 65, no. 4 (2018): 456–83.

Carleton, Gregory. *Sexual Revolution in Bolshevik Russia*. Pittsburgh: University of Pittsburgh Press, 2005.

———. "A Tale of Two Wars: Sex and Death in *9th Company* and *Cargo 200*." *Studies in Russian and Soviet Cinema* 3, no. 2 (2009): 215–28.

Cassiday, Julie A. "Post-Soviet Pop Goes Gay: Russia's Trajectory to Eurovision Victory." *The Russian Review* 73 (January 2014): 1–23.

———. "Sacrifice and Self in *Everybody Dies but Me*." In *The "Other" Martyrs: Women and the Poetics of Sexuality, Sacrifice, and Death in World Literatures*, edited by Alireza Korangy and Leyla Rouhi, 23–37. Wiesbaden: Harrassowitz Verlag, 2019.

———. "Vladislav Mamyshev-Monroe, Frog-Princess of Neoacademism." *The Russian Review* 78 (April 2019): 221–44.

———. "A World without Safe Words: Fifty Shades of Russian Grey." *Journal of Popular Romance Studies* 9 (30 March 2020): 1–16. http://www.jprstudies.org/2020/03/a-world-without-safe-words-fifty-shades-of-russian-grey.

Cassiday, Julie A., Helena Goscilo, and Jonathan Brooks Platt. "Introduction: The Allure of Retro: Neoacademism After the Fall." *The Russian Review* 78 (April 2019): 183–200.

Cassiday, Julie A., and Emily D. Johnson. "A Personality Cult for the Post-modern Age: Reading Vladimir Putin's Public Persona." In *Putin as Celebrity and Cultural Icon*, edited by Helena Goscilo, 37–64. London: Routledge, 2013.

Charochkina, Viktoriia. "'Raduzhnyi Milonov' i drugie: avtor iz"iatykh politsiei kartin predpochel pokinut' stranu." *The New Times*, 27 August 2013. http://newtimes.ru/articles/detail/70385/.

Chernitsyna, Mariia. "Ledi pod grifom 'Sekretno': 'MK' raskryvaet semeinye tainy Liudmily Putinoi." *Kompromat.ru*, 9 September 2005. http://www.compromat.ru/page_17355.htm.

Cicero. "Orator." In *Cicero V*, Loeb Classical Library. Translated by H. M. Hubbell, edited by Jeffery Henderson, 356–57. Cambridge, MA: Harvard University Press, 1939.

Clark, Katerina. "The Stalinist Myth of the 'Great Family.'" In *The Soviet Novel: History as Ritual*. 3rd ed. Bloomington: Indiana University Press, 2000.

Cleto, Fabio. "Introduction: Queering the Camp." *Camp: Queer Aesthetics and the Performing Subject: A Reader*. Ann Arbor: University of Michigan Press, 1999.

Coad, David. *The Metrosexual: Gender, Sexuality, and Sport*. Albany: SUNY Press, 2008.

Coalson, Robert. "Echoes of War and Collapse: Russia's Demographic Decline as Small 1990s Generation Comes of Age." *RadioFreeEurope/RadioLiberty*, 12 January 2020. https://www.rferl.org/a/russia-demographic-data-dip-as-small-1990s-generation-comes-of-age/30373049.html.

Cohen, Ben. "RuPaul on the RuNet: 'Drag Race' Catches On in Russia." *Global Voices*, 28 March 2017. https://globalvoices.org/2017/03/28/rupaul-on-the-runet-drag-race-catches-on-in-russia/.

Collier, Stephen J. *Post-Soviet Social: Neoliberalism, Social Modernity, Biopolitics*. Princeton, NJ: Princeton University Press, 2011.

"Conchita Wurst Tops Russian iTunes Chart." *PinkNews*, 12 May 2014. https://www.pinknews.co.uk/2014/05/12/conchita-wurst-tops-russian-itunes-chart/.

Condee, Nancy. *The Imperial Trace: Recent Russian Cinema*. Oxford: Oxford University Press, 2009.

Crescente, Joseph James. "Performing Post-Sovietness: Verka Serduchka and the Hybridization of Post-Soviet Identity in Ukraine." *Ab Imperio* 2 (2007): 405–30.

Danilov, Anton. "Kakim poluchilsia pervyi vypusk dreg-shou 'Korolevskie kobry Nasti Ivleevoi': Shantay you stay ili sashay away?" *Wonderzine*, 29 September 2021. https://www.wonderzine.com/wonderzine/entertainment/entertainment-opinion/259157-ivleeva-and-drag.

de Beauvoir, Simone. *The Second Sex*. Translated by Constance Borde and Sheila Malovany-Chevallier. New York: Alfred A. Knopf, 2010.

Denisova, Anastasia. "How Vladimir Putin's Divorce Story Was Constructed and Received, or When the President Divorced His Wife and Married the Country Instead." *M/C Journal* 17, no. 3 (June 2014). https://journal.media-culture.org.au/index.php/mcjournal/article/view/813.

Doane, Mary Ann. *Femmes Fatales: Feminism, Film Theory, Psychoanalysis*. New York: Routledge, 1991.

"'Dolzhna byt' zakryta, unichtozhena, sterta navsegda': Kak osnovatelia proekta 'Deti-404' nakazali za 'gei-propagandu.'" *Meduza*, 26 January 2015. https://meduza.io/feature/2015/01/26/dolzhna-byt-zakryta-unichtozhena-sterta-navsegda.

Dostoevsky, Fyodor. "Pushkin (A Sketch)." In *A Writer's Diary*. Translated by Kenneth Lantz. Evanston, IL: Northwestern University Press, 1994.

"Dreg-artisty v Irkustske: O razorvannykh lifchikax, grudi s AliExpress i reaktsii okruzhaiushchykh." *The Village*, 5 June 2020. https://www.the-village.ru/people/people-city/384105-dragqueen.

Dubin, B. V. "Kruzhkovyi steb i massovye kommunikatsii: k sotsiologii kul'turnogo perekhoda." In *Slovo–pis'mo–literatura: Ocherki po sotsiologii sovremennoi kul'ture*, 163–74. Moscow: NLO, 2001.

Dumančić, Marko. "Feliks Mikhailov: Jolly Fellows (Vesel'chaki, 2009)." *KinoKultura* 29 (2010). http://www.kinokultura.com/2010/29r-veselchaki.shtml.

Dzagoeva, Zarina. "'Korolevskie kobry' Ivleevoi: Chto za shou i pochemu o nem gudit ves' internet." *News.ru*, 1 October 2021. https://news.ru/culture/korolevskie-kobry-ivleevojchto-za-shou-i-pochemu-o-nyom-gudit-ves-internet/.

Edenborg, Emil. "Homophobia as Geopolitics: 'Traditional Values' and the Negotiation of Russia's Place in the World." In *Gendering Nationalism: Intersections of Nation, Gender and Sexuality*, edited by Jon Mulholland, Nicola Montagna, and Erin Sanders-McDonagh, 67–87. Cham, Switzerland: Palgrave Macmillan, 2018.

———. "'Homosexual Propaganda': Regulating Queer Visibility." In *Politics of Visibility and Belonging: From Russia's 'Homosexual Propaganda' Laws to the Ukraine War*. London: Routledge, 2017.

Edgar, James. "Putin Attacks Eurovision Drag Artist Conchita for Putting Her Lifestyle 'Up for Show.'" *The Telegraph*, 25 May 2014. https://www.telegraph.co.uk

/news/worldnews/europe/russia/10856197/Putin-attacks-Eurovision-drag-artist-Conchita-for-putting-her-lifestyle-up-for-show.html.

Edkins, Jenny, and Adrian Kear, ed. *International Politics and Performance: Critical Aesthetics and Creative Practice*. London: Routledge, 2013.

Egorova, El'vira. "Rossianki nachali krasit' tufli 'pod labuteny' kak v klipe gruppy 'Leningrad.'" *Metro*, 20 January 2016. https://www.metronews.ru/novosti/russia/reviews/rossiyanki-nachali-krasit-tufli-pod-labuteny-kak-v-klipe-gruppy-leningrad-1182887/.

Elder, Miriam. "Vladimir Putin Mocks Moscow's 'Condom-Wearing' Protesters." *The Guardian*, 15 December 2011.

Engström, Maria. "Little Big: Neo-camp and a New Generation of Russian Identity." *Riddle*, 20 May 2019. https://www.ridl.io/en/little-big-neo-camp-and-a-new-generation-of-russian-identity/.

Epshtein, Mikhail. "Vpervye v Rossii vybrany slova i antislova goda." *SpbTalk.Ru*, 21 June 2008. http://www.gramma.ru/RUS/?id=1.39.

Erofeev, Viktor. *Muzhchiny*. Moscow: Izdatel'skii Dom Podkova, 1997.

———. *Shchel'*. Moscow: RIPOL klassik, 2018.

Essig, Laurie. "'Bury Their Hearts': Some Thoughts on the Specter of Homosexuality Haunting Russia." *QED* 1, no. 3 (Fall 2014): 39–58.

———. *Queer in Russia: A Story of Sex, Self, and Other*. Durham, NC: Duke University Press, 1999.

Essig, Laurie, and Alexander Kondakov. "A Cold War for the Twenty-first Century: Homosexualism vs. Heterosexualism." In *Soviet and Post-Soviet Sexualities*, edited by Richard C. M. Mole, 79–102. London: Routledge, 2019.

Etkind, Alexander. "The Decay of the Russian Public Sphere." *Current History* 114, no. 774 (2015): 278–81.

———. "Introduction: Genres and Genders of Protest in Russia's Petrostate." In *Cultural Forms of Protest in Russia*, edited by Birgit Beumers, Alexander Etkind, Olga Gurova, and Sanna Turoma, 1–16. London: Routledge, 2018.

———. "Post-Soviet Russia: The Land of the Oil Curse, Pussy Riot, and Magical Historicism." *boundary 2* 41, no. 1 (2014): 153–70.

"Eurovision: Russia Banned from Competing at 2022 Song Contest." *BBC News*, 25 February 2022. https://www.bbc.com/news/entertainment-arts-60530513.

"Eurovision 2010 Ratings Follow Trend of 2007, 2008." *Eurovision Song Contest*, 8 July 2010. https://eurovision.tv/story/eurovision-2010-ratings-follow-trend-of-2007-2008.

Evdokimov Show Theater. Accessed 4 November 2022. https://www.evdokimov-show.com/.

Evreinov, Nikolai. *V shkole ostroumiia: Vospominaniia o teatre "Krivoe zerkalo."* Moscow: Iskusstvo, 1998.

Faller, Helen. *Nation, Language, Islam: Tatarstan's Sovereignty Movement*. New York: Central European University Press, 2011.

Fanailova, Elena. "Nikto iz nas ne vyidet otsiuda zhivym." *Seans* 37/38 (8 July 2010). https://seance.ru/articles/nikto-iz-nas-ne-vyiydet-otsyuda-zhivyim/.

Fedorova, Anastasiia. "Dragzina: Join the Queer Artists Claiming Russia's Summer Houses as Their Own." *The Calvert Journal*, 22 September 2020. https://www.calvertjournal.com/features/show/12154/dragzina-dacha-russia-z.

———. "For These Queer Young Russians, Makeup Is Both Armour and a Weapon." *The Calvert Journal*, 1 April 2019. https://www.calvertjournal.com/features/show/11099/genderless-makeup-russia-miliyollie.

———. "Queer Moscow: Dispatches from the Front Lines of Russia's LGBTQ Creative Revolution." *The Calvert Journal*, 31 July 2019. https://www.calvertjournal.com/features/show/11285/queer-moscow-o-zine-lgbtq-revolution.

———. "Queer Petersburg: Dispatches from the Front Lines of Russia's LGBTQ Creative Revolution." *The Calvert Journal*, 1 August 2019. https://www.calvertjournal.com/features/show/11287/queer-st-petersburg-o-zine-lgbtq-revolution.

Feminist Anti-War Resistance. "Russia's Feminists Are in the Streets Protesting Putin's War." Translated by Anastasia Kalk and Jan Surman. *Jacobin*, 27 February 2022. https://jacobinmag.com/2022/02/russian-feminist-antiwar-resistance-ukraine-putin.

Fiks, Yevgeniy. *Moscow*. Brooklyn: Ugly Duckling Presse, 2013.

———. *Mother Tongue*. Pleshka Press, 2018.

Fiorito, Lorenzo. "On Performatives in Legal Discourse." *Metalogicon* 19, no. 2 (2006): 101–12.

Flood, Rebecca. "Resurfaced Clip of Volodymyr Zelensky Dancing in High Heels Goes Viral." *Newsweek*, 4 March 2022. https://www.newsweek.com/volodymyr-zelensky-dancing-high-heels-viral-resurfaced-viral-clip-ukraine-russia-war-1684820.

Folomeeva, Anastasiia. "'U nas vse po Stanislavskomu': Dreg-artisty–o teatre, svobode i shizofrenii." *Teatralii*, 15 December 2020. https://teatralium.com/interviews/drag_queens/.

Fox, Emily Jane. "Putin Works Out in a $3220 Sweatsuit as Only Putin Would." *Vanity Fair*, 2 September 2015.

Freidin, Gregory. *A Coat of Many Colors: Osip Mandelshtam and His Mythologies of Self-Presentation*. Berkeley: University of California Press, 1987.

Fricker, Karen, Elena Moreo, and Brian Singleton. "Part of the Show: The Global Networking of Irish Eurovision Song Contest Fans." In *Performing Global Networks*, edited by Karen Fricker and Roni Lentin, 139–62. Newcastle: Cambridge Scholars Publishing, 2007.

Friedman, Misha. *Lyudmila and Natasha: Russian Lives*. New York: New Press, 2014.

Frye, Northrop. *The Well-Tempered Critic*. Bloomington: Indiana University Press, 1963.

Gabowitsch, Mischa. "Fascism as *Stiob*." *kultura* 4 (December 2009): 3–8.

———. *Protest in Putin's Russia*. Cambridge: Polity Press, 2016.

Galperina, Marina. "An Interview with Petr Pavlensky: Anarchist Artist Nails His Balls to Red Square, So You Don't Have To." *Animal*, 18 November 2013. http://animalnewyork.com/2013/interview-petr-pavlensky-anarchist-artist-nailed-balls-red-square-dont/.

Gapova, Elena. "Polnyi Fuko: Telo kak pole vlasti." *Neprikosnovennyi zapas* 76, no. 2 (2011). *ZhZ*. https://magazines.gorky.media/nz/2011/2/polnyj-fuko-telo-kak-pole-vlasti.html.

Garber, Marjorie. *Vested Interests: Cross-Dressing and Cultural Anxiety*. New York: Routledge, 1992.

"Gay Clown Putin." *Know Your Meme*. Accessed 2 November 2022. https://knowyourmeme.com/memes/gay-clown-putin.

Gessen, Masha. "How Russia's Hilarious, Homoerotic 'Satisfaction' Became a Nationwide Meme of Solidarity." *New Yorker*, 22 January 2018.

———. *Words Will Break Cement: The Passion of Pussy Riot.* New York: Riverhead Books, 2013.

Gessen, Masha, and Joseph Huff-Hannon, eds. *Gay Propaganda: Russian Love Stories.* New York: OR Books, 2014.

Gevorkian, N., A. Kolesnikov, and N. Timakova. *Ot pervogo litsa: Razgovory s Vladimirom Putinym.* Moscow: Vagrius, 2000.

Gill, Rosalind. "The Affective, Cultural and Psychic Life of Postfeminism: A Postfeminist Sensibility 10 Years On." *European Journal of Cultural Studies* 20, no. 6 (2017): 606–26.

———. "Postfeminist Media Culture: Elements of a Sensibility." *European Journal of Cultural Studies* 10 (2007): 147–66.

Gitelman, Zvi. *Jewish Identities in Postcommunist Russia and Ukraine: An Uncertain Ethnicity.* New York: Cambridge University Press, 2012.

Glenn, Clinton. "'IA GEI! (I Am Gay!)': Russian Coming Out Video Narratives on YouTube." *Digital Icons: Studies in Russian, Eurasian and Central European New Media,* no. 21 (2021): 131–47.

———. "My ne oshibka (We Are Not an Error): Documentary Film and LGBT Activism against the Russian Anti-'Gay Propaganda' Campaign." In *LGBTQ+ Activism in Central and Eastern Europe: Resistance, Representation and Identity,* edited by Radzhana Buyantueva and Maryna Shevtsova, 77–100. Cham, Switzerland: Palgrave Macmillan, 2020.

Goldstein, Joshua S. "War and Gender." In *Encyclopedia of Sex and Gender,* vol. 1, *Topics and Cultures A-K,* edited by Carol R. Ember and Melvin Ember, 107–16. New York: Kluwer Academic/Plenum Publishers, 2003.

———. *War and Gender: How Gender Shapes the War System and Vice Versa.* New York: Cambridge University Press, 2001.

Golynko-Vol'fson, Dmitrii. "Agressivno-passivnyi glamur." *Khudozhestvennyi zhurnal* 60 (December 2005). https://moscowartmagazine.com/issue/35/article/668.

Gorbachev, Aleksandr, ed. *Ne nado stesniat'sia: Istoriia postsovetskoi pop-muzyki v 169 pesniakh (1991–2021).* Moscow: Institut muzykal'nykh initsiativ, 2021.

Gorbachev, Nikolai. "Proizvodstvo normativnosti v diskurse zapreta 'propagandy gomoseksualizma.'" In *Na pereput'e: Metodologiia, teoriia i praktika LGBT i kvir-issledovanii,* edited by A. A. Kondakov, 86–110. St. Petersburg: Tsentr nezavisimikh sotsiologicheskikh issledovanii, 2014.

Gorbunova, Yulia. "The Chilling Inaction on Domestic Violence in Russia Is Endangering Women's Lives." *euronews,* 29 July 2019. https://www.euronews.com/2019/07/29/the-chilling-inaction-on-domestic-violence-in-russia-is-endangering-women-s-lives-view?utm_medium=Social&utm_source=Twitter#Echobox=1564419588.

Goreslavskaia, Nelli. *Vladimir Putin i Liudmila Putina: Vne politiki.* Moscow: Algoritm, 2008.

Goscilo, Helena, ed. *Putin as Celebrity and Cultural Icon.* London: Routledge, 2013.

———. "Putin's Performance of Masculinity: The Action Hero and Macho Sex-Object." In *Putin as Celebrity and Cultural Icon,* edited by Helena Goscilo, 180–207. London: Routledge, 2013.

———. "Style and S(t)imulation: Popular Magazines, or the Aestheticization of Postsoviet Russia." *Studies in 20th Century Literature* 24, no. 1 (2000): 15–50.

Goscilo, Helena, and Vlad Strukov, eds. *Celebrity and Glamour in Contemporary Russia: Shocking Chic*. London: Routledge, 2011.

Gradskova, Yulia. *Soviet People with Female Bodies: Performing Beauty and Maternity in Soviet Russia in the mid-1930–1960s*. Stockholm: Stockholm University, 2007.

Greenberg, Clement. "Avant-Garde and Kitsch." In *Art and Culture: Critical Essays*. Boston: Beacon Press, 1961.

Grigorashenko, Sergei. "Retsenziia na fil'm *Potselui ne dlia pressy*." *MirSovetov*. Accessed 5 December 2008. http://mirsovetov.ru/a/miscellaneous/movies/kiss-no-press.html.

Gudkov, Lev. "Raspolzaiushcheesia obshchestvo." *Iskusstvo kino*, no. 7 (June 2007). http://old.kinoart.ru/archive/2007/07/n7-article4.

Guliaeva, Shura. "'Dreg kak protest v Rossii nikomu ne nuzhen': 4 problemy predstoiashchego shou Anastasii Ivleevoi. Ob"iasniaiut aktivisty i feministskaia issledovatel'nitsa." *The Village*, 27 September 2021. https://www.the-village.ru/weekend/opinions/kobry.

Günther, Hans. "Wise Father Stalin and His Family in Soviet Cinema." In *Socialist Realism without Shores*, edited by Thomas Lahusen and Evgeny Dobrenko, 178–90. Durham, NC: Duke University Press, 1997.

Gurova, Olga. *Fashion and the Consumer Revolution in Contemporary Russia*. London: Routledge, 2015.

Gusiatinskii, Evgenii. "Aleksei Balabanov: 'Vsegda zhivem v Rossii.'" *Iskusstvo kino*, no. 7 (June 2007). https://old.kinoart.ru/archive/2007/07/n7-article2.

Halberstam, Judith. "Shame and White Gay Masculinity." *Social Text* 23, nos. 3–4 (Winter 2005): 219–33.

Halperin, David M., and Valerie Traub. "Beyond Gay Pride." In *Gay Shame*. Chicago: Chicago University Press, 2009.

Healey, Dan. *Bolshevik Sexual Forensics: Diagnosing Disorder in the Clinic and Courtroom, 1917–1939*. DeKalb: Northern Illinois University Press, 2009.

———. *Homosexual Desire in Revolutionary Russia: The Regulation of Sexual and Gender Dissent*. Chicago: University of Chicago Press, 2001.

———. "Russian Gay Propaganda Law." In *Global Encyclopedia of Lesbian, Gay, Bisexual, Transgender, and Queer (LGBTQ) History*, vol. 3, edited by Howard Chiang, Anjali Arondekar, Marc Epprecht, Jennifer Evans, Ross G. Forman and Hanadi Al-Samman, 1400–1403. New York: Gale, 2019.

———. *Russian Homophobia from Stalin to Sochi*. London: Bloomsbury, 2018.

———. "'Untraditional Sex' and the 'Simple Russian': Nostalgia for Soviet Innocence in the Polemics of Diliia Enikeeva." In *What Is Soviet Now? Identities, Legacies, and Memories*, edited by Thomas Lahusen and Peter H. Solomon, 173–91. Berlin: Lit Verlag, 2008.

Heller, Dana. "t.A.T.u. You! Russia, the Global Politics of Eurovision, and Lesbian Pop." *Popular Music* 26, no. 2 (May 2007): 195–210.

Hemment, Julie. *Youth Politics in Putin's Russia: Producing Patriots and Entrepreneurs*. Bloomington: Indiana University Press, 2015.

Hsu, Tiffany, and Michael Greenbaum. "'Minute-to-Minute Triage': Weighing News against Safety in Russia." *New York Times*, 15 March 2022.

Hutchings, Stephen. *Projecting Russia in a Mediatized World: Recursive Nationhood*. London: Routledge, 2022.

———. "Serializing National Cohesion: Channel 1's 'Shkola' and the Contradictions of Post-Soviet 'Consensus Management.'" *The Russian Review* 72 (July 2013): 470–91.

"'Ia mogu vstat' i skazat'': Tak bol'she ne budet': 27 istorii iz zhizni rossiiskikh geev." *Afisha*, 22 February 2013. https://daily.afisha.ru/archive/gorod/archive/gay-issue/.

Ilic, Melanie. "Women and Competition in State Socialist Societies: Soviet Beauty Contests." In *Competition in Socialist Society*, edited by Katalin Miklóssy and Melanie Ilic, 159–75. New York: Routledge, 2014.

Isajanyanm, Nerses. "Russian Federation: Decriminalization of Domestic Violence." Law Library of Congress, June 2017. https://permanent.fdlp.gov/gpo87191/russia-decriminalization-domestic-violence.pdf.

Isin, Engin. "Performative Citizenship." In *The Oxford Handbook of Citizenship*, edited by Ayelet Shachar, Rainer Bauböck, Irene Bloemraad, and Maarten Vink, 500–523. New York: Oxford University Press, 2017.

Ivanova, Elena. "'Ona otlichno vladeet iazykom': Ivleeva rasskazala, ponravilsia li ei potselui s Sobchak." *Radio Komsomol'skaia Pravda*, 22 October 2021. https://radiokp.ru/znamenitosti/ona-otlichno-vladeet-yazykom-ivleeva-rasskazala-ponravilsya-li-ey-poceluy-s-sobchak_nid492065_au37688au.

James, E. L. *Fifty Shades Darker*. New York: Vintage Books 2011.

———. *Fifty Shades Freed*. New York: Vintage Books, 2012.

———. *Fifty Shades of Grey*. New York: Vintage Books, 2011.

Jameson, Fredric. *Postmodernism, or, The Cultural Logic of Late Capitalism*. Durham, NC: Duke University Press, 1991.

Johnson, Emily. "Exploring His/Her Library: Reading and Books in Russian Romance." *Journal of Popular Romance Studies* 9 (30 March 2020). http://www.jprstudies.org/2020/03/exploring-his-her-library-reading-and-books-in-russian-romance/.

———. "Multiculturalism Timati-Style: Ethnicity and Masculinity in Black Star Videos." Presentation at the Annual Convention of the Association for Slavic, East European, and Eurasian Studies on the panel "Gender, Ethnicity, and Queerness in East European Popular Music," November 2017.

———. "A New Song for a New Motherland: Eurovision and the Rhetoric of Post-Soviet National Identity." *The Russian Review* 73, no. 1 (January 2014): 24–46.

Johnson, Janet Elise. *The Gender of Informal Politics: Russia, Iceland, and Twenty-First Century Male Dominance*. Cham, Switzerland: Palgrave Macmillan, 2018.

Johnson, Lena. *Art and Protest in Putin's Russia*. London: Routledge, 2015.

Kaganovsky, Lilya. *How the Soviet Man Was Unmade: Cultural Fantasy and Male Subjectivity under Stalin*. Pittsburgh: University of Pittsburgh Press, 2008.

———. "*Vystuplenie i nakazanie*: Performing Political Protest in Putin's Russia (Voina, Pussy Riot, Pavlensky)." In *Russian Performances: Word, Object, Action*, edited by Julie A. Buckler, Julie A. Cassiday, and Boris Wolfson, 148–55. Madison: University of Wisconsin Press, 2018.

Kalinin, Ilya. "Why 'Two Russians' Are Less Than 'United Russia': Cultural Distinctions and Political Similarities: Dialectics of Defeat." In *Cultural Forms of Protest in Russia*, edited by Birgit Beumers, Alexander Etkind, Olga Gurova, and Sanna Turoma, 48–67. London: Routledge, 2018.

Kamitdinov, Nikita. "'Esli styditsia orientatsii, liudi uvidiat slaboe mesto i budut pol'zovat'sia': Monologi LGBT-predprinimatelei o gomofobii, 'gei-lobbi' i vykhode iz shkafa." *Inc.*, 25 February 2020. https://incrussia.ru/understand/lgbt-entrepreneurs/.

Karagodina, Anastasiya, and Aizhan Kazak. "Why Russian Boys Dream of Having a Beard." *Russia Beyond*, 31 August 2017. https://www.rbth.com/multimedia/pictures/2017/08/31/why-russian-boys-dream-beard-831916.

Khachaturov, Sergei. "Umom nash gender ne poniat': Sovremennoe izobrazitel'noe iskusstvo Rossii i problematika 'kvir.'" *Dialog iskusstv*, no. 4 (April 2013): 110–11.

Khazan, Olga. "Why Homophobic Russia Loves Gender-Bending Pop Stars." *The Atlantic*, 20 August 2013. https://www.theatlantic.com/international/archive/2013/08/why-homophobic-russia-loves-gender-bending-pop-stars/278833/.

Khoroshilova, Ol'ga. *Russkie travesti v istorii, kul'ture i povsednevnosti*. Moscow: "Mann, Ivanov i Ferber," 2021.

Kirei-Sitnikova, Iana. *Politicheskie vzgliady trans* soobshchetva: Rezul'taty oprosa*. N.p.: Trans* Koallitsiia, 2015.

Kirsanov, Vladimir. 69. *Russkie gei, lesbiianki, biseksualy i transseksualy*. Tver': GanimeD, 2005.

Kishkovsky, Sophia. "A Love Letter to Putin (but It's Not Addressed to Him)." *New York Times*, 6 February 2008.

Klever, Alisa. *Chetyre storony sveta i odna zhenshchina: Roman*. Moscow: Eksmo, 2015.

———. *Dva mesiatsa i tri dnia: Roman*. Moscow: Eksmo, 2015.

———. *Piatnadtsatyi rai: Roman*. Moscow: Eksmo, 2015.

Klimova, Lena. *Nastoiashchaia devchonka: Kniga o tebe*. N.p.: Izdatel'stvo "Samokat," 2019.

———. *Stranitsa naidena*. N.p.: Izdatel'skie resheniia, 2017.

———. *Vyzhit' i zhit': Dolgo i schastlivo*. N.p.: Izdatel'skie resheniia, 2020.

Klingseis, Katharina. "The Power of Dress in Contemporary Russian Society: On Glamour Discourse and the Everyday Practice of Getting Dressed in Russian Cities." *Laboratorium* 3, no. 1 (2011): 84–115.

Knox, Patrick. "First Mistress? Who Is Vladimir Putin's Rumored Girlfriend Alina Kabaeva?" *The U.S. Sun*, 22 February 2022. https://www.the-sun.com/news/1601251/alina-kabaeva-vladimir-putin-rumoured-girlfriend-wedding-gymnast/.

Kolbovskii, Aleksandr. "Valeriia Gai-Germanika: *Everybody Dies but Me* (*Vse umrut, a ia ostanus'*, 2008)." *KinoKultura*, 15 October 2008. http://www.kinokultura.com/2008/22r-vseumrut.shtml.

Kolstø, Pål. "The Ethnification of Russian Nationalism." In *The New Russian Nationalism: Imperialism, Ethnicity and Authoritarianism, 2000–2015*, edited by Pål Kolstø and Helge Blakkisrud, 18–45. Edinburgh: Edinburgh University Press, 2016.

Kon, I. S. *Seksual'naia kul'tura v Rossii: Klubnichka na berezke*. Moscow: O.G.I., 1997.

Kon, Igor S. *The Sexual Revolution in Russia: From the Age of the Czars to Today*. Translated by James Riordan. New York: Free Press, 1995.

Kondakov, Aleksandr A. "The Censorship 'Propaganda' Legislation in Russia." In *State Sponsored Homophobia 2019*, edited by Lucas Ramón Mendos, 213–15. Geneva: ILGA, 2019.

———. "Crip Kinship: A Political Strategy of People Who Were Deemed Contagious by the Shirtless Putin." *Feminist Formations* 30, no. 1 (2018): 71–90.

———. "Eksperty v oblasti netraditsionnykh seksual'nykh otnoshenii: Sudebnaia nauka o gomoseksual'nosti posle priniatii zakona o 'propaganda.'" Manuscript in author's possession.

———. "The Influence of the 'Gay-Propaganda' Law on Violence against LGBTIQ People in Russia: Evidence from Criminal Court Rulings." *European Journal of Criminology* (2019): 1–20.

———. "Konfiguratsiia prava: Kak deistvuet zakon o 'propagande' v shkolakh." *Zhurnal sotsiologii i sotsial'noi antropologii* 20, no. 5 (2017): 187–206.

———. "Kvir-arkhiv, LGBT-muzei i poteriannye mal'chiki: dve versii istorii seksual'nosti." In *Politika affekta: Muzei kak prostranstvo publichnoi istorii*, edited by A. Zavadskii, V. Sklez, and K. Suverina, 123–47. Moscow: Novoe literaturnoe obozrenie, 2019.

———. "Mezhdunarodnye diskussii o gomoseksual'nosti: effekty bumeranga v potokakh vlasti." *Sotsiologiia vlasti* 30, no. 1 (2018): 14–32.

———, ed. *Na pereput'e: Metodologiia, teoriia i praktika LGBT i kvir-issledovanii.* St. Petersburg: Tsentr nezavisimikh sotsiologicheskikh issledovanii, 2014.

———. "Pereopredelenie moral'nykh granits grazhdanstva v Rossii: Diskurs o gomoseksual'nosti posle raspada SSSR." In *XV aprel'skaia mezhdunarodnaia nauchnaia konferentsiia po problemam razvitiia ekonomiki i obshchestva* 3, edited by E. G. Iasin, 43–51. Moscow: Izdatel'skii dom Vysshei shkoly ekonomiki, 2015.

———. "Poriadok diskurskov v formirovanii deviantnykh chert gomoseksual'noi sub"ektivnosti." *Paradigma* 16 (2011): 65–74.

———. *Prestuplenie na pochve nenavisti protiv LGBT v Rossii: Otchet.* St. Petersburg: Tsentr nezavisimykh sotsiologicheskikh issledovanii, 2017.

———. "The Queer Epistemologies: Challenges to the Modes of Knowing about Sexuality in Russia." In *The Sage Handbook of Global Sexualities*, vol. 1, edited by Zowie Davy, Ana Cristina Santos, Chiara Bertone, Ryan Thoreson, and Saskia E. Wieringa, 82–98. Los Angeles: SAGE, 2020.

———. "Regulating Desire in Russia." In *Research Handbook on Gender, Sexuality and the Law*, edited by Chris Ashford and Alexander Main, 396–408. Cheltenham: Edward Elgar Publishing Limited, 2020.

———. "Resisting the Silence: The Use of Tolerance and Equality Arguments by Gay and Lesbian Activist Groups in Russia." *Canadian Journal of Law and Society* 28, no. 3 (2013): 403–24.

———. "Rethinking the Sexual Citizenship from Queer and Post-Soviet Perspectives: Queer Urban Spaces and the Right to the Socialist City." *Sexualities* 1, no. 17 (2017): 1–17.

———. "The Silenced Citizens of Russia: Exclusion of Non-heterosexual Subjects from Rights-Based Citizenship." *Social & Legal Studies* 23, no. 2 (2014): 151–74.

———. *Violent Affections: Queer Sexuality, Techniques of Power, and Law in Russia.* London: UCL Press, 2022.

Kondakov, Alexander Sasha, and Evgeny Shtorn. "Sex, Alcohol, and Soul: Violent Reactions to Coming Out after the 'Gay Propaganda' Law in Russia." *The Russian Review* 80 (January 2021): 37–55.

"KoAP RF Stat'ia 6.21. Propoganda netraditsionnykh seksual'nykh otnoshenii i (ili) predpochtenii, smeny pola." *Konsul'tantPlius*, 14 April 2023. https://www.consultant.ru/document/cons_doc_LAW_34661/d43445 68bd586d541d39273855ba64ba9d18e84a/.

Kottasova, Ivana. "Protests over Russia, Belarus and Kazakhstan 'Ban' on Lacy Underwear." *CNN*, 21 February 2014. https://www.cnn.com/2014/02/21/business/kazakhstan-lace-underwear-ban/index.html.

Kozachenko, Dimitry. "These LGBTQ Instagram Accounts Show That Queer Life in Russia Is Vibrant, Loving, and Defiant." *The Calvert Journal*, 5 June 2019. https://www.calvertjournal.com/features/show/11212/lgbtq-instagram-russia-kozachenko.

"Kratkaia Russkaia Pravda (po Akademicheskomu spisku poloviny XV v." *hist.msu.ru*. Accessed 4 November 2022. http://www.hist.msu.ru/ER/Etext/RP/krp.htm.

Krieg, Gregory. "Donald Trump Defends Size of His Penis." *CNN Politics*, 4 March 2016. https://www.cnn.com/2016/03/03/politics/donald-trump-small-hands-marco-rubio/index.html.

Kriukova, Polina. "Pevyi rossiiskii zhurnal o drege: Dragzina." *Blueprint*, 30 November 2020. https://theblueprint.ru/fashion/magazines/dragzina.

Kupfer, Matthew, and Bradley Jardine. "Defying State Conservatism, Russia's Drag Queens Strut On: Despite Homophobic Laws, Declining Wages and the Threat of Physical Violence, a Distinctly Gay Art Form Perseveres." *The Moscow Times*, 17 February 2017. https://www.themoscowtimes.com/2017/02/17/russian-drag-queens-a57177.

Kurkin, Dmitrii. "'Deti-404': Kak ia sozdala gruppu poderzhki LGBT-podrostkov." *Wonder*, 6 March 2018. https://www.wonderzine.com/wonderzine/life/experience/233597-404.

Kuzio, Taras. "Nationalism and Authoritarianism in Russia: Introduction to the Special Issue." *Communist and Post-Communist Studies* 49 (2016): 1–11.

Kuznetsov, Sergey. "'Pyl" Sergeia Lobana, kak by retsenziia." *LiveJournal*, 15 February 2007. https://skuzn.livejournal.com/398345.html.

Kvasha, Semen. "Retsenziia na fil'm 'Vesel'chaki': Razbitoe serdtse donny Rozy." *film.ru*, 13 October 2009. http://www.film.ru/articles/razbitoe-serdce-donny-rozy.

Lane, Anthony. "Letter from Oslo. Only Mr. God Knows Why. The Meaning of the Eurovision Song Contest." *New Yorker*, 28 June 2010, 38–47.

Lanoux, Andrea. "Laundry, Potatoes, and the Everlasting Soul: Russian Advice Literature for Girls after Communism." *The Russian Review* 73, no. 3 (2014): 404–26.

Laruelle, Marlene. "Misinterpreting Nationalism: Why Russkii Is Not a Sign of Ethnonationalism." *PONARS Eurasia*, 27 January 2016. https://www.ponarseurasia.org/misinterpreting-nationalism-why-russkii-is-not-a-sign-of-ethnonationalism/.

———. "Russia as an Anti-liberal European Civilization." In *The New Russian Nationalism: Imperialism, Ethnicity, and Authoritarianism, 2000–2015*, edited by Pål Kolstø and Helge Blakkisrud, 275–97. Edinburgh: Edinburgh University Press, 2016.

———. *The "Russian World": Russia's Soft Power and Geopolitical Imagination*. Washington, DC: Center on Global Interests, 2015.

Le Guern, Philippe. "From Global Kitsch to National Pride: The Eurovision Song Contest." *The Web Journal of French Media Studies* 3 (October 2000). http://wjfms.ncl.ac.uk/leguWJ.htm.

Leksikov, Roman, and Dafna Rachok. "Beyond Western Theories: On the Use and Abuse of 'Homonationalism' in Eastern Europe." In *LGBTQ+ Activism in Central and Eastern Europe*, edited by R. Buyantueva and M. Shevtsova, 25–49. New York: Palgrave Macmillan, 2020.

Liderman, Iuliia. "Balabanov snial 'tot' fil'm." *Iskusstvo kino*, no. 7 (June 2007). http://old.kinoart.ru/archive/2007/07/n7-article5.

Litovskaia, Maria, and Olga Shaburova. "Russian Glamour and Its Representations in Post-Soviet Mass Media." In *Russian Mass Media and Changing Values*, edited by Arja Rosenholm, Kaarle Nordenstreng, and Elena Trubina, 193–208. London: Routledge, 2013.

"Liubov' ne umiraet: K vystavke v Galeree Marata Gel'mana." In *Arkhiv M*, edited by Elena Selina and Antonio Dzheuza, 88–90. Moscow: Artguide Editions, 2015.

Lokot, Tetyana. "Affective Resistance against Online Misogyny and Homophobia on the RuNet." In *Gender Hate Online*, edited by Debbie Ging and Eugenia Siapera, 213–32. Cham, Switzerland: Springer International, 2019.

Longworth, Karina. "Cargo 200 Review." *IMDb*, 2 January 2009. https://www.imdb.com/news/ni0642080.

Makarychev, Andrey, and Sergei Medvedev. "Biopolitics and Power in Putin's Russia." *Problems of Post-Communism* 62 (2015): 45–54.

Mamyshev-Monro, Vladislav. "Konets snezhnoi korolevy: Vladik Mamyshev-Monro dlia Eleny Selinoi i varshavskoi vystavki." In *Arkhiv M*, edited by Elena Selina and Antonio Dzheuza, 91. Moscow: Artguide Editions, 2015.

———. "Kuda ia popal? Gde moi veshchi? Stabil'naia mobil'nost' i mobil'naia stabil'nost' ob"ektivnogo sub"ektivizma Vladislava Mamysheva." In *Arkhiv M*, edited by Elena Selina and Antonio Dzheuza, 56–61. Moscow: Artguide Editions, 2015.

———. "Monrologiia: Prakticheskoe znachenie issledovaniia dlia udobstv i v silu deistviia na dannyi moment signala M.M., nazvannogo monrologiei." In *Arkhiv M*, edited by Elena Selina and Antonio Dzheuza, 48–51. Moscow: Artguide Editions, 2015.

———. "Transvestizm v traditsii russkogo messianstva." In *Arkhiv M*, edited by Elena Selina and Antonio Dzheuza, 69–71. Moscow: Artguide Editions, 2015.

Matveev, Ilya. "Between Political and Economic Imperialism: Russia's Shifting Global Strategy." *Journal of Labor and Society* (2021): 1–22.

———. "Big Business in Putin's Russia: Structural and Instrumental Power." *Demokratizatsiya* 27, no. 4 (2019): 401–22.

Mavromatti, Oleg. "Director's Statement." *Oleg Mavromatti* (2014). Accessed 5 November 2022. https://olegmavromatti.com/sample-page/.

McReynolds, Louise. *Russia at Play: Leisure Activities at the End of the Tsarist Era*. Ithaca, NY: Cornell University Press, 2003.

McThomas, Mary. *Performing Citizenship: Undocumented Migrants in the United States*. New York: Routledge, 2016.

Medvedev, Aleksei. "Pro liudei i urodov. Kruglyi stol 'IK'." *Iskusstvo kino*, no. 7 (June 2007). http://old.kinoart.ru/archive/2007/07/n7-article3.

Meerzon, Yana, and Dmitri Priven. "Back to the Future: Imagining a New Russia at the Eurovision Song Contest." In *Performing the 'New' Europe: Identities, Feelings and Politics in the Eurovision Song Contest*, edited by Karen Fricker and Milija Gluhovic, 111–24. London: Palgrave Macmillan, 2013.

Meklina, Margarita, and Anne O. Fisher, eds. "Life Stories, Death Sentences." *In Translation*, June 2019. https://intranslation.brooklynrail.org/2019/06.

Menzel, Birgit. "Russian Discourse on Glamour." *kultura* 6 (December 2008): 4–8.

Mesropova, Olga. "I Choose Russia—I Choose Glamour." *kultura* 6 (December 2008): 12–14.

Meyer, Moe. "Introduction: Reclaiming the Discourse of Camp." In *The Politics and Poetics of Camp*. London: Routledge, 1994.

Miazhevich, Galina. "An Innocent Provocation or Homoerotic Challenge? Mediations of the 'Satisfaction' Video Parody in the Russian Mediascape." *Information, Communication & Society* (2020): 1–17.

———. "Sexual Excess in Russia's Eurovision Performances as a Nation Branding Tool." *Russian Journal of Communication* 3, nos. 3–4 (Summer/Fall 2010): 248–64.

Mihailovic, Alexandar. *The Mitki and the Art of Postmodern Protest in Russia*. Madison: University of Wisconsin Press, 2018.

Milienko, Elena. "Sergei Zarubin: 'Lora—eto vsego lish' obraz!'" *Teatral*, 1 September 2008. http://www.teatral-online.ru/news/1668/.

"Milonov potreboval vvesti pozhiznennyi zapret na v"ezd Konchity Vurst v RF." *Izvestiia*, 17 November 2017. https://iz.ru/672327/2017-11-17/milonov-potreboval-vvesti-pozhiznennyi-zapret-na-vezd-konchity-vurst-v-rf.

Ministry of Justice of the Russian Federation. "Ekstremistskie materialy." *Ministerstvo iustitsii Rossiiskoi Federatsii*. Accessed 25 February 2022. https://minjust.gov.ru/ru/extremist-materials.

Minkova, Yuliya. *Making Martyrs: The Language of Sacrifice in Russian Culture from Stalin to Putin*. Rochester, NY: University of Rochester Press, 2018.

Mizulina, E. B. "Kontseptsiia semeinoi politiki imeni Mizulinoi." *Advokat Anton Zharov*. Accessed 1 November 2022. https://zharov.info/guestbook/koncepciya-semejnoj-politiki-imeni-mizulinoj.

Mogutin, Slava. *Food Chain*. New York: ITNA Press, 2014.

Mole, Richard C. M. "Constructing Soviet and Post-Soviet Sexualities." In *Soviet and Post-Soviet Sexualities*, edited by Richard C. M. Mole, 1–15. London: Routledge, 2019.

———, ed. *Soviet and Post-Soviet Sexualities*. London: Routledge, 2019.

Moran, Dominique, Judith Pallot, and Laura Piacentini. "Lipstick, Lace, and Longing: Constructions of Femininity inside a Russian Prison." *Environment and Planning D: Society and Space* 27 (2009): 700–720.

Morgan, Joe. "Russians Shave Off Beards to Protest against Conchita Wurst." *GayStarNews*, 13 May 2014. https://web.archive.org/web/20150626234440/http://www.gaystarnews.com/article/russians-shave-beards-protest-against-conchita-wurst130514.

Morris, Jeremy. "Elevating Verka Serdiuchka: A Star-Study in Excess Performativity." In *Celebrity and Glamour in Contemporary Russia: Shocking Chic*, edited by Helena Goscilo and Vlad Strukov, 195–218. London: Routledge, 2011.

Moss, Kevin. "Russia as the Saviour of European Civilization: Gender and the Geopolitics of Traditional Values." In *Anti-Gender Campaigns in Europe: Mobilizing against Equality*, edited by Roman Kuhar and David Patternotte, 195–214. London: Rowman & Littlefield, 2017.

———. "Russia's Queer Science, or How Anti-LGBT Scholarship is Made." *The Russian Review* 80 (January 2021): 17–36.

Mossopp. "tATu Flame Out! ("Face" Magazine—UK)." *Tatysite.net*, 9 December 2003. http://eng.tatysite.net/press/press.php?id=%201168_0_7_0_M.

Motschenbacher, Heiko. "The Discursive Interface of National, European and Sexual Identities: Preliminary Evidence from the Eurovision Song Contest." In *Intercultural Europe: Arenas of Difference, Communication and Mediation*, edited by Barbara Lewandowska-Tomaszczyk, 85–103. Stuttgart: Ibidem-Verlag, 2010.

Murav'eva, Marianna. "'(Ne)traditsionnye seksual'nye otnosheniia kak iuridicheskaiia kategoriia istoriko-pravovoi analiz." In *Na pereput'e: Metodologiia, teoriia i praktika LGBT i kvir-issledovanii*, edited by A. A. Kondakov, 68–85. St. Petersburg: Tsentr nezavisimikh sotsiologicheskikh issledovanii, 2014.

Muzei istorii LGBT v Rossii. Accessed 5 November 2022. http://lgbtru.com.

Nabokov, Vladimir. *Nikolai Gogol*. New York: New Directions, 1961.

Naiman, Eric. *Sex in Public: The Incarnation of Early Soviet Ideology*. Princeton, NJ: Princeton University Press, 1997.

Noordenbos, Boris. *Post-Soviet Literature and the Search for a Russian Identity*. New York: Palgrave Macmillan, 2016.

Norris, Stephen M. "Playing with History." In *Blockbuster History in the New Russia: Movies, Memory, and Patriotism*. Bloomington: Indiana University Press, 2012.

Novitskaya, Alexandra. "Patriotism, Sentiment, and Male Hysteria: Putin's Masculinity Politics and the Persecution of Non-heterosexual Russians." *NORMA: International Journal of Masculinity Studies* 12, nos. 3–4 (2017): 302–18.

———. "Sexual Citizens in Exile: State-Sponsored Homophobia and Post-Soviet LGBTQI+ Migration." *The Russian Review* 80 (January 2021): 56–76.

Novoselova, Elena, Iadviga Iuferova, and Nataliia Iachmennikova. "Roditel'skoe sobranie s Liudmiloi Putinoi." *RGRU*, 6 January 2006. http://www.rg.ru/2006/06/01/lyudmila-putina.html.

"Novyi trek 'Leningrada' vozglavil charty rossiiskogo iTunes." *Lenta.ru*, 25 January 2016. https://lenta.ru/news/2016/01/25/leningrad/.

"O saite." *Wonderzine*. Accessed 7 November 2022. https://www.wonderzine.com/pages/about.

Obukhova, Aleksandra, ed. *Performans v Rossii, 1910–2010: Kartografiia istorii, katalog*. Moscow: Tsentr sovremennoii kul'tury "Garazh," 2014.

O'Connor, John Kennedy. *The Eurovision Song Contest: The Official History*. London: Carlton Publishing, 2007.

Ol'bik, Aleksandr. *Prezident*. Donetsk: Izdatel'stvo "Stalker," 2002.

Osborn, Andrew. "From Russia, without Love: New Movie Slams Soviet Union." *Wall Street Journal*, 21 June 2007. https://www.wsj.com/articles/SB118239157195142942.

Oushakine, Serguei Alex. "Performative Objects: How Things Do Things without Words." In *Russian Performances: Word, Object, Action*, edited by Julie A. Buckler, Julie A. Cassiday, and Boris Wolfson, 54–63. Madison: University of Wisconsin Press, 2018.

"Parodist stal litsom kompanii 'L'Etual'.'" *Sostav.ru*, 11 August 2010. http://www.sostav.ru/news/2010/08/11/r5/.

Patlay, Anastasia. "In Search of Complexities: Documentary Theatre in Today's Russia." *Extended Play*, 7 July 2020. https://extendedplay.thecivilians.org/in-search-of-complexities-documentary-theatre-in-todays-russia-7720/.

Patteson, Callie. "Who Is Alina Kabaeva, Putin's Alleged Lover and Mother of His Secret Twins?" *New York Post*, 20 April 2022. https://nypost.com/article/who-is-alina-kabaeva-putin-alleged-lover/.

Pavlenko, Anastasiia, and Svetlana Medvedeva. "'Devochki prikalivaiutsia': mogut li nakazat' Sobchak i Ivleevu za strastnyi potselui." *Moskva24*, 20 October 2021. https://www.m24.ru/articles/kultura/20102021/158747.

Pecheikin, Valerii. "Viktor Erofeev: Rossiia kak transvestit." *Kvir* 75, (1 June 2014). http://www.kvir.ru/articles/viktor-erofeev-rossiya.html.

pene4ka. "Konkurs krasoty v zhenskoi kolonii (28 foto)." *Bugaga*, 6 December 2013. http://www.bugaga.ru/interesting/1146741638-konkurs-krasoty-v-zhenskoy-kolonii.html.

Persson, Emil. "Banning 'Homosexual Propaganda': Belonging and Visibility in Contemporary Russian Media." *Sexuality & Culture* 19, no. 2 (June 2015): 256–74.

Peskov Productions. Accessed 4 November 2022. http://peskov-show.com.

Petrova, Anna. "Nemnogo o glamure." *Baza dannykh FOM*, 13 September 2007. https://bd.fom.ru/report/map/d073724.

"Pevitsa Manizha predstavliaet Rossiiu na 'Evrovidenie-2021': Ona ispolnit pesniu 'Russkaia zhenshchina'." *TASS*, 8 March 2021. https://tass.ru/kultura/10857225.

Plato. *The Republic of Plato*. Translated by Francis Macdonald Cornford. London: Oxford University Press, 1941.

Platt, Jonathan Brooks. "Hysteria or Enjoyment? Recent Russian Actionism." In *Cultural Forms of Protest in Russia*, edited by Birgit Beumers, Alexander Etkind, Olga Gurova, and Sanna Turoma, 141–59. London: Routledge, 2018.

Platt, Kevin M. F. "Russian Empire of Pop: Post-Socialist Nostalgia and Soviet Retro at the 'New Wave' Competition." *The Russian Review* 72 (July 2013): 447–69.

Porteous, Holly. "From Barbie to the Oligarch's Wife: Reading Fantasy Femininity and Globalisation in Post-Soviet Russian Women's Magazines." *European Journal of Cultural Studies* 20, no. 2 (2017): 180–98.

———. "'There Are No Ugly Women, Only Lazy Ones': The Duty of Beauty Labour in Contemporary Russian Women's Magazines." In *Körper—Geschlecht—Wahrnehmung. Geistes- Und Sozialwissenschaftliche Beiträge Zur Genderforschung*, edited by Helle Ehlers, Gabriele Linke, Nadja Milewski, Beate Rudlof and Heike Trappe, 133–56. Berlin: Lit Verlag, 2013.

———. "'A Woman Isn't a Woman When She's Not Concerned about the Way She Looks': Beauty Labour and Femininity in Post-Soviet Russia." In *The Palgrave Handbook of Women and Gender in Twentieth-Century Russia and the Soviet Union*, edited by M. Ilic, 413–28. London: Palgrave Macmillan, 2018.

Prina, Federic. *National Minorities in Putin's Russia*. New York: Routledge, 2016.

Probyn, Elspeth. *Blush: Faces of Shame*. Minneapolis: University of Minnesota Press, 2005.

Prokhorova, Elena. "Sergei Loban: Dust (Pyl'), 2005." *KinoKultura*, 14 January 2006. http://www.kinokultura.com/2006/11r-dust.shtml.

Puar, Jasbir. *Terrorist Assemblages: Homonationalism in Queer Times*. Durham, NC: Duke University Press, 2007.

Pushkin, Alexander. *Eugene Onegin*. Trans. Charles Johnston. New York: Penguin Books, 1977.

"Putin: itogi vyborov otrazhaiut real'nyi rasklad sil." *BBC News/Russkaia sluzhba*, 15 December 2011. https://www.bbc.com/russian/russia/2011/12/111215_putin_line_preview.

"Putin schitaet fil'm '9-aia rota' talantlivoi i udachnoi rabotoi." *RIA Novosti*, 7 November 2005. https://ria.ru/20051107/42016802.html.

"Raduzhnye novosti: Zaza Napoli ustraivaet 'Seksual'nuiu Revoliutsiiu' v priamom efire." *xGay.ru*, 11 October 2004. https://www.xgay.ru/news/rainbow/2004/10/11-4213.htm.

Rai, Shirin M. "The Dilemmas of Performative Citizenship." In *Gendered Citizenship: Manifestations and Performance*, edited by Bishnupriya Dutt, Janelle Reinelt, and Shrinkhla Sahai, 25–43. Cham, Switzerland: Palgrave Macmillan, 2017.

Rai, Shirin M., and Janelle Reinelt, eds. *The Grammar of Politics and Performance*. London: Routledge, 2015.

Rajagopalan, Sudha. "Misogyny, Solidarity and Postfeminism on Social Media: The Work of Being Diana Shurygina, Survivor-Celebrity." *European Journal of Cultural Studies* 22, nos. 5–6 (2019): 739–62.

Raspopina, Sasha. "Beauty Trauma: Tajik Singer Manizha Starts Campaign against Toxic Beauty Standards." *Calvert Journal*, 26 September 2017, https://www.calvertjournal.com/articles/show/9035/beauty-trauma-tajik-singer-starts-campaign-against-toxic-beauty-standards.

Rehberg, Peter, and Mikko Tuhkanen. "Danzing Time: Dissociative Camp and European Synchrony." *SQS* 2, no. 7 (2007): 43–59.

RFE/RL's North Caucasus Service. "'Content Unavailable': Facebook Again Blocks Kadyrov's Instagram Account." *RadioFreeEurope/RadioLiberty*, 14 May 2020. https://www.rferl.org/a/content-unavailable-facebook-again-blocks-kadyrov-s-instagram-account/30611740.html.

RFE/RL's Russian Service. "Russian Lawmakers Approve First Reading of Amendments to Tighten 'Gay Propaganda' Law." *RadioFreeEurope/RadioLiberty*, 27 October 2022. https://www.rferl.org/a/russia-gay-propaganda-amendments-duma-approved/32103685.html.

Riabov, Oleg, and Tatiana Riabova. "The Decline of Gayropa? How Russia Intends to Save the World." *Eurozine*, 5 February 2014. https://www.eurozine.com/the-decline-of-gayropa/.

———. "The Real Man of Politics in Russia (On Gender Discourse as a Resource for the Authority)." *Social Sciences* 42, no. 3 (2011): 58–71.

———. "The 'Remasculinization' of Russia? Gender, Nationalism, and the Legitimation of Power under Vladimir Putin." *Problems of Post-Communism* 61, no. 2 (2014): 23–35.

Rivkin-Fish, Michele. "Pronatalism, Gender Politics, and the Renewal of Family Support in Russia: Toward a Feminist Anthropology of 'Maternity Capital.'" *Slavic Review* 69, no. 3 (2010): 701–24.

Rivkin-Fish, Michele, and Cassandra Hartblay. "When Global LGBTQ Advocacy Became Entangled with New Cold War Sentiment: A Call for Examining Russian Queer Experience." *The Brown Journal of World Affairs* 21, no. 1 (Fall/Winter 2014): 95–111.

Roberts, Graham H. *Consumer Culture, Branding and Identity in the New Russia: From Five-Year Plan to 4×4*. London: Routledge, 2016.

Roldugina, Irina. "Vernacular Queer and Shifting Power in Russia: From the Late Imperial Era up to the 1930s." Ph.D. diss. Oxford University, 2021.

Ross, Andrew. "Uses of Camp." In *Camp: Queer Aesthetics and the Performing Subject. A Reader*. Ann Arbor: University of Michigan Press, 1999.

"Rossiiskie staroobriadtsy sviazali gomoseksualizm s otsutsviem borody." *Natsional'naia Sluzhba Novostei* (8 June 2017). https://nsn.fm/lenta-novostei/hots-rossiyskie-starоobryadcy-svyazali-gomoseksualizm-s-otsutstviem-borody.

"Rossiiskii telekanal otkazalsia pokazyvat' Verku Serduchku iz-za gei-propagandy." *LB.ua*, 13 August 2013. http://society.lb.ua/culture/2013/08/13/219488_rossiyskiy_telekanal_otkazalsya.html.

Rossman, Ella. "Kak pridumali 'novuiu etiku': fragment iz istorii poniatii." *syg.ma*, 27 September 2020. https://syg.ma/@ella-rossman/kak-pridumali-novuiu-etiku-fraghmient-iz-istorii-poniatii.

Rostova, Nataliia. "Pervoe litso—na prokat: V Moskve proshla prem'era prezidentskoi kinobiografii 'Potselui ne dlia pressy.'" *Novaia Gazeta*, 13 February 2008. https://novayagazeta.ru/articles/2008/02/14/39327-pervoe-litso-na-prokat.

Roth, Andrew. "'I Won't Allow Myself to Be Broken': Russia's Eurovision Candidate Manizha Takes on 'the Haters.'" *The Guardian*, 9 April 2021.

Rotkirch, Anna. *The Man Question: Loves and Lives in Late 20th Century Russia*. Helsinki: University of Helsinki—Department of Social Policy, 2000.

Roudakova, Natalia. *Losing Pravda: Ethics and the Press in Post-Truth Russia*. Cambridge: Cambridge University Press, 2017.

Rubin, Dominic. *Russia's Muslim Heartlands: Islam in the Putin Era*. London: Hurst & Company, 2018.

Rudova, Larissa. "Uniting Russia in Glamour." *kultura* 6 (December 2008): 2–3.

———. "'Who's the Fairest of Them All?' Beauty and Femininity in Contemporary Russian Adolescent Girl Fiction." *The Russian Review* 73, no. 3 (2014): 389–403.

Russell, Emily. *Reading Embodied Citizenship: Disability, Narrative, and the Body Politic*. New Brunswick, NJ: Rutgers University Press, 2011.

"Russia Gay Blood Donation Ban, Free Conversion Therapy Proposed by Moscow Mayoral Candidate." *HuffPost*, 2 February 2016. https://www.huffingtonpost.com/2013/08/26/russia-gay-blood-ban-_n_3816935.html.

Rutland, Peter. "Petronation? Oil, Gas, and National Identity in Russia." *Post-Soviet Affairs* 31, no. 1 (2015): 66–89.

Rutland, Peter, and Andrei Kazantsev. "The Limits of Russia's 'Soft Power.'" *Journal of Political Power* 9, no. 3 (2016): 395–413.

Ryabovolova, Alina, and Julie Hemment. "'Je Suis Satisfaction:' Russian Politics in the Age of Hybrid Media." *East European Politics* 36, no. 1 (2020): 9–26.

Sabonis-Chafee, Theresa. "Communism as Kitsch: Soviet Symbols in Post-Soviet Society." In *Consuming Russia: Popular Culture, Sex, and Society Since Gorbachev*, edited by Adele Marie Barker, 362–82. Durham, NC: Duke University Press, 1999.

Salmenniemi, Suvi. "In Search of a 'New Wo(Man)': Gender and Sexuality in Contemporary Russian Self-help Literature." In *Russian Media and Changing Values*, edited by A. Rosenholm, Kaarle Nordenstreng, and Elena Trubina, 134–53. London: Routledge, 2013.

Salys, Rimgaila. "Chapter 3: *Volga-Volga*." In *The Musical Comedy Films of Grigorii Aleksandrov: Laughing Matters*. Bristol: Intellect, 2009.

Savina, Aleksandra. "Roskomnadzor zapretil piat' LGBT pablikov." *Wonder*, 21 September 2015. https://www.wonderzine.com/wonderzine/life/news/215229-deti-404.

Scherker, Amanda. "Artist of Painting Showing Putin in Lingerie Reportedly Flees Russia." *Huffington Post*, 28 August 2013. http://www.huffingtonpost.com/2013/08/28/artist-putin-in-lingerie_n_3830773.html.

Scholl, Tim. "Queer Performance: 'Male Ballet.'" In *Consuming Russia: Popular Culture, Sex, and Society since Gorbachev*, edited by Adele Marie Baker, 303–17. Durham, NC: Duke University Press, 1999.

Seckler, Dawn. "Fedor Bondarchuk: Company 9 (9-aia rota), 2005." *Kinokultura*, 26 April 2006. http://kinokultura.com/2006/12r-company9.shtml.

Sedgwick, Eve Kosofsky. *Tendencies*. Durham, NC: Duke University Press, 1993.

———. *Touching, Feeling: Affect, Pedagogy, Performativity*. Durham, NC: Duke University Press, 2003.

Sedov, Sergei. "Sergei Zarubin: Lora Kolli sushchestvuet otdel'no ot menia." *xGay.ru*, 29 September 2005. http://www.gay.ru/people/view/zarubin2005.html.

Selina, Elena, and Antonio Dzheuza, eds. *Arkhiv M*. Moscow: Artguide Editions, 2015.

Selk, Avi, and David Filipov. "It's Now Illegal in Russia to Share an Image of Putin as a Gay Clown." *Washington Post*, 5 April 2017.

Senelick, Laurence. *The Changing Room: Sex, Drag, and Theatre*. New York: Routledge, 2000.

Sergeeva, Kira. "Anatolii Evdokimov: 'Travesti-shou—eto ne prosto muzhchiny v iubkakh." *Internet-Gazeta Newslab.ru*, 18 April 2011. http://newslab.ru/article/376381.

Shatskaia, Evgeniia. *Bibliia Stervy: Kratkii kurs*. Moscow: 1000 Bestsellerov, 2012.

———. *Stervologiia: Kratkii kurs dlia znatnoi stervy*. Moscow: 1000 Bestsellerov, 2010.

Shatskaia, Evgeniia, and Eliza Tanaka. *Shkola geishi: Mudrost' vostoka dlia sovremennoi zhenshchiny*. Moscow: Eksmo, 2006.

Shiianov, Mikhail. "'Volga-Volga' Mamysheva-Monro: nedootsenennyi rimeik mrachnoi komedii." *RIA Novosti*, 23 April 2013. https://ria.ru/20130423/934067958.html.

Simon, Mark. "Why Manizha's 2021 Eurovision Entry Touched a Raw Nerve in Russia." *ZOIS*, 12 May 2021. https://en.zois-berlin.de/publications/why-manizhas-2021-eurovision-entry-touched-a-raw-nerve-in-russia.

Simpson, Mark. "MetroDaddy Speaks!" *Salon.com*, 5 January 2004. http://www.salon.com/2004/01/05/metrosexual_ii/.

Singh, Ethan. "From Russia with Glove: Despot Putin's Lavish Fashion Choices Include £10,000 Coat, £2,400 Roll-neck—and Luxury Watch Collection." *The Sun*, 21 March 2022. https://www.thesun.co.uk/news/18023066/despot-putins-lavish-fashion-choices/.

Skladanowski, Marcin. "The Myth of Russian Exceptionalism: Russia as a Civilization and Its Uniqueness in Aleksandr G. Dugin's Thought." *Politics, Religion & Ideology* 20, no. 4 (2019): 423–46.

Sleptcov, Nikita. "Political Homophobia as a State Strategy in Russia." *Journal of Global Initiatives* 132, no. 1 (2017): 140–61.

Soboleva, Irina V., and Yaroslav A. Bakhmetjev. "Political Awareness and Self-Blame in the Explanatory Narratives of LGBT People amid the Anti-LGBT Campaign in Russia." *Sexuality & Culture* 19 (2015): 275–96.

Sontag, Susan. "Notes on 'Camp.'" In *Against Interpretation and Other Essays*. New York: Farrar, Straus & Giroux, 1966.

———. "Zametki o kempe." *Photographer.ru*. Accessed 2 November 2022. http://www.photographer.ru/forum/view_messages.htm?topic=10517.

Sotnik, Nastia. "Istoriia odnogo plat'ia: plat'e Manizha na 'Evrovidenii-2021.'" *Blueprint*, 18 May 2021. https://theblueprint.ru/fashion/industry/istoriya-odnogo-platya-manizha.

Sozankova, Zhenia. "Dreg-artisty: Ob obraze, rabote, kosmetike i reaktsii okruzhaiushchykh." *The Village*, 21 February 2020. https://www.the-village.ru/people/people-city/374901-drag-artists.

Sperling, Valerie. *Sex, Politics, Putin: Political Legitimacy in Russia*. New York: Oxford University Press, 2015.

Steel, Catherine. "Divisions of Speech." In *The Cambridge Companion in Ancient Rhetoric*, edited by Erik Gunderson. Cambridge: Cambridge University Press, 2009.

Stella, Francesca. *Lesbian Lives in Soviet and Post-Soviet Russia: Post/Socialism and Gendered Sexualities*. New York: Palgrave Macmillan, 2015.

———. "The Right to Be Different? Sexual Citizenship and Its Politics in Post-Soviet Russia." In *Gender, Equality and Difference during and after State Socialism*, edited by Rebecca Kay, 146–66. Basingstoke: Palgrave Macmillan, 2007.

Stella, Francesca, and Nadya Nartova. "Sexual Citizenship, Nationalism, and Biopolitics in Putin's Russia." In *Sexuality, Citizenship and Belonging: Trans-National and Intersectional Perspectives*, edited by Francesca Stella, Yvette Taylor, Tracey Reynolds, Antoine Rogers, 17–36. New York: Routledge, 2016.

Stepnova, Svetlana. "O zhizni i liubvi (retsenziia na fil'm 'Vesel'chaki')." *Ruskino*, 25 October 2009. https://ruskino.ru/item/2009/10/25/o-zhizni-i-lubvi.

———. "Zhenskoe schast'e—byl by milyi riadom . . . : Retsenziia na fil'm 'Potselui ne dlia pressy.'" *Ruskino*, 15 February 2008. https://ruskino.ru/item/2008/2/15/zhenskoe-schaste-byl-by-milyj-ryadom.

Suchland, Jennifer. "The LGBT Specter in Russia: Refusing Queerness, Claiming 'Whiteness.'" *Gender, Place & Culture* 25, no. 7 (2018): 1073–88.

Taylor, Alan. "Beauty in the Ceasefire: A Pageant in Donetsk." *The Atlantic*, 9 March 2015. http://www.theatlantic.com/photo/2015/03/beauty-in-the-ceasefire-a-pageant-in-donetsk/387247/?utm_source=Russian+Life&utm_campaign=adedbe3616-Russia_File_Mar_19&utm_medium=email&utm_term=0_2e99ba62b2-adedbe3616-84240921&mc_cid=adedbe3616&mc_eid=424dc42cda#.

"Tekst pesni Zaza Napoli—Lenin." *Lyricsonline.ru*. Accessed 2 November 2022. https://lyricsonline.ru/45134-zaza-napoli-lenin.html.

"Telekanal 'Rossiia' poiasnil, pochemu Danilko ne vedet 'Subbotnii vecher.'" *RIA Novosti*, 13 August 2013. https://ria.ru/20130813/956036083.html.

Temkina, A., and A. Rotkirkh. "Sovetskie gendernye kontrakty i ikh transformatsiia v sovremennoi Rossii." *SotsIs* 11 (2002). http://www.isras.ru/files/File/Socis/2002-11/Tyomkina_Rotkirx.pdf.

Temkina, Anna, and Elena Zdravomyslova. "The Sexual Scripts and Identity of Middle-Class Russian Women." *Sexuality & Culture* 19 (2015): 297–320.

Testometrika Team. "Naskol'ko ty poshlyi(aia)?" *Testometrika*. Accessed 2 November 2022. https://testometrika.com/funny/how-vulgar-can-you/.

Tilly, Charles. *Contentious Performances*. Cambridge: Cambridge University Press, 2008.

Tolstaia, Tat'iana. "Ia planov nashikh liubliu glamur'e." In *Den': lichnoe*. Moscow: Eksmo, 2012.

———. "Tat'iana Tolstaia. Noch', Peters." *Ark.ru*, 8 November 2016. https://ark.ru/zapoved/tigr/tatyana-tolstaya-noch-peters/2/.

———. *White Walls: Collected Stories*. Trans. Antonina W. Bouis and Jamey Gambrell. New York: New York Review of Books, 2007.

Trofimenkov, Mikhail. "'Pyl'': Zagrobnaia zhizn'—eto vechnyi prosmotr televizora s pripliasyvaiushchim Petrosianom." *KinoKafe*. Accessed 3 November 2022. https://www.kinocafe.ru/reviews/?rid=32573.

Tsirkun, Nina. "Transformatsiia kempa i retseptsiia kino." *Iskusstvo kino*, no. 1 (January 2013). https://old.kinoart.ru/archive/2013/01/transformatsiya-kempa-i-retseptsiya-kino.

Tuller, David. *Cracks in the Iron Closet: Travels in Gay and Lesbian Russia*. Boston: Faber and Faber, 1996.

"Ukraine War: Editor Interrupts Russian TV News Show." *BBC*, 14 March 2022. https://www.bbc.com/news/world-europe-60744605.

University of Pittsburgh. "Camp Cinema: Russian Style." 2012 Russian Film Symposium. https://rusfilm.pitt.edu/2012-camp-cinema-russian-style/.

Utkin, Roman. "Introduction. Illegal Queerness: Russian Culture and Society in the Age of the 'Gay Propaganda' Law." *The Russian Review* 80 (January 2021): 7–16.

Vainshtein, Ol'ga. "Female Fashion, Soviet Style: Bodies of Ideology." Trans. Helena Goscilo. In *Russia, Women, Culture*, edited by Helena Goscilo and Beth Holmgren, 64–93. Bloomington: Indiana University Press, 1996.

Vassilieva, Julia. "'Becoming-Girl' in the New Russian Cinema: Youth and Valeria Gai Germanika's Films and Television." *Camera Obscura* 29, no. 1 (2014): 59–79.

Volpp, Leti. "Feminist, Sexual, and Queer Citizenship." In *The Oxford Handbook of Citizenship*, edited by Ayelet Shachar, Rainer Bauböck, Irene Bloemraad, and Maarten Vink. New York: Oxford University Press, 2017. http://www.oxfordhandbooks.com/view/10.1093/oxfordhb/9780198805854.001.0001/oxfordhb-9780198805854-e-7.

von Drehle, David. "Opinion: The Man Known as 'Putin's Brain' Envisions the Splitting of Europe—and the Fall of China." *Washington Post*, 22 March 2022.

"Voprosy i otvety: Otryvki iz razlichnykh interv'iu s Vladislavom Mamyshevym-Monro." In *Arkhiv M*, edited by Elena Selina and Antonio Dzheuza, 318–31. Moscow: Artguide Editions, 2015.

"Vyiti iz shkafa." *Teatr.doc*. Accessed 5 November 2022. https://teatrdoc.ru/events.php?id=186.

Vyrypaev, Ivan. "Vozvrashchenie 'pokhishchennogo' Zapada: Otvet na stat'iu Konstantina Bogomolova 'Pokhishchenie Evropy 2.0.'" *Novaia gazeta*, 11 February 2021. https://novayagazeta.ru/articles/2021/02/11/89158-vozvraschenie-pohischennogo-zapada.

Walker, Shaun. "Transgender People in Russia Banned from Driving, Says Legal Amendment." *The Guardian*, 9 January 2015.

Waters, Elizabeth. "Soviet Beauty Contests." In *Sex and Russian Society*, edited by Igor Kon and James Riordan, 116–34. London: Pluto, 1993.

Weber, Max. *From Max Weber: Essays in Sociology*. Translated by H. H. Gerth and C. Wright Mills. New York: Oxford University Press, 1946.

———. *The Theory of Social and Economic Organization*. Translated by A. M. Henderson and Talcott Parsons. New York: Cornell University Press, 1947.

Weichert, Stefan, and Emil Filtenborg. "For Ukraine's Female Soldiers, Armed Conflict Is Not the Only Danger." *euronews*, 11 May 2021. https://www.euronews.com/my-europe/2021/05/07/for-ukraine-s-female-soldiers-armed-conflict-is-not-the-only-danger.

Weidlack, M. Katharina. "Gays vs. Russia: Media Representations, Vulnerable Bodies and the Construction of a (Post)modern West." *European Journal of English Studies* 21, no. 3 (2017): 241–57.

———. "Quantum Leap 2.0 or the Western Gaze on Russian homophobia." *Adeptus* 11 (2018): 1–20.

Whalley, Zita. "The Controversial History of Russian Beards." *Culture Trip*, 30 March 2018. https://theculturetrip.com/europe/russia/articles/the-controversial-history-of-russian-beards/.

White, Alan. "Russians Are Shaving Their Beards In Reaction to Conchita Wurst's Eurovision Win." *BuzzFeed*, 12 May 2014. https://www.buzzfeed.com/alanwhite/russians-are-shaving-their-beards-in-reaction-to-conchita-wu.

Wilkinson, Cai. "Putting 'Traditional Values' into Practice: The Rise and Contestation of Anti-Homopropaganda Laws in Russia." *Journal of Human Rights* 13 (2014): 363–79.

Wofford, Susanne L. "The Social Aesthetics of Rape: Closural Violence in Boccaccio and Botticelli." In *Creative Imitation: New Essays on Renaissance Literature in Honor of Thomas M. Greene*, edited by David Quint, Margaret W. Ferguson, G. W. Pigman III, and Wayne A. Rebhorn, 189–239. Binghamton, NY: Medieval and Renaissance Texts and Studies, 1992.

Wolfson, Boris. "Juggernaut in Drag: Theater for Stalin's Children." In *Russian Children's Literature and Culture*, edited by Marina Balina and Larissa Rudova, 173–91. New York: Routledge, 2008.

Wood, Elizabeth A. "Hypermasculinity as a Scenario of Power." *International Feminist Journal of Politics* 18, no. 3 (2016): 329–50.

Yekelchyk, Serhy. "What Is Ukrainian about Ukraine's Pop Culture? The Strange Case of Verka Serduchka." *Canadian-American Slavic Studies* 44 (2010): 217–32.

Yoffe, Mark. "The *Stiob* of Ages: Carnivalesque Traditions in Soviet Rock and Related Counterculture." *Russian Literature* 74 (2013): 207–25.

Youngblood, Denise J. *Russian War Films: On the Cinema Front, 1914–2005*. Lawrence: University Press of Kansas, 2007.

Yurchak, Alexei. *Everything Was Forever, Until It Was No More: The Last Soviet Generation*. Princeton, NJ: Princeton University Press, 2013.

Yurtaev, Alexey. "Inside the Fight over Russia's Domestic Violence Law." *openDemocracy*, 17 February 2020. https://www.opendemocracy.net/en/odr/russia-domestic-violence-law/.

Zakharovich, Yuri. "A Movie Valentine for Putin." *Time*, 13 February 2008. http://content.time.com/time/arts/article/0,8599,1712848,00.html.

Zaslavskii, Grigorii. "Valentinka." *Nezavisimaia gazeta*, 13 February 2008. https://www.ng.ru/culture/2008-02-13/16_valentinka.html.

Zaza Napoli. Accessed 4 November 2022. http://www.zazanapoli.ru/.

Zdravomyslova, Elena. "Gendered Citizenship in Soviet and Post-Soviet Societies." In *Nation and Gender in Contemporary Europe*, edited by Vera Tolz and Stephenie Booth, 96–113. New York: Palgrave, 2005.

———. "Gendernoe grazhdanstvo i abortnaia kul'tura." In *Zdorov'e i doveria: gendernyi podkhod k reproduktivnoi meditsine*, edited by Elena Zdravomyslova and Anna Temkina, 108–35. St. Petersburg: Izd. Evropeiskogo universiteta v Sankt-Peterburge, 2009.

Zdravomyslova, Elena, and Anna Temkina. "Krizis maskulinnosti v pozdnesovetskom diskurse." In *O muzhe(n)stvennosti: Sbornik statei*, edited by S. Ushakin, 432–51. Moscow: Novoe literaturnoe obozrenie, 2002.

———. "Sovetskii etakraticheskii gendernyi poriadok." In *Sotsial'naia istoriia. Ezhegodnik, 2003. Zhenskaia i gendernaia istoriia*, edited by N. L. Pushkareva, 437–63. Moscow: ROSSPEN, 2003.

———. "Transformatsiia gendernogo grazhdanstva v sovremennoi Rossii." In *Kuda prishla Rossiia? Itogi sotsietal'noi transformatsii*, edited by T. I. Zaslavskaia, 140–50. Moscow: MVShSEN, 2003.

Zigon, Jarrett. *'HIV Is God's Blessing': Rehabilitating Morality in Neoliberal Russia*. Berkeley: University of California Press, 2011.

Zvereva, Vera. "Pozyvnye glamura. Glamur: kul'turnaia ekspansiia ili novaia ideologiia?" *Iskusstvo kino*, no. 11 (November 2006). http://old.kinoart.ru/archive/2006/11/n11-article3.

Video and Filmography

Aleksandrov, Grigorii, dir. *Volga-Volga*. Russia: Mosfil'm, 1938.

"Aleksandr Peskov—Pesnia goda (Sol'noe shou)." Peskov Show, 12 May 2012. YouTube video, 1:46:58. https://www.youtube.com/watch?v=hxuBO7B_G58.

"ALL THE SINGLE VLADY'S | Volodymyr Zelenskyy Dancing to Beyonce In women's heels | WW3." *The Last Trump*, 1 March 2022. YouTube video, 1:15. https://www.youtube.com/watch?v=PKHGp1XPv48.

ArmiaPutina. "Tortik dlia Putina! Chocolate cake!" ArmiaPutina, 7 October 2011. YouTube video, 1:04. https://www.youtube.com/watch?v=rVCiwYqX18o.

Astakhov, Sergii. "Astakhov Sergii." YouTube channel. Accessed 13 March 2022. https://www.youtube.com/channel/UCba4jRsoLIOklXXd6ZAyzNA.

Balabanov, Aleksei, dir. *Gruz 200*. St. Petersburg: STV Film Company, 2007.

Benassi, Benny. "'Satisfaction' (Official Video)." GOK1Music, 7 April 2012. YouTube video, 2:25. https://www.youtube.com/watch?v=aZcSCT34H84.

Bilan, Dima. "Dima bilan—Never Let You Go (Eurovision 2006 Russia)." Sekaisin, 19 September 2007. YouTube video, 3:05. http://www.youtube.com/watch?v=HMyK0018ECo.

BitchVEVo. "Madonna, Britney Spears & Christina Aguilera Kiss!!! HD." BitchVEVo, 24 July 2012. YouTube video, 0:19. https://www.youtube.com/watch?v=MAy-NtCQCB8.

Bondarchuk, Fedor, dir. *9 rota*. Moscow: Art Pictures Group, 2005.

Claypool, Les, Stewart Copeland, Eugene Hütz, Sean Lennon, Sergey Ryabstev, and Billy Strings. "Claypool, Hütz, Copeland, Lennon, Ryabtsev, & Strings—'Zelensky: The Man with the Iron Balls.'" officialprimus, 20 April 2022. YouTube video, 4:40. https://www.youtube.com/watch?v=BowjATQloVA.

Doni. "Doni ft Timati—Boroda (Prem'era klipa, 2014)." Doni, 10 June 2013. YouTube video, 3:53. https://www.youtube.com/watch?v=7mvqAEe58°M.

Elin, Aleksandr. "*Takogo kak Putin*/Someone Like Putin, English Subs." Ilya Landa, 6 December 2008. YouTube video, 3:13. https://www.youtube.com/watch?v=zk_VszbZa_s.

Eurovision Song Contest: Moscow 2009. Moscow: "M'iuzik Treid," 2009.

Evdokimov Show. "Anatolii Evdokimov v programme 'Otkrytyi razgovor'." Evdokimov Show, 2 November 2012. YouTube video, 44:37. https://www.youtube.com/watch?v=TFAX_gn_uO4.

———. "Evolution by Evdokimov Show Theater—DVD Concert." Evdokimov Show, 5 October 2012. YouTube video, 51:48. https://www.youtube.com/watch?v=qFXOWWpCdVo.

———. "Pravda.ru—Anatolii Evdokimov v gostiakh u glavreda." Evdokimov Show, 21 March 2012. YouTube video, 39:16. https://www.youtube.com/watch?v=mvu6VPv8N_8.

fensi prodakshen. "Ia idu iskat' | veb-serial | pervyi sezon," fensi prodakshen, last updated 13 August 2021. YouTube playlist. https://www.youtube.com/playlist?list=PLX_ysH5jGc2GjLUHmfHBl6nHwMSYvDbnY.

France, David, dir. *Welcome to Chechnya*. Chicago: Music Box Films, 2020.

Gai Germanika, Valeriia, dir. *Devochki*. Moscow: Kinoteatr.doc, 2005.

———. *Shkola*. Russia: Profit and Russia's Channel One, 2010.

———. *Vse umrut, a ia ostanus'*. Russia: Profit, 2008.

hgwb2009. "Slavic Pride 2009: 40 Arrested." hgwb2009, 16 May 2009. YouTube video, 3:11. http://www.youtube.com/watch?v=HGmEayo8ZK4.

Ivleeva, Nastia. "Drag–shou Korolevskie Kobry." Nastia Ivleeva, last updated 13 January 2022. YouTube playlist. https://www.youtube.com/playlist?list=PLn2SiPuzV6DtYLeVyCaiuyLZS12-bCbcq.

johnnychs07. "Army Satisfaction." johnnychs07, 9 February 2013. YouTube video, 2:46. https://www.youtube.com/watch?v=ucOhx09ivg0.

Komel'kov, Dmitrii. "Potselui Kandelaki i Sobchak." Dmitrii Komel'kov, 7 February 2012. YouTube video, 0:49. https://www.youtube.com/watch?v=9XWYPvsrimM.

Kurov, Askold, and Pavel Loparev, dirs. *Children-404*. Berlin: Rise and Shine, 2014.

Leningrad. "Leningrad–Exhibit (aka Louboutins)." Leningrad, 13 January 2016. YouTube video, 6:57. https://www.youtube.com/watch?v=et281UHNoOU.

Lerner, Mike, and Maxim Pozdorovkin, dir. *Pussy Riot: A Punk Prayer*. UK: Docuramafilms and Cinedigm Entertainment, 2013.

Little Big. "Little Big—Uno—Russia—Official Music Video—Eurovision 2020." Eurovision Song Contest, 12 March 2020. YouTube video, 3:13. https://www.youtube.com/watch?v=L_dWvTCdDQ4.

"Liudmila Putina: Nash brak s Vladimirom Putinym zavershen." *RT na russkom*, 6 June 2013. https://www.youtube.com/watch?v=3zhdJnKEvJU.

Livnev, Sergei, dir. *Serp i Molot*. Moscow: MMM-Studiia, 1994.

Loban, Sergei, dir. *Pyl'.* Moscow: SVOI2000, 2005.

Lorina Rey. "Lorina Rey." YouTube channel. Accessed 4 November 2022. https://www.youtube.com/channel/UCeV8tIxlRopIiRvBoBWYHbQ.

Mamyshev-Monro, Vladislav. *Volga-Volga*, dir. Pavel Labazov and Andrey Sil'vestrov. Russia: Studiia Videodom and Dom Sine Fantom, 2006.

Manizha. "Manizha–Russian Woman–LIVE–Russia–Grand Final–Eurovision 2021." *dailymotion* video, 3:26. Posted by Greek—TTV. Accessed 11 February 2022. https://www.dailymotion.com/video/x81g3nx.

Mavromatti, Oleg, dir. *Durakam zdes' ne mesto.* Russia/Bulgaria: Supernova, 2015.

Mikhailov, Feliks, dir. *Vesel'chaki.* Russia: Studio Timeline, Survive Entertainment, 2009.

Mikhalkov, Nikita, dir. "55. Dokumental'nyi fil'm o Vladimire Putine. Nikita Mikhalkov." Aleksandr C, 22 September 2014. YouTube video, 21:50. https://www.youtube.com/watch?v=afmYJULOkQc.

Mikheeva, Katia, and Illuminator, dir. "Pogovorim? Shall We Talk?" Private account. Accessed 5 November 2022. YouTube video, 5:00. https://www.youtube.com/watch?v=xAbq22gS-RM&feature=emb_logo.

Pavlov, Yurii, dir. *Sotvorenie Adama.* Russia: Lenfil'm, 1993.

perviirazpolubvi. "Otkrovenie devushki pro ee pervyi raz." perviirazpolubvi, 10 February 2012. YouTube video, 0:50. https://www.youtube.com/watch?v=MbIzj21XotU.

Poliakova, Olia. "Olia Poliakova—Russian Style (Full HD)." Ol'ga Ivanova, 12 June 2014. YouTube video, 3:43. https://www.youtube.com/watch?v=sK8dVWhUCqM.

Prikhod'ko, Anastasiia. "Anastasia Prikhodko—Mamo (Russia)—Eurovision 2009 (The Final)." MrTechnologic, 17 May 2009. YouTube video, 3:10. http://www.youtube.com/watch?v=K5kKOVoO55g.

Pussy Riot. "Pussy Riot—Punk Prayer 'Virgin Mary, Put Putin Away' (English Subtitles)." Freedom Requires Wings, 17 August 2012. YouTube video, 1:59. https://www.youtube.com/watch?v=lPDkJbTQRCY.

———. "Pussy Riot's Action—Putin Has Pissed Himself!" Pussy Riot, 18 January 2021. YouTube video, 1:37. https://www.youtube.com/watch?v=5C4ZvODrazE.

Rabfak. "Nash durdom (golosuet za putina)." Thomas Lamber, 13 October, 2011. YouTube video, 3:44. https://www.youtube.com/watch?v=zVxyBMCd4qY.

Rudnitskaya, Alina, dir. *Den' pobedy.* Russia: 317-Film, 2014.

———. "Kak stat' stervoi (2008)." Otechestvennaia Dokumentalistika, 5 March 2017. YouTube video, 30:45. https://www.youtube.com/watch?v=jYPmdRBvAsQ.

———. *School of Seduction: Three Stories from Russia.* Denmark: Danish Documentary, 2019.

Ruki Vverkh. "Ruki Vverkh—On tebia tseluet (HQ)." vnuchara, 7 May 2009. YouTube video, 3:31. http://www.youtube.com/watch?v=Kkx8iqCuscc.

Sasha Chest feat. Timati. "Luchshii drug (Prem'era klipa, 2015)." Timati, October 6, 2015. YouTube video, 3:21. https://www.youtube.com/watch?v=jp9pfvneKf4.

"Scantily-clad Girls in Putin's 'Army' Wash Russian-made Cars." Unknown channel, 21 July 2011. YouTube video, length unavailable. https://www.youtube.com/watch?v=aOe4Jrry5j8.

Serebrennikov, Kirill, dir. *Uchenik.* Russia: Hype Film, 2016.

Shainian, Karen. "Russkii dreg, besstrashnyi i besposhchadnyi (18+)." Karen Shainian, 10 December 2020. YouTube video, 1:18:21. https://www.youtube.com/watch?v=X8qgovs45NU&t=51s.

Shevel'kov, Vladimir. *Sterva*. Ukraine and Russia: Kinokompaniia "Shpil'," 2009.

Shpil'ki and Sergei Zverev. "Bol'she glamura." Retro klipy, 4 February 2015. YouTube video, 3:22. https://www.youtube.com/watch?v=AFJRbrXDxtk.

Spektr Online. "Ul'ianovskie kursanty—Satisfaction." Spektr Online, 20 January 2018. YouTube video, 2:01. https://www.youtube.com/watch?v=k7y2AdtBhFc.

Steele, Ben, dir. *Cold Fear: Gay Life in Russia*. London: BBC Worldwide, 2014.

———. *Hunted: The War against Gays in Russia*. UK: Blakeway Productions, 2014.

Stolpovskaia, Ol'ga, and Dmitrii Troitskii, dirs. *Ia liubliu tebia*. Russia: Malevich Prodakshnz, 2004.

Suvorkin, Anton. "MAKEEVA I KVANTOVYI RAZBOR ALEKSA KURS ZA ODIN RUBL'. TAINY VDOVY GRADSKOGO DETALI PARNIA DIMY BILANA." Anton S Live, 28 January 2022. YouTube video, 23:42. https://www.youtube.com/watch?v=cZulSDHWjok.

Talbot, Stephen, dir. *Sound Tracks*. Season 1, episode 1, "Sound Tracks Pilot Episode." PBS, 25 January 2010. https://www.pbs.org/video/sound-tracks-sound-tracks-pilot-episode/.

Tamaraev, Sergei, and Liubov' L'vova, dirs. *Zimnii put'*. Russia: Mika Film, 2013.

t.A.T.u. "t.A.T.u.—All The Things She Said (Official Music Video)." tatu, 24 December 2009. YouTube video, 3:46. https://www.youtube.com/watch?v=8mGBaXPlri8.

———. "TaTu Eurovision 2003." Burhan Ozdemirci, 21 November 2006. YouTube video, 3:09. http://www.youtube.com/watch?v=94FYrYJF16E.

———. "Tatu—Nas Ne Dogoniat." xtatyRU, 29 July 2010. YouTube video, 3:57. Accessed 12 March 2022. https://www.youtube.com/watch?v=Oe4Wp8DQRYo.

———. "t.A.T.u.—Nas ne dogoniat 'fil'm LED 2'." T.A.T.u. Music, 27 February 2020. YouTube video, 3:30. https://www.youtube.com/watch?v=qdzmzkzwOfg.

———. "t.A.T.u.—'Nas Ne Dogoniat' Live @ Winter Olympics Games 2014." tATu Official, 5 March 2014. YouTube video, 3:41. https://www.youtube.com/watch?v=iNrvmHPDOic&t=212s.

———. "t.A.T.u. Ne ver', ne boisia Eurovision 2009." MyKlownS, 11 May 2009. YouTube video, 2:59. https://www.youtube.com/watch?v=dtdA2-YRv78.

———. "t.A.T.u. Not Gonna Get Us Eurovision 2009 Semifinal 1." LauiiiTV, 12 May 2009. YouTube video, 1:50. https://www.youtube.com/watch?v=TypdkNGoYvo.

ThePubliciti. "Putin's Army [English subs]." ThePubliciti, 19 July 2011. YouTube video, 1:27. https://www.youtube.com/watch?v=klcyPNIA698.

The Telegraph. "Putin Attacks Church of England for Considering Gender-Neutral God." *The Telegraph*, 21 February 2023. YouTube video, 1:28. https://www.youtube.com/watch?v=I-FjJnFpuwQ.

"Tumany (ტუმანი)—Na labutenakh, Vakh!" Leningrad, 6 February 2016. YouTube video, 0:54. https://www.youtube.com/watch?v=WAX4r-gH8ao.

"Ukrainian Woman Offers Seeds to Russian Soldiers so 'Sunflowers Grow When They Die'—Video." *The Guardian*, 25 February 2022.

Ulianov, Anatolii. "My New Orthodox Video/Moe novoe pravoslavnoe video (2013)." Looo.ch, 13 October 2013. YouTube video, 19:21. https://www.youtube.com/watch?v=OX27UrIvrLQ.

Verka Serduchka. "Eurovision 2007 Final Ukraine Verka Serduchka Dancing." VLAD, 14 May 2007. YouTube video, 4:35. http://www.youtube.com/watch?v=GP5YOhQZtlA.

———. "Verka Serduchka—Russia Goodbye & Make It Rain Champagne|Embrace Ukraine—#StrivingTogether." Atlas Festival, 22 June 2022. YouTube video, 8:22. https://www.youtube.com/watch?v=hvXUeHwDoRU.

VICE. "Young and Gay in Putin's Russia." VICE, 2014. YouTube series, Parts 1–4. Part 1, https://www.youtube.com/watch?v=AZ_aSl3ktjg.

Vice News. "A Rebel Beauty Pageant: Russian Roulette (Dispatch 98)." Vice News, 9 March 2015. YouTube video, 6:10. https://www.youtube.com/watch?v=_9glPPNLQyg.

Vice News Tonight. "Inside the Chechen Prison Where Gay Men Say They Were Tortured." Vice News Tonight. Accessed 5 November 2022. Vice video, 9:08. https://video.vice.com/en_us/video/inside-the-prison-in-chechnya-where-gay-men-say-they-were-tortured/59482279ca2298ec7e99a69f?latest=1.

Wholphin, No. 11, DVD Magazine of Rare and Unseen Short Films. San Francisco: McSweeney's, 2010.

Zaza Napoli. "Zaza Napoli—Lenin/Ofitsial'noe video/Versiia 1." Denis Sokolov, 26 October 2010. YouTube video, 4:32. https://www.youtube.com/watch?v=K8vJp1S2ioU.

———. "Zaza Napoli, Anastasiia Volochkova. Ispoved'. . . " Denis Sokolov, November 5, 2010. YouTube video, 3:48. https://www.youtube.com/watch?v=EUZjVjr4KA4.

zhirinovskij. "Zhirinovskii—Konchita Vurst eto konets dlia vsei Evropy. Evrovidenie 2014." zhirinovskij, 12 May 2014. YouTube video, 1:21. https://www.youtube.com/watch?v=8BtbuNCkFGU.

Zhulina, Ol'ga, dir. *Potselui ne dlia pressy*. Russia: Prodiuserskaia kompaniia Anatoliia Voropaeva, 2005.

Index

abortion, 10–13, 16. *See also* reproductive labor
Adamson, Maria, 89, 131, 140–41
Adventures of Priscilla, Queen of the Desert, The (Elliot), 96
Afghanistan war, 61–70
agency, 45–47, 51–56
Aguilera, Christina, 167–68
alcoholism, 61
Aleksandrov, Grigorii, 83
Alekseev, Nikolai, 113, 167
"All the Things She Said" (t.A.T.u.), 108
Altunin, Konstantin, 80
ambivalence: affective ambivalence, 74, 105; of camp, 36; epistemological ambivalence, 63, 65, 69; of irony, 29, 57; of *stiob*, 47; of *travesti*, 55, 102
Andriukova, Valentina, 68
androgyny, 36, 47, 51, 59, 80, 86, 151, 156–57. *See also* gender
Aristotle, 27
Article 6.21 of the Russian Administrative Code. *See* "gay propaganda" law
Astakhov, Sergii, 122–26
Austin, J. L., 17, 117
Austria, 100, 107
authoritarianism: desire for, 32; rise of, 41
"Avant-Garde and Kitsch" (Greenberg), 29

Balabanov, Aleksei, 61, 66–70
Barabanov, Nikolai, 79
Bartlett, Djurdja, 59
Baum, Frank, 192n27
BDSM, 144–50, 157
"Beard" (Timati and MC Doni), 101
"Beautiful People and What They Say to Me" (Klimova), 118
beauty contests, 158–60. *See also* prison pageants
beauty labor, 131
Beckham, Victoria, 161
"Believe" (Bilan), 110–13
Berlant, Lauren, 16–17
"Best Friend" (Timati), 7, 32
Bichevin, Leonid, 68
Bilan, Dima, 106–14, 172, 179, 200n33
Bin Laden, Osama, 82
biopolitics, 5, 7
Birdcage, The (Nichols), 96
bitchology, 139–43, 145, 150, 157, 159–60, 162, 209n60. *See also* postfeminism
Black Star Inc., 32
body: commodification of, 19–20; weaponization of, 60–61. *See also* embodied citizenship
Bogomolov, Konstantin, 174–75
Boileau-Despréaux, Nicolas, 28
Bolshevik Revolution of 1917, 10, 46–47
Bondarchuk, Fedor, 61–66
Borenstein, Eliot, 9, 29, 43, 173, 179n4, 179n6, 186n26
Boyer, Dominic, 47, 50–51

Boym, Svetlana, 45, 187n43, 188n69
Brother (Balabanov), 67
Buranovskie Babushki, 169
Burgess, Anthony, 175
Bush, George W., 173
Butler, Judith, 17, 34, 87, 104, 116–17

Cage aux Folles, La (Molinaro), 90, 96
Calvert Journal, The, 166
camp: aesthetics of, 33, 48, 51, 107; and affluence, 40–41, 187n43; as apolitical, 34; and exaggeration, 36–37; and gender, 53, 89, 104; and nostalgia, 53; perceptions of, 107–8; similarities to *stiob*, 46–47; and stereotypes, 170; strategic use of, 8–9, 36, 110, 112; and *travesti*, 55; as Western mode, 28, 40. *See also* charisma; *glamur*; kitsch; *poshlost'*; *stiob*
Cargo 200 (Balabanov), 61, 66–70, 97, 148
celebrity, 21, 31–32, 39, 48, 81–82, 130, 166–69
censorship, 6, 15, 80, 115, 117–18, 175–77. *See also* free expression
Chadov, Aleksei, 64
charisma: boundaries of, 33, 37; challenges to, 48; and future orientation, 35; as global mode of performance, 28; and hypermasculinity, 31; and leadership, 45; and politics, 34–35; universal appeal of, 8. *See also* camp; *glamur*; kitsch; *poshlost'*; *stiob*
Chechnya antigay purges, 129
Chekhov, Anton, 45–46, 174
Cher, 92
Cherry Orchard (Chekhov), 174
childhood, 70, 150–57
Children-404 (Kurov and Loparev), 118
Chvanov, Sergei, 79
Cicero, 27–28
cisgender drag: and abject masculinity, 71–72; ambivalence of, 66, 73–75; and androgyny, 153; failures of, 67, 69, 76–77; goals of, xii, 52, 55–56, 61; and hypergender, 59–62, 67. *See also* cross-gender drag; drag; *travesti*
citizenship: and discipline, 5, 16; ideal forms of, 9–17, 162, 177; and obligations to the state, 18; and Othering, 23; passivity of, 16–19; performance of, xi, 6, 8, 26, 29, 59, 103–4; rights of, 183n53. *See also* embodied citizenship; privatization of citizenship
Claypool, Les, 176
Clinton, Hillary, 34
Clockwork Orange, A (Kubrick), 174
Colbert Report, The, 47
Cold War, xii, 12, 26
coming-of-age stories, 150–57
Coming Out of the Closet (Patlay), 121
coming-out stories, 103, 121
compensatory heterosexuality, 114, 122
Condé Nast, 48
constructivism, 115
consumerism, 40, 49, 60
Covid-19 pandemic, 170
Creation of Adam, The (Pavlov), 107–8
Crimea, seizure of, 7–8, 55, 128
crisis of masculinity: anxieties of, 70–71; and citizenship, 78; responses to, 12, 15, 81–82, 141; responsibility for, 12, 20, 99, 104, 131–32, 175; and women's emancipation, 61. *See also* masculinity; Russia
cross-gender drag: perceptions of, 82, 96–97, 116; politicization of, 167; professional history of, 79–80, 92, 95; and same-sex desire, 90, 104; and vulnerability, 81–86, 195n30. *See also* cisgender drag; drag; drag queens; *travesti*

Daily Show, The, 47
Dana International, 107, 172
"Dancing Lasha Tumbai" (Serduchka), 87–88
Danilov, Anton, 167
Danylko, Andriy, 80, 87–88, 195n30. *See also* Serduchka, Verka
Davis, Angela, 102
de Beauvoir, Simone, 141
"Deputy Mizulina's Dreams" (Altunin), 80
disability studies, 171n21

Donbas conflict, 55, 158
Donskaia-Khil'ko, Vera, 80
"Don't Believe, Don't Fear, Don't Beg" (t.A.T.u.), 108–9
Dorokhov, Denis, 167
Dostoevsky, Fyodor, 135–36
drag, 51–52. *See also* cisgender drag; cross-gender drag; *travesti*
drag kings, 78
drag queens: and agency, xi, 51–56; depictions of politicians as, 39, 51; growing number of performers, 166; performance modes of, 36, 78, 89–90, 93; performer's distance from persona, 88, 95–97; reinforcing gender norms, 78–81, 86–96; similarities with other cultural products, 25; and Soviet trauma, 81–86. *See also* cross-gender drag; *travesti*; *specific performers*
Dragzina, 166
Dugin, Aleksandr, 7
Duncan, Isadora, 79
Dust (Loban), 62, 70–75, 78, 102, 107, 120

Echo of Moscow, 52–53
Eisenstein, Sergei, 187n43
Elin, Aleksandr, 33, 48, 50
emasculation, 12–13, 61–62, 73. *See also* masculinity
embodied citizenship, 9–17, 24–25, 57, 181n21. *See also* body; citizenship; hypergender; Russia
English language, 120, 169, 204n82
Engström, Maria, 170
Epistemology of the Closet (Sedgwick), 37
Erofeev, Viktor, 20, 22–24, 27, 29, 55, 70, 76, 163
essentialism, 115–16
estrada, 89–90, 107
Etkind, Alexander, 19
Euromaidan, 55
European Union, 107
Eurovision Song Contest: and camp, 170–71; drag at, 80, 87–88, 100; influence of, 169; performances of queerness at, 106–14, 200n31; politics at, 172; Russia's participation in, xii, 106–14
Evdokimov, Anatolii, 90–95, 98, 166
Everage, Dame Edna, 80. *See also* Humpries, Barry
Everybody Dies but Me (Gai Germanika), 150–57
Everything was Forever, Until It Was No More (Yurchak), 46
Evgenii Onegin (Pushkin), 135–36
"Evolution, or Woman Through the Eyes of Man" (Evdokimov), 92–93
"Exhibit" (Leningrad), 160–62

Facebook, 118
facial hair, 100–101
family code of 1968, 12
Farmer, Mylène, 93
fascism, 165, 175
fashion, 71–72, 76; fast fashion, 60; socialist fashion, 59–60. *See also* haute couture
Federal Security Service (FSB), 71–73
femininity: and abjection, 88; and bitchiness, 139–43; and camp, 53; and charisma, 34–35; and fashion, 59–60, 80; and *glamur*, 49; markers of, 91–93, 101, 135–36, 139; and maternity, 9–10, 12; as Other, 22; performances of, 52, 95–96, 209n60; and seductiveness, 82; and *stiob*, 88; and submission, 144–50; traditional forms of, 5, 11, 59, 91, 99, 139–43; *travesti* of, 172; and vulnerability, 152, 157. *See also* gender; hyperfemininity; masculinity
feminism, 9, 26, 43–44, 140–41, 172. *See also* postfeminism
Feminist Antiwar Resistance, 177
Fifteenth Paradise, The (Klever), 144–50
55 (Mikhalkov), 32
Fifty Shades of Grey (James), xii, 144–50
Fiks, Yevgeniy, 121
Filonenko, Polina, 150–57
"Fixation" (Pavlensky), 164
Four Ends of the Earth, The (Klever), 144–50

free expression, 18, 32–33, 57. *See also* censorship
Friedin, Gregory, 35
Friedman, Misha, 127
"From a Confession" (Altunin), 80
Frye, Northrop, 28
Full Metal Jacket (Kubrick), 62

G20 summit, 80
Gagarina, Polina, 169
Gai Germanika, Valeriia, 132, 150–57
Galinskii, Aleksandr, 79
"Gangnam Style" (Psy), 53
Garber, Marjorie, 87
Gay Propaganda (Huff-Hannon and Gessen), 121
"gay propaganda" law: contradictions of, 114–20; expansion of, 164–65, 168; and moral panic, 3–4, 129; motivations for, 44, 126–27, 200n43; perceived transmission of homosexuality, 23–24; as performative utterance, 106, 117–19; responses to, xii, 102–4, 120, 127–28; and *travesti*, 125–26
gaze, 29, 60–61, 76, 111, 143
Geisha School (Shatskaia and Tanaka), 143
gender: ambiguity of, 51–53, 60, 200n31; binaries of, 29, 33–34, 61, 79, 87, 90, 95, 99, 101, 106, 138; equity of, 22–23; essentialism of, 22, 131; and ideal citizenship, 9–17; local experiences of, 26; performance of, 13, 131; policing of, 60–61, 93, 105; and sexual differences, 131, 134, 140; social construction of, 17, 22, 34, 77; traditional roles, xii, 14–15, 59–60. *See also* androgyny; femininity; hypergender; masculinity; sexuality
gender-affirming care, 184n62
gender dysphoria, 21
Gender Trouble (Butler), 116
Genet, Jean, 79
Gentlemen of Fortune (Seryi), 81
Gessen, Masha, 9, 121
Gill, Rosalind, 131
Girls (Gai Germanika), 160
Glamour (magazine), 48
glamur: demonstration of, 134, 160; and excess, 48–49; and *poshlost'*, 93; Russian versions of, 8, 48; as Western mode of performance, 28. *See also* camp; charisma; kitsch; *poshlost'*
glasnost, 28
Gloss (Konchalovskii), 49
Goncharova, Natal'ia, 171
Gorbachev, Mikhail, 132
Goscilo, Helena, 48–49, 184n55
Greenberg, Clement, 29
Gulag Archipelago, The (Solzhenitsyn), 109

Haapasala, Ville, 97, 99
Hammer and Sickle (Livnev), 107, 184n62
Hands Up! (musical group), 92
"Happy Love (Liubov' Orlova)" (Mamyshev-Monro), 83–84, 194n17
hate crimes, 119
haute couture, 49–50. *See also* fashion
Healey, Dan, 10, 16, 121, 128
Hegel, 37
Heifits, Iosif, 45
"He Kisses You" (Hands Up!), 92
Heller, Dana, 108
Hello! I'm Your Aunt (Titov), 81
Here I Come, 103–4
heteronormativity, 5, 9, 24, 37, 103–4, 112–13, 120, 122, 181n19. *See also* homophobia; neotraditionalism
heterosexuality, 19, 23, 52, 114, 122. *See also* homophobia; homosexuality; sexuality
High Heels (musical group), 50
Hitler, Adolph, 82–83
HIV/AIDS, 42, 98
Hollywood, 62, 81, 85, 96
homoeroticism, 64, 73, 112
homonationalism, 16–17, 107–8, 113, 205n95
homophobia: amplification of, 22–23, 99, 164; and gender essentialism, 141; and hypermasculinity, 16; institutionalization of, 11, 106, 114; and Othering, 105–6; perceptions of, 109, 122; as quotidian, 14, 122–23; responses to, 42, 96,

102, 127; and Russian identity, 4, 80, 119; violence of, 96–97, 113, 129, 166. *See also* heteronormativity; heterosexuality; LGBTQ+ subjects; transphobia
homosexuality: growing interest in, 103; lesbianism, 12–13, 108–9, 168, 183n53; perceptions of, 9–10, 23–24, 97–98, 201n49; as performative utterance, 117; stereotypes of, 3–4, 112; tolerance of, 11; and transness, 55. *See also* heterosexuality; LGBTQ+ subjects
How the Soviet Man Was Unmade (Kaganovsky), 184n62
How to Become a Bitch (Rudnitskaya), 142
Huff-Hannon, Joseph, 121
Humpries, Barry, 80. *See also* Everage, Dame Edna
hyperfemininity: clothing of, 153; and gender binary, 90; performances of, 55, 87, 157–58; stereotypes of, 130; and *travesti*, 61; and vulnerability, 68, 97. *See also* femininity
hypergender: and cisgender drag, 61, 67, 69–70; and gender norms, 22–24, 82; media representations of, 50; and Othering, 23–24; rejection of, 80, 176; requirements of, 52, 59, 127; and traditional values, 26, 164; uses of, 17, 77–79, 100. *See also* embodied citizenship; gender
hypermasculinity, 30; and ambivalence, 75; as compensatory, 15–16; construction of, 52, 62; and drag, 80; and multiple performative modes, 33; and *travesti*, 63, 65; *travesti* of, 129. *See also* masculinity

Il'inskii, Il'ia, 85
illiberalism, 4, 16–18, 179n7. *See also* liberalism
I Love You (Stolpovskaia and Troitskii), 107
Inc. (magazine), 121
intergenerational trauma, 62
International Children's Day, 138
International Women's Day, 92
internet, 6–7, 15, 46, 103, 105, 118, 165–66
irony, xi, 29, 34, 41, 46, 50, 56. *See also* self-irony
It Gets Better Project, 118
Ivan the Terrible (Eisenstein), 187n43
"I've Done Everyone" (Evdokimov), 92
Ivleeva, Nastia, 103, 166, 168–69

James, E. L., 144–50
Jameson, Frederic, 29
"Je t'aime mélancholie" (Evdokimov), 93
Johnson, Emily, 32–33, 112
Johnson, Janet Elise, 5
Jolly Fellows (Mikhailov), 96–99, 107, 167

Kadyrov, Ramzan, 32
Kaganovsky, Lilya, 184n62
Kalustian, Loran, 102. *See also* Rey, Lorina
Kandelaki, Tina, 168
Kandinsky Prize, 85
Kasilov, Igor', 79
Katina, Lena, 108. *See also* t.A.T.u.
Kazantsev, Vladim, 52, 93. *See also* Napoli, Zaza
Khrushchev, Nikita, 32
Kirill, Patriarch, 80
Kirkorov, Filipp, 80, 107
kitsch: boundaries of, 33, 37–38, 53; and gender, 89; perceptions of, 107; and *poshlost'*, 44–45, 188n69; as Western mode, 8, 28. *See also* camp; charisma; *glamur*; *poshlost'*; *stiob*
Klever, Alisa, 144
Klimova, Lena, 118
Klimushkin, Aleksei, 97
Klingseis, Katerina, 60
Kolli, Lora, 89–90, 93. *See also* Zarubin, Sergei
Konchalovskii, Andrei, 49
Kondakov, Alexander, 14, 115–16
Kozlovskii, Danila, 99
Krasilov, Dima, 170
Krid, Egor, 166
Krusanov, Pavel, 47
Kubasov, Dmitrii, 69

Kubrick, Stanley, 62–63, 174–75
Kurekhin, Sergei, 46–47
Kurov, Askold, 118
Kuznetsova, Agniia, 67, 150–57
Kvir (web portal), 21

Labazov, Pavel, 85
"Lady with Lapdog" (Chekhov), 45–46
"LaLa-Lei" (Tsoi), 91
Lanoux, Andrea, 131
Lazarev, Sergei, 169
Lel', Katya, 91
"Lenin" (Napoli), 93
Lenin, Vladimir, 8, 10, 46–47, 52–53, 80
Leningrad (musical group), 164
Lenna, Anastasiia, 176
lesbianism, 12–13, 108–9, 168, 183n53
L'Etoile (cosmetics store), 92
LGBTQ+ activism, 113, 117, 120–23, 166. *See also* protests
LGBTQ+ subjects: censorship of, 114–15; and drag, 51, 90; exclusion of, 9, 12, 16; and the internet, 105, 118; and queerness, 198n10; *stiob* of, 108–9; sympathy with, 98–99, 107, 126. *See also* homophobia; homosexuality; queerness
liberalism, 4–5. *See also* illiberalism
Limonov, Eduard, 47
LitRes, 208n41
Little Big (musical group), 170–71
Livnev, Sergei, 107, 184n62
Loban, Sergei, 62, 70–75, 107
Lollobrigida, Gina, 36–37
Loparev, Pavel, 118
Love Bitch, 95
Luzhkov, Iurii, 113
L'vova, Liubov', 107
Lyudmila and Natasha (Friedman), 127

Madonna, 92, 168
Maids, The (Viktiuk), 79, 90
Makarychev, Andrey, 5
"Mamo" (Prikhod'ko), 112
Mamonov, Petr, 73–74
Mamyshev-Monro, Vladislav, 79, 81–86, 95, 100, 102, 105
Mandelshtam, Osip, 35
Manizha, 170
Mansfield, Jayne, 36–37
"Many-Faces Peskov, The" (Peskov), 90
marriage, 5, 10, 138–39
Marton, Edvin, 111
masculinity: and abjection, 70–72, 75, 124, 164; and charisma, 34–35, 37, 49; and desire, 21, 143; and deviance, 9, 111–12; and dominance, 146, 149–50; failures of, 11–12, 62, 71–72; fragility of, 14, 24, 76–77; markers of, 91–93, 95, 99, 101; performances of, 17, 52, 111; and politics, 134, 138; presumption of, 181n19; and sexism, 42–43; toxic forms of, 68–69, 82, 165; traditional forms of, 5, 33, 59, 76. *See also* crisis of masculinity; emasculation; femininity; gender; hypermasculinity; military masculinity; *muzhik*
"Mask, I Know You" (Peskov), 90–91
master-slave dialectic, 37
masturbation, 63
maternity capital, 15, 114, 129, 207n18. *See also* reproductive labor
Mature, Victor, 37–38
Mavrikievna, Veronika, 79, 88
Mavromatti, Oleg, 122, 124–25
May, Theresa, 34
Mayo, Virginia, 36–37
MC Doni, 101
McDowell, Malcolm, 174
Medvedev, Dmitrii, 80, 99, 135
Medvedev, Sergei, 5
memes: and camp, 42–43; circulation of, 7, 162; and kitsch, 38; and performing citizenship, xi; and political legitimation, 176. *See also* Putin "gay clown" meme
Men (Erofeev), 20–21
Menzel, Birgit, 49
Merkel, Angela, 34
#MeToo movement, 5, 105
metrosexuality, 110–11
Miazhevich, Galina, 199n16
Mikhailov, Feliks, 96–99, 107, 167

Mikhailovskii, Valerii, 79
Mikhalkov, Nikita, 32
Mikheeva, Katia, 121
military masculinity, 63–64. *See also* masculinity
Milonov, Vitalii, 80, 118, 166–68
Minelli, Liza, 92
misogyny, 22–23. *See also* sexism
Mizulina, Elena, 80
Mogutin, Slava, 121
Moiseev, Boris, 80
Monroe, Marilyn, 81–83, 92, 169
Monsoon, Edina, 102
moral panic, 115, 129
"More Glamour" (High Heels), 50
Moscow (Fiks), 121
Mother Tongue (Fiks), 121
Motschenbacher, Heiko, 200n31
Museum of the History of LGBT in Russia, 121
muzhik, 72, 125, 164. *See also* masculinity
"My Marmalade Man" (Lel'), 91
My New Orthodox Video (Ul'ianov), 124

Nabokov, Vladimir, 45
Napoli, Zaza, 52, 54, 57–58, 61, 90, 93, 98, 166. *See also* Kazantsev, Vladim
narcissism, 35, 47, 112, 143, 174
National Bolshevik Party, 47
nationalism, 7, 109, 122
Navalnyi, Aleksei, 18–19, 41
Nazism, 174–75
Nedos, 102
Neoacademism, 81. *See also* New Academy of Fine Arts
neoconservatism, 15
neoliberalism, 16, 47, 130–31
neonationalism, 55
neotraditionalism, 5, 14, 17, 26, 104, 164. *See also* heteronormativity
Neuwirth, Thomas. *See* Wurst, Conchita
"Never Let You Go" (Bilan), 110
New Academy of Fine Arts, 81, 189n81. *See also* Neoacademism
New Russian Grannies, 79–80, 88
New Russians, 27, 76
Nigmatullina, Matrena Ivanovna, 79
Nikitichna, Avdot'ia, 79, 88
9th Company (Bondarchuk), 61–66, 154
No Place for Fools (Mavromatti), 122–26
nostalgia, 36, 53, 62, 69, 83, 91
"Notes on 'Camp'" (Sontag), 29, 34, 36
"Not Gonna Get Us" (t.A.T.u.), 109
Novikov, Timur, 81, 189n81

Obama, Barack, 80
Occupy Gerontophilia, 117
Occupy Pedophilia, 117
October Revolution, 10, 46–47
Orange Revolution, 87
Orlov, Andrei, 93
Orlova, Liubov', 83–84, 86
Othering, 5, 11–12, 16, 21–23, 55, 60–61, 73, 81, 104
Otherness: acceptance of, 96; appropriation of, 28, 173; and blame, 22–23; and gaze, 76, 163; and the self, 29, 77, 82
"Our Madhouse Votes for Putin" (Rabfak), 48
Ovsiannikova, Marina, 177

pan-Slavism, 55
paternalism, 14, 137
Patlay, Anastasia, 121
patriarchy, 11
patriotism, 62–63, 65, 67, 125
Pavlensky, Petr, 16, 164
Pavlov, Yurii, 107–8
pedophilia, 55, 97–98, 164
perestroika, 28
performative contradictions, 118–19, 128
performative utterances, 17, 106, 117–19
performativity: and the audience, 37; and contradictions, 114–20; distinct modes of, 8–9, 36, 45–46, 50, 56–57; and gender essentialism, 141; individual motives for, 81; and productivity, 19–20; and queerness, 26, 104–5; Russian modes of, 44–45; and stylistic slippage, 28, 33, 38–39, 163, 165; and *travesti*, 52. *See also* style

Peskov, Aleksandr, 90–91
"Peters" (Tolstaia), 70
Petersburg Fundamentalists, 47
Peter the Great, 20, 100
phallic metaphors, 23–24, 42, 101
Plato, 27
Platoon (Stone), 62
Platt, Kevin, 29
pleshki, 12–13
Pliushchenko, Evgenii, 111
Pliushchev, Aleksandr, 52–53
Podol'skii, Aleksei, 71, 75
Poliakova, Olia, 53–55, 57–58
political masculinity, 17. *See also* masculinity
political party names, 186n26
Poluian, Aleksei, 67
porn tropes, 108, 130
Porteous, Holly, 131
poshlost': and agency, 45–46; and bitchiness, 142–43; as distinctly Russian, 8, 28, 50; and glamour, 93; and kitsch, 44–45, 89, 188n69. *See also* camp; charisma; *glamur*; kitsch; *stiob*
postfeminism, 130–31, 134, 139–50, 157–58, 162. *See also* bitchology; feminism
power vertical, 23, 42, 80
Pride parades, 44, 105, 113, 122
Prigov, Dmitrii, 41
Prikhod'ko, Anastasia, 112
prison pageants, 159–60. *See also* beauty contests
privacy, 11–13, 18, 116
privatization of citizenship, 16–17. *See also* citizenship
professional theater, 79
protests: as content-free, 24–25, 41–42; forms of, 212n5; infrequency of, 17. *See also* LGBTQ+ activism
Puar, Jasbir, 16–17, 205n95
public-private divide, 116
Pugacheva, Alla, 82, 86–87, 91, 107
punk aesthetics, 43
"Punk Prayer" (Pussy Riot), 43–44
Pushkin, Alexander, 135–36
Pussy Riot, 3–4, 16, 42–44, 57–58, 164
Putin, Vladimir: anti-Western rhetoric, 164; and camp absurdity, 42; and cisgender drag, 17, 24, 30, 52, 76–77, 129; cult of personality, 15, 30–33, 52–53, 132–33; lack of political substance, xi, 7–8, 25, 38–39; marriage and divorce, 138–39; memes of, xi, 4, 33, 38–39, 42–44, 50–52, 57–58, 80, 187n42; as *muzhik*, 15, 31, 164; plastic surgery, 55; political career, 6–7, 30, 41, 44, 83; staged photo-ops, 21, 30–31, 133; and toxic masculinity, 165; and *travesti*, 56–57; use of social media, 175–76. *See also* Putinism
Putina, Liudmila, 132–34, 138–39, 157
Putin "gay clown" meme, 4, 39, 44, 50–52, 57–58, 80, 187n42. *See also* memes
Putinism: challenges to, 104; and *glamur*, 49–50; and hypergender, 15–16, 99, 164; and the ideal citizen, 16–18, 177; pedagogy of shame, 165; sexism of, 43; as style, xi–xii, 8–9, 56; as stylistic void, 21, 163, 173; violence of, 148. *See also* Putin, Vladimir
"Putin Pissed Himself" (Pussy Riot), 42–43
Putin's Army, 130

queer archive, 120–26
queerness, xii, 12–13; and camp, 40; and definitional slippages, xii, 30, 120, 125–26; embrace of, 51, 113–14, 119; and LGBTQ+ subjects, 198n10; perceptions of, 12–14, 81, 102; and performative precarity, 165–66; and performativity, 26, 53, 104–5, 108–10; and shame, 104. *See also* LGBTQ+ subjects
Queerography (Shainian), 103
queer theory, 26, 116

Rabfak (musical group), 48, 164
"Rainbow Milonov" (Altunin), 80
Rajagopalan, Sudha, 131
Rakhmanova, Irina, 64
Rakovskii, Vladimir, 142, 162
rape, 14, 64, 67, 155
Reeves, Steve, 37

reproductive labor, 9–11, 13, 15–16, 114, 134. *See also* abortion; maternity capital; sex
Rey, Lorina, 102, 166. *See also* Kalustian, Loran
right to claim rights, 17–18
"Rise Like a Phoenix" (Wurst), 100
Robski, Oksana, 48
Roskomnadzor, 118, 175–76
Ross, Andrew, 40
rossiiskii, 7–8. *See also* Russian identity; *russkii*
Royal Cobras, 103–4, 166–69
Ruckus in a Henhouse, 90
Rudnitskaya, Alina, 122–23, 142, 160–61
Rudova, Larissa, 131
RuPaul's Drag Race, 51, 87, 101–3, 166
Russell, Jane, 36–37
Russia: appropriation of *stiob*, 47–48; consumerism in, 40; continuation of the Soviet Union, 18–19; counterculture in, 81–82; distinction from Europe, 108; global perceptions of, 4, 41, 118, 127, 170; growing queerness in, xi–xii, 14, 106–7; illiberality of, 4, 163–64, 179n7, 183n53; life expectancy in, 61, 114; limited queer archive in, 120–26; limited role of leader's wives, 132–33; mediascape of, 15, 25, 31, 175; military aggression of, 17, 24, 76; as motherland or fatherland, 22, 44, 138; oil and gas boom, 5, 16, 19; participation in Eurovision, 106–14, 172, 199n14; perceptions as trans, 21–24, 55, 163, 184n62; political parties, 186n26; precarity in, 19, 76; protecting traditions of, 5, 16, 164–65; and shame, 70, 72, 108; significance of facial hair, 100. *See also* crisis of masculinity; embodied citizenship; Soviet Union
Russian exceptionalism, 28
Russian identity, xii, 5–8, 29, 56, 146, 173–77. See also *rossiiskii*; *russkii*
Russian language, 120, 145, 203n76
Russian Ministry of Health, 14
Russian National Music Awards, 162
Russian Orthodox Church, 5, 13, 15, 43, 80
"Russian Style" (Poliakova), 53–55
"Russian Woman" (Manizha), 172
russkii, 7–8. See also *rossiiskii*; Russian identity

sacrifice, 137, 150–57
Salmenniemi, Suvi, 89, 131, 140–41
same-sex marriage, 5
satire, 73–75
"Satisfaction" parodies, 3–4, 8–9, 21, 179n6
Saunders, Jennifer, 102
School (Gai Germanika), 150
School of Seduction (Rudnitskaya), 160–61
Sedgwick, Eve, 34, 37–38, 104, 116, 198n10
self-help literature, 131, 140, 142
self-irony, 4–5. *See also* irony
Senelick, Laurence, 87
Serbia, 107
Serduchka, Verka, 80, 87–90, 95, 108, 167. *See also* Danylko, Andriy
Serebrennikov, Kirill, 127, 129, 150
Šerifović, Maria, 107
Seven Year Itch, The (Wilder), 82
sex: attitudes toward, 46; and bitchiness, 139–43; and coming of age, 64; depictions of, 63, 154; education about, 16; and impotency, 68–69; masturbation, 63; and power, 64, 67–68, 144–50. *See also* reproductive labor; sodomy
sexism, 42, 79. *See also* misogyny
sexual differences, 131, 134, 140
sexual exceptionalism, 16
sexuality: clichés of, 3–4, 50; definitions of deviance, 11, 13–14, 16; and essentialism, 115; exaggeration of, 36–37; local experiences of, 26; rigid norms of, 105–6, 114; and tolerance, 128. *See also* gender; heterosexuality
Sexual Revolution (television show), 93–94
sexual revolutions, 10–13, 15
sexual subjectivity, 115–16, 131, 201n45
Sex with Anfisa Chekhova, 49
sex work, 14–15

Shainian, Karen, 103
shame, 75, 104–6, 108, 123–24, 128, 142, 159–60, 164–65
Shapalov, Ivan, 108
Shatskaia, Evgeniia, 139–43
Shiianov, Mikhail, 85
Shklovskii, Viktor, xiii
Shnurov, Sergei "Shnur," 160
Shuvalova, Olga, 150–57
Sil'vestrov, Andrei, 85
"Simply the Best" (Turner), 93
Simpson, Mark, 110
simulacra, 8, 28
Singing Together (musical group), 33
Siniavskii, Andrei, 41
slogans, 35, 41–42, 71–72
Smol'ianinov, Artur, 64
Snow Revolution, 16, 20–21, 41, 44, 48, 57–58, 164
Sobchak, Kseniia, 48, 166, 168
social criticism, 66, 75
socialist fashion, 59–60
social violence, 148–49
sodomy: decriminalization of, 10–11, 13–14; recriminalization of, 11, 182n27. *See also* sex
Solzhenitsyn, Aleksandr, 109
Some Like It Hot (Wilder), 81
"Someone Like Putin" (Singing Together), 33, 53
"Songs of the Year" (Peskov), 90–91
Sontag, Susan, 8–9, 29, 34, 36, 38, 40, 51, 187n43
"Soundtrack" (Evdokimov), 92
Soviet Union: collapse of, 13–14, 24, 40–41; counterculture in, 81–82; crisis of masculinity, 10–13; cultural isolation of, 28; drag in, 79, 81, 85–86; fashion styles in, 59–60; and gender equity, 10, 22–23, 61–62; housing boom of the 1960s, 12; irony in, 46; material culture, 67–68; nostalgia for, 69, 83, 106; precarity in, 18–19; and reproductive labor, 10–12; significance of facial hair, 100; and Socialist Realism, 20. *See also* Russia
Spears, Britney, 168
Sperling, Valerie, 5, 130, 176
Stalin, Joseph, 8, 11–12, 32–33, 80, 85
Steele, Ben, 127
Stella, Francesca, 181n20
stervologiia. *See* bitchology
stiob: and affect, 81–82; and agency, 47–48; and camp, 46–47; as distinctly Russian, 8, 21, 28, 47; and double-messaging, 47–49, 108, 113; and excess, 169, 199n16; of postfeminism, 162; and queer performativity, 108–9. *See also* camp; charisma; kitsch; *poshlost'*
Stolpovskaia, Ol'ga, 107
Stone, Oliver, 62
St. Petersburg Male Ballet, 79
Straight Talk with Gay People (Shainian), 103
Strukov, Vlad, 48–49
Student, The (Serebrennikov), 127, 129, 150
style: as appropriating Otherness, 23, 28, 173; definitions of, 27–28, 173; lack of, 173–74; overload of, 169; and slippage, 39–41, 50, 56, 163, 165; and subjectivity, 20, 116; and substance, xi, 27. *See also* performativity
Suk@ liubov', 95
Syria, 17, 128

Tamaraev, Sergei, 107
Tanaka, Eliza, 143
Tatchell, Peter, 113
t.A.T.u., 106–14, 168, 172. *See also* Katina, Lena; Volkova, Iuliia
Teatr.doc, 121
Temkina, Anna, 209n60
temporality, 51, 104
This Kiss Is Off the Record (Zhulina), xii, 133–39
Tilly, Charles, 18
Timati, 7, 32, 101
Tolstaia, Tat'iana, 49, 70
Tonkov, Vadim, 79
To Wong Foo, Thanks for Everything, Julie Newmar (Kidron), 96

transphobia, 4, 22–23, 97, 163. *See also* homophobia
trauma, 62, 64–65, 69, 75–76, 81, 100, 148–49, 172
travesti: and abject masculinity, 71–72; and ambivalence, 63, 66, 74–75, 102; and bitchiness, 139–43; and double-messaging, 113; of heterosexuality, 116, 120; of hyperfemininity, 157–58, 172; of hypermasculinity, 24, 65, 129; as meta-mode, 56–57, 59; as profession, 80, 86–96, 98–99; rejection of, 176; strategic use of, 25, 78, 104, 167. *See also* cis-gender drag; cross-gender drag; drag; drag queens
"Travesti" (Altunin), 80, 99
Trevor Project, The, 118
Troitskii, Dmitrii, 107
Trump, Donald, 34, 38–39
Tsoi, Anita, 91
Tsvetochek, Klavdia Ivanovna, 79
tucking, 93, 95
Turner, Tina, 93
Two Months and Three Days (Klever), 144–50
2011–2012 election fraud protests. *See* Snow Revolution

Udmurt language, 169
Ukraine, 17, 19, 24, 26, 55, 80, 87, 117, 128, 172–77
Ukrainophobia, 173–77
Ul'ianov, Anatolii, 124
Ulianovsk Institute of Aeronautical Engineering, 3–4, 8–9, 21, 179n6
Union of Orthodox Women, 172
United Russia Party, 35
United States, 16, 34–35, 39–40, 91–92
"Uno" (Little Big), 170–71
"Uses of Camp, The" (Ross), 40

vaudeville, 79
Vendenskaia, Tat'iana. *See* Klever, Alisa
verisimilitude, 91
Victory Day (Rudnitskaya), 121–23, 126
Viktiuk, Roman, 79
VKontakte, 118
Vladimirov, Boris, 79
Volga-Volga (Mamyshev-Monro), 83–86, 105
Volkova, Iuliia, 108. *See also* t.A.T.u.
Volochkova, Anastasiia, 93
Voropaev, Anatolii, 135
Vyrypaev, Ivan, 175

Weber, Max, 30–31, 33–35, 37
white ribbons, 42
Wilder, Billy, 81–82
Wilkinson, Cai, 115
Winter Journey (Tamaraev and L'vova), 107
Winter Olympics in Sochi (2014), 109
Wizard of Oz, The (Fleming), 68, 192n27
Women on the Brink (Rakovskii), 142
Wonderzine (web portal), 166–67
World Health Organization, 14
World War II, 174
"Wrestling" (Donskaia-Khil'ko), 80
Wurst, Conchita, 100–102, 104, 107

Yandex, 162
Yeltsin, Boris, 13–14, 132, 164
Yeltsina, Naina, 132
YouTube, 166
Yurchak, Alexei, 19–21, 24, 46, 50–51, 57, 105

zAiBi, 75
Zarubin, Sergei, 89–90. *See also* Kolli, Lora
Zdravomyslova, Elena, 209n60
"Zelensky: The Man with the Iron Balls" (Claypool), 176
Zelenskyy, Volodymyr, 175–76
Zhirinovskii, Vladimir, 100
Zhulina, Ol'ga, 134–35
Zverev, Sergei, 50